Dulwich
and
Beyond

To Sam with best wishes

Neil J Smith.

June 2006

A History of Dulwich College Preparatory School

Neil Smith

Before The Beginning

The site of DCPS as seen from College Road when painted by Camille Pissaro in 1871. The whisp of white smoke (centre right) is from the railway which had been opened in 1863. The twin pointed roof building in the centre is 35 Alleyn Park currently owned by DCPS and occupied by the Headmaster. It is thus one of the first Victorian buildings in Alleyn Park and also one of the last.

View from Sydenham Hill (Pissaro 1871)   Original held in Kimbell Art Museum, Fort Worth, Texas, USA

Contents

Acknowledgements

First and foremost, I am indebted to Mandy Peat (mother of Alexander Peat DCPS 1992-2000) who has encouraged me throughout and has minuted so many conversations that there is a large dossier entitled the 'Mandy Peat Interviews'. Without her support this book would never have been written. George Marsh has rubbed his hands in eager anticipation for a very long time and his patience has made the writing of this book a pleasure. I must also thank the Board of Governors for financing its production and Margaret Battley at Cantate Press for her wisdom and guidance. I am grateful too for the many hours given by Ann Revell, of the school's IT department, for arranging the typesetting and the layout of the pages, and the assistance given by David Lewis and Matthew Betts. Tricia Rusling kindly provided the postcard of the school in 1909 and Diana Hendriks (mother of Tom Hendriks DCPS 1998-2004) has edited and proofread the script and, despite every effort to spot errors, I apologise if the computer has got the better of any of us at any stage.

I must also thank Gordon Chubb and his wartime contemporaries for their input into Chapters 4 and 5, John Hendy of DPS, Cranbrook, for his background information relating to Chapter 9 and Roderick Suddaby, Keeper of Documents at the Imperial War Museum, whom I approached to verify the accuracy of Chapter 7. Thanks are also due to Dr Jan Piggott, Archivist at Dulwich College, who has given me free access to all relevant documents held in his department.

Finally I must thank the vast number of former pupils and staff, as well as many current ones, who have provided a mountain of reminiscences and information. Where this has been used in the text reference has been made, but there are many hidden contributors who are much appreciated but have gone without mention. This includes many boys and colleagues, past and present, who have willingly contributed ideas and read drafts. I am grateful to them all. Some of the text is a personal reflection of life at DCPS as I saw it and where this is the case I have used the first person. Other aspects are my own interpretation and any errors of fact are therefore entirely mine.

Introduction

Researching the school's history has been exciting and meeting and sharing experiences with former pupils has been exhilarating to say the least. Memories, mementos, treasures, photographs and contemporary documents have all been made available, some of which have been donated to the school archive for future generations to enjoy.

The principal source of information has been the school magazine which has run continuously since the first edition appeared in December 1919. Before then, and from the school's foundation in 1885, information about 'The Preparatory School' appeared in the back pages of *The Alleynian*, the magazine for Dulwich College. John Leakey's book (Headmaster 1932-1961) *School Errant* described the school's trials and tribulations during the Second War and this has provided detailed information about that period. Unless otherwise stated, references are taken from *The Alleynian* (by kind permission of Dulwich College), various editions of the school magazine or from documents and letters held in the school's archives. Similarly, photographs and illustrations, unless captioned otherwise where this has been possible, are the property of the DCPS Archive.

Early information about DCPS from *The Alleynian* is scant and is devoted almost entirely to matches, with little or no reference being made to life at the school in general. The Honours Boards in the school hall, and in the corridor behind, show the names of boys who gained scholarships to public schools and these are complete from the school's foundation. Sadly there are no complete lists of other boys who attended the school between 1885 and 1961, although some of the Valete sections from magazines after 1919 are reasonably detailed and a few class lists and form timetables from the 1890s have survived. As we begin the 21st century, there are obviously no surviving pupils who attended the school at the beginning; one of the boys who was there, W F Hudson, heard that the school was starting a school magazine and, in the second issue, he wrote at length from Poona in India about his early experiences. He was clearly an enthusiast for DCPS for in the summer issue of 1950, and now as Sir Frank Hudson, he wrote again for the thirtieth birthday number. These are valuable sources of information.

There are several discrepancies within the text. During the Second War DCPS evacuated to Betws-y-Coed in North Wales and an explanation of the spelling of the word is called for – is it 'Bettws' or 'Betws'? During the war the English version spelt the word with two Ts, but the current Welsh version has only one. All documents and quotations in the text from the time are spelt with two Ts, but references to the place since the war are spelt with one T.

Until the 1960s it was not unusual for staff and boys to refer to each other using the surname only and to differentiate brothers, each carried the numbers i, ii or iii after the surname. Boys with common surnames, such as my own, carried initials in the same way – hence Smith N D. In the text, staff from the early days are referred to by surnames only, with forenames or initials added if they are known. References to boys have forenames added whenever possible. Once the forename of a more recent member of staff has been established, surnames only are used to avoid repetition. The forenames by which they were commonly known by their colleagues (and probably by some of the boys too) have not been used on their own to avoid ambiguity.

In 1985 the school celebrated its centenary, the occasion being marked by a visit from His Royal Highness The Duke of Gloucester. The Headmaster at the time, Hugh Woodcock, devoted many hours trying to trace as many former pupils as he could and he encouraged them to come back and visit the school at some stage during its centenary year. They provided valuable and personal information in writing about the school's early years and this has been used extensively for the first two chapters. Although much of it appears in the Centenary Issue of the school magazine, I am much indebted to Hugh Woodcock for allowing me to make use of it again.

Foreword

It was fifty years ago, and I was an anxious new boy of ten who had previously only known life at a quiet little local dame school. DCPS, by contrast, seemed to me like the real world, big and noisy and exciting.

As I stood outside Mr Sheppard's office, waiting to be taken to my new classroom, the bell rang for morning break. A river of boys in grey and dark blue came pouring down the metalled stairs, jumping and calling out and pushing each other. 'What are the boys like at your new school?' someone asked me that night, when I got home. 'They're a bit rough,' I answered.

But they weren't really rough at all, as I soon came to understand; they were lively, boisterous, enthusiastic. Then as now, Dulwich Prep was one of the best schools in the country, and the boys were bright and highly motivated. Walking round the school now, I find it recognizably the same place, with the same ethos; and yet it seems remarkably different too.

It's easy to spot the old playground, where, in my first term, I caught out the captain of the school cricket during an improvised game played with a tennis ball, and was so embarrassed I dropped it deliberately. There are one or two classrooms and staircases which are familiar to me, even down to the floorboards and handrails. There is the Hall, with its honour boards for the same prizes and awards we competed for, though none of the winners goes back to my impossibly ancient time.

Other things remain totally unchanged: all the arcane business of tribes and good slips and so on. Sadly, though, my nephew Rees tells me that the old custom of getting rid of unwanted things by holding them up and calling 'Quis?' ('Who?') and giving them to the first person who shouts 'Ego!' ('I!') has disappeared. So, apparently, have most of the intricate games we played.

But the kids look just the same, and the teaching is, if anything, better than it was half a century ago. It's certainly a great deal more imaginative. Relations with the staff are much friendlier and more relaxed: no surnames now, just first names, and no physical punishment. None of the sense of terror, either, that followed some masters around like a whiff of sulphur; we had one, I remember, who was known to us simply as 'Satan'.

But there were also teachers even then who knew how to catch a child's imagination, including one marvellous old boy who would swear us to secrecy in English lessons and read us ghost stories, excellent ones, too, which taught me more than any amount of grammar could, and another called Captain Fleming, whose tales of the North-West Frontier and the attacks of blood-crazed Afghan tribesmen set my imagination on fire and made me long to travel.

Former pupils of my generation, like me, owe a good deal to DCPS, and are deeply grateful for what we learned there. Now this excellent school has a fitting tribute in an equally excellent and enthralling book; and it just surprises me that the untidy, ink-stained character I once was should be lucky enough, fifty years later, to have the considerable privilege of writing the foreword to it.

John Simpson

Preface

When I was on my very first visit to the Prep way back in 1989, Hugh Woodcock showed me round and told me why I should allow my name to go onto the list of candidates to replace him. He talked of the academic excellence, the drama, the sport and the loyal staff. He told me I would be moving to one of the best-known prep schools in London and in England. I am sure he was right in all he said, but it was not what he said that decided me to meet the Chairman of Governors and explore a move to SE21. When I met the Chairman and his Deputy they too spoke with passion and conviction about DCPS, but again it was not what they said that persuaded me to agree to being interviewed. The governors were courteous and rigorous in their probing and questioning, but it was not they that decided me to accept the post they offered me. No, it was none of those; it was the boys. On that first visit I sensed their everyday enthusiasm and their pride for their school. Even today, some sixteen years later, I cross Alleyn Park every morning and delight in the boys and their approach to life. This book is about The Prep and at the centre of every page are the boys. The narrative is about generations of boys in their formative years when attitudes to life and learning are formed. Look at the earliest photographs of prep boys and see the twinkle in their eyes, read about their exploits over the years, meet the old boys who came to the Prep but who were evacuated to Betws-y-Coed during the Second War, and meet the prep boys of today and you will sense that there is a prep ethos. There is never any lack of conversation, never a lack of desire to learn and always a warm welcome for newcomers. Above all the boys cherish fairness, fair play and form the courage to 'have a go'.

Although this book is a look at the past, I very much hope that the same prep ethos will be evident when the next history of the Prep comes to be written, and my successors will enjoy the great pleasure the boys of the Prep have given me.

George Marsh

First Published 2005

Published in the United Kingdom by
 DULWICH COLLEGE PREPARATORY SCHOOL
42 Alleyn Park, Dulwich, London SE 21 7AA

Typesetting and layout by Ann Revell of DCPS IT Department

Printed in the UK by Cantate Press
Cantate Centre
Culvert Place
London SW11 5DZ
www.cantate.biz

ISBN   0-9551718-0-6   (978-0-9551718-0-2 from January 1st 2007)

DCPS Boarders Summer Term 1910

1   How it all began

Any number of important events occurred in 1885. *The Mikado* was first performed at the Savoy Theatre on 14th March; a German engineer called Gottlieb Daimler, who pioneered the modern car, produced his first motor vehicle and motor cycle in that year, and at least two schools were founded, one for girls, the other for boys, both of which have prospered greatly. Roedean received its first girls, and a boys' school, the subject of this history, opened its doors at the bottom of Alleyn Park, West Dulwich on 18th January 1885.

One of the small number of boys who were enrolled on that winter's day was W F Hudson who wrote much later recalling the day it all began:

> *When Dr Welldon came to Dulwich College as Master in 1883 he found that the only recognised Prep School was Miss Shorter's, about four houses up from the bottom of Alleyn Park. It was owned by two middle-aged sisters, Miss Bessie Shorter and Mrs Brown, and was a typical mid-Victorian Dame School with antiquated methods and a ridiculous curriculum. To the youths of Dulwich it was known as Bessie's. Dr Welldon saw that something must be done and he invited Mr T H Mason MA (Cantab) to start a school which was to be allowed to call itself Dulwich College Preparatory School, although entirely independent of the College Governors. Accordingly, Mr Mason took up residence in No 1 Alleyn Park, just opposite the Alleyn's Head and the railway bridge, and started*

Portrait by H H La Thangue of Thomas Henry Mason
First Headmaster 1885 – 1887

operations in 1885 with about 13 small boys, of whom I was one aged 9½. We met at 9 o'clock on the morning of 18th January in the single room of Whitfield Lodge, and so launched the Prep on its great and glorious career. There was only one classroom, and Mr MASON did all the teaching until, a term later, he was joined by Mr Bickmore, a charming man and a splendid teacher, who afterwards made a great success of his own school, Yardley Court at Tonbridge.

W F Hudson must have made a sound impression from the start for he was the first of a number of former pupils to return as a member of staff. After a most successful career at Oxford, he became what was loosely called a 'stopgap teacher' at DCPS from 1896 to 1898. Later he joined the Indian Civil Service and led the Bombay Legislative Council.

As soon as Mason received Dr Welldon's invitation and had gained the lease on Whitfield Lodge from the Dulwich Estate Governors, he made application to use the building as a school. As the Master had instigated the idea in the first place, he was unlikely to be refused, but the normal channels had to be followed. At a meeting in February 1885, the Estate Governors reported thus:[1]

The Solicitors of the Estate reported an application by Mr T.H. Mason of Whitfield Lodge, Alleyne Park, West Dulwich, for licence to carry on a Preparatory School for Dulwich College on the premises in his occupation. We recommend that licence be given to Mr Mason personally during his occupation of the premises, subject to such regulations as the Governors and Master of Dulwich College shall require.

The school had been open for almost three weeks when the Estate Governors recommended that Mason be given a licence but it would not be until May of the following year before it was formally ratified. During this time it is likely that Mason and his school were on probation. These then are the bare bones of the start of the Prep more than a hundred years ago.

Lest there be confusion about the numbering of the houses and the exact location of Whitfield Lodge (all houses had names before they had numbers), an explanation may be useful. In 1885 the odd numbered houses in Alleyn Park (then as now on the opposite side of the road to the present school) found Number 1 (Whitfield Lodge) at the bottom of Alleyn Park and 77 at the Gypsy Hill end. Whitfield Lodge was situated where the Alleyn's Head now stands, which itself was then beside the railway bridge on the corner of Acacia Grove. It was destroyed in the Second War and eventually rebuilt across the road on its present site. In 1892 the numbers were reordered with 1 becoming the house nearest the roundabout at the South Croxted Road end and 77 at the bottom. The original houses at Numbers 1 and 3 have since disappeared. The odd numbers were then able to continue later on under the railway bridge with houses built on land facing Dulwich College, with Alleyn Park continuing to the junction with Dulwich Common. The odd numbers then

---

1 Minutes from meeting of Estate Governors 12th February 1885. Courtesy Dulwich College Archives.

came into line with the even numbers which were always arranged as they are now. The present 71 Alleyn Park (Number 7 in 1885) was called Brightlands, the name having been brought by Bessie Shorter from her '*establishment*' in Rosendale Road which had opened in 1874, and it was here that she pursued her '*antiquated methods*', though such words may be rather a harsh commentary on such a well established school. As well as her sister, Mrs Brown, there was also a Mrs Growse who was a partner, and by 1885 when the rival school opened only four doors away, Bessie may well have been thinking about retirement. Just what her views were on this new school taking her pupils is not known, but she continued for a while and actually moved to Whitfield Lodge for a year after the Prep had found larger premises further up Alleyn Park. When Bessie moved into Whitfield Lodge, what is now 71 Alleyn Park was vacated, but whereas Whitfield Lodge was destroyed, 71 survives and is one of the few remaining Victorian buildings in Alleyn Park. It is currently occupied by Chris and Charlotte King whose three sons subsequently became boarders at DCPS Brightlands virtually a hundred years after their own home had been the original Brightlands for a short time after it moved there from Rosendale Road.

With Bickmore to assist him, Mason's school flourished at Whitfield Lodge from the start and the first pupils were well grounded, some becoming eminent doctors in their day. W F Hudson relates that the boys' playground was the small back garden, but as the configuration of the present Alleyn's Head is quite different from the original house, it is hard to tell

The present Alleyn's Head is on the site of Whitfield Lodge where the school started in 1885. The original Alleyn's Head was on the other side of the road.

where this might have been. Virtually all the original boys had come from Miss Shorter's establishment '*under whose auspices,*' he writes '*and awe inspiring presence the previous generation of boys had started their education*'. These reflections from Hudson imply that Dr Welldon felt that there was need for some kind of Junior School in the Dulwich area to feed boys to the College. Glad as he was to receive boys from 'Bessie's', he clearly considered that educationally there was room for some improvement. Dr Welldon also thought that Mason's new school would benefit from having the words 'Dulwich College' incorporated into its title as it was a name which already had a well established reputation in the locality. Mason worked in close collaboration with the College and used its crest on all his documents, but his school, which was to become DCPS, was not an integral part of Dulwich College nor has it ever been. For the first few years, not surprisingly, all the pupils from 'The Preparatory School', as it was initially called, went on to the College at the age of 13. Mason also instigated a school motto '*Deus adest laborantibus*' ('God is with those who work') and this survived for some years after him. From September 1885 and just as the school was beginning to establish itself, Dr Welldon moved to become Headmaster of Harrow, so much of Mason's time in Dulwich was under the auspices of the new Master at the College, Herman Gilkes. He too would play a significant role in the development of DCPS. Then came a second unexpected move. Mason himself decided that he wanted to leave Dulwich and move on, although his reasons for doing so are not clear. One may have been that his close friend and confidant, Dr Welldon, was no longer at Dulwich. Whatever the reason, Mason was on his way at the end of the autumn term in 1886 (then called 'The Third Term') and moved to Rottingdean to join his brother George and a Mr James Hewitt at a school called Field House. He became its Headmaster in the summer term 1887, soon moved it to new premises and renamed it Rottingdean School, which grew and flourished until its eventual closure in 1962. Mason did not turn his back on the Prep though, and when he was invited to give away the prizes in December 1900 he was pleased to return and was no doubt impressed and gratified by the way the school had grown.

Thomas Henry Mason must therefore be regarded as the founder of DCPS, backed by the encouragement, but not the financial support, from the Master of Dulwich College. He was born on 7th May 1854, the son of Revd Mason Mason of Whitfield Rectory, Carlisle. As the houses at the lower end of Alleyn Park had only recently been built when Mason arrived, it is logical to assume that he gave the name Whitfield Lodge to Number 1 after his family home. There is no evidence that the house ever held any other name. It must also be assumed that he had the financial wherewithal to take out the lease in the first place, although as it happened it would only be in his name for a short time. He went briefly to Rugby School and then Pembroke College, Cambridge, and taught at Aysgarth School in Yorkshire from 1878-1882 before spending a year in France. From 1883 he taught for two years at Lambrook School (now amalgamated with Haileybury Junior School) before answering Dr Welldon's invitation to come to Dulwich, and it is almost certain that the two men met at Cambridge. Mason died on 5th February 1905 and through the pages of

The Alleynian in the following year an appeal was made to parents and former pupils for money to be raised for some kind of lasting tribute to be made for him. As a result a portrait was commissioned and this hangs in the school hall to this day. It was painted by H H La Thangue, a painter of landscapes and a Gold Medallist in 1879, who had studied in Paris and exhibited at the Royal Academy. For the portrait of Henry Mason, £34-4s was collected from well wishers. Of this £21 went to the artist, £7 was paid for the frame and 7 shillings was the cost of carriage. The hire of an MA hood cost a further 16 shillings and £1-3-2d was spent on postage. The portrait was unveiled on 21st July 1906 by Dr Welldon (who by this time was Dean of Manchester) following thirteen years as Headmaster of Harrow (1885-1898) and four years as Bishop of Calcutta (1898-1902). In his address, Bishop Welldon commended Mason to the boys telling them that he was a good schoolmaster, a good friend and a good man. He continued by saying that in his experience of the British Empire, he had always found that it was character that told in favour of the British race, and it was not always the cleverest boys who became the most successful in their later lives, but those who showed the most honourable and trustworthy characters.

Finally, no better epitaph is available than that which appeared in the *Rottingdean Magazine* for December 1905. Referring to Thomas Mason, it read:

> *We all feel we have lost a very dear friend. To the younger members of our society he was as gentle as a father, ever solicitous for their welfare, ever interested in their pursuits, ever ready with wise and kindly counsel, and to his colleagues the kindest and most genial of comrades, the truest friend that a man could have. The example of his blameless life will not fade from our memories, and with all reverence we may say of the beloved headmaster whom we have lost: he being dead, yet liveth.*

What a tribute! What a man he must have been and what a school he sent on its way in January 1885.

2   Forward with Mallinson

When Henry Mason announced his forthcoming departure, the parents petitioned the Master of the College to appoint Bickmore in his place but Herman Gilkes, who in 1885 had followed F as Master, had other ideas. He turned, as his predecessor had done, to Aysgarth, a Yorkshire preparatory school founded in 1877, where both Mason and Bickmore had taught. Although the College did not actually own 'The Preparatory School', it had instigated it only a few years earlier and clearly had every intention of maintaining a strong influence over who was to be responsible for it. In consequence, Gilkes appointed the Revd J H Mallinson, aged a mere 26, who had been educated at St Peter's School in York and was a graduate from Christ's College, Cambridge. While at university he was known on the river and rowed for his college for three consecutive years. He was introduced as a good teacher, a first rate administrator and an excellent preacher. In January 1887 he came to live at Whitfield Lodge to take over the school, which already numbered 71 boys, and he was conspicuously successful from the start. By the start of his third term, in September 1887, there were 83 boys and he was assisted by four staff including Bickmore. Music and singing were in the hands of E D Rendall, who was an assistant Master at Dulwich College and H Michaelis, who remained at the school for much of Mallinson's time and taught French.

The school timetable for the summer of 1888, which was Mallinson's second term, showed the nature of work covered by the

Revd J H Mallinson Headmaster 1887 - 1909

" Deus adest laborantibus."

DULWICH COLLEGE PREPARATORY SCHOOL.—LIST OF WORK.

SIXTH FORM, SECOND TERM, 1888.

Hours.	MONDAY.	TUESDAY.	WEDNESDAY.	THURSDAY.	FRIDAY.	SATURDAY
9—9.15.	Psalms. Prayers.	Hymn. Prayers.	Psalms. Litany.	Hymn. Prayers.	Psalms. Litany.	Hymn. Prayers.
9-15—10.	Algebra.	Arithmetic.	Euclid.	Algebra.	Arithmetic.	Euclid.
10—10-45.	Greek.	Latin.	Latin.	Latin.	Latin.	Latin.
11—11-45.	Latin.	Latin.	Swimming.	Latin.	Latin.	Swimming.
11-45—12-30.	French.	History.	Greek.	French.	History.	Greek.
2—2-55.	Bible.	Greek.	French.	Geography.	Greek.	French.
3-5 —4.	Latin.	English.	Half Holiday.	Singing.	English.	Half Holiday.
Preparation.	Latin. Arithmetic. History.	Greek. Euclid. French.	Latin. Algebra. French.	Latin. Arithmetic. History.	Greek. Euclid. French.	Latin. Algebra. History.

On Wednesday and Saturday the hours are from 9—1.

Fifth Form (Year 7) timetable for the summer term 1888

then Fifth Form (Year 7) and the length of the school day. Classes were quite small but Whitfield Lodge must have been bursting at the seams. The problem of providing sufficient space was a recurring theme from the very start and Dr Welldon's view that there was scope for a new school to be established in the area was clearly vindicated. At the beginning, the boys gathered for the first fifteen minutes of each day in a large room for Morning Prayers, a practice which has continued more or less ever since. There was an extensive amount of time devoted to Latin and in the afternoons the top two year groups had the same lessons so invariably worked together. These afternoon lessons lasted for fifty-five minutes each and school ended, as it does now, at 4 p.m. There was school on Wednesday and Saturday mornings but from 2.45 p.m. on these days there was a 'half holiday' as it was called, when seasonal games were played on the fields of Dulwich College. History and Geography were included in the syllabus and there were two periods of French per week which was progressive for the time. Swimming was held at Dulwich College, only a short walk away. Of note, too, was that in the final year some of the time allocated to Arithmetic was given to Algebra and Euclid would have been an introduction to Geometry. Mention is also made of boys being put into sets according to their ability for Arithmetic, but it would be some time before there would be any mention of Science. This pattern for the school timetable seems to be the way it was from the very start and remained little altered until the 1920s. A curt note advised boys of the start date of each term when a punctual attendance was required and expected, and the youngest age of entry was at 8.

By the third term in 1889 the school numbered 119 boys in nine classes, and the staff had grown to seven in addition to the Headmaster and the music teacher. In the top form, Form VI, were Hugh de Selincourt, who went on to captain the cricket XI at Dulwich College and who later gained renown for his book *The Cricket Match*, and Gordon Campbell, who was to win the Victoria Cross in the Great War. One of Mallinson's earliest appointments to the staff in 1886 was H O Glenn, who remained at the Prep until his death in 1922. The Lent term in 1890 started on Saturday 18th January at 9.00 a.m., a strange day to choose, the reason presumably being that it was the fifth anniversary of the founding of the School.

With such a large number of boys, Whitfield Lodge was totally inadequate so in 1891 Mallinson took a lease on 46 Alleyn Park, a house called Oakside, on the lower corner of Union Road, now Hunts Slip Road, where modern houses now stand. Mallinson kept Whitfield Lodge as his own home, and the 1891 Census Return[1] shows it being occupied by Mallinson himself, seven pupils aged 7 to 12 (who were therefore the first boarders), his mother, his sister and five servants. Later in the same year he married a Miss Powell and in due course raised a family of six children, a daughter Muriel, and five sons.

Such was the rise and popularity of the new school that the larger premises at 46 Alleyn Park quickly proved to be inadequate as well and DCPS did not stay there long. Mallinson had further expansion in mind and set his eye on two houses further up Alleyn Park, the leases of which were becoming available. In 1893 he took over Number 44 (now part of the Lower School) for school premises, but continued to live with his family in Whitfield Lodge. By 1897 he had secured the lease on neighbouring 42, a house which went by the name of Hillsborough and that is where he took his growing family. It remained the 'private' side for many years and to begin with there was no physical link between the two buildings. The leases on Numbers 1 (Whitfield Lodge) and 46 (Oakside) were surrendered in 1897 and from that date forward the school has been on its present site. Some time in 1895, the boys first wore a school cap, a practice which remained in force until 1973. The school grew quickly and when it re-commenced on 20th September 1899 there were 196 boys in twelve classes. There were only five boys in the top form but the average class size was 17 or 18 boys. The Headmaster led a staff of twelve, six of whom, in addition to himself, were graduates of Oxford or Cambridge. Bickmore, who had been the parents' choice as headmaster to succeed Mason, stayed until 1891 when he followed Mason to Rottingdean. Two years later, at the invitation of Dr Wood, Headmaster of Tonbridge School, he moved again to take over responsibility for that school's junior boys, with additional duties of headmaster's secretary and local representative of the Skinners' Company. Dr Wood felt that it would be better to house and educate younger boys at an entirely separate establishment, so in May 1898 he wrote to parents informing them that a new junior school, to be known as Yardley Court, would open in September. Bickmore's

1 *The Houses In-Between* by Patrick Darby (2000)

struggle to establish his school has no part in a history of DCPS, but in due course it thrived and grew and the Bickmore family led a most successful school until eventually a Trust was formed. It moved to a new site in 1990.

Among Mallinson's staff of twelve was Montagu Mason Snow, Second Master from 1895-1908. He was married on New Year's Day 1900 at St Stephen's Church by the Chaplain of Dulwich College, who was assisted by Mallinson. Snow's colleagues presented him with a handsome American roll-top self-locking writing table which was on display with many other presents in the recently built school hall, where two hundred people were invited to an *'At Home'* by permission of the Headmaster and were entertained by the Viennese Salon Orchestra. Soon Mr and Mrs Snow were 'conducting' a boarding house of nine boys from their home. Their son Edward is recorded as writing:

> *When I arrived upon this earth on 24th January 1901 my father was Second Master of Dulwich College Preparatory School, whose headmaster was a parson, John Henry Mallinson, severe and steeped in heavy Victorian morality. "I think so, and God thinks so too", was a remark he once made to one of the boys.*

Monty Snow with his wife Lilian, son Edward and some of the DCPS boys in 1905

One of the pupils who was at the school in Mallinson's early days was H Martin-Leake (DCPS 1889-1891), who was the brother of the Headmaster-to-be. He remembered being completely overawed by Mallinson, recalling that:

> *… he was rather a small man but with a severe countenance and a pointed wax moustache. He entered a classroom bearing a cane which he deposited on the desk in front of him with a resounding bang - he never used it on me!*

news of the school was confined to one or two paragraphs at the back of *The Alleynian*, the magazine for Dulwich College. Most of this information was simply the results of matches and games played, and there is little mention of any other activities or day-to-day routine. In 1894 a concert was held in a hall in West Norwood, and two years later the school had its own song. In 1896 the staff defeated Crystal Palace FC 4-1, and a year later an old boy, Lieutenant H E Rennick, entered the Navy and joined HMS *Imperieuse*. He was in Captain Scott's last expedition and took soundings during the voyage on the *Terra Nova*. He brought back a sledge which had been used on that expedition and presented it to the school, where it remains to this day.

No sooner had the lease on Number 42 been acquired, than Mallinson set about planning a link between that building and Number 44. Planning and construction must have been somewhat quicker in those days since the hall which was built between them was opened by the Master, Herman Gilkes, on 12th July 1897, less than a year since the lease on 42 had been secured. A small entry from *The Alleynian* revealed Gilkes' approval:

> *The Master expressed his pleasure and satisfaction with the new arrangements, showing how important it was for the school to have good surroundings, and urging boys to make the most of their privileges and advantage.*

During the same term, a sanatorium was opened on ground which had formerly been the rear of the gardens of both 42 and 44, this being needed to isolate boarders suffering from infectious diseases. Mallinson cannot be accused of being slow in coming forward, either by the way he expanded the school or by the money he chose to spend. It must be

The two houses, Numbers 44 (left) and 42 Alleyn Park in 1909, both of which Mallinson had leased by 1897. Mallinson and his family lived in 42.

assumed that he had private means since no money was forthcoming from the College and the rapid growth of his school gave him confidence to expand and cater for an ever-increasing market. Just one year later, in 1898, a large dormitory was built over the hall to house the boarders, the number of which was also increasing. Their day started with a cold bath followed by a run to the tollgate, and on their return they were given an apple by Matron, whose sitting room was on the first floor at the top of the stairs in 42 (now the PE office). This house was still the private home of Mallinson and his family, but the construction of the hall meant that it was connected on the ground and first floors to the school rooms in 44, access to which was gained through green baize doors. The hall stayed in its original form until 1959 when it was doubled in length to its present size. The former boarders' dormitory above had been converted into two classrooms much earlier.

Mallinson hardly had a moment to himself on a Sunday for it was his practice to lead his boarders on two long walks before arriving at St Stephen's Church for the 11 a.m. and the 3.30 p.m. services. The morning walk took the group up Dulwich Wood Park to Crystal Palace Parade and down College Road to church. In the afternoon, and it must have helped to walk off a large lunch, they went up Union (now Hunts Slip) Road along College Road, and then via Dulwich Common through the woods to Sydenham Hill and Crescent Wood Road and down to church. How did they all manage to keep awake during the sermon! A letter home would have been written earlier in the day and in the evening the Headmaster read to the boys, any remaining time being spent learning the Collect for that day or the Catechism. Mrs Mallinson supervised all domestic matters and, with her husband, served breakfast, lunch and supper. Eton suits were worn on Sundays and boys wore top hats which Matron brushed on a Monday morning before returning each to its box. Both the staff and boys worked hard, discipline was firm and corporal punishment was almost certainly frequent but the school gave pupils the education their parents expected and it grew and flourished, as did Mallinson's own family.

Mallinson's oldest child, Muriel, who died in 1980, had visited the school earlier after returning from a life in India. She had worked there as a missionary and a school at Srinagar in Kashmir is named after her. She recalled Matron supervising baths for the boarders in the bathroom after which she would cut a boy's toenails and give him a biscuit. Muriel went to Dulwich High School (now Rosemead School) when she was eight and walked both ways. The family had a home in Eastbourne, and H O Glenn, one of the staff, sometimes cycled there during the holidays to spend a night or two with them.

On 20th December 1898, Mallinson invited Dr Welldon, who by this time was the Bishop of Calcutta, to give away the prizes at the end of the autumn term. Bishop Welldon must have spent much of his time in the United Kingdom for he was asked again the following year and this time T H Mason, the school's founder, was invited with him. Before Bishop Welldon awarded the prizes, Mason gave a talk on the beginnings of the school fourteen years earlier. If only it had been recorded! The Mallinsons had five sons, although the youngest, Theodore, was born after his father died. John (known as Jack), the eldest, won a scholarship to Marlborough and then joined the Rifle Brigade. He had been in France for just one week when he was killed at Ypres, but that was long enough for him to be mentioned in despatches. The second son, Ernest Mallinson, known as Simon, won a foundation scholarship to Fettes and joined the Indian Army in 1916. Many years later he recalled his life as a boy at the Prep at the time:

> *I slept in the dormitory over the hall and can well remember the excellent view we got of the world-famous Brock's fireworks. They took place at the Crystal Palace and on a clear night we had a magnificent view not only of the rockets but even of the set pieces. Although my father was a rowing man he was very keen on games, especially cricket. I remember him taking us to the Oval in 1905 to watch a Test Match against the Australians. On another occasion I can recollect going to the Crystal Palace to see the redoubtable W.G. Grace. With two courts in the school grounds we got plenty of tennis and used to earn a penny an hour for rolling the courts. Threepence a week was our pocket money, so these earnings greatly helped our finances. The asphalt playground was a great place for games. Stump cricket was the great game in the summer and soccer in the winter. The San. (sanatorium) was at the paddock where also was one of the tennis courts and some lovely big trees. The playground was also used for punishment drill. I have quite a vivid memory of being a member of P.D. (Punishment Drill) one day when there was a shot followed by some shouting. A boy ran up to Glenn, who, I think, was in charge of us, and then Glenn immediately ran off to the shooting range which adjoined the playground. I can't recall what happened after that, though a few days later I can distinctly recall the whole School being assembled in Hall and my father telling us what had happened. Apparently one of the masters had accidentally shot a boy as the latter was taking his bike from the bike shed, which was close to the shooting range targets. The boy was killed, and there were all sorts of rumours flying about the place. It was a terrible tragedy and a great shock to everyone, especially to my father and the master concerned. Not surprisingly, no more shooting took place in my time.*

A silver challenge cup for rifle shooting had been given to the school in 1906, but the accident to which Simon Mallinson refers, put a stop to it. He continued:

> *Lunch in the hall was quite an occasion with over 200 boys to cater for. I remember my mother and father coping with huge joints and the masters helping too. We always had to eat up everything served to us. Sago and rice pudding were more than many of us could stomach, especially the former, which we called frogs' eyes. I can remember surreptitiously depositing these unwelcome foods into an envelope held beneath the table. We did not get away with it very often! My older brother John was my hero in those days. He was always better than I was at everything, but at one annual Sports Day I managed to pip him at the post and win the half-mile race. I still have the cup. Alas John was killed in the First World War, shortly after a fine record at Marlborough and winning a Scholarship at Cambridge. Bertie (now called Bob), a year younger than me, obtained a scholarship to King's Canterbury. My younger brothers Hugh and Theodore never went to the Prep; they were too young.*

For the pupils of DCPS at the turn of the century the week was an arduous one. For many there was a long journey to school on foot arriving in good time for Prayers every morning from 9 a.m. until 9.15. The expansion in numbers and the additional space available in 44 Alleyn Park meant that the timetable could be broadened slightly, although there were no major changes from twelve years earlier. During their week, Form VI (Year 8) had seven periods of Greek, with German appearing as an alternative on four of them. There were still six periods of Latin, four of French, four of Arithmetic, two of Algebra, two of Euclid and two of English. History lessons had increased from one to two, but Geography remained at one. Singing, Drawing, and two lessons of Gymnastics which preceded games on Wednesday and Saturday afternoons, appeared on the timetable and were innovations during the last decade of the nineteenth century. Nor were the holidays without their demands as boys were always given a task for each school holiday. In 1899, for example, the task for the older boys was to read *The Talisman* by Sir Walter Scott while the younger boys were expected to read *The Heroes* by Charles Kingsley. No mention is made anywhere of boys who failed to achieve the necessary standards in these tasks, so presumably all succeeded. As an analogy to Trafalgar, DCPS clearly expected every boy to do his duty. From 1890 to 1899 twenty-seven scholarships were gained, most of them to Dulwich College, but among the others were awards to Malvern, Oundle and King's College School, Wimbledon. Two 13-year olds gained Naval Cadetships at HMS Britannia.

So much for the Mallinson family, and what an able group they were; but it all came to an end abruptly and sadly when Mallinson died at home after a short illness on Monday 28th June 1909. He was only 48 and one can only imagine how his family, the staff, the boys and his many friends must have felt at the beginning of a new school week. During his twenty-two years as headmaster, he had seen the school grow from 78 boys to over 250, it had gained new premises and had developed out of all recognition. The funeral service, held at St Stephen's Church on 1st July, was attended by the whole school at Mrs Mallinson's request. Many former pupils were present and the large congregation testified to the great respect and esteem in which Mallinson was held. There were many floral tributes, the wreath sent by the boys being particularly moving, having a white background of flowers upon which the letters DCPS were picked out in cornflowers. Interment was at the Crystal Palace Cemetery (now Beckenham), at Elmer's End.

The widow and family were soon without a home in Alleyn Park and moved to Eastbourne during the summer holiday. Although no longer in residence, the school remained in the hands of the Mallinson family until the necessary financial formalities had been completed, this being emphasised by the front of the school list for the autumn term in 1909. This showed that Mallinson was still technically the Headmaster although deceased. The school had earlier produced a prospectus in 1906, and there can be no better postscript to Mallinson's reign than to reproduce it verbatim.

Dulwich College Preparatory School
Hillsboro', Alleyn Park,
West Dulwich, SE
Headmaster: Rev. J. H. Mallinson, M.A.
Late Scholar and Prizeman of Christ's College, Cambridge, 2nd Class in Classical Tripos

The subjects of instruction are: Divinity, Latin, English, Arithmetic and Mathematics, French, History and Geography, Drawing, Singing, Gymnastics, Drilling, and for the more advanced boys Greek or German. The mode of teaching and the choice of books are regulated by the system of Dulwich College. The School hours are: Week-days (except Wednesdays and Saturdays), Morning, 9 to 12-30; Afternoon, 2 to 3-30; Wednesday and Saturday, 9 to 1. Gymnastics, Drilling, Swimming and Singing form part of the School Curriculum, and the lessons take place in School hours.

The afternoon lessons for young boys in the three lowest forms are Gymnastics and Preparation. The School is officially recognised by the Board of Education.

The Fees are:-   For Day boys, **£7 a term.**
These fees are inclusive and no extra charge is made for use of books, stationery, school games or gymnasium.

For Boarders, **£25 a term.**
For Weekly Boarders, **£23 a term**

These Fees include tuition, laundress, seat in Church, sanatorium, and all extras as for day boys. Entrance Scholarships have been gained every year by boys in the School, and Senior Scholarships at the College by boys who received their early training at the Preparatory School.

Boarders are in the Headmaster's house; they receive every possible help and encouragement in their work; and they live with, and are under the personal supervision of Mr. and Mrs. Mallinson.

The School buildings are on high, open ground, and well drained; the new Hall, Dormitory, Class Rooms and Sanatorium have been specially planned and built on the most approved principles of modern sanitary science.

Both Boarders and Day boys have the advantage of using the College Swimming Bath, Gymnasium, Music Rooms and Playing Fields; and every care is taken to develop a sound mind in a sound, healthy body.

A part of the College grounds is reserved for the use of the boys at the Preparatory School, and masters are always present on half-holidays, and after four o'clock on other days, to organise the games.

All Fees are due in advance.

Half a term's notice must be given before the withdrawal of a boy from the School, or half the term's Fees paid.

In case of illness, if a boy is absent for six consecutive weeks, half the fees for the half term will be remitted, i.e. £1 15s.

No boy is admitted to the School before seven, or allowed to remain in it after the term or holiday in which he is thirteen years of age; and boys will be promoted to the College when they are fit to go.

All boys are required to wear a cap or straw hat with the School colours, to be obtained at the School. It is specially requested that all clothing, umbrellas, or property of any description brought to the School, should be clearly marked with the owner's name.

Every boy must be in attendance on all School days, from the first day of term until the formal dismissal of the School by the Head Master on the last day of term.

No boy is allowed to attend School from any house in which there is a case of infectious disease.

Parents are requested to notify the existence of such cases.

The holidays are seven weeks at Midsummer, a month at Christmas, and three weeks in April. There is also a holiday given on the Monday nearest to the middle of each term.

Boys living at a distance can dine at the school, at an inclusive charge of one shilling per day; and the number of dinners is entered in the following term's account.

There is also a preparation class every evening for boys who require help and supervision in preparing their work for next day.

Fee: two guineas a term.

The Fee for Instrumental Music is two guineas a term.

Applications for information, or for the admission of boys, should be made to the Head Master, who may be seen on School business, at his private house, in the morning of the two days previous to the commencement of each term and on Wednesday and Saturday morning at ten o'clock during term; and any evening by appointment.

Dulwich College Preparatory School

Masters of the School
Head Master: Rev. J. H. Mallinson, M.A. Christ's College, Cambridge

Assistant Masters
Mr. M. M. Snow, M.A., Selwyn College, Cambridge

Mr. F. H. Simpson, M.A., St. John's College, Oxford

Mr. W. R. Lewis, M.A., St. John's College, Cambridge

Mr. J. H. Stevens, M.A., St. John's College, Oxford

Mr. W. D. Monro, M.A., Trinity College, Cambridge

Mr. R. Johnstone, B.A., Keble College, Oxford

Mr. Sholto Douglas, Dulwich College

Mr. H. Michaelis, University of France and Germany

Mr. H. O. Glenn, Trained Certificated Teacher

Mr. W. L. Foxworthy, Trained Certificated Teacher

Music and Singing
Mr. H. W. Russell, Music Master at Dulwich College

Gymnastics and Drilling
Quarter-Master Sergeant Hawkins, Gymnastic Instructor at Dulwich College

HONOURS

1896	Inglis, C.S.	Scholarship, Dulwich College
	Douglas, P.W.	1st place, Naval Cadetships
	Campbell, J.D.	9th place, H.M.S. Britannia
1897	Clark, F.L.	Scholarship, Dulwich College
	Archer, T	Scholarship, Dulwich College
	Orgill, T.C.	Scholarship, Dulwich College
	French, D.G.	Scholarship, Dulwich College
1898	Nicholson, M.A.	Scholarship, Dulwich College
	Walker, W.A.	Scholarship, King's College School
1899	Firth, R.B.	Scholarship, Dulwich College
	Clark, E.C.	Scholarship, Dulwich College
	Haydon, G.S.	Scholarship, Dulwich College
	Mair, E.M.	Scholarship, St. Paul's School
	Ingrams, A.H.	Scholarship, K.E.S., Birmingham
1900	Cox, T.F.W.	Scholarship, Dulwich College
	Grogan, W.M.	Scholarship, Dulwich College

	Clifton, E.M.V.	Scholarship, Dulwich College
1901	Wheeler, A.M.	Scholarship, Dulwich College
	Aitchison, J.G.	Scholarship, Dulwich College
	Collinson, W.E.	Scholarship, Dulwich College
	Spurgeon, R	Scholarship, Dulwich College
	Ashwin, M.F.	Scholarship, Westminster School
	Ratcliffe-Cousins, E.R.J.	Scholarship, Westminster School
1902	Martin, W.H.	Scholarship, Dulwich College
1903	Goddard, C.S.	Scholarship, Dover College
	Smith, E.C.	Scholarship, Dulwich College
	Wissmann, J.R.	Scholarship, Dulwich College
1904	Dobbyn, A.F.	Scholarship, Dulwich College
1905	Attwater, A.H.	Scholarship, Dulwich College
	Thompson, D.C.	Scholarship, Dulwich College
	Gray, E.H.	Scholarship, Westminster School

N.B. The Scholarships at Dulwich College are open to all boys under 13 years of age on May 1.

1904	Courtney, G.S.	Passed into R.N.C. Osborne
	Dobbyn, A.F.	Passed into R.N.C. Osborne
	Berry, H.H.	Passed into R.N.C. Osborne
	Tomkinson, L.E.	Passed into R.N.C. Osborne

3   Leake – A Golden Era

The death of J H Mallinson came as a great shock and for a while the school was stunned. Montagu Snow, the Second Master, had left in 1908 and until Mallinson's successor could be appointed, one of the staff, the Revd Rupert Johnstone, became acting Headmaster. Mallinson's son Simon was a boy when his father died and he remembered Johnstone as being a very strict disciplinarian who showed him no favours.

One person who was very interested in the appointment was the Revd W R M Leake who was the housemaster at The Orchard, one of the boarding houses for Dulwich College. He had the wherewithal both academically and financially to secure control of the Preparatory School, and to all intents and purposes he was the ideal person. The vacancy which had thus arisen presented him with a great challenge and opportunity. Born on 31st December 1865, he entered Dulwich College in 1879 and while there captained both the 1st XV

DULWICH COLLEGE PREPARATORY SCHOOL.

MASTERS OF THE SCHOOL.

Late Head Master:
Rev. J. H. MALLINSON, M.A.,
Christ's College, Cambridge.

Acting Head Master:
Mr. R. JOHNSTONE, M.A.,
Keble College, Oxford.

Assistant Masters:
Mr. R. PRATT, B.A., Hertford College, Oxford.
Mr. G. S. DAVIDSON, M.A., Queen's College, Cambridge.
Mr. W. S. BELL, B.A., Peterhouse, Cambridge.
Mr. R. A. BRANDRAM, M.A., Christ's College, Cambridge.
Mr. B. H. JOHNSON, B.A., University of Oxford.
Mr. E. C. CLARK, B.A., London University.
Mr. R. E. A. CHESSEX, B.A., Caius College, Cambridge.
Mr. E. WALLING, B.A., Magdalen College, Oxford.
Mr. H. O. GLENN, Trained Certificated Teacher.
Mr. E. P. GRAHAM BARROW, Trained Certificated Teacher.
Mr. S. A. WRIGHT, Trained Certificated Teacher.

Music and Singing:
Mr. H. W. RUSSELL, Music Master at Dulwich College.

Gymnastics and Drilling:
Quarter-Master Sergeant HAWKINS, Gymnastic Instructor at Dulwich College.

List of staff for the Autumn Term 1909, showing Rupert Johnstone as Acting Headmaster

and the 1st XI, as well as being Editor of *The Alleynian*. From 1885 until 1888 he was at Selwyn College, Cambridge, where he gained a Third in the Classics Tripos and achieved three rugby blues. He returned to Dulwich College in 1889 as a junior member of staff and while there played rugby for England on three occasions in 1891. Not surprisingly, he quickly made a favourable impression on the Master, A H Gilkes. Leake married in 1901, had three sons and a daughter, and was ordained in 1909.

Gilkes was not in a position to appoint Leake, nor indeed to prevent him from applying, but he was able to sanction the appointment and it is clear that without the Master's approval, the appointment would never have been made. That being so, Leake still had to gain the approval of the College Governors and be obliged to follow their requirements. He must have been quick off the mark for on 16th July 1909, just over a fortnight after Mallinson's death, there was a meeting of the College Governors at which reference was made to Leake's application. The following is minuted:[1]

> *(a) On condition that the appointment of a new Headmaster of the Preparatory School is approved by the Master of Dulwich College, the Governors are prepared to continue the arrangement sanctioned by the Minute passed on the meeting held on 18th May 1886, provided that the Headmaster undertakes that boys will not be retained in the Preparatory School after the age of 13 years.*
>
> *(b) The Governors reserve the right to cancel these arrangements upon giving the Headmaster one term's notice of their intention of doing so.*

So from the beginning of the spring term in 1910 the Revd W R M Leake became the Prep's third headmaster, a position he would hold for twenty-four years: a period which was to be a golden age in the school's history.

Leake had impressed Gilkes while a young master at the College and felt that he owed much of his success to the encouragement given to him by his former mentor. In later years

Leake with his staff – Summer 1911

1 Minutes of Dulwich College Governors: Courtesy Dulwich College Archives

Leake was to write a lengthy appreciation of the life of A H Gilkes in his book *Gilkes and Dulwich*, and this gives an interesting insight into the great respect which Leake held for Gilkes. That said, and from early on there were strains in their relationships. In her book on the History of Dulwich College, Sheila Hodges makes it apparent that the College was not prosperous in 1910 and the number of day boys, though not boarders, had fallen:[2]

> *The governors had allowed to slip through their fingers one way of increasing the income which had been urged by Gilkes – the purchase of the Preparatory School by the College when the Headmaster (Mallinson) died in 1909. This would, he felt, have put the finances on a sound basis and to quote Gilkes "it would do away with a kind of competition between the Preparatory School and the College which is disagreeable".*

Gilkes privately recorded his disappointment that, for the second time in twenty-five years, the College Governors had missed the opportunity of making what is now DCPS the official preparatory school for Dulwich College. He considered that in 1885 Dr Welldon should not have invited his friend Thomas Mason to start a school which could use the name of Dulwich College in its title, but he should have created it outright and appointed Mason as Headmaster. Patrick Darby[3] suggests that the correct reading of DCPS is not as the Preparatory School FOR Dulwich College but the College Preparatory School OF Dulwich, yet the word 'for' was the word used by the Dulwich Estate Governors at their meeting in February 1886 when the school was granted a licence. This ambiguity hardly removes the confusion which has existed ever since. Darby continues:

> *Gilkes was considerably consoled by the knowledge that Leake was taking over the establishment, and for the next twenty-five years that confidence was fully justified.*

So Leake left the College and became Headmaster and sole owner of the Prep from 1910. But that was not all. Gilkes felt that the sum of money paid to Mallinson's executors for the goodwill of the school should rightfully belong to the College. About £3000 was involved, a lot of money in those days, and Gilkes felt very strongly about it, for in his own hand he wrote:[4]

> *The College made the Preparatory School and could at any time destroy it.*

A little later he relents and continues:

> *The payment of this sum by Mr Leake makes this difficult . . . Mr Leake has been a useful master here and will make an excellent master of The Preparatory School.*

To be fair, the quarrel was between Gilkes and the executors of Mallinson's will and not directly with Leake himself and the matter was left unresolved. Sheila Hodges emphasises that despite these apparent problems *'competition behind the scenes was not apparent to outsiders or the boys, many of whom came on to the college from the prep school'.*

2 *God's Gift* by Sheila Hodges (1981)
3 *The Houses In-Between* by Patrick Darby (2002)
4 Courtesy Dulwich College Archives

Whereas Leake generally enjoyed reasonably cordial relations with the College and was thought of highly by those with influence there, the same cannot always be said for the Estate Governors, for just over a year after he had become Headmaster, the following statement is minuted:[5]

> *The Revd W R M Leake, proprietor of Dulwich College Preparatory School, has erected at the rear of the school house a building constructed of corrugated iron and wood for the purpose of providing changing accommodation for the pupils of the school, and was not aware that the Governors' sanction to such building was necessary. I called Mr Leake's attention to the matter, and now he writes that he erected the building in entire ignorance of the terms of his lease and asks for the sanction of the Governors to the retention of the building as it has proved so useful in connection with the school. I see no objection to the application being granted but think Mr Leake should pay the usual surveyors' fees.*

The Estate Governors had not wasted much time in discovering the arrival of a new building without their approval but permission was duly granted and the fee paid. The building served several purposes and in the 1920s was being used as two classrooms, the only division being a low wooden partition with a curtain as a door. On Wednesdays and Saturdays the partition was pulled back and the space used as a changing room for games. Later it became a small gymnasium and a changing room, with a boiler for hot water being added in 1935. It was demolished in 1971 when it made way for the then new Annexe building.

The corrugated building which was used as a gymnasium for which Leake had to gain the approval of the Colllege Estate Governors. It was demolished in 1971. The Paddock is in the foreground.

5 *Minutes of the Estate Governors' meeting, 26th February 1911 (courtesy Dulwich College Archives)*

With greater independence than his predecessors, Leake soon became his own man, running his school in his own way. Almost immediately he created two prizes for General Knowledge to commemorate the name of Mallinson who in Leake's own words '*made the school what it is to-day*'. These prizes are still awarded but are given now for achievement. The words 'Dulwich College Preparatory School' had been shown on school lists from the start and Leake began to emphasise this title, and the letters DCPS as the formal name of the school, although the College continued to refer to it as 'The Preparatory School'. After all, why should it continue to give its name to a school of which it had never been a part and which seemed to be flourishing in its own right, even though it had, by invitation, created the embryo from which it had developed in the first place? Leake quickly made his mark and established many of the traditions which survive today. In his first year, on 17th November, he introduced something totally new to the school in the form of a cinematograph exhibition in the hall. This was very progressive for the time and was rated as a great success. A year later, on 30th September 1911, he introduced what was to become a long-standing tradition at DCPS - Hobbies Day. This was a day when boys brought their hobbies to school for all to see and it soon became a social occasion for parents and friends. Later it became healthily competitive.

Apart from the Mallinson prizes, many awarded each year have their origins in the Leake era as do four words associated with DCPS – Chippeways, Deerfeet, Mohicans and Ojibwas. All schools are sub-divided into smaller units not only for convenience but also for healthy competition between them. First mention is made of the tribes in 1916, so it must be assumed that Leake instigated them about then. How satisfied, and perhaps surprised, he would be to know that they are still going strong in the next millennium. But why North American Indian tribes? The poems about Hiawatha by Longfellow were popular at the beginning of the last century. They had been set to music by Coleridge Taylor and were performed frequently at the Albert Hall. Leake personally chose the four names because he felt that the characteristics of the tribes portrayed were worthy of imitation. But there is a flaw. Chippeway, Mohican and Ojibwas are all names of North American Indian tribes which can be traced, and one in particular is well known from the book *The Last of the Mohicans*. The odd one out is Deerfeet. Research shows that there is no such tribe and Deerfoot was actually a man called Louis Bennett, who was a tribe chief in the USA in 1862. Edward S Ellis subsequently wrote stories about him and a copy of *Deerfoot on the Prairies* is in the school archive. Leake must have been well aware of this anomaly, as covers of the first magazines show three symbols and one head, each representing one of the four tribes.

Each tribe was divided into a number of patrols and the senior boys in each patrol were known as Patrol Leaders. There were also a number of Tribe Leaders. These were the forerunners of the Prefects and Senior Boys which were to follow in later years. The tribes almost came to grief only a few years after they had been created. Towards the end of the First War, a few members of staff suggested that the names of the tribes be changed to those of the great generals of the day – Haig, Kitchener and Rawlinson etc. Fortunately Leake resisted this idea because he felt the tribe names had an enduring appeal and were applicable in peace and war. So the tribes live on.

One of the people to make contact with the school many years later was Leake's daughter Marjorie, who was only four years old when her father became headmaster and who was able to offer some vivid recollections of the school in those early years. She believed there were about 200 boys when her father took over, of whom 30 were boarders. The buildings were used very much as they had been in Mallinson's time: 42 Alleyn Park continued principally to be the Headmaster's residence, with 44 being used by the boys as classrooms. The hall had been built between them (then half its present size) in 1897 and above was a large dormitory where most of the boarders were housed. The hall was used for lunch and for Morning Prayers which were held between 9.00 and 9.15 each morning and were an important part of the day. Each day, Leake read an appropriate collection of Collects and the boys and staff responded with the Lord's Prayer or the General Confession. There was a hymn and a reading from the Bible, sometimes read by a senior boy. Finally Leake read out any relevant announcements and commendations about boys who had done particularly well.

Leake's wife was always involved in the welfare of the boys and for her it was a full-time job. She was responsible for the catering and engaged domestic staff. The classrooms as well as the other rooms were heated by coal fires in those days and Mrs Leake went round to every classroom before school to make sure the fires were burning well. The first central heating system using coal boilers and iron radiators was not installed until 1919 and what a luxury that was – for Mrs Leake if for no one else! Before then rumour had it that it was often the practice of a master taking a lesson to stand in front of the fire, thus warming himself, but preventing the heat from reaching the rest of the room. Masters wore academic gowns in those days and it was the habit of the wickedest boys to try to cause a draft behind the master so that his gown became engulfed in flames from the fireplace. Apparently this happened more than once but such antics came to an end when central heating arrived. In 1916 the school fee for a day boy was £7 a term inclusive, with no extra charge for the use of books, games or the gymnasium. Boarders were charged £25 per term. By 1920 this had increased to £10 for day boys over 11 and to £26 for boarders.

During the First World War, the number of boarders did not decrease, although the possibility of aerial bombardment was a real threat. Although slight compared with what was to follow in the Second War, it was nevertheless taken seriously at the time. If an air raid was anticipated, the boarders were led down to the cellar of 42 Alleyn Park where it was usual for the older boys to read stories to the younger ones. The sanatorium was approximately where the present Annexe (2004) now stands and was in the charge of Mrs Marshall, who had a connection with the main building by a simple field telephone. If there was an air raid and there were sick boys in the sanatorium, Mrs Leake would go over there and stay until the raid was over. If, on the other hand, Mrs Marshall was alone in the sanatorium because there were no sick boys, she would come over to the main house, usually after much hesitation, and on the way across would wear a metal dish cover on her head as a protection from the possibility of falling shrapnel.

The war years brought sadness and grief to many homes. In those days Morning Assembly was conducted in the hall and many of the boys whom Leake had known, mainly from the College but from the Prep too, went to France and never returned. The Kingsdale Estate was yet to be built so the railway was clearly visible from the hall. Leake said years later that when he saw a train load of railway trucks passing the school on their way to France, some of which were carrying the first tanks to be used in warfare, he became full of emotion because he knew that many of the young men apportioned to them would be among those not to return. One such example was R B Firth, after whom the History Prize is named and dedicated. Robert Firth was born in 1887 and was a boy at the Prep until 1899, when he gained a scholarship to Dulwich College. While there he became captain of cricket and football and was later awarded a scholarship to King's College, Cambridge where he gained a First Class in the Classical Tripos. Leake had obviously been impressed with Firth while they were at Dulwich together and invited him to join the staff at the Prep as soon as he became headmaster. Firth stayed for six years, and at the end of the summer term in 1916 he answered the call and joined the London Rifle Brigade. Just over a year later on 26th September 1917, he died from wounds sustained at St Julien, not far from Ypres a few days earlier, leaving a wife and two children. The large War Memorial in front of Dulwich College shows that many boys from there lost their lives in the First War. There are no precise records to show which of those boys had come from the Prep, but obviously a fair proportion had done so. The war brought its heroes, as well as its victims, and no less than four former Prep boys gained that most prestigious of all awards, the Victoria Cross.

Captain (later Rear Admiral) Gordon Campbell had been at DCPS from 1894 until 1898 when he went on to Dulwich College. He made a name for himself during the First War with what became known as Q-ships. At the time, submarines were considered to be inhumane weapons of war and there were no scruples about sinking them. Q-ships were innocent looking merchant ships which were secretly armed and despatched to lure submarines. When challenged by a submarine, some of the crew of the merchant Q-ship (the panic party) appeared to abandon ship. When the submarine surfaced to deal the final blow, the remainder of the crew quickly uncovered guns and opened fire. On 17th February 1917, the merchant ship *Farnborough*, a Q-ship under Campbell's command, was struck by a torpedo from a submarine off Southern Ireland. The panic party left and the submarine surfaced. Then when the U-boat was very close, the Q-ship opened fire with devastating results. A fearful battle ensued resulting in the surrender of the submarine's crew and a struggle to keep the Q-ship afloat. For this action, and for the bravery shown, Captain Gordon Campbell was awarded the Victoria Cross.

Born in 1891, Benjamin Geary was at DCPS from 1900-1904 and went on to St Edmund's School, Canterbury. He subsequently joined the East Surrey Regiment, was commissioned in August 1914 and was sent to France a month later. On 20th December 1915, he was at Hill 60 near Ypres, which was being constantly attacked by German forces, resulting in fierce fighting. At one point he was the only unwounded officer. He was severely wounded the next day but survived. His citation reads: *'mainly owing to the splendid gallantry and example of Second Lieutenant Geary who exposed himself with entire disregard to danger, he showed conspicuous bravery and determination.'* Much of his life thereafter was spent in Canada where he was a leading administrator in Parliament. He also served in the Second World War.

Arthur James Fleming Sandes was also from the East Surrey Regiment and was at DCPS from 1903 until 1907, going on to King's School, Canterbury. He joined up in the Artists' Rifles in August 1914 and was commissioned with the East Surrey Regiment in 1915. On 15th September during the Battle of Loos, he showed extreme courage by throwing bombs at the enemy by hand from a parapet in full view of the enemy who were only twenty yards away. This most gallant act, for which he gained the VC, put new heart into his men, rallied them and saved the situation.

The fourth recipient of the VC was Richard Basil Jones, who had been at DCPS from 1906 to 1910 but he was not so fortunate. On leaving Dulwich College, Jones joined the Loyal North Lancashire Regiment as a Second Lieutenant in September 1914. He went to France in September 1915 and a year later on 21st May 1916, at Vimy Ridge, kept his men together by a *'splendid display of courage'*. When he had no ammunition left, he threw stones at the enemy, *'thus inspiring and encouraging his men'*. Sadly, and one might say almost inevitably, he was killed. His men fought on and one of them said afterwards: *'We could not help doing our best as he was so brave and cheerful'*. He was just 19 years of age and his VC was awarded posthumously. The Headmaster and his family were so moved by this tragic event that a prize was established in his memory, and the Jones VC prize for Geography is still awarded each year.

Although the school did not leave London as it did in 1939, the First War influenced school life. As an example, rather than award prizes in 1916, £60 was given to the Red Cross instead. War, and the terrible loss of life which resulted from it, cast a shadow over the following years. There were some fortunate survivors though, including two of Leake's staff, C P Hamilton and A E J Inglis, both of whom volunteered for service in 1915 and were lucky enough to return to school when war ended.

As time went on, the College began to have less influence over the Prep. News about it in *The Alleynian* became sparse, with more and more space being devoted to Alleynians who had lost their lives in the Great War. In 1919, Leake decided that the time had come for the Prep to have a magazine of its own and the first issue appeared in the autumn term of that year. The first editor was W W Butler, a member of staff who was also keen for the Prep to have its own magazine. Not long before he died in 1957, and referring to the magazine from the previous year, he wrote '*the magazine has grown in size and influence far beyond the wildest dreams of its originators*'. One wonders what he would make of the modern editions.

Although enjoying a close relationship with Dulwich College, Leake appears to have chosen this moment to stop using the College crest and motto on concert programmes and other literature produced by the school. At the same time he devised the interwoven letters DCPS which have been used by the school ever since. By retaining the word College in the formal title, he was obviously keen that the close links established over the years should not be lost. As a further move towards total independence, DCPS was visited by His Majesty's Inspectors during the spring term in 1921 and as a result the school was separately recognized by the Board of Education.

Whether or not it was a new dawn brought about by the ending of the Great War which gave Leake the impetus to get things done we shall never know, but the school magazine was not the only aspect of DCPS life to be introduced in 1919. On 19th October the school held its first Harvest Festival Service in the hall, a practice which has continued ever since, the war years aside. It was clearly a great success, but a magazine article showed there was some doubt beforehand :

Cover of the first magazine, autumn term 1919, showing three symbols and a head (Deerfoot)

> *We wondered whether it would be a success. We hoped it would be, but as it was our first attempt, no-one was quite sure. However since the notice on the board said, "Bring anything from a pea to a pumpkin," we thought we would help and bring what we could. At the beginning of the day, Room 3 was just an ordinary classroom, but at the end of the afternoon it resembled an extraordinary greengrocer's shop. Sometimes as we watched boys staggering along with extra large marrows, we wondered whether they were bringing the marrows or the marrows were bringing them. Lessons in Room 3 became more and more difficult as the day progressed.*

Alan Wesencraft (DCPS 1921-1925) remembered Butler as a talented teacher of English literature who suffered from severe arthritis brought on by the appalling conditions he suffered in the trenches during the First War, yet remaining cheerful and even-tempered. The first magazine cover illustrated the totems of the four tribes and was designed by

M A Glenn, daughter of H O Glenn, who was a master at the time. From 1919 there are therefore more accurate records about the school's achievements and events. Leake took the opportunity in the first issue to pen a piece of verse which appeared as a frontispiece. It reveals a great deal about his philosophy, his attitude to life in general and to the school in particular.

> *To Our Team*
>
> *All God's world's His Team*
> *And we are merely players*
> *Doers and not sayers*
> *One for another.*
>
> *Life is not a dream,*
> *Where each one drifts apart*
> *Seeking his own self chart,*
> *One from another*
>
> *Follow down that stream*
> *Whose current more and more*
> *Sets to that distant shore*
> *One in the other*
>
> *Hope doth brightest gleam*
> *Where sanctifies each soul*
> *This truth as its goal*
> *All for the other*
>
> *God bless this school, our team,*
> *Where each one strives his best*
> *To make this manifest*
> *To one another.*

After the Harvest service all the produce was taken to the British Home for the Incurables on Crown Point on the following day. The large items like pumpkins were put into a hand cart and dragged by boys along Alleyn Park and up Salter's Hill, the rest being carried in small baskets. Glenn chose eighteen boarders to do this and on arrival at the Home, they received a great welcome from the Matron-in-Charge. The whole exercise was a tremendous success, to say nothing of the goodwill which the school generated in the local area and an annual Harvest Festival Service, when boys bring in garden produce from home, has been held ever since. A few years later, in 1923, some of the vegetables and fruit were taken to the Home after the service by a member of staff in his motorbike and side car, but many of the smaller items were still carried by a group of boys. Interestingly, gifts brought to school for the Harvest Festival Service are still taken to the Home for the Incurables to this day, although there are other outlets too. Today the PTA is much involved, as boys cannot be taken out of lessons for activities like that now.

Links with Dulwich College were not totally severed in 1919. There was much patriotism after the First War and, for some years after, DCPS boys went to the College each year on Armistice Day to place a wreath on the War Memorial. A two minute silence was observed during which time the Union Flag was lowered to half mast. Leake also instigated the practice of finishing school one hour earlier on Empire Day (May 24th) although this was not always the case, for in 1924 he decided that the standard of work in the school was not high enough and the hour off was postponed until later in the term.

Another idea instigated by Leake at this time, and which lasted for many years, quickly became known as *Charity Shillings*. In 1923 Leake decided that the school should maintain (or sponsor - to use the modern term) a bed at King's College Hospital for patients who would not otherwise have the means to pay for medical care. For the first few years this was for a child's cot but the scope was widened to become a bed. To pay for its upkeep, each boy in the school was encouraged to bring one shilling (5p) to school on a fixed day each term. The bed became known as the 'Dulwich Prep Bed' and as Leake obviously valued this link with the local community, the dedication of the bed was done in style.

> On Tuesday June 24th the whole school down to 2B journeyed to the hospital for the dedication of the bed. A large number of boys marched down from the school in tribes and others went by bus, cycled or walked. When everybody had arrived, we formed up in tribes outside the hospital and marched in. Having traversed a broad passage, we found ourselves in the hospital chapel which is in the centre of the building, and the light which filtered through the beautiful stained glass windows of the chapel was very restful after the glare in the noisy streets. Prayers were said by the Revd W R M Leake and there was an address from the Revd R U Galer, the hospital chaplain and himself an old Preparatory boy.

For a few years thereafter, a group of boys went to the Chapel at King's College Hospital each year for a service of rededication and continuing commitment to the bed, this invariably occurring on Ascension Day. In May 1926 these plans were thwarted and the service was held in the school hall instead because the General Strike made transport arrangements difficult. The practice for each boy to bring a shilling to school each term continued long after health care became free with the arrival of the National Health Service after the Second War. After then, the money went to other worthy causes, but Charity

Shillings did not end until shortly before decimalisation in 1972. By that time a shilling would not have gone anywhere like as far as it would have done in 1923, and the fact that the sum asked remained at a shilling for so long shows that whatever problems there may have been over the years, inflation was not one of them. After 1972, the school raised money for charity in other ways.

Although the school began to recover from the gloom of the First World War, sorrow sometimes came from other directions. One date when tragedy struck was a most unusual one – 22nd February 1922, or 22-2-22. On that day, the school received news of the death of not one but two of its serving masters. The first was H O Glenn who had joined the school under Mallinson in 1887 and his obituary in the school magazine tells that '*he devoted his life to the service of the school and the boys he loved. It is only with the passing of time that we shall realise how much he will be missed, both in the form room and in the playground*'. He had been unwell only for a week or so and his death from pneumonia was totally unexpected. A picture donated after his death described him as '*a shepherd to the school*' and it is clear that he was much respected. The following account of him from Alan Wesencraft illustrates not only the great respect that Glenn had for the boys and they for him, but it is also a social cameo of the time. Wesencraft had lost his cap after a Christmas play at St Barnabas Hall and was concerned that his mother would chastise him for the expense of a new cap and be worried about his risk of catching cold without head cover on a bitter evening:

H O Glenn

As I stood in the now deserted cloakroom wondering with considerable anxiety how best to deal with the situation, I became aware of an elderly bearded gentleman standing by my side. It was Mr Glenn whom I recognised from morning assemblies although we had never met. 'You don't look very happy', he said, in a kindly voice, 'Can I be of any help?' With immense relief, I told him my problem. 'Don't worry about your cap', he said, 'it will be handed in. Meanwhile my hand will serve as a cap.' He then placed his hand gently on my head, told me to take him to my home and that all would be well. This plan at once removed all my fears and together we set

off through Dulwich Village, Half Moon Lane and to Norwood Road where I lived, and not once did
he remove his hand. Giving me a cheerful goodbye and a final injunction not to worry, he turned and
disappeared into the gloom and cold night air. There is no possible way by which Mr Glenn could have
known who I was nor where I lived. He had come across a small unhappy boy, and without any thought
for himself, had taken the only way possible for removing that unhappiness: he was truly a remarkable
man performing an act of kindness.

The other death that day in February 1922 was not quite so unexpected, although it was a cruel blow that the two should occur on the same day. W J Ward, who had undergone a major operation in King's College Hospital, had joined the staff in 1914. His magazine tribute stated that '*he will long be remembered for his almost stern adherence to duty and his keen sense of humour*'. Somehow these few words give an idea of the sort of person he was.

Nor was it just the staff. On 5th May 1925 the school learnt of the death of Charles Goodwin, who was just ten years old. Again the magazine tells that: '*Little Goodwin died at the beginning of the term after a severe illness. He has been greatly missed by his school, his cheery smile and gentle manners making him loved by all*'. In the days before penicillin and antibiotics, such events were not that rare. The rest of his tribute is of particular interest. '*His brother, L. F. H. Goodwin, founded the Deerfeet in 1916 before entering the College with a Junior Scholarship*'. This presumably means he was the first Deerfeet Tribe Leader, so from this the birth of the tribe system can be ascertained. L F H Goodwin was later to become an Admiral and a DCPS Governor.

Leake employed several members of staff who were to be at DCPS for many years. Among his most loyal were the two wartime survivors, A E J Inglis and C P Hamilton. Inglis had been a boy at the Prep before moving on to the College, and while there he became editor of *The Alleynian*, a member of the 1st XV and head boy at Ivyholme[5] when Leake was its housemaster. In 1906 he went on to King's College, Cambridge and not long after he graduated, Leake became Headmaster at DCPS. One of the first things he did was to offer Inglis a job. He stayed until 1915, when he volunteered for military service, returning afterwards to DCPS for a short while. From 1920 to 1921 he taught at Uppingham for four terms, but he cannot have been particularly happy there because the lure of Dulwich brought him back again. At the time most of the boarders were being looked after by Leake himself with their dormitory over the hall. Leake needed this space for an ever-growing school and he had it in mind to move them to somewhere nearby. He must have been disappointed when Inglis went to Uppingham, and it is not unreasonable to suppose that he invited him back with the added incentive of giving him greater responsibility. On his immediate return Inglis agreed to take an overflow of boarders into his home at 28 Alleyn Park, a large Victorian house called St Agnes, and from the autumn term of 1922

---

5 Ivyholme is one of the Dulwich College boarding houses, but in 1906 was in a different building from that of today.

Leake's boarders joined them. This house does not exist today and after being damaged in the Second War the site was subsequently swallowed up by Kingsdale School. In 1929 Inglis left again, this time to start a preparatory school of his own, called Lanesborough, in Guildford, taking with him in a joint venture W Walker from the DCPS staff. In typical style, and no doubt with a tinge of sadness to see them go, Leake gave both these gentlemen his blessing. Charles Hamilton joined the staff in 1913 as a junior sports master and subsequently taught History for a long time. He too volunteered for military service in 1915, having reached the rank of major, soon after becoming Leake's second master. Known affectionately as 'Hammy', he was Leake's right-hand man for many years.

When Inglis and Hamilton went to war in 1915 Leake employed a colourful Swiss called Paul Meyrat to teach French. Although they returned, he outstayed them both and remained at the school until the day of his death in 1949. Meyrat's boisterous and flamboyant nature meant that he terrified at the beginning those who did not know him, but he came to be loved and respected by boys as they came to know him better. K C Bishop (DCPS 1920-1925) remembered him as '*Monsieur Meyrat – the dashing blond Frenchman with his fast motorbike*'. No doubt being regarded as French was better for his image. Wesencraft also remembered him for his passion for fast motor bikes and his cheerful disregard for the speed limit which at that time was 20 mph. W W Butler remembered Meyrat even more colourfully one Sports Day: '*Meyrat, hyacinthine locks waving in the breeze and emulating the colour of his flag, as with Gallic enthusiasm, he urged the Ojibwas to triumph in the pole race*'. Meyrat instigated the trips to Paris (described in Chapter 14) and he became an influential figure in the school generally. Meyrat spent the rest of his working life at DCPS and many years later taught me to remember for life those French verbs which take *être* in the past tense. He died suddenly, when I was a boy in his form, in 1949.

Bishop's report for the summer term in 1922, when he was ten, showed that History, Geography, Composition, Grammar and Repetition were all listed under English, and in the report a one word summary for each subject was adequate. Latin, French and Maths were listed separately, everything else being classified under Extra Subjects. Science was still far away on the horizon as a classroom subject, although it had been introduced as a club. A similar report for M S Lumsden (DCPS 1926-1930), almost a decade later, showed the format to be exactly the same. Lumsden's school fees for the summer term in 1930 were £9-14-6d.

Another person to become devoted to DCPS until he retired was W A Sheppard, 'Shep', who joined the staff in January 1924. Like Meyrat he played a significant role in the development of DCPS, especially during the war years in Wales, and became Leakey's trusted Deputy. Close on the heels of Shep came Freddie Taylor, 'FNT', who joined the staff just eighteen months later in September 1925. He too would give the rest of his working life to DCPS and the three men worked together as a team, taking the Prep through some of its most

DULWICH COLLEGE PREPARATORY SCHOOL.

REPORT FOR THE 2 TERM, 1922

Name.....Bishop K.C.....................Form III B   No. of Boys 24

Age....10....yrs....2....mo.   Average age of Form.....11....yrs....7....mo.

Days absent 1.........   Days late 2.........   Conduct.....V. good.....

FORM SUBJECTS.	TERM'S ORDER.	EXAMTN. ORDER.	FINAL ~~ORDER~~ Place	REMARKS.
ENGLISH	7	6		Hist. Good. *CMl.* Geo. Good. *WH.B.W.* Comp. Good *Huff* Gr. and Rep. Fairly good *WW* Writing Reading } Good *RO.* Spelling
LATIN	1	1	1st	Very good indeed. Has done a splendid term's work. *AGg.*
FRENCH	21	4 avg.		Has worked well in spite of low place in term. Slow in oral work Exam: quite good.
MATHEMATICS Class 4 Middle School No. of boys 17	9	6	8	Geom. Quite satisfactory *AG* Alg. Has much improved, especially Arith. during the latter part of term. *J.J.*
EXTRA SUBJECTS (if any) Drawing				Fair

PHYSICAL DEVELOPMENT : Weight

GENERAL REMARKS : Capital. deserves his triumph. I am very pleased with him. *GRush.*

Next term begins on.....Friday 22nd.....~~the~~ day of.....September.....and ends on.....December 20th.....
All Boys must return punctually on the day named.   The only ground for exemption allowed by School Rules is sickness or exposure to infection.   Notice of this must be sent before the opening of the School to the Head Master.

Each Boy must bring with him on the first his heath certificate signed.   A Boy who fails to do this will be sent home and his tribe will lose a mark.   No boy shall return to School from a house in which there has been any infectious disorder during the previous month.

Boarders *must* return before 7 p.m. on the EVENING BEFORE the day of Commencement.

School Report for K C Bishop – Summer Term 1922

troubled times fifteen or so years later. Shep, Taylor and Meyrat came to be known and loved by generations of boys, many of whom later on would recognise the contribution to their lives these men had made. Taylor quickly became known for his sense of humour. In 1938, for example, he tried to convince the school (and his own mother) that he had a twin. He managed to do this by sitting at one end of a row when the school photograph was being taken by a slow rotating camera. Then quickly he slipped around the back just in time to be seated again when the camera reached the other end of the row. One hears of this prank being performed by pupils from time to time but never by a member of staff. Shep and Taylor became firm friends, and in 1926 they were joined by W G Doig Gibb. Gavin Gibb had been a pupil at DCPS from 1913 until 1916 and had clearly impressed Leake by his enthusiasm and skill for sport, especially rugby football. Although he took a share in the academic curriculum, specialising in Maths and Modern Languages, it was on the sports field and as Chippeway tribemaster that Gibb made his mark. As coach to the 1st XV through the 1930s he had a splendid record of successes. He left the school in 1939 for the duration of the war to be a special constable in London and returned in 1945, until forced to retire through ill health in 1950. In 1929 another duo arrived. Russell Taylor was appointed as the first Director of Music and David Livingston came to teach Art and Drama. The two worked closely as a pair in the 1930s and more will be heard of them later. Reg Hatton also joined the staff in 1929. He accompanied the school to Wales during its evacuation in the Second War and played a major part there, leaving DCPS in 1946 to take up a post at the City of London School. Leake was beginning to create a nucleus of staff around him who would serve the school for many years.

Fortunately Sheppard put some of his memories into writing[6] and from these some idea can be gained of a typical school day in the 1920s. In 1924 school started at 9.00 and finished at 3.30. From 3.30 until 4.00 there was Punishment Drill and Corrections and also practices for rugby and cricket in the appropriate seasons. A P Hemming (DCPS 1921-27) recalls that Punishment Drill was taken by Monsieur Meyrat (again referred to as being French) whom he dreaded. After school, boys could stay and do their prep as happens now, but at lunch time things were very different. About half a dozen junior staff stayed to lunch in the hall and carved huge joints of meat, served the puddings and supervised the boys generally, eating their own lunch at intervals between the carving. Out of almost 500 boys in the school at the time, about 140 stayed to lunch while the rest went home and returned for afternoon school. Shepherd describes a typical school lunch in Leake's day:

> *At 12.30 morning school ended and those taking their lunch at school made their way to the hall. A good standard of manners was expected. At each table one boy was chosen to 'buttle' as it was called by the Head. At two large marble-topped tables were set four carving places at which the Head, two dinner masters and one of Mrs Leake's domestics carved huge joints of meat or served out large meat pies. 'Butlers' would then ask for 'knuckle-end please' or 'lean please'. 'Butlers' would then serve from*

plates with vegetables as requested by the boys, return to their tables and then receive their next orders. At the end of the meal the Head called a roll, asked for a blessing on the meal and the boys were free for the rest of the dinner hour until afternoon school.

As well as Punishment Drill, the boys received regular drill of a different kind as recalled by J B F Brackenbury (DCPS 1924-1929):

Every Wednesday and Saturday morning we had five periods, and from 11.00 until 11.30 on those days, an enormous Sergeant Major, whose name was Wyatt, came from the College to drill us in tribes in turn. We always did exactly the same drill. It included forming patrols from line, close order to extended order. Half at least of what he shouted was not distinguishable as English words, but we got to know the tune and usually turned the right way. There was a termly tribe competition for drill and competition was fierce.

There was no proper gymnasium at the school and many forms went to the College to the old gymnasium for physical training (PT) which was taken by a College PT master. Every Wednesday and Saturday morning the school worked in tribes from 11 a.m. until 11.30. The Sergeant Major came to the Prep to give drill to one tribe at a time. Sheppard recalled what happened:

Twice a week, the College Sergeant Major came to give one tribe platoon drill, each patrol leader commanding his own patrol. At this time, the other three tribes were given lessons in PT, first aid or

The Hall set out for lunch in Leake's time. The pillars are still there but little else remains the same.

singing. Each half day, there would be a change so that all tribes took part in each in rotation. At the
end of each term drill competitions took place to determine the best tribe and the best patrol leader.

As the number of boys in the school grew, its reputation grew with it and the demand for space became ever more pressing. Every corner was occupied, and there were some strange makeshift arrangements in the urgent need to find suitable teaching areas. The hall, then half its present size as we have seen, could be divided into two classrooms by a clever but somewhat cumbersome arrangement. Housed in the ceiling were four collapsible shutters. Vertical wooden racks were fixed in place and the shutters were then pulled down by a long pole, thus creating two reasonably self-contained classrooms. The long flat tables used at lunch doubled up as desks, and benches were placed on each side. The whole procedure of raising and lowering the shutters came down to a fine art, and little time was lost from a 45-minute lesson when this performance of lowering the shutters was necessary. Elsewhere in the school large rooms were divided into smaller ones by more permanent glass partitions, but these were not very sound proof and not entirely satisfactory, as teaching staff had to talk more softly than usual so as not to disturb the class next door. Sheppard recalled how one particular member of staff had the habit of throwing open the door on his side of the partition if the adjacent room was becoming noisy, and inviting his own class to join in!

One room which must get special mention is what was known as Room 13. Looking today at the area which it once occupied makes it hard to believe that it could ever have been a classroom. Leading into what is now the Lower School playground and near the entrance to the kitchen, is a small door not much used by boys now. In the 1920s that door did not exist, and the small area now occupied by a passageway and a storeroom was a dark and dingy classroom - Room 13. It was known as the Black Hole of Calcutta, partly because of its dismal aspect and partly because it had been the place where the boarders had cleaned their shoes when they were accommodated in the building. Lockers remained around three sides of the room and with boys sitting on these and a wooden bench placed in the middle of the room, it was just possible to teach a class of twenty-four boys. The master had a small desk with a space for two or three boys behind him and the only radiator, so these places were highly sought after. The Black Hole of Calcutta measured just 18 feet by 10 feet, far too small to be adequate for a classroom, even on standards prevailing at the time. By comparison, a classroom in the modern Betws Building is more than twice that size for the same number of boys, a luxury unheard of in 1920 and even today almost excessive. After the war, by which time the door to the playground had been made, the area was used as a small tuck shop.

One popular activity in the 1920s and 1930s was lectures given by outside speakers who were invited to visit the school. Derek Ray (1922-1927) wrote:

How excited we were when Lawrence, the handyman, was seen putting up brown paper sheets over the windows to black out the Hall. This meant that we were to have a lantern lecture in the afternoon and thus a relief from normal lessons.

Sheppard also makes mention of these afternoon lectures. As examples, in the autumn term in 1925, there was an illustrated lecture with lantern slides, on *The King's Highways*, followed in later weeks by lectures on *Butterflies*, the *Tower of London* and *David Copperfield*. Lectures were also arranged for the Annexe and Lower School boys. Amazingly a set of these lantern slides has survived but sadly not the means of projecting them. Always anxious to find more space Leake approached the Estate Governors in 1929 with a view to obtaining a lease on 39 Alleyn Park directly

One of the lantern slides used in the 1920s lectures

opposite the school and which had become vacant. His plan was to use this principally for classrooms and he specifically stated in his application that the garden would not be used as a playground. He was however outbid by a subsequent lessee and the property never became a part of the school.

There is no doubt that Leake was an exceptional headmaster and DCPS was fortunate to have a man of such calibre at its helm for so many years. He was held in the greatest esteem by his pupils and colleagues and he too had an affection and regard for them which would be rare today. Of the many former pupils who have made contact with the school over the years, not one has ever said a word about Leake which is anything other than complimentary. One who thought highly of him was John Bazalgette (DCPS 1930-1936) who wrote:

> *The Rev W. R. M. Leake was (to me) the finest type of headmaster for a boys' school. I thought so then and am even surer now. Stern at times but with a twinkle in his eye, he exerted discipline splendidly but at the same time created a very pleasant atmosphere in the school. When you were in the presence of WRML, you realised you were with a very powerful high class human being. His influence was to remain with me all my life and I look back on him with the greatest respect, admiration and affection.*

David Brewer was at DCPS at approximately the same time and he too held Leake in high regard. Correspondence which he kept illustrates the care and affection which Leake held for his pupils. In January 1931, Leake wrote to David Brewer who was missing school as a result of measles:

Poor Old Brewer

May the Spots be fewer

I will have some Greek sent on.

What books have you?

Cheer Thee - WRM Leake

P.S. You can return as soon as doctor gives you leave - this depends on the spots and their scabs.

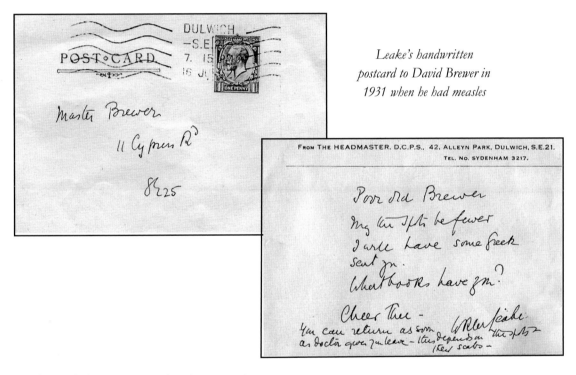

Leake's handwritten postcard to David Brewer in 1931 when he had measles

And a little later on, another letter arrives.

My dear Brewer

Rascal! To get the measles. Let me know if thou canst do work and will see that thou art supplied with needed refreshment. I do sympathise with you and hope the doctor will soon have you back.

Keep up thine pecker and we will supply the food.

Thine - W. R. M. Leake

A boy did not have to be ill to receive one of Leake's handwritten notes and Alan Wesencraft received one at the end of 1925 when he passed the exam into Dulwich College, in spite of what he himself described as a rather mediocre academic record. Leake wrote:

Bravo Wesen!

Thou hast done it and got a good start.

We shall rejoice to see you.

Of Leake himself, Wesencraft wrote many years later:

There can be no doubt that Leake was a truly remarkable person, a born teacher to whom education meant much more than passing exams and stuffing one's head with facts. He abhorred any form of snobbery and once at morning assembly gave a severe lecture on how wrong and disgraceful it was for those of us who had laughed and scorned a boy who had confessed to cleaning his own boots. He cared passionately for the welfare of both boys and staff, knew the name of every pupil and any boy kept at home through illness received an encouraging post card.

Many stories have been handed down about the legacy of Leake, one being that he would set holiday work in Greek and Latin and go around Dulwich days later collecting it in and giving out more. Sometimes, it was said, he would go round on a horse to conduct these errands although where the horse came from, and how much truth there was in this, has never been substantiated. K C Bishop (DCPS 1920-1925) remembered Leake giving him extra coaching in Latin and Greek in his study during the lunchtime break. He remembered the room as being large and dark and lined with bookcases on which were photos and rugby caps from Cambridge, Harlequin and England teams. In lighter mood, G H Goodman (DCPS 1933-1937) remembered Leake as an elderly distinguished gentleman who looked like Bismarck and told his mother what an awful lot the Prussians were! Sheppard held him in high regard for all his teaching career and remembered that it was Leake's custom to shake the hand of every boy after the break up at the end of every term. Clearly there was no great rush to start the holidays as there is now. Later, Sheppard related one incident about Leake which tells so much about him:

The only cricket played in break was on the playground and there would be several games in progress at any one time played with tennis balls. It was thus somewhat risky to walk across the playground unless one kept a sharp look-out. During one break, Leake was looking for a boy when a batsman took a heavy swing to leg and the ball, travelling very fast to the boy's dismay, hit the Headmaster full on the side of his head and rebounded off for quite a long way. Half stunned by the impact the Head called out 'Who did that?' Then a very nervous boy appeared and faltered, 'I did, Sir.' 'Well, what do you say?' 'Sorry Sir,' said the boy, wondering what was going to happen next. 'All right,' said the Head, 'that is all. Off you go.' That ball must have hurt.

All these characteristics and qualities made Leake a headmaster of the old school and we shall not see his like again. Although he continued as full-time headmaster until 1934, this is perhaps the best place to include an appreciation of him which was written by an anonymous old boy after he died in 1942:

In our memories of the days when we were very young, Mr Leake Senior will always remain an outstanding figure. He once said, 'You will come back a few times after you leave us, and notice later doings, but we are soon forgotten. It's natural that this should be - we're only the nursery.' But he remains the centre and focus of our affection, the friend who guided and encouraged our studies, sports and hobbies. He knew each one of us by name and character, and remembered each after we had passed on from his care. Looking back, we begin to realise what a great headmaster can mean from his grasp of any situation: and those who won inspiration from his courage when his school was under the battle-front saw his strength in facing each emergency as it arose. Mr Leake will long be remembered with affection, yea and with pride.

A few words written by G H Hammer (DCPS 1920-1924) many years later said it all:

I do not think there was anyone famous among the boys. The Reverend W R M Leake was the celebrity.

By 1930, Leake had been sole owner of the Prep for twenty years and, although his son Philip had joined him as co-headmaster, retirement of some kind was clearly in his mind. In the autumn of 1929 he made a decision which was to shape and alter the complexion of DCPS for ever. He appointed a man called John Leakey to his staff. Leakey's father had been the headmaster of a prep school in Westward Ho!, Devon, a school which he himself had attended before going on to Bedford School and then Pembroke College, Cambridge. He was also related to the famous anthropologist of that name. His first teaching appointment was at Berkhamsted School and after two years there, he joined the Revd W R M Leake at DCPS. To start with, he was an assistant master and the school magazine makes only slight reference to his arrival. Before long, Leakey had made a most

Leake with a group of senior boys outside his study in 1930. The wisteria is still there.

favourable impression on Leake and when Leakey offered to put money into the school, Leake invited him to become a partner. It is not clear if this proposition was on the cards in the first place when Leakey applied in 1929, but it must be considered as a possibility. The early 1930s were the years of recession and although DCPS does not appear to have suffered unduly at the time by a noticeable drop in numbers, this injection of cash must have been most welcome. Unorthodox in many ways, Leakey was a charismatic man who was destined to become a legend at the school and a great headmaster. Lean and difficult years lay ahead and without him it is highly probable that the school of today would almost certainly not have survived.

Leake's days were not quite over in 1934, but as Leakey's influence grew more and more, so 'Old Man Leake', as he was affectionately called by this time, began to play a lesser part. His influence in the background was never far away and as things worked out, he had another important and decisive role to play.

4   Prelude to War

The year 1930 saw the Revd W R M Leake start his twentieth year as headmaster, and it was to be an eventful decade, finishing in a way which no one could then envisage. The last term of the decade, autumn term 1939, saw the Alleyn Park buildings desolate and empty with the school forced to flee elsewhere.

No such thoughts were in anyone's mind when term started in the spring of 1930. The main problem then was space, with numbers already exceeding 500. Despite the recession of the early thirties the demand for places grew constantly, and Leake was concerned that many good boys were being turned away. One big decision which eased the situation was taken in 1932 when he decided, with semi-retirement in mind, to vacate 42 Alleyn Park and live away from the premises. This released two storeys of rooms and provided much needed classroom space. Until then there had been a green baize door outside what is now the Headmaster's Secretary's office, which separated the 'boys' side' from the 'private side'. There was a similar door in the corridor over the hall, which served the same purpose, although the construction of the present science rooms has removed all trace of this. At the same time a large room was provided for staff, a much needed improvement and although the configuration has changed, this room was more or less where the staff room is now. Sometimes small groups of boys were shown films in there and, on one occasion, so rumour had it, the projector caught fire. The only room available for staff until that time, and for male staff only, was the small room at the top of the stairs, for many years the book room. The Headmaster's study remained where it had always been, and a large room was also set aside for a library. This room is currently the secretaries' office.

Outside the school, things were very different as well. As many as a hundred boys came to school by bicycle, and David Mann (DCPS 1935-1939) spoke with pride of his arrival at the school each day by tricycle from his home formerly in Annexe Gate, renamed Dulwich Wood Park in 1932. Alleyn Park itself was distinctly rural with large Victorian houses running the full length of the road on the DCPS side, of which only the school buildings remain today. On the other side there were fewer houses, although one of the oldest, now Number 35 and presently occupied by the Headmaster, was very much to the fore as the frontispiece to this book shows. Until 1930 the road itself was of gravel, and there were so many trees and bushes that it was difficult for a stranger to know that a school existed unless boys were arriving or going home. A significant landmark was a tall flagpole in the front of Number 44, now the Lower School car park. On special days the Union Flag was hoisted, but normally a Tribe Flag (red, blue, green or yellow) was hoisted denoting which tribe was on duty that week. Among the various duties for the Tribe of the Week was the placing of a chain through all the bicycle wheels in the cycle shed in the playground before Prayers each morning. Two tribe patrol leaders were responsible for this and they were excused ten minutes of the first lesson for this purpose. Other boys came to school by the Number 3 bus, like DCPS still going strong, although in those days they were 'General' buses with open top decks. When it rained, tarpaulins attached to the back of the seat in front provided protection. A prospectus for the early thirties stated that boys could come to school by omnibus, train, tram or trolleybus and much advice was given about the various options for reaching the school from outlying districts by public transport.

W A Sheppard remembered life at the Prep in the early 1930s:

> *The Hall was the scene of Assembly, or Prayers as it was then called; each morning at 9 o'clock when between 400 and 500 boys were sardine-packed to sing a lusty hymn, listen to a short passage read from the Bible and prayers from the Book of Common Prayer. Certain boys did not attend because of religious reasons, and these boys waited in a room and filed in after Prayers. The Head then gave out any relevant notices. These may have included results of a match when all the boys applauded in the Prep. manner by what was known as 'flipping'. This was done by letting the forefinger of each hand hang loose and then shaking the hands quickly up and down. Thus the forefinger was made to hit with force the second finger on each hand so a clicking noise was produced. The result of several hundred pairs of hands so engaged produced a quite surprising noise. This custom continued in the Prep. until somewhere about 1950. Just how it then died out, no one seems to know. In order further to improve the standard of work, each boy had a fortnightly report as well as the customary monthly and termly ones. Thus in a long term it was possible to have seven reports to issue for each boy along with the appropriate lists. The fortnightly report was a simple affair showing the age of the boy, average age of the form, and a letter A, B or C for each of the main subjects to show the boy's effort. All boys were placed in sets for mathematics irrespective of the forms they graced. When the monthly reports were due, the top boy in each subject stood in the front of the Hall at Prayers and took the subject list up to the Headmaster. English and Maths lists were taken up one day and Latin and French the next. Then, on the day the reports were to be given out, the boy who was top of the form in combined order took up the complete list. Boys taking up these lists considered it an honour to do so and the Head, with his remarkable memory, was able by means of the lists to keep a very good idea of each boy's progress. The report was taken home by the boy, who had to show it next day to his form master complete with parent's signature.*

Latin played a major part in the curriculum and made a lasting impression. One reflection came from David Marshall (DCPS 1932-1937) who remembered his DCPS Latin well – with good cause. He recalled that if verbs were conjugated incorrectly, appropriate use of a ruler was taken to the offender's hand with the result that the same mistake was seldom made twice. Latin was obligatory for all classes from the Lower School upwards and the emphasis was heavily slanted towards Caesar's Gallic Wars, lessons being filled with useful tips about ramparts and javelins. Mention of rulers as a means of punishment leads to this unhappy memoir from John Bazalgette (the Bazalgette family has long-standing connections with DCPS through several generations):

> *I remember the first time I was caned by anyone from a school. (Lots more were to follow at Dulwich College). I reported to the Headmaster's study but he could not find a cane, so he took out a pocket penknife from his desk and went outside to cut one from a tree and used that. It hurt.*

Bearing in mind that John was only about eight years old at the time, such behaviour seems barbaric now, but it was very much the practice at the time. Beatings were an accepted means of dealing with minor offences, even for just talking in class, as David Mann recalled:

> *Beatings were so commonplace that they went without comment. Several boys were beaten every lesson for talking, for getting their tables wrong, or for eating in class. Lady teachers were popular because they did not beat.*

School photographs from the 1930s show that lady teachers, certainly among the older boys, were a rarity. For many years, canings were known as 'Tolly' and usually took place in the little room on the first floor of Number 42 at the top of the main stairs, then the staff room. Just how this name came about is not clear, but caning was also known by this name at Dulwich College at the time so presumably it was brought over by Leake when he became Headmaster. It may even have been the terminology used during Mallinson's time, his daughter Muriel remembering many years later that canings were frequent and usual at the time. Gordon Chubb (DCPS 1933-1941) wrote that not all masters needed canes to instil discipline and good order, and one withering look or word was often enough. Canings were not the only punishments and there were other sanctions for miscreants. 'Punishment Drill' for misbehaviour and 'Corrections' for work being poorly done were in full swing in the 1930s. These were held immediately after afternoon school, between 3.30 and 4 p.m. The term 'Corrections' is self-explanatory and continues, but punishment drill, which went back to early days, involved boys being drilled around the playground by a master. Sheppard said that it was a problem to make the punishment suitable for older boys without being too harsh on the younger ones. In due course drill was replaced by punishment detention, and when it moved indoors it was considered a very soft option. Whereas such practices have been swept aside and replaced by kinder and more gentle sanctions, the procedure for rewards has continued in much the same way. In the 1930s the four tribes were well established and there were good and bad slips, and a termly competition as now. At that time, boys who gained an Honours Certificate were entitled to miss half a day of school and the tribe results for every term since 1919, the war years aside, appear on a board in the hall.

When Leakey became a partner to Leake and his son Philip in 1932, the school was owned and managed by Leake, Leake and Leakey, a venerable triumvirate if ever there were one, and one which Leakey often joked about saying they sounded like a firm of corrupt solicitors. In 1934, Leake Senior went into semi-retirement leaving Philip and Leakey to run the school between them. Technically he still owned the school and maintained close links with it from behind the scenes, the magazine for the summer of that year making little mention of his departure other than saying that he made a 'remarkable speech' on Sports Day. From then on, Leakey was the dominant partner and the day-to-day running of the school was in his hands, although the 1937 prospectus still showed the school as having three co-headmasters. As well as putting his own money into the school, Leakey also managed to make his mark elsewhere. He was a man of grand ideas and when he secured a large plot of land on Sydenham Hill, he approached an eminent architect of the day, Berthold Lubetkin, to draw up plans for a house which would be strikingly different. Lubetkin had already made his name by designing the Penguin Pool at London Zoo, considered then to be a masterpiece of the time and Leakey only wanted the best. The commission to design Leakey's house was given to Valentine Harding, one of Lubetkin's younger partners, and as a result a remarkable building was constructed. Six Pillars in Crescent Wood Road still stands today and is a Grade II listed building. Within a couple of years Harding, who was killed at Dunkirk in 1940, was commissioned by Leakey for further work at the school and subsequently he designed a building, no longer in existence, which was used as a nursery school.

Although links with Dulwich College were not as strong as they had been two decades earlier, there were still close ties, especially as the majority of boys who left the Prep continued

Leakey's home in Crescent Wood Road – Six Pillars

to go there, and the academic syllabus was suited to its requirements. There were periodic meetings between the Heads of Maths, English, French and Latin from both schools, then regarded as the four main subjects, and F N Taylor, who taught Maths at the time, remembered that these meetings led to difficulties. C Boon was the Head of Maths at the College and his methods of the multiplication and division of decimals could not be found in any current text books. As a result duplicated sets of examples were distributed to the boys and these were strictly followed. Taylor must have made a good job of it, for Paul Bazalgette (DCPS 1930–1934), who went on to the College, remembered Taylor as one of the best teachers he had ever known. He considered that he had the ability of knowing instantly when a member of the class was not understanding a particular point and '*his scrutiny radiated round the room like a searchlight*'. Academically, the school's reputation and achievements grew during the 1930s with scholarships gained regularly to leading public schools and also to the Royal Naval College at Dartmouth which had a 13+ entry at the time. 1936 in particular proved to be a memorable year. Out of 18 boys in the top form (6A1), 16 returned for a reunion fifty years later, one having been killed and one who could not be traced. The reunion was held in the same room which had been their classroom and Bryan Thwaites (DCPS 1934-1936), who was one of them, considered this to be a huge tribute to the school and the affection held for it by the boys of his time.

Just as the 1920s saw the arrival of several members of staff who were to serve the school for many years, so did the 1930s. Barbara Herbertson joined DCPS in May 1934 to teach Maths to the younger boys. When the war came she evacuated with it and looked after the boys who were too old for the Annexe but who needed greater supervision than the older boys. She soon became a stalwart of the school and is remembered now with affection and trepidation by many who passed through her hands. After the war she became Head of the Lower School.

J B 'Hamish' Maclean joined the staff in 1938 and soon after war was declared joined the London Scottish Regiment. After distinguished military service, principally in North Africa, he returned to DCPS in 1946 and two years later became the Master-in-Charge at the school Leakey subsequently created at Cranbrook. He returned to London again in 1960 becoming Housemaster at Brightlands until 1965. He retired in 1980. Another member of staff worthy of mention from this time was Jack Chapman. Chapman, a talented linguist and musician, joined DCPS in 1935. He evacuated with the school for a short while and was called up for military service in 1942 during which time he served in the Intelligence Corps performing sterling work as an interpreter, principally with the Free French. He returned to DCPS in 1946 and when Paul Meyrat died unexpectedly in 1949, he took over the Modern Languages department, a position he held until his own death in 1958.

At DCPS two events dominated the second half of the 1930s. First there was the continuing problem of a lack of space and once again room was needed for expansion. The other, and common to everyone at the time, was the ever-threatening and worsening political situation in Europe. By the middle of the 1930s, and certainly after Leake's partial departure, the school was again turning away boys because it was full and there was no further accommodation available, although this did not prevent him from offering a few places without fees to bright boys who would benefit from the education which the school offered and who would not otherwise have had the chance to receive it. He also felt that such boys could help to raise the standards of the others. One former pupil to benefit in this way subsequently established for the school a Charitable Trust, offering scholarships to similar boys in the future.

Leakey, supported by the elder Leake, thought that buying out the nearby Brightlands School could solve the problem of a lack of space, and cash was accumulated with this in mind. School records are by no means complete as Leakey took most of them away with him when he retired, but one book which escaped contains minutes of private meetings in the 1930s at which the three headmasters were present. As these go beyond 1934 that is clear evidence in itself that the elder Leake continued to exercise considerable influence in the day-to-day running of the school. On 2nd December 1936 an interesting entry is made amongst an otherwise dull agenda. The Headmaster/owner of Brightlands School (S de M Bucknall) was offered £5,000 for Brightlands, £3,150 being for the lease of the building and the balance for goodwill. Bucknall, however, was not prepared to sell and Leake wrote in his own hand that despite this set-back, DCPS still wished to acquire extra premises. Brightlands School would have been convenient, as its purchase would, to some extent, have cut out local competition. A minute entry goes on to say that if the purchase of Brightlands did not prove possible, the school would then negotiate for the purchase of the lease of 36 Alleyn Park which was currently available. It should be borne in mind that at that time neither 38 nor 40 Alleyn Park were part of the school, so 36 would have been well away from the main school complex. In the event this did not happen, which is just as well, since it was badly damaged in the war. The house was later pulled down and the land became part of Kingsdale School. Now it is the site of the Betws Building, so DCPS got there in the end. Frustrated by the inability to lease nearby property, the headmasters decided in the end to construct a building within the school grounds.

Although former pupils from the late 1930s made little mention of the threat to peace by Hitler's expansionist ideas, there was nevertheless concern. Many people hoped, as did the government of the day, that peace would prevail but Leakey was one of an increasing number who was not convinced about the certainty of a prolonged peace. If it came to war, he contemplated, London would be a prime target and what then? All his ambitions would be set to nought if DCPS was suddenly forced to close and this, he reasoned, would be the inevitable consequence if London became a principal target area. Fortunately, he had harboured these thoughts in his mind for some time and how beneficial they were to prove to be. In 1932 he had married Muff who was to be his first wife and was the daughter of Claude Lemon, a stockbroker. The Lemons owned *'an exceedingly fine Georgian Residence'* set in eighteen acres of its own grounds at Coursehorn, near Cranbrook in Kent. This they had purchased in 1927 when its asking price had been reduced from £5,500 to £4000, a considerable reduction at the time. Interestingly, when the Lemons bought the house the word *'Coursehorn'* was spelt with an added 'e', thus *'Coursehorne'*, allegedly a derivation from *'Cow's Horn'*, but why the Lemons dropped the 'e' is not known. At the perimeter of the property was a four acre orchard and with the full sanction of his in-laws, Leakey decided to erect a camp there where the boys could go and spend a part of their summer holidays. His idea was that should worse come to worst and the threat of war become a reality, boys from Dulwich could go there quickly and thus be relatively safe away from the dangers in London. As conditions became steadily worse, his foresight was put to the test when Germany invaded Czechoslovakia in late September

CRANBROOK, KENT

"COURSEHORNE"

For Sale by Private Treaty

BY

Messrs. GEERING & COLYER,
HAWKHURST and Ashford, Kent;
Rye, Sussex; and 2, King Street, St. James's, S.W. 1.

Brochure for the sale of 'Coursehorne' – purchased by the Lemon family in 1927

1938. On the 26th of that month a circular, signed by all three headmasters, was hurriedly sent to those parents who had opted for their sons to go to Cranbrook should an emergency arise. This advised that the camp would open the following day and that boys should arrive at school early in the morning fully prepared. The circular concluded, *'Should there be a marked improvement in the situation, the journey will be cancelled and boys should attend school as usual.'* This was giving very short notice and involved about 130 boys and for those who chose to remain behind there was no school and no alternative.

For a short time it appeared as if war was about to be declared, but the crisis passed with Prime Minister Neville Chamberlain returning from Munich with his famous 'Peace in our Time' agreement which declared that Hitler had fulfilled his ambitions and there would be no more aggression. Within a week another circular was sent from the camp to parents

The front hall of Coursehorne when the house was privately owned

saying that the boys had behaved themselves admirably, although there had been some homesickness and doleful letters home, and that school in Alleyn Park would shortly be resuming. The Munich Crisis, as it became known, had been a false alarm with the threat of war temporarily in abeyance, but the exercise had not been entirely wasted. It had become evident that the camp at Cranbrook had been woefully inadequate for a major evacuation of a large part of the school to relocate from Dulwich should it become necessary. Leakey felt that Munich was merely a crisis deferred and he set about dismantling the camp and building a new and better one for the day which he felt would surely arrive.

Leakey was very proud of the new camp he created at Coursehorn, so much so that this letter to *The Times* appeared in June 1939. It gives a very clear picture of what the camp was like, how it had been funded and how it was to operate:

A PRIVATE SCHOOL'S CAMP

To the Editor of THE TIMES

Sir,

Owing to the prominence accorded to evacuation schemes at the present time, I thought the following might be of interest to you as showing what has been done by a private school with no grants or public money, the only help received being the offer of a site in their orchard by the owners of the land. We have built on the Kent/Sussex borders a camp to accommodate 300 boys at the cost of £2,600, this cost including such equipment as army stoves, two 100-gallon hot water boilers, palliasse covers, a large store of non-perishable foodstuffs and all medical necessities.

The cost of the scheme, which is voluntary, has been met by a capital loan, and parents joining have been asked to pay ten shillings per term towards repaying this sum. In addition, two camps each lasting a fortnight will be held every summer at a cost of £2. 10 shillings a fortnight for members of the scheme and £4.10 shillings for non-members. Any profit from these camps will be used for reducing the debt.

The camp consists of an oasthouse, recently re-roofed and repointed, 11 wooden huts varying in size, interlined for warmth and raised from the ground by concrete posts, a wooden dining hall with kitchen attached to accommodate 150 boys at a time, and separate domestic quarters, the whole being connected by a covered way. In addition to earth latrines situated away from the camp, there are chemical closets for each hut. The boys will sleep on palliasses which will be stacked during the day, being replaced by folding tables for work. The camp will be run by members of the scholastic and domestic staff from the school who have already volunteered and have received their instructions.

Transport in the event of an emergency will be provided by the LCC and two lorries have been officially earmarked for us to move necessary school furniture. The scheme has at present 273 members, their ages varying from six to thirteen.

Finally this camp in a smaller form was, I believe, the only private one used during the crisis of September last, when we evacuated 130 boys for one week

I remain, Sir, yours faithfully

J. H. Leakey Headmaster

42 Alleyn Park, Dulwich, SE21

No one could say that Leakey and his school were not prepared.

The 1938 summer camp

The need to establish a semi-permanent school at Coursehorn became more and more likely as each month passed, but Leakey did not hold the freehold of the house or its grounds which were still in the hands of his wife's parents. At this stage, Leakey decided to make his in-laws an offer. They had apparently expressed a wish to move away – perhaps the threat of so many school children on their doorstep was more than they were prepared to put up with, although they had given their blessing to the orchard being used as a camp in the first place. The property was put up for sale and Leakey was happy to pay the asking price which was not a great deal higher than the Lemons had paid over a decade earlier. One condition was that the Lemons could continue to use the garden behind the house and, although it was included in the sale, it was not used by the school until many years later. Having procured the land, setting up a camp in the orchard was far from straightforward. Drainage and electricity had to be supplied and, most important of all, planning permission had to be obtained. This was not immediately forthcoming as Kent County Council considered the area to be one of conservation. Planning permission was refused twice, even as late as March 1939, but once the school became registered as part of the London County Council (LCC) Evacuation Scheme and war appeared imminent, things changed dramatically and permission was finally granted.

Before Munich, the LCC had already devised a scheme whereby all London schoolchildren could be taken out of the capital relatively quickly by a mass evacuation scheme. It was not compulsory but many parents all over London considered it to be a welcome necessity even though it meant that children would be separated from their families and homes. Almost at once, Leakey saw the advantage of joining the LCC scheme as a school, so he registered with it. Many children who were ultimately evacuated were destined to stay with families as individuals, in some cases as far away as Canada, and the 1942 Christmas edition of the school magazine told of the experiences of one such boy, Paul Harvey, who was sent to Newfoundland to escape the anticipated war zone. He made no mention of the problems of the time but bemoaned the fact that he had to play baseball and there was no cricket! He was the exception though, and because Leakey had registered the school as a single unit, most of the boys had the advantage of being kept together with friends and contemporaries and this made the separation from parents much easier. DCPS was not the only school to do this and many other big London day schools including Dulwich College, St Paul's and Westminster had set similar plans in motion. Many smaller schools, and prep schools in particular, moved away from London, and for one reason or another never returned and are now just a memory. The former Abbey Prep School in Beckenham was one such example. While Leakey was planning to set up part of the school in Kent should the need arise, some of the boys took part in an important piece of research. David Mann (DCPS 1935–1939), from a medical family and later to become a parent and school doctor himself, wrote most interestingly of this:

> *With war looming, there was concern about how a small industrial island could feed itself if blockaded*
> *by enemy submarines. At DCPS there was a boy called Colin McCance whose father was Professor*

of Nutritional Biochemistry at King's College Hospital. Professor McCance arranged for about one hundred DCPS boys to volunteer as guinea pigs. The boys were first weighed and measured and then everything they ate over the course of two months was meticulously measured and weighed and recorded as well. This became a dreadful bind and I remember porridge being weighed and sticking to the scales. There was some coercion to 'eat it all up' because anything left also had to be weighed and recorded. At the end of the time, all participants were taken to King's for a blood test. I was so scared of the needle that I sneaked to the end of the line and pretended I had already been done but I was caught. The result of this research was that Professor McCance played a key part in the planning of the rationing system whereby Britain was kept adequately fed during the war. I am sure that other schools must have been involved as well, but the system worked so well that after the war Britain's children were renowned for being not too fat, not too thin and rosey cheeked.

As a result of what became known as the Munich Crisis, the autumn term in 1938 started almost three weeks late, but Leakey wrote that the school soon made up for lost time and all boys entered for the College that term were successful. The editorial of the magazine stated that thanks to Herr Hitler the term had been spoilt *'because of our little holiday in Kent'* and in consequence there was no Christmas Entertainment that year. The rugby and soccer teams did well though, the soccer XI not losing a single match, and the threat of war did not stop a party of boys going on a ski-ing trip to Champery in January. In the term which followed, chicken pox appeared to be the greatest disruption to school life which otherwise continued in much the usual way. In the summer, Sports Day was held on a warm and sunny day, there were plenty of cricket matches and the prospectus for 1939 gave no indication of any special precautions being taken or being deemed necessary. Comments in the magazine about cricket during that glorious summer seemed to anticipate the fortitude which was going to be needed in the years ahead:

The aim of a coach at a Preparatory School should not only be to see the sides victorious, but to plant the right seed, so that when a boy goes on to his Public School, he has the spirit of sportsmanship and team work, giving of his best, and with the will to win firmly implanted in his mind. To do one's best, the umpire's decision should be taken without question and with a smile – that's cricket.

Within five years the boys to whom those remarks were made would be eligible for military service. Fees for boarders in 1939 were £38-10s per term, and for dayboys over 13 the charge was just £12. There were extra charges for the use of the school library and the College Bath and there were Dancing Classes at one and a half guineas per term (£1.57). Even as late as 28th July 1939, with impending gloom only weeks away, no mention is made in the minutes from the end of term staff meeting of anything untoward. It had been an agreeable summer and though lacking in detail, plans were being formulated for the following term. Little did they know that the halcyon days of Leake's influence over the school were coming to a close, and soon life at DCPS would never be quite the same again. Perhaps the form master of Keith Fairweather (DCPS 1936-1944) had something else on his mind at the end of that summer term when he wrote, in a slip of the pen, that the forthcoming term would end two days before it started! By the anticipated date, Fairweather's parents had taken him to the comparative safety of Clitheroe in Lancashire. The summer term report itself is of interest for although it is a little more detailed than that written for K C Bishop almost two decades earlier, there is no great change in format and the word 'good' continued to be an adequate summary for each subject conveying nothing about the work covered or any application in class. Biology had made an appearance as an 'extra' subject and, although not mentioned on Fairweather's report, a science club had been started earlier, the cost of which was one shilling per term.

Also in January 1939, for reasons which are not entirely clear, Philip Leake left the school to join His Majesty's Inspectorate for Schools. Maybe he preferred a more academic existence than working with John Leakey and his frenetic life style. Philip's father was living in Godalming by this time so, to all intents and purposes, Leakey was at last the sole headmaster.

For the summer holidays in 1939, 130 boys spent a fortnight's holiday at the camp, the principal purpose being to test its weaknesses and strengths. Cranbrook School offered the use of its playing fields and swimming bath and to all intents and purposes it was a dress rehearsal. Then, just as the summer holidays were ending, it became obvious that the situation had worsened and the prospect of war seemed likely. This emergency procedure and somewhat abrupt circular was sent to parents by DCPS on 25th August 1939.

> EVACUATION URGENT
>
> *The school staff are all standing by now. In the case of an Emergency, the Evacuation Order will be announced on the wireless and in the newspapers. Boys who are at home at the time will come to the school at 5pm on the first day of the evacuation, bringing their personal kit, gas mask and sandwiches for one meal. Boys on holiday will come to Cranbrook in their own time, parents being responsible for their transport. It would be a help if all bicycles could be brought to the school on the morning of Evacuation where they will be stored until they can be taken to the camp later.*
>
> *J. H. Leakey.*

They did not have to wait long, for Germany invaded Poland on 1st September and Britain presented the ultimatum that unless Germany agreed to withdraw from Poland by 11 a.m. on Sunday 3rd September, a state of war would then exist. This had been foreseen in official circles too and on the Friday before the ultimatum actually came into effect, the LCC Evacuation Scheme swung into force. The school was notified on Thursday 31st August that some time during the following day would be zero hour, and all boys going to the evacuation camp should be at school by 8.30 in the morning, and not at 5 p.m. as had originally been planned. An advance party had already gone to Cranbrook with provisions and equipment which the school would need and, when it became difficult to obtain lorries through official channels, parents came to the rescue as they often do, and private cars and vans were used

DULWICH COLLEGE PREPARATORY SCHOOL.

MIDDLE SCHOOL.

REPORT FOR *Summer* TERM, 1939.

Name *Fairweather*   Form *L3c*   No. of Boys *24*

Age : *9* years *2* months.   Standard Age of Form : *10* years *6* months.

Conduct *Fair. Rather talkative*   Days Absent *1*   Days Late *1*

English Subjects :	
COMPOSITION ...	*With the exception of Grammar, (which is weak)*
SPELLING ...	*his English subjects are all good and*
REPETITION ...	*he has worked well and steadily.*
WRITING ...	*I have nothing but praise for him.*
GRAMMAR ...	
HISTORY ...	*A very good worker.*
GEOGRAPHY ...	*Good.*
SCRIPTURE ...	*V. good.*

Languages :	
FRENCH ...	*Excellent. He has worked hard.*
LATIN ...	*An excellent term's work.*

Mathematics :	
ARITHMETIC ...	*An excellent term's work. He must keep an*
ALGEBRA ...	*eye on neatness though*
GEOMETRY ...	*Good.*

Extra Subjects :	
ART ...	
SINGING ...	*Good.*
BIOLOGY ...	*Good. He is keen.*
HANDWORK ...	
P.T. ...	

	TERM ORDER.	EXAM. ORDER.	TERM AND EXAM.	FINAL ORDER.
ENGLISH	16	10	15	
HISTORY and GEOGRAPHY	3	1	2	2
FRENCH	1	2	1	
LATIN	6	11	7	
MATHEMATICS Set *G* of *12* boys	2	5	2	

General Remarks : *Excellent. He has shewn great keenness both in and out of the form room.*

J. H. L.

Next Term begins on *Sept 20th* and ends on *Sept 18th*

All boys must return punctually on the day named. The only ground for exemption allowed by School Rules is sickness or exposure to infection. Notice of this must be sent before the opening of the School to the Head Master.

Each boy must bring with him on the first day his health certificate signed. A Boy who fails to do this will be sent home and his Tribe will lose a mark.

No boy shall return to School from a house in which there has been any infectious disorder during the previous month.

Boarders **must** return before 7 p.m. on the EVENING BEFORE the day of commencement.

Fairweather's Report for the Summer Term 1939. Note the date for the end of term.

instead. Friday 1st September turned out to be a long day. On what is now the Lower School playground, the boys were divided into groups depending upon which hut they would be using at the camp. To use Leakey's own words:[1]

I addressed the parents and told them that the way they could be of the greatest assistance would be for them to go away at once. This they nobly agreed to do, and after the boys had given three cheers for their parents and the parents had given a somewhat forlorn answering cheer, they moved off and we were left to our vigil.

Such a statement would not go down too well today and the parting of boys from their parents cannot have been an easy or happy one. The threat of war and the uncertainty of what might happen next caused a very different kind of emotion. The school had a long wait and after several false alarms, the message eventually came through at 6 p.m. that a special train would be leaving West Dulwich for Cranbrook at 6.35 p.m. and the school

The P246 Evacuation banner being raised by two Year 8 boys, Milo Sumner and John Owen, in 2004. This playground is where the boys assembled in 1939 before evacuating to Cranbrook.

1 *School Errant* by J H Leakey (published 1951: Reprinted 1997)

should proceed to the station without delay. What a sight they must have been! With John Leakey at the front, armed with a large megaphone and wearing two armlets, the school marched proudly, almost defiantly, down Alleyn Park in groups, each boy carrying a suitcase with his belongings and his gas mask. The master or mistress of the hut to which each boy had been assigned accompanied each group. At the fore, and held high by two of the older boys, was the large banner which had been provided by the LCC proclaiming the school's evacuation number – P246. The train left punctually and once it was on its way there was a general feeling of relief. The staff with 135 boys were on their way at last. As there were almost 400 boys in the school at the time, this represented a fairly small percentage and, although another hundred or so soon followed, there was no DCPS in Dulwich for those left behind. Of those, some went to stay with friends out of London, but for those whose parents, for various reasons, chose to remain behind there was a problem. With the government urging children to leave London, where should these boys go to school? Within a few months that problem would be partially resolved.

The 1939 camp was not built on the same site as the earlier one, but among trees, which offered a degree of camouflage. The area was once an orchard and a few of the original fruit trees remain today. The entrance was from The Lane where The Lodge has been built, and much of the camp itself was on ground now occupied by all weather pitches used by

Inside one of the huts of the 1939 camp – note the shutter over the window.

Dulwich Preparatory School Cranbrook. The administrative buildings were nearest to the lane, these including a large hut for dining and the kitchens. Further in among the trees were huts for classrooms, which could be adapted as dormitories, as well as several huts which were for recreational purposes. There were shutters at all the windows which could be lowered at night during the 'black out' when no lights were to be shown.

Moving the boys was one thing. Finding suitable staff to accompany them was another. Not all the staff in Dulwich wished to accompany the school to Cranbrook and young men such as Maclean and Gibb, who expected to be called up at any moment, chose not to go. Principal staff among those who did go included Sheppard, Taylor, Meyrat and Barbara Herbertson. Others were Reg Hatton, Edward Gardner, Jack Chapman and 'Hippo' Linck but it was not too long before Gardner and Chapman were called into military service. Elaine Barnett, who had a son at the school in Dulwich, joined the staff at the camp, stayed with the school during the war and continued long afterwards. Maggie Glenn, daughter of H O Glenn, went to the camp as did Leakey's cook, Mabel Drewry, who quickly learnt to adapt her skills to cater for large numbers. Helen Dickson, about whom more will follow, looked after the younger boys at The Parsonage at Benenden as there was insufficient room at the camp, and Phyllis Glazier, who had worked at the school in London for a short time before the war, quickly became responsible for the general well being of the boys in the capacity of what today would be called a Matron. Helen Dickson and Phyllis Glazier remained at the school for many years.

When the boys and their staff arrived at Cranbrook Station, which was three miles from the camp, it was raining and because of the black out which had been enforced, it was pitch black. Somehow vans, cars, and a lorry provided by a local farmer ran a shuttle service, taking the younger boys first, the older ones beginning to walk. It had been a very long day and everyone was weary, but even at this stage the problems were not quite yet over. To use Sheppard's own words:

> *As boys arrived, we took them into the big dining hall and served them with a hot meal. This was much appreciated, but while we were thus engaged, working by the dim light of a few hurricane lamps, an air raid warden arrived and ordered all lights to be extinguished or be obscured. This was the first day of the official 'black out' which was to last nearly six years and it had not been possible to complete shutters for the windows by the time of our arrival. A compromise was reached and we were allowed to continue with one lamp only, and the windows, which were numerous, were covered as well as possible with coats. Everyone was fed at last and assigned to appropriate huts where all eventually got to sleep.*

The evacuation had begun, and at Alleyn Park the 1939 autumn term never started. One person who thought DCPS would never return was David Livingston who had been on the staff since 1929. He wondered what would happen to those boys whose parents had decided that their sons should not go to the camp. Surely there would be a need for them

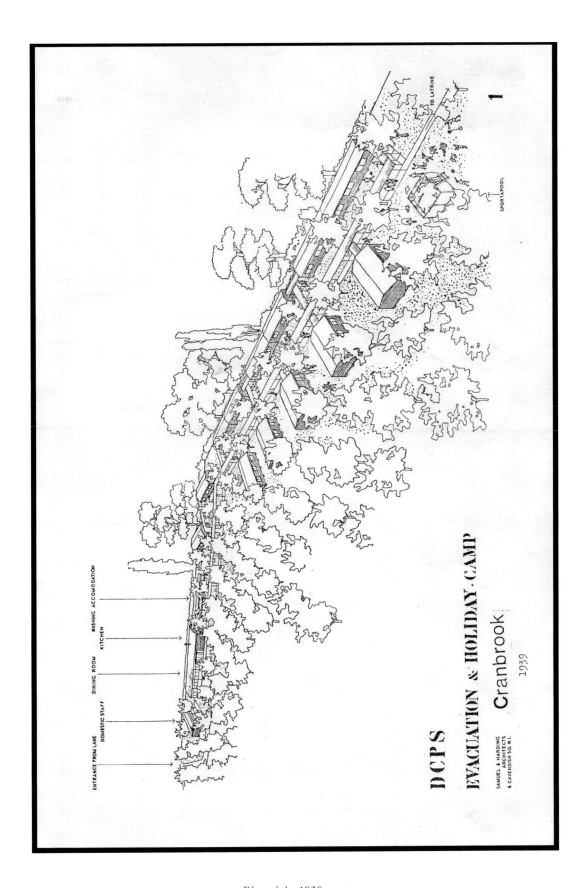

Plan of the 1939 camp

The 1939 camp was better organised and set among trees.

In 2003 a few of the original fruit trees remain on the site which is now occupied by all weather pitches.

to continue to be educated in Dulwich. Seizing what he thought was a golden opportunity, he made approaches to various members of staff to join him in the creation of a new school. Maclean was amongst those who were approached and although Leakey did not require him to go to the camp at Cranbrook, he remained loyal to DCPS and did not take up the offer. There had been a girls' school at Oakfield House at the junction of Croxted Road and Thurlow Park Road before the war and when these premises became vacant, Livingston gained the lease from the Estate Governors and the present Oakfield School was born. Presumably Livingston was dismayed when DCPS re-opened in 1940, albeit somewhat haphazardly, and even more dismayed when it re-established itself in 1945, but by then his school was well under way and flourishes today, Livingston remaining as headmaster for many years.

Meanwhile DCPS was struggling to provide some kind of education under very difficult circumstances at Cranbrook. For purposes of continuity, minutes from the termly Tribemasters' meeting show a hurried entry which made no reference to a war, but that the usual tribe activities in Dulwich had not been able to take place as a result. At the camp, there was a semblance of normality towards school life within a very short time, despite the hardships, and thanks to the kindness of Cranbrook School which provided the pitches, three 1st XV rugby matches were played there instead. Leakey was determined to carry on undaunted, but it was not going to be easy.'

Autumn Term 1939 in Dulwich.

Entry for the Tribemaster's meeting for that term.

5   Evacuation -
Leakey's foresight prevails

The first day at the camp was spent getting things straight. Facilities were, to say the least, basic and although the camp had been rebuilt after the Munich Crisis a year earlier, there were still serious shortcomings and much had to be done if the school were to survive the winter. There was no accommodation for teaching, apart from the huts themselves, no bathing facilities and no medical room. The kitchen and dining facilities were also inadequate and there was nowhere to store the boys' clothes. Winter was approaching, and if the camp were to be anything approaching a normal school, all these things would have to be provided. Fortunately it was still school holiday time and only 135 boys had gone to the camp instead of the 200 who were in the scheme, so at least initially there was no shortage of space.

The second day was Sunday 3rd September, and the day when the Government's ultimatum to Germany to cease hostilities against Poland expired. Boys and staff gathered in the dining hut to hear Chamberlain's statement that as no such undertaking from Germany had been received, a state of war would then exist. Gordon Chubb, who was a boy at the camp, wrote many years later that he did not quite know what to make of it at the time, nor what it would mean in the future, but he came to consider it to be one of the most serious moments of his life. After the Prime Minister's broadcast, boys and staff returned to their huts and then heard the first air raid warning of the war. They put on gas masks, went to emergency stations and prepared themselves for some kind of onslaught. Everyone believed that Germany would react instantly and there would soon be air raids and the threat of gas. Consequently, and for some time, boys carried their gas masks in cumbersome cardboard boxes with them wherever they went. Black enamelled cylindrical containers, the surfaces of which were then artistically etched to denote their respective owners' names, subsequently replaced these. As is now well known, nothing happened either on that Sunday or for many days thereafter, and it was all a bit of an anticlimax. Leakey decided it was time to organise the camp and sort things out while he had the chance.

One of the first things to be considered was that school work was going to be difficult, so Leakey approached Russell Scott, the Headmaster of nearby Cranbrook School. Scott had been very helpful and supportive during the earlier Munich Crisis Camp when he had made playing fields and several other amenities at his school available to Prep boys. This time Leakey required classroom space. Fortunately Scott welcomed the idea as it had already been suggested to him that his school would be merged with another school of similar type and he considered that an arrangement to co-operate with a school of younger children would be preferable. Accordingly, Kent County Council, under whose jurisdiction Cranbrook School was administered, was approached and an agreement was reached. The plan was to share the facilities and some of the teaching. One school would have organised games while the other had classroom work, and vice-versa. Soon staff from both schools were called for military service, so those who were left held the school together. Some DCPS staff were able to teach the boys from Cranbrook School, especially in games, and in return Cranbrook staff offered to teach the DCPS boys Music, Art and Handiwork. This was one of the best aspects of the operation in Cranbrook at this time as Prep boys gained benefit from the more mature approach offered by staff accustomed to teaching at 14+. The co-operation of Russell Scott was another essential link in the survival chain of DCPS for, without his help and co-operation, it is unlikely that DCPS would have been able to offer anything like a full academic timetable at the camp.

Very soon the camp became better organised, and as the proper date for starting term arrived, so numbers swelled to 225 and the camp was full. A regular routine was established and a boy at the time, J P Thompson, wrote as follows:

> *About 9.10 we start for school. We walk over in twos by forms. Cranbrook School has very kindly*
> *allowed us to work at their school. Some of the forms work at the boarding houses. The number of*

Freddie Taylor serving out food in the dining hut at the camp shortly after arrival, autumn term 1939

forms has naturally been cut down. The names of the forms are 6A, 5A, 5B, 4A, 4B, 3A, 3B, and form 2 usually works at the camp but occasionally works with 3B. We have mostly three quarters of an hour periods. At 11.10 a.m. we have a quarter of an hour's break. We have P.T. and singing with Cranbrook School masters. At 12.45 we stop morning school and walk back to camp for lunch. We start school again at 2.15. Our games holidays are Tuesdays and Fridays, and our free afternoons are Thursdays. Both school and games end at 4p.m.

Peter Milton sent this letter to his parents from the camp on 4th October 1939, when he was 10 years old:

> *Hut A, D.C.P.S. Camp, Coursehorn, Cranbrook, Kent*
> *Wednesday 4.10.39*

Dear Mummy and Daddy,

I got my camp bed yesterday; it is very comfortable, and will be better still when the opportunity comes for you to bring down my mattress. The camp is being improved in many ways: the covered way is being walled in so that it will form little lobbies at the door of each hut, in which will be kept our macs etc. Electric light and wireless and heating will soon be installed; also telephone. As soon as the lighting is in, the stamp club will be formed; probably of only a few senior boys, chief of whom will be Linck, whose father will no doubt run it. That means when you next come down please bring all my stamps.

I am so sorry Mummy's birthday present was a bit late but when I should have been getting it I was in the Sick Hut. Mrs Linck said I needed some sort of tonic … I am running short of Magnesia Tablets and money, most of the latter having been spent on stamps and things. Please put 'Hut A' on all correspondence.

Lots of love and xxx from Peter.

Gordon Chubb wrote that despite all the efforts to make the boys as comfortable as they could, conditions were still harsh. Initially they slept on the floor on straw palliasses until parents produced camp beds and mattresses. Without proper beds, sleeping was uncomfortable and dusty, and during the daytime there was no real place to sit. Getting up in freezing conditions and rushing to the one ablution block which had hot water was, Chubb said, like introducing army life well before its time. By the end of October, electric lighting and heating had been installed, a room in the oast house had been set aside as a sick bay and the camp was as ready as it could be for the forthcoming winter.

The use of Cranbrook School, which was about a mile from the camp, resulted in a fair amount of walking, for boys had to return to the camp for lunch each day and then walk back again for afternoon school. Most members of staff acquired bicycles since long distances were involved between the various locations within Cranbrook School. Sometimes a lesson would begin while the master taking it would be peddling furiously between one building of Cranbrook School and another. The younger boys in the Annexe and those with Barbara Herbertson remained at the camp and did their lessons there. Soon, when the camp was becoming cramped, boys of Annexe age stayed at the Old Parsonage at Benenden School. Helen Dickson had once taught there and it was almost certain that it was her contacts which had made the place available to these younger boys. In any case, the winter conditions at the camp were considered likely to be too severe for the very small children. Another stalwart was Phyllis Glazier. Like Helen Dickson, Phyllis Glazier had been employed in Dulwich by Leakey before the war and when the move to the camp came, both went with him. It was a boy called Baynon, one of the younger boys at Benenden, who started what became almost a legend. Young Baynon was an asthmatic and when he was given his nightly medication, he always replied by saying, 'Thank you Glazybones'. This was quickly picked up by others to become 'Lazybones', and then soon abbreviated to just 'Bones'. From that day forward, Phyllis Glazier became known by staff, parents and generations of boys alike simply by that name and the place where she worked looking after the boys' clothes and their medicinal comforts became known as 'The Bonery'.

Although Cranbrook was relatively safer than London, there was always the nagging question of air raids, and the staff were much exercised by the thought that from the air, the camp could look like a military installation. Sheppard wrote as follows:

> *The camp had been well-designed to hide in the orchard and was well hidden by the trees and the roofs*
> *of the huts were well camouflaged which also helped to make us unlikely to be seen. It was arranged that*

Boys returning to the camp after lessons at Cranbrook School. Note the gas masks (March 1940).

*in the case of an attack the boys should
assemble in the lobbies of the large huts.
These we tried to make a little stronger by
throwing up banks of earth along the sides
of the lobbies and by covering the roofs with
three inch thick breeze blocks. All this was
done by the Staff in their spare time and
while we hoped that we should never have
to put our defences to the test we felt that we
had done the best we could and had some
satisfaction in having done so.*

In November a Tannoy broadcasting system
was installed and this made the working
of the camp much easier. Not only could
messages be sent to the various huts through
loudspeakers, but it was also possible to relay
records and wireless programmes as well. In
the evenings, 'Bones' used to walk around
the camp to listen to the boys and to ensure
that all was well.

*Leakey at the microphone
of the loudspeaker system
at the camp*

The passage way between the huts with the trees above

The long passage between some of the huts had a corrugated iron roof and hessian down the sides. Every now and then apples fell on the roof from the trees above making a thunderous sound which in the still of the night was quite frightening.

Another problem in the early days was that of homesickness. Normally boys who are homesick are in the minority and, in most cases, overcome it by being kept occupied and fully involved in school life. In this case, the whole school was homesick and the pupils, of all ages, were evacuated day boys not boarders and it was hard work to keep the boys constantly occupied, especially at weekends. The problem was compounded by the fact that the parents were suffering withdrawal symptoms as well, especially as their sons had only become boarders in the first place by necessity.

By November, everything was working as smoothly as it could under the circumstances, but on the war front nothing happened. Bombing was bound to come sooner or later but in the meantime another problem arose. Pressure was building up to have the children home again. In London large numbers of children had returned from families in the country where they had not been very happy but found that many of the capital's schools were closed. A number of DCPS parents who had declined to send their children to the Cranbrook camp were anxious for the school in Alleyn Park to be re-opened. Most of the boys at the camp went home for Christmas in 1939, but given the pressure and the need, Leakey relented and a small section re-opened in Dulwich in January 1940. A few boys returned from the camp, but most remained in the comparative safety at Cranbrook.

The following extract, which sums up all that had been achieved in the first term, appeared in the *Kentish Express*:

> *The only School Evacuation Camp at present fully established and working in England is to be found in the rural district of the Weald at Coursehorn, Cranbrook, where two hundred boys of Dulwich College Preparatory School have an encampment on most modern and up-to-date lines on an eighteen acre estate. The encampment is composed of fifteen huts, or what can more suitably be described as temporary wooden buildings. They are of various sizes ranging from the smaller domestic to larger ones suitable for dormitories and commodious halls. All are linked together by roofed-in corridors, the sides of which are protected by tightly stretched hop netting of a narrow mesh which acts as an effective screen against wind and rain, and admits a maximum amount of light and air, while it secures dry access to any part of the encampment independent of climatic conditions. The buildings are electrically heated and are very cosy and comfortable. The whole of the encampment is linked up by wireless so that announcements and any other communications can be given to each building by microphone. A large oast house has been converted into a recreation room where boys can occupy their leisure in billiards, ping pong etc., while one hut has been set apart for draughts, and other table games. Work is carried on at Cranbrook School, where the boys attend daily and where separate accommodation has been provided. The purity of the country air has had a beneficial effect on the boys, which is shown by the high standard of health maintained by them during the several months they have been in their new quarters, the maximum*

amount of illness having been at the extremely low figure of one per cent. as against ten per cent. for the
same period of the year in London.

January and February were exceptionally cold and the boys trudged to their lessons at
Cranbrook School through heavy snow. Of the winter, Leakey wrote:

All of us who took night duty during those unforgettable weeks will remember the brilliant moons whose
light glittered on the snow-covered branches of the orchard giving a scene of incredible beauty. The extreme
cold made the timbers of the camp creak. As we patrolled the covered way we could see the dim glow of
the Ferranti heaters going full blast in the huts, and hear the sigh and mutter of over a hundred children
sleeping. It was hard to believe that we were at war – everything was so peaceful and calm. The days were
bitter but the sun shone brilliantly, and we had some wonderful tobogganing on Sissinghurst Hill. The
staff felt the cold but the children revelled in it and no one was ill throughout all those bitter weeks.

When at last the thaw came, there was an outbreak of German measles and quite a lot
of 'flu – the latter affecting the staff badly. Still nothing happened on the war front, but
pressure was growing all the time for the school to be brought back to Dulwich. Dulwich
College, which had evacuated to Tonbridge, announced that the whole thing had been a
failure, and they were intending to return to London for the summer term. John Leakey
still refused, saying that bombing was bound to come and besides, the camp was now
running smoothly and he did not want to give it up. The Easter holidays arrived but in
April 1940 there came a dramatic change in circumstances when Germany invaded Norway
and Denmark. As the summer term started, news from Europe became worse by the
day, and there was an atmosphere of unease and uncertainty. Then in May the Germans
crossed the Maginot Line and swept into France, eventually forcing the British Army to
evacuate from the beaches of Dunkirk at the end of the month. The fact that it did so
more or less completely but without its equipment, was said at the time to be nothing less
than a miracle.

With the total fall of France seeming imminent, the plight of the boys at Cranbrook took on
a new twist. Everything had suddenly changed and parents who had supported the school
so loyally began to have second thoughts. Leakey was loathe to give up his beloved camp,
but the inevitable became clearer by the hour. There was now a threat of invasion. Having
walked through France and the Low Countries, it was generally felt locally that the enemy
would soon land on Romney Marsh and move inland from there. Enemy planes had even
been seen over the camp and as Cranbrook could then be described as being in the front
line, everyone's nerves were on edge. Meyrat, being Swiss, hurried back to London on his
motor bike and sidecar, and one evening shortly afterwards when the boys had gone to
bed, the school was visited by a perspiring police sergeant from Cranbrook who said that
he had to interview some boys whom he had heard were aliens. These consisted of two
Czech boys and a little Dutch boy who had lived in London all his life and who couldn't
speak a word of Dutch. After a tremendous argument, the strength of Leakey's presence

was enough to persuade the policeman that the little boys aged nine were innocent of any form of sabotage and would be terrified if they were woken up to be interviewed. The time had clearly come for DCPS to move and uproot itself all over again, and to move quickly if it were to survive as an entity, but where to this time? The Leakeys had family connections in Devon, so that is where Muff, Leakey's wife, first went. She soon discovered that the Leigh Abbey Hotel at the Valley of the Rocks near Lynton was empty. DCPS could have it, a rent was agreed verbally and preparations were made for the move.

Lorries were acquired, the equipment was loaded into railway trucks at Cranbrook station, and everything was prepared as best it could be. Then a telegram came from Devon:

> ARRANGEMENTS FALLEN THROUGH. DO NOT EVACUATE TO THE ABBEY.

What had happened was that the hotel was in the hands of the Bankruptcy Commissioners who had acted without notifying Leakey. A wealthy prep school headmaster had made a higher offer for the premises, and in modern parlance, DCPS had been gazumped! With everything packed, and with the trucks waiting at Cranbrook station, what was to be done? The railway was very understanding and allowed the trucks to stay where they were and cancelled the journey. Leakey dared not unpack them because the state Britain was in at the time may have meant that he might never get any trucks again. So it was not bombing which frustrated his plans, but clearly at this time the whole future of the school was again hanging by a very fine thread. Somehow recommendations were made about North Wales, and Leakey's wife heard that the Waterloo Hotel in Betws-y-Coed in Snowdonia was empty and available. A £300 deposit was agreed and Mrs Leakey went post-haste to Wales to sort it out. By the time she arrived, she discovered that the hotel had been requisitioned by the army in Chester, and the Royal Army Medical Corps (RAMC) intended using it as a hospital.

But all was not lost. The nearby Royal Oak Hotel was available and was willing to offer the school accommodation. A rent of £1000 per year was agreed, the only stipulation being that DCPS did not take the bar as that, from the owner's point of view, was the only part of his business which was profitable. So that was agreed – no bar for DCPS! At last the path was clear to get moving again. Senior members of staff went on ahead in lorries with some of the senior boys who had passed their exams by this time, and the trucks were released from Cranbrook station and sent on their way to their new destination. Coaches were arranged to take the rest of the boys and the staff to the station from where a special train was provided to Victoria. More coaches were needed from there to Euston, and then another special train conveyed the weary party to Llandudno Junction and down the branch line to Betws-y-Coed.

With all the troubles of war, it seems amazing that all this was achieved at such short notice, but somehow it was and the removal of children from London obviously had some kind of priority. A party of boys from Dulwich also joined at Euston. At this point we have Leakey at his very best – autocrat as he was. He decided that after the Leigh Abbey affair he would not give the parents any further information about evacuation as it might only lead to disillusionment and trouble. There had been too many false starts already, so circulars were prepared beforehand to be sent out to parents on arrival in Wales. This is what they said:

> *Your boy has now arrived safely in Wales, and I have undertaken the whole matter on my own responsibility. If you wish to remove your boy, you are at perfect liberty to do so and I will charge you no fees in lieu of notice.*

Just two boys returned to London and later Leakey admitted himself that his action had been a bit high handed. Friday 16th June, the day of departure, dawned bright and fine and buses arrived at the camp. When the party reached Euston, news had got out that the school was on the move and as a number of boys had come in from Dulwich, those families were obviously in the know. The journey was long and difficult. Although many boys were

Boys at Victoria, arriving from the camp en route to Betws (Friday June 16th 1940).
The coaches to take them to Euston are parked on the extreme left.

excited, many of those from Dulwich who had not been away before were fretful and homesick. Furthermore they had been provided with far too much food by their parents and were frequently sick. As Leakey put it rather delicately, '*they were often violently ill in the most inconvenient of places*'. Eventually the train reached Llandudno Junction and made its way down the Conway Valley branch with the hills of Snowdonia towering above. The advance party was waiting on the platform to greet them, and unlike Cranbrook, the distance to the accommodation was only yards away. Paul Gray (DCPS 1938-1943), who was eight years old at the time, wrote a letter home not long after his arrival. He described the long train journey and declared that the area was 'lovely', and there was nothing untoward in the letter which might have caused his parents concern with regard to homesickness.

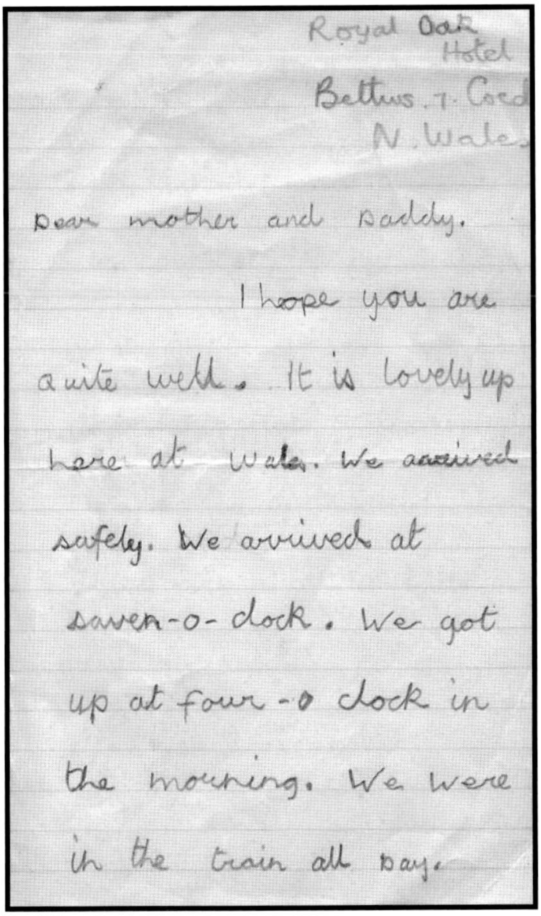

Letter from Paul Gray telling his family that he had arrived safely

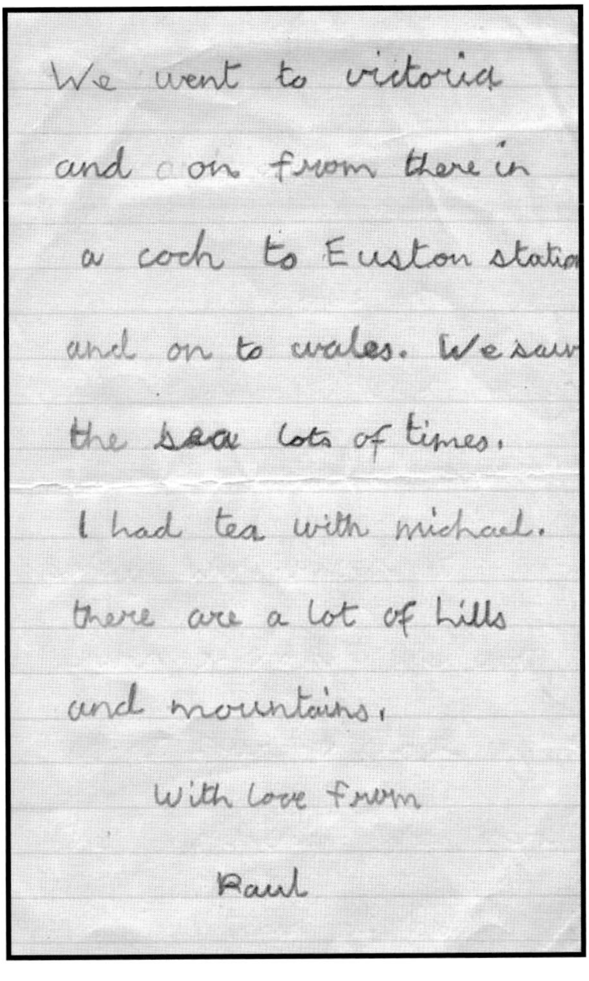

Royal Oak Hotel
Bettws . y. Coed
N. Wales

Dear mother and Daddy,

I hope you are quite well. It is lovely up here at Wales. We arrived safely. We arrived at saven-o-clock. We got up at four -o clock in the mourning. We were in the train all day.

We went to victoria and a on from there in a coch to Euston station and on to wales. We saw the sea lots of times. I had tea with michael. there are a lot of hills and mountains.

With love from

Paul

The second evacuation had thus been completed, and although the boys had arrived safely, some of the items which had been sent with the advance party had not. Leakey had taken the precaution of ensuring that there would be enough food for the first twenty-four hours, so among the items he had sent were tins of golden syrup and some biscuits. As a result of some injudicious shunting somewhere en route, Chubb remembered spending several hours at the goods yard clearing up a very sticky mess and eating lots of biscuits. France fell the very next day so the decision to move the school away from Kent proved to be a wise one. In Cranbrook, the camp which had been left so hurriedly was soon requisitioned by the army. Leakey visited it once in 1942 when it was being used as a base by the Royal Army Service Corps (RASC), and when he learnt they were delighted with its layout, it was some consolation to know that his earlier efforts had been of use to the country. The main house at Coursehorn was used as the Sergeants' Mess, and later in the war, a unit from the RAMC was based there.

With the arrival in Wales of extra boys from Dulwich it was soon realised that a mistake had been made – the Royal Oak Hotel was not big enough. Very quickly a further lease was taken on the Llugwy Tea Rooms further up the High Street, and that is where the five and six-year-olds were housed – in effect an Annexe. Yet again boys of younger age lived away from the main body of the school. The Royal Oak had originally been a stopping place on the London to Holyhead Road which runs through Betws, and also a place where the horses were rested and changed. The former coaching stables were available and were used as classrooms and were about two hundred yards from the hotel itself. The school had

The stables at the Royal Oak which were used as classrooms

not been there very long when a boy rushed into the hotel saying that a group of soldiers had arrived at the stables. Leakey went over to see the major in charge, who informed him that the stables and the outhouses were being requisitioned for army use. Leakey, who was not slow in coming forward and who had tremendous presence, explained that the school simply had to have them as there was nowhere else it could go. The major was not moved but Leakey stood his ground:[1]

> *"These are the only premises we have in which we can work", I said.*
>
> *"I can't help that", the major replied, "we have just got to have them."*
>
> *I was in despair and thought we really had lost them when one of the boys came in.*
>
> *"My God!" said the major. "Isn't that a Prep cap?" When I said that it was, he told me that he was an old Prep boy.*
>
> *"Don't worry," the major said, "we will go and find somewhere else."*

And he did. Another problem had been solved.

Having secured the use of the stables was one thing, but making them serviceable as classrooms was another. Finding labour, skilled or otherwise, at that time was nigh on impossible, as young men had been called to military service and older men in reserved occupations were busy and much in demand. So the conversion of the stables, hacking out spaces in the walls for windows and then glazing them, as well as heaving up desks through open windows, was left to the staff, principally Sheppard and Taylor, who displayed skills well beyond their normal classroom obligations. The Tannoy system which had been in use at the camp was carefully dismantled by Taylor and taken to the Royal Oak where he re-assembled the loudspeakers and the wiring piece by piece. He must have made a good job of it, for the whole system was dismantled after the war and re-installed for a third time at Brightlands, the school's post-war boarding house, and did valiant service there for some years. The original microphone still exists. Sheppard became adept at cutting boys' hair and aided by 'Bones' Glazier, he also learnt how to repair boys' shoes from the very limited amount of leather and other materials which were available at the time. Paul Gray remembered that haircutting was such a problem at the camp that it was done by the boys themselves on occasions, news of which even reached the local press. These were problems solved by willing hands, and years later Sheppard wrote [2] about them illustrating the point that boys and staff often worked together, invariably finding a way if they could:

> *One of the British troops stationed at Bettws was a barber in civilian life and he dealt with the hair of a number of boys on his free afternoon each week. This was another interruption to lessons as boys went from class up the village street to a spare room in the annexe to have their haircut and this meant that quite a large part of a lesson was lost. The time boys were away steadily became longer and longer, until*

1 *School Errant* by J H Leakey. (1951 - Reprinted 1997)

2 *41 Years at The Prep* – W A Sheppard. (DCPS Magazines 1969-1974)

we found out what was happening. The barber, to save time, sat several boys in a row and cut their hair,
first by doing all the left sides, then the backs and then the right sides. This saved his time but wasted it
for the boys, hence the long delays. In due course, this man was posted elsewhere and a member of staff
carried out some of the more pressing needs of hair trimming.

Sheppard, somewhat modestly, does not say that the member of staff was actually him! Nor was it just the teaching staff. Leakey's personal cook before the war was Mabel Drewry, and when the school went first to the camp and then to Wales, she went with it and soon turned her hand to producing meals on a far larger scale. So successful was she that she became the cook at Brightlands for over twenty years after the war had ended. Another veteran from pre-war days was Charlie Beasley, who had been employed by Leake in Dulwich as the school gardener in 1930. He accompanied the school to Cranbrook and he too went on to Wales. One of his hardest times was in January 1941 when there was a measles epidemic. At one time, there were sixty boys in beds in different rooms and some thirty fires throughout the buildings which had to be kept burning with very little coal and a great deal of wood, for which he himself often had to forage. As jobs needed doing, everyone turned their hands to dealing with them for the common cause. Not only was this the 'grin and bear it' attitude of war, but also the result of the great respect held for Leakey by those who worked for him. After the war Beasley attended to the garden and grounds at Brightlands for some years.

Despite all these vicissitudes, a near normal programme of school work was carried out almost from the start. In Geography, the boys were taken to the Conway Valley, and in History the Welsh wars of Edward I were popular, with Conway and Caernarvon Castles being near at hand. The district was also ideally suited for Biology and Botany. Snowdonia is a beautiful place and the boys took full advantage of the many attractions in the area, especially during holiday time for those who remained, as without the demands of a daily school timetable, these were more relaxed occasions. In those days, boys were able to be given far more freedom than they can be now. On Sundays in term time, and more often in the holidays, they were often free for the whole day and were able to do much as they pleased without supervision. There were organised outings as well and boys were taken up Snowdon and the mountains around, had picnics by the lakes and despite transport difficulties were taken to the sea at Llandudno from time to time. It was fortunate that the Royal Oak was near the railway station at Betws-y-Coed, so access to Llandudno was possible. The branch line remained open during the war and, incidentally, remains open today. Outdoor pursuits were limitless and there was always plenty to do. In those days before television and piped entertainment, boys were far more innovative than they are now. Paul Gray's report for the end of the spring term in 1941 showed that the report format remained virtually unchanged and the words 'Lower School' were being used, with art and singing lessons included for boys of that age. A near normal school programme was being carried out and clearly the summer term was being made as long as it could

DULWICH COLLEGE PREPARATORY SCHOOL.

LOWER SCHOOL.

REPORT FOR ⅛ TERM, 1941

Name _Gray 2_ Form _3A_ No. of Boys _16 (12 placed)_

Age: _9_ years _2_ months. Average Age of Form: _9_ years _5_ months.

Conduct _Very good_ Days Absent _____ Days Late _____

READING	... Improved, but must still 'plod away'!	W.H.
REPETITION	... Fairly good.	W.H.
WRITING ...	... Usually neat & careful.	M.G.
SPELLING ...	... Only fair.	W.H.
ORAL COMPOSITION	Good. RDH.	
GEOGRAPHY ...	} Good. He is very keen, & his work is neat & accurate. RDH.	
HISTORY		
SCRIPTURE ...	Good. RDH.	
French	Good: especially oral work.	
ART	Fairly good. Neat careful work.	
SINGING	Excellent. RDH.	
~~LATIN~~ NATURE STUDY ...	Good. He is very keen indeed	
HANDWORK ...	Very good. RDH.	
P.T.	Very good indeed. W.H.	WEIGHT ...

Arithmetic Set _____ of _____ boys.

ARITHMETIC ...	Very good. He has worked well.	M.G.
~~GEOMETRY~~ ...		

	TERM ORDER.	TERM ~~DRAW.~~ ORDER.		TERM ~~FINAL~~ ORDER.	
FORM	4	Latin:	5	English:	6
ARITHMETIC ~~Set~~ ...	2.	French:	7	Hist. & Geog:	8

General Remarks: _A most satisfactory term in every way. J.H.L._

Next Term begins on _Friday 2nd. May_ and ends on _1st. August._

All boys must return punctually on the day named. The only ground for exemption allowed by School Rules is sickness or exposure to infection. Notice of this must be sent before the opening of the School to the Head Master.

Each boy must bring with him on the first day his health certificate signed. A Boy who fails to do this will be sent home and his Tribe will lose a mark.

No boy shall return to School from a house in which there has been any infectious disorder during the previous month.

Boarders **must** return before 7 p.m. on the EVENING BEFORE the day of commencement.

Paul Gray's Report for the Spring Term 1941

be, not ending until August 1st[t]. The deletion of Nature Study in favour of Latin is an interesting development. Presumably there was plenty of time to study flora and fauna in the surrounding area during out of school hours.

All in all things went well in Wales. Although wartime conditions meant that there were many diversions, it was never forgotten that DCPS was a school and its prime purpose of moving to Wales was not only to escape from the bombing, but also to continue operating, albeit under different conditions, as an educational establishment, maintaining the highest standards it possibly could under the difficulties prevailing at the time. School life did not continue as it had in Dulwich, but it did continue. An internal competitive spirit operated, but it was considered prudent to dispense with tribes and in their place the school was divided into four houses with names of Welsh origin. The familiar tribe names were suspended until the war ended, and in came 'Tryfan', 'Snowdon', 'Garmon' and 'Conway'. There were still good and bad slips, and there were 'tribe matches' and 'tribe meetings'. Although the boys at Betws were shielded from the bombing and the immediate atrocities of war, what was going on was never far from their thoughts or activities. Sheppard organised a most successful War Savings Scheme throughout the duration and although boys had access to limited amounts of money, a percentage of what they had was saved for the war effort. In this way each boy felt he was making his own contribution. At the beginning of 1941, when DCPS had been in Wales for less than a year, Sheppard wrote:

> *In eight months, we have obtained 100% membership from the school, and more than a 100 of these members have gained at least one savings certificate. So far we have raised £471 which is just £29 short of our target of £500. Even so, we will have paid for 90,000 rounds of ammunition, or we will have provided 24 infantrymen with items of equipment each. This is a result of which we can feel justly proud.*

At the same time a boy, (CGS aged 13), saw his war effort being made in a different way:

> *The very fact that we are here in the Royal Oak is helping to win the war; because the government has asked us to evacuate from London, so as to make the work of the Civil Defence Workers easier, who will then not have so many people in their charge. Also our parents do not have to worry for us, and can give all their attention to their work.*

By the time the boys left Betws, they had raised over £4000 which was a commendable effort. Contributions to the war effort were made in other ways. There was a piece of neglected land near the old stables which was put to good use by giving each boy a small plot to cultivate his own vegetables such as lettuces, radishes and tomatoes. The more enterprising boys sold their produce to Mrs Leakey, thus supplementing their own funds, and enabling the school to gain extra produce at relatively less cost. The school was once approached by Bangor University and the boys urged to gather hips for the making of rose hip syrup. These, they were told, replaced vitamins which they should have obtained from oranges, so many boys went out to collect rose hips. They also helped with forestry and a plantation of conifers was planted which ultimately became known as 'The Dulwich Plantation'. The younger Annexe children made their contributions in a less conventional way and one which would not be considered at all suitable now. In 1943 they sent a parcel of cigarettes to a central point for distribution to soldiers by the army authorities. Recipients of these parcels were encouraged to reply to the donors and L/C J Higginson acknowledged some cigarettes which he had received.

To the Pupils of Dulwich College Prep School Annexe.
'Many thanks for the cigs. Appreciated by all ranks in Unit.'

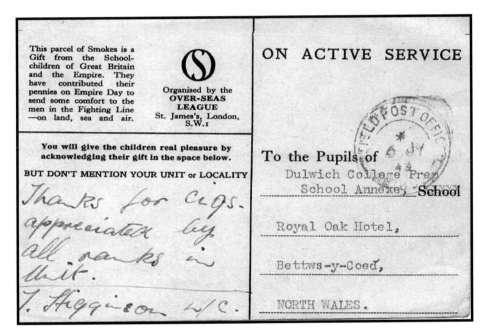

The letter received by boys at the Annexe from a soldier
thanking them for the cigarettes they had sent

Happily it was not always packets of cigarettes which the boys sent and in this case just a letter to a soldier at the front produced the following reply:

7007503 /Cpl D J Dykes
HQ Squadron
7th Army Division
MEF
August 3rd 1943

Dear Kids,
Many thanks for your letter. It was certainly a pleasant surprise to hear from you boys of the Annexe and I must tell you how much I appreciate receiving mail from home. I am enclosing a snapshot of myself and my comrade taken in front of our tank just before the great battle of El-Alamein.

The first year at Betws drew to a close with a service of lessons and carols in the local church, and many boys stayed on for Christmas – a very wise move as it happened, as December 1940, immediately after Christmas, saw some of the heaviest bombing of London during the entire war. This was the time of the blitz and much damage was done. Parents had earlier been given the option of either having their sons home for Christmas or leaving them in the comparative safety of North Wales. Even this was not straightforward as this excerpt from a circular sent to parents from Betws in November 1940 illustrated:

CHRISTMAS HOLIDAYS.

Term ends on Friday December 19th and next term begins on Friday January 16th. We shall only take a conducted party as far as Crewe, owing to the Government's desire that children shall not be taken back to evacuation areas.

The Railway Company have kindly arranged for us to have a special train as far as Llandudno Junction, as the early morning train has been withdrawn. Those parents who are forced to leave their children here during the holidays may rest assured that we shall do everything in our power to see they have a happy Christmas.

The circular goes on to explain that because of increased prices and the fact that boys would be staying on over Christmas, fees would be increased from £5 to £8 per term, quite a stiff relative increase. Leakey and members of his staff gave up their holidays quite voluntarily to keep the school open and they went out of their way to ensure that those boys who remained had a memorable Christmas. Chubb, Hull and others who were there, remember it with much affection, even though they were separated from their own families.

Later on, as the war front eased, it was possible for boys to go home in larger numbers at the end of every term, and staff always travelled on the trains with them. Leakey described these journeys as being exceedingly difficult. It was always a fierce battle to keep the coaches to themselves as the trains were full to bursting point. The boys were no help as they encouraged soldiers to come and join them and, as now, they all started gobbling their packed lunches within the first few minutes of the journey. The journeys back were no better as the boys were invariably over-supplied with vast quantities of tuck which the parents had managed to procure, even in wartime, and this was consumed throughout the journey with the usual dire results. This article, written by WB (aged 12.6) shows one such journey back to school from a boy's point of view:

COMING BACK TO SCHOOL

At Euston every boy's face is a study. Some boys, glad of the thoughts of seeing their chums again, are laughing. Others, very glum because the holidays are over, just stand about looking miserable. The majority, however, are quite cheerful, and when the train comes in, rush to get seats. The windows are crowded with faces of boys waving to their parents and saying goodbye. Then the train goes, and everybody finds something to do. Some boys stand at the windows and count the miles. Others play such card games as 'Pontoon' or 'Patience'. Lunch is eaten at about 1 o'clock, and so the train continues through the stations, Rugby, Crewe, Chester, to Llandudno Junction, where our coaches are shunted on to the little train going to Bettws-y-Coed. This little train is known as the 'coffee-pot', owing to the very high funnel of the engine. The little train starts off, and within another hour or two we are at the Royal Oak Hotel. We put our cases in room seven, room eight or the sun-lounge, and go in to supper. Nobody ever eats much after the long journey, and when tea is finished and the list of bedrooms read, we all get our night things and go to bed. The next day we start to unpack and are finished, with our cases over at the garage by the end of the day. The next day ordinary school begins and the term has started.

Not all the boys returning to Wales to start a new term came from London. Peter Dawson (DCPS 1938-1943) remembered waiting on the platform at Crewe, complete with gas mask, with his friend Robert O'Neill to join the DCPS party on the train from London in April 1941, having come from Edinburgh where his family was then in residence. It is interesting to note that gas was still considered a threat when the war was well into its second year. Sometimes parents came to Wales for the school holidays instead. One such example was the mother of Bruce Shilstone who rented a cottage in Penmachno, not far from Betws, for the summer holidays in 1941. This meant that Bruce, and his brother Brian who had

Peter Dawson (left) and Robert O'Neill waiting on the platform at Crewe for the arrival of the DCPS train for Betws. Note the gas mask (1941).

been at DCPS in London earlier, and his sister as well, could spend the summer holiday together as a family. Bruce Shilstone had a very interrupted education and was one of only a few boys to experience all the wartime moves. He joined DCPS in 1935 and in 1939 went with the evacuated school to Cranbrook. He was on the train from Cranbrook to Betws on 16th July 1940 and stayed there until 1942 when his father gained a war-based appointment in Bath so he moved there, it being considered a safe place to be. He returned to London in 1943 and was at the Dulwich section until July 1944 when he went on to the College. Close links with the school had been formed and, for a short while in 1949, Bruce's mother taught at the DCPS Kindergarten when it was back in London again.

There can be no doubt that the time when the school was exiled in Wales made a lasting impression on those who were there, and at present the 1939-45 period is the only time in the school's history for which reunions of former pupils are held periodically, sometimes in London but more usually back in Betws at the Royal Oak itself. Instrumental in this has been Gordon Chubb, who was at the camp and at Betws for the first couple of years, and his enthusiasm has led to the establishing of the John Leakey Memorial Fund. This furthers the relationship between the present school, whose Year 8 regularly visit Snowdonia, and the current community at Betws by maintaining records of the school's wartime stay at the village. Chubb has been assisted by several others, notably Giles Flint whose own sons followed him at the Prep many years later, but under very different circumstances, and Ken Hull, a remarkable old boy if ever there were one, because his enthusiasm for the school as a whole stems from the fact that he was never at Alleyn Park as a pupil and spent all his DCPS years at Betws. The circumstances prevailing at the time led to a camaraderie within the school which has not been matched before or since.

Gradually the school became absorbed and accepted as a part of the local community and, to use Leakey's words, '*the inhabitants began to take an interest in the boys instead of regarding them as an invasion of heathen Barbarians*'. Several local people in particular were most welcoming. W Bennett Hughes, the vicar of the local church, which happened to be virtually next door to the Royal Oak, was willing to allow the school to use his church for morning assembly each day. He also invigilated exams and was always willing to lend a hand to the school when it was necessary. After the war, Leakey placed a plaque to commemorate this happy union between school and church just inside the church door, and there it remains. Another local was 'Jones the Grocer', who was not only helpful to the school professionally, but later allowed the school to use his field for games. This was nearby and one of the few flat pieces of land in the area. Jones worked with a Mr Roberts, the butcher, and Leakey describes them both as being towers of strength for the school during a difficult time. This Mr Roberts is of particular interest. When the Leakeys first arrived, they found him dour and evasive and somewhat suspicious of this invasion of London schoolchildren. They were therefore surprised when one day during the week before the first Christmas, he drew up in front of the Royal Oak in his pony and trap, bearing two enormous turkeys which he said were a present for the boys. Every Christmas for the rest of the evacuation he did the same. This was a generous gesture and Leakey was pleased to realise that the school was being accepted into the local community. Although the boys in Wales generally fared better for food than their counterparts in London, Malcolm Lees (DCPS Betws 1943-1945) remembered that conditions generally were fairly spartan and that rationing was so severe that a whole week's ration of cheese could go in a single meal. Visits by boys to see parents in London during the holidays were fairly common when they could be arranged, and Lees remembered cycling in the area and fishing for salmon – a ration-free bonus. Later on a field almost in the centre of the village was rented from the same Mr Roberts, the butcher. Though not entirely level, games of rugby and soccer were played, and cricket too in the summer, and this field was a great asset. Occasionally matches were arranged with local schools and Leakey recalled a wonderful story about transport to matches, which in wartime was exceedingly difficult. For the first part of the war at least, limited amounts of petrol were available. The school had two cars, a Triumph and a Morris, and in one match against Ruthin School these were the only means of transport available. Somehow the entire rugby team managed to squeeze into these two cars. The boys were incredibly cramped and stops were made every half hour or so to ease limbs and reshuffle positions. Any speed would have damaged the springs so the journeys were slow as well. There were many astonished faces when the entire team disgorged itself from two cars. Such a practice would be frowned on from all quarters today, but in wartime rules and regulations can always be stretched.

The plaque on the wall of the parish church at Betws-y-Coed.
The church was used for morning assembly each day during the evacuation.

One big event which everyone remembered was on 11th October 1940 when Betws itself was bombed. At the time Leakey was returning to Betws after a fortnight at the school in Dulwich, during which time the blitz had been particularly severe. To be told, as he approached Betws, that an air raid was on seemed almost unbelievable, but it was true. The bombing of Merseyside was in full force at the time, and on this occasion a German plane, damaged by Spitfires near Snowdon, escaped by diving down the valley which carries the A5 from Capel Curig. Seeing Mount Garmon rising before him and to gain more height, the pilot jettisoned his load of bombs which fell in a field not far from Betws railway station, and thus near the Royal Oak. In fading light he was able to make his escape. No serious damage was done and a few windows were broken. Later, Gordon Chubb related what happened at the Royal Oak that evening:

> *The normal refined hubbub of the Prep. at supper was suddenly shattered by the roar of a damaged German plane at roof level followed by the explosion of bombs not far from Mr Leakey's house. Few who were there will ever forget the noise made by that plane or the swiftness of action by the entire school as it jointly dived for cover under the dining tables and benches. The instinct for survival has always been strong at the Prep.*

The air raid at Betws was obviously a major event during the Prep's time in Wales, but memories from the boys who were there are many and varied. John Hetherington (Betws 1940-1942), for example, remembered that if a boy was caught smoking, Leakey would make him smoke his worst cigar under his supervision, in the hope it would put him off for life. Punishments and correction for misdemeanours continued to rely on the cane and former pupils, for some reason, seem to recall its use with glee all these years on. David Mushlin (Betws 1942-1945) remembered an occasion when one of the masters, R A Forster, heard some talking in one of the bedrooms after 'lights out'. When no one owned up, all eight boys in the room were taken downstairs and given three of the best. It was unheard of in those days for anyone to betray the culprit and loyalty to one's friends was far more honourable than the discomfort of the cane.

Memories from wartime Wales are generally happy ones, as less happy experiences fade from the mind with the passing of time. Gordon Dearing (Betws 1940-1941) remembered collecting peat for the hotel fires and the wonderful smell when it burned. He also recalled being told to pump the organ in church one day, but when he let it die on a sustained chord he was not asked again. All remembered the hills, the mountains, the streams, the woods and the magnificence of Snowdonia, all so very different from the suburbia they had left behind. Then there were the slate quarries at Blaenau Ffestiniog, where it never stopped raining. John Hedwell (Betws 1940-1945) remembered the US Army Corps passing the Royal Oak towards the end of the war, surrounded by DCPS boys begging for chocolate and chewing gum. He remembered too how Leakey assembled the school together to hear the hushed announcement that D-Day had arrived and a landing had been made on the coast of France in Normandy. Euphoria soon turned to dismay when the first flying bomb fell on London just over a week later. South London suffered badly from the doodlebugs and rockets and the need to keep the boys in Wales grew very strong again. For the last part of 1944, London became a battleground once more, but it was comparatively short lived. Peter Vernon (Betws 1940-1944) remembered well one of Leakey's habitual traits – his absent-mindedness. He recalled how one morning Leakey came into the dining room from his study which was in the next room, clapped his hands and told everyone to be quiet because he had something important to say. Silence followed and then Leakey left the room looking somewhat confused because he had forgotten what he had come in to say! David Weaver (Betws 1941–1944) remembered a very different side to Leakey's character which on reflection he considered justified:

> *At the Royal Oak, two other boys and I lived in a second floor bedroom immediately over the hotel entrance. One day, upstairs in our room, we decided to have fun by dropping balls of paper, of ever increasing size, onto boys standing in the entrance below. But it wasn't exciting enough and I was 'encouraged' to pour a bucket of water onto them. But disaster struck. Just as I emptied the bucket, the boys below stepped to one side to let Mrs Leakey leave the hotel. She collected the bucketful on her head and shoulders – precise marksmanship – but within a few minutes I was in the headmaster's study for a stern reprimand and a well deserved caning!*

The front of the Royal Oak in 2003 showing the second floor window from which
David Weaver emptied his bucket of water

On the other hand the memories of William Gruby (Betws 1941-1944) were not entirely happy ones. He recalled being read to by Freddie Taylor, but thinking to himself '*He's doing his best to be kind, but why isn't it one of our parents and where are they?*' Furthermore, he recalled a feeling that he and the other boys were not being accepted into the local community. '*I sang solo in a choir*', he wrote, '*which gave concerts in the church to the Betws townsfolk, yet I cannot remember crossing a single Welsh threshold into a Betws home*'. As we have seen, Leakey felt differently. Gruby loved the mountains but loathed the rain. He remembered sheltering in caves because he was not allowed back indoors for many hours each day, no doubt for some character-forming reason he thought, no matter how hard it rained. Yet he blamed no one but wondered if parents today would wash their hands of their responsibility and hand such young children over into a place like the camp and that terrible first winter of war. He sincerely hoped not and he is probably right. But war conditions bring about very different emotions and reactions.

Each year new arrivals came, usually but not always, from Dulwich to replace those who had reached leaving age. The school had gained a reputation in the area and boys began to arrive from other parts of the country, some becoming members of DCPS without ever setting foot inside Dulwich itself. Ken Hull and brothers Basil and Raymond Bathurst were among those. This meant that the schools to which boys went became more varied and away from London and the South East, and Common Entrance and scholarship exams were taken with a remarkable success rate given the circumstances. Leakey's philosophy as well as what he achieved can best be summed up in the newsletter written to parents at the end of the summer term in 1942:

SCHOOL NOTES

On June 16th, we completed our second year at Bettws, and it is perhaps a good opportunity of reviewing our achievements during these two crowded and adventurous years.

We have obtained a most gratifying list of scholarships, 16 boys being successful in 1941, and 14 up to the present this year. In games, in spite of initial difficulties, we have turned out Rugger and Soccer, Cricket and Tennis teams which have been worthy of the traditions of the Prep.

These are concrete results which are obvious and easily tabulated, but the School attempts to achieve less definable and more important things than these. The Prep wants to send boys to the College and Public Schools who are self-reliant, capable of standing on their own feet and thinking for themselves.

Boys who consider others before self and who are always ready to help those not so strong as themselves. Unlike most Prep Schools, older boys are allowed to go out on their own and have a great deal of freedom. This is because we feel that we can trust them and, up to now that trust has not been abused.

Men's lives are based on two things, work and leisure, and it is now that your sons are building up their capacities for both.

The habit of hard work is learned in the School Curriculum but the enjoyment of leisure in the right way is not so easily learned. The habit of reading, of enjoying good music, of forming hobbies, of learning about nature and the world in which we live – these things are of real value. Evacuation has helped us in all these things. We have had to learn to live together for the common good and that is the basis of good citizenship. We have had to learn to rely on ourselves and to help those who cannot and that is the basis of a good Englishman.

We are surrounded by beautiful mountains, moors and rivers and we are entirely dependent on ourselves for our amusements. This has taught us to occupy our leisure in the best possible way and this will stand us in good stead in the days to come. I shall miss those boys who are leaving, but I can be sure that they will grow up to be good citizens in a new world and that is all a schoolmaster can ask.

J. H. L.

While the main part of DCPS was functioning in Wales, there was also a section of the school in Dulwich, for those boys whose parents for various reasons had chosen not to send their sons to Wales. It was important that the two schools, or rather the two sections of the same school, should have common standards and common goals, so Leakey spent a part of his time in Dulwich each term to ensure that these things were achieved. When Leake died in 1942, Leakey's visits were even more important, as Leake's successor as Master-in-Charge in London, O E Watson, was not so familiar with the DCPS routine.

At the beginning of the war, both Dulwich and Betws shared the same magazine but as the war progressed there were times when each produced its own. For the summer of 1943, for example, there were two DCPS magazines, one from Betws and the other from London but with printing restrictions and a shortage of paper, it was more usual for the magazine to be printed in Wales with a small Dulwich section at the back. These magazines were used as a channel of communication between the two schools, and each issue always included a letter to the other. In July 1940 the following letter from Betws appeared in the London section:

Dulwich College Preparatory School
Royal Oak Hotel, Bettws-y-Coed
North Wales.
July, 1940

Dear Stay-at-homes,
Perhaps you think that you would rather remain in Dulwich than be down here with us, but if you were to visit North Wales, we are sure that you would think differently. What with climbing, bathing, walking, cycling, and ping-pong and billiards, we enjoy ourselves very much during our spare time, and even school is not so bad. Our form-rooms are situated in various places: four are over at the hotel

garage, which was formerly the courtyard for the coaches of the olden days, and two more are at some private rooms that Mr Leakey has taken. The remaining ones are in the hotel. The history of the hotel itself is very interesting. Opposite us is the river Llugwy, and we are able to play and paddle in it, as part of the river is the property of the hotel. We hear from Mr Leakey that the Camp at Cranbrook is going to be occupied by soldiers. We certainly didn't leave anything for them except for the huts, and the vegetables that were growing as a result of our "Dig for Victory" efforts. Owing to various difficulties, it appears that some of us will be remaining here during the holidays, but there is no doubt that these people will have an enjoyable time. It is certainly as good as a holiday by the sea.

Finally, we would like to thank the masters and other members of the staff, and, above all, Mr and Mrs Leakey, for making this term the happy one it has been.

Cheerio and Best of Luck,

All at Bettws

Three years later in 1943, this letter was sent from Dulwich to those at Betws. It has been abridged, but has been chosen because it conveys a clear picture of school life at the time:

DULWICH NEWS LETTER

Dear Bettws,

Thank you for your News Letter. We were interested to read about so many of your activities. It is impossible to tell you everything we do as only part of our time is spent at school and the many interesting things done at home do not come into this letter. We are working hard and trying to raise our standard to what the College expect. Two boys have gone to the College and a third goes at the beginning of next term.

We have a busy time, and many of us rise early and have a long journey to school. During school hours we are occupied all the time in various ways. After dinner on Tuesdays the Music Makers meet and some play their recorders while others play the piano or violin. We have only been in the air raid shelters two or three times this term. Once it was most exciting when a plane started firing its machine gun just beyond the Paddock. We were glad to have Mr Leakey with us at the beginning of term and then again later for a fortnight. This gave an opportunity for the newer boys to know him better, and he helps us to bring our work in line with Bettws.

Those of you who remember the Annexe may be interested to hear that it has been de-requisitioned, and its Blitz scars mended ready for occupation next term. The Paddock crocuses and daffodils are at their best, while the big chestnuts are already in bud.

Happy holidays to you all – DULWICH

DCPS taking exercise at the Royal Oak Hotel in 1942

The same place in 2004

With the coming of peace in May 1945, Leakey's bonhomie came to the fore in style. He celebrated with a display of fireworks, although nobody ever knew from where he had obtained them. As in all things, he had found a way. So the last term at Betws drew to a close. Boys taking the Common Entrance Examination returned to Dulwich in June and both there and in Wales it was decided to finish the term early as all were in urgent need of a rest. Those boys remaining at Betws helped to pack up the stores and the furniture, until little was left except their beds and the clothes they stood up in. Although elated by the end of the war, there was sadness that the organization which had been built up with such effort under almost impossible conditions, was about to be disbanded. It had been a supreme effort, not only by the irrepressible and unstoppable John Leakey, but also by his team of dedicated staff who kept the DCPS ship afloat during this most difficult time. The school of today is unquestionably the fruit of their labours – people like Sheppard, Taylor, Meyrat and Barbara Herbertson as well as Leakey himself. At the end, the village turned out to say goodbye. DCPS had left its mark in this beautiful little corner of Wales.

The last word should go to Peter Fairley, who was a boy at Betws, later to become Science Correspondent for Independent Television News. He later wrote about his stay in Wales during the war:

> It is testimony to our way of life at the Royal Oak Hotel that 17 scholarships were gained in one year, and between 1949 and 1951, 16 of us became head boys at public schools around Britain. (DCPS has no proof of this, but who are we to argue?) For us boys Snowdonia became Adventureland, and thanks to our inspired Headmaster, I believe we were the Outward Bound movement before it was even thought of.

6   Dulwich under Fire!

Just before war was declared on 3rd September 1939, parents had a number of choices. Their sons could either be evacuated to the camp which had been established at Cranbrook, or they could remain in London, against government advice it should be added, or they could go elsewhere to what was deemed to be a safe place. DCPS did not operate in London for the autumn term of 1939, although the buildings were not just abandoned. Russell Taylor, the school's Director of Music, decided not to go to the camp and with a handful of pupils who had also remained, kept an eye on the place. However, even the best laid plans can be overtaken by the unexpected and, although the evacuation of London's children had been meticulously arranged and carried out, the unexpected brought about a welcome surprise. There was no immediate onslaught as had been expected and as each day passed this period of comparative quiet, which lasted well into 1940, became known as the 'Phoney War'. It seemed as if both sides were bracing themselves and preparing for the conflict which would surely follow, but so far as the evacuees were concerned, it led to problems of a different kind.

Not all evacuees were as fortunate as the boys from DCPS, who had evacuated as a school unit and not as individuals. They had their friends around them and this made life more agreeable than it might otherwise have been, although obviously they missed their families and the comforts of home. Many other children had gone to live with families in the country, often on their own or just with a brother or sister, and they were not happy about being away from home when, in their eyes, there seemed no good reason. As early as January 1940, a number of evacuated children had returned to London and, as many schools were closed, were roaming the streets. Government policy was to keep the children away from London as bombing and, worse still, the threat from gas both remained distinct possibilities. But there was no legal compulsion for parents to keep their children away in the country and although there was a strong publicity campaign advising against it, many children drifted back to London. In consequence there was pressure for the London County Council (LCC) to re-open some of the schools which had closed.

Leakey found himself under similar pressure and, almost certainly against his better judgement, he agreed to re-open a part of the school in Alleyn Park in January 1940, although the main part remained at the camp at Cranbrook. Leake, who had retired as full-time headmaster in 1934, stepped in to supervise matters and Miss Osborne, who had played a prominent part before the war as Head of the Kindergarten and had not gone to

Government posters urging parents not to bring their
children back to London in 1940
(Courtesy Imperial War Museum)

Government Evacuation Scheme.

EASTER HOLIDAYS.

Dangers of air attack are in no way less.

You are earnestly advised not to bring your children back to the evacuation areas.

March, 1940.

MINISTRY OF HEALTH,
LONDON, S.W.1.

[77458] 50854 3/40 706

Cranbrook, was thus able to help in Dulwich as well. Other former staff, including a Mr Davies, returned and Russell Taylor was already there. Only a handful of boys came back from Cranbrook and the London section generally catered for those who had not gone to Cranbrook in the first place. There were also some boys totally new to DCPS who came from other schools in the area which had closed and had not re-opened. By April 1940, there were 112 boys in London and 180 at Cranbrook. Of the situation, Leakey wrote:

> *We are in the happy position of knowing that whatever happens the School will carry on either in London and Cranbrook, or in Cranbrook alone.*

As he wrote, arrangements were made to enlarge the camp at Cranbrook so it could receive more boys should the need arise. In London there were problems when the term started. Although there had been no bombing, the buildings had been empty for four months and there were burst pipes and no heating. Angus Greig (DCPS 1937–1943) remembered going to school in January 1940 armed with sticks and lumps of coal, these being his contribution to maintain a fire in one of the classrooms. Frequent raids to the handwork room were made to forage other pieces of small wood and every effort was made to keep the boys warm. Although central heating had been installed in most rooms much earlier, there was no fuel for it and it was fortunate that the chimneys and fireplaces were still serviceable. There were other surprises. The boys arrived at school one Wednesday to be confronted by a strong smell of petrol everywhere. Some suggested that Mr Leakey's car had sprung a leak, but they were told later that all the windows had been painted with a rubber solution to prevent them from splintering in the event of blast. There were also shortages of furniture and books as many of these had gone to the camp at Cranbrook. These problems had to be sorted out and it was a tense time. Everyone knew that bombing would come sooner or later, but nobody knew when. To add to the anxiety, 'flu took its usual toll and the weather was exceptionally cold.

The period of uncertainty could not last and May brought the big event which was to change everything so dramatically: the evacuation of a large part of the British Army from Dunkirk followed by the fall of France in mid-June. As we have seen, DCPS was forced to uproot itself all over again, this time from Cranbrook, luckily finding itself another new home at Betws-y-Coed in North Wales. With the distinct possibility that war would soon come to London, some boys from Dulwich joined the evacuation party at Euston while it was en route for Betws. Yet despite all the problems the school in London continued to function during the summer of 1940. There were cricket matches and Russell Taylor, who incidentally chose this term to be married, said that the school's singing had improved and boys learning the piano continued '*to do good work*'. Of Sports Day, on 22nd June, by which time German air activity over England had started, Russell Taylor (obviously a master of all trades) wrote:

> *You see, we will not let any of our time-honoured institutions lapse in spite of the Blitz and the scars we bear. Gone were the rows of gleaming white shorts and the immaculate blazers: gone were the championship cups, and the prizes: gone was the feeling of a state occasion. What, therefore, remained? That indomitable spirit of the old Prep - sportsmanship, good comradeship and friendly rivalry each with the other. So that, although shorn of its finery, we had our 100 yards and our quarter mile and our Tribe relays as well as some new and amusing events, which included one for our parents. The weather, as usual, rose to the occasion and the proceedings closed with the usual rounds of cheering. Congratulations are due to the organisers (and the organised) for the splendid result of a memorable day.*

The boys commented that air raid practices were particularly popular when they occurred in French or Latin lessons and even more popular was the decision that if there had been an air raid during the night, boys could come to school one hour later in the morning. This was not a privilege just for DCPS but national practice, and at no time does it appear to have been abused. In the summer of 1940 the Deerfeet won the slip competition and a handful of boys took exams and passed successfully to the College. At this time Leakey wrote:

> *The boys who have stayed in London have worked manfully to keep the flag flying in the old school, and I am glad to say that Hitler permitting, there will be an increased number of boys next term.*

By the time the autumn term started, the situation had deteriorated and bombing intensified. The number of boys fell and it was considered impracticable to continue with four tribes, so the school was divided into two new tribes, Mohawks and Sioux. Later in the war, when the number of boys had increased, the usual tribe system was adopted again. There are no tribe results on the boards in the hall for the war period as there was no continuity. Despite the tribulations, the school carried on. Soccer and rugby were reduced to 7-a-side and in November the soccer tribe match was abandoned, firstly because of an air raid and then, when that was over, heavy rain made the pitch so sodden that it was not possible to resume. One early casualty of the war was the original house which had once been Number 1 Alleyn Park and where the school had started in 1885. This received a direct hit from a bomb on 15th September 1940 and was totally destroyed. The Alleyn's Head, which was then on the other side of the road, was also damaged beyond repair and the adjacent railway bridge was severely damaged, disrupting train services for a while. The heaviest raids of all came just after Christmas 1940 and, although the school was closed at the time, some damage was done. After the war the Alleyn's Head was rebuilt on the site of the original Number 1, the sequence of numbering having been subsequently changed. A bomb also

Alleyn Park Railway Bridge destroyed by enemy action 15th Sept 1940.
The building where the school had started was destroyed at the same time. (Courtesy R C Riley Collection)

fell near Hamilton's former house at 28 Alleyn Park which had been the principal home for boarders before the war. It was damaged beyond repair and blast caused much damage to school property, particularly the recently built Nursery School.

The principal buildings in use at the time were 42 Alleyn Park, which was the main school building where the staff room and offices are now, and 44, the Victorian part of the present

Lower School. The rest of the buildings facing onto Alleyn Park, including Number 40, had yet to be purchased. The hall was half its present size and the stage was where the servery is now. As well as the original Annexe and Nursery School, there was a ramshackle old brick building which had a multitude of uses, and the corrugated gymnasium which had caused problems for Leake when it was built. There was also a brick outdoor air raid shelter with a reinforced concrete roof, but this was dark and smelly and was not very popular with the boys who considered the cellars to be much better. None of these buildings remain today. It must be said that Leakey was not the only one to make preparations for war long before it came. The father of Angus Greig, mentioned earlier, was an architect and had had the foresight to incorporate a basement air raid shelter under three feet of concrete at his home at 5 Alleyn Park. There the family lived each night during the blitz.

There was a flow of correspondence in the school magazine between the evacuated DCPS in Wales and the London DCPS. Extracts from one such letter sent from Dulwich to Betws in July 1940 give an interesting insight into the priorities of the day:

July, 1940

Dear Pioneers at Bettws-y-Coed,

We have had, here at Dulwich, a very successful and enjoyable term under the guidance of the Revd W. R. M. Leake. We have played three cricket fixtures, so far, and there is one still to follow, in which we may say, we have a good chance of winning. During the term we have had a visit from Monsieur Meyrat, and his car, which now, owing to the Darkness Regulations, he has to push to school. At the moment St. Swithin seems to have turned over in his grave and we have been having a good deal of rain. We hope that you enjoy swimming in the streams around Mount Snowdon and we also hope that you do not use hot water bottles as well as water wings. Throughout the term we have been having air raid practices, which are most welcome in the Latin and French lessons. Another most popular decision is that when there is an air raid in the night we come to school one hour later. That is one up on you, we think. Anyway, we hope you are having a jolly good time and we will probably see some of you in the holidays.

So until we next meet,

Cheerio

THE STAY AT HOMES.

In December 1940 Leakey wrote these words for the school magazine:

With the beginning of this term, we entered our second year of the war. A year ago the Prep in London was closed and we were just beginning to settle into the camp at Cranbrook. This year there are fifty boys in the bomb-scarred school in London and 200 at Bettws-y-Coed. The difficulties in London have been overcome by the heroic work of Revd Leake, Miss Osborne and the staff. The shelter has been fitted up with heating, tables and benches, so work can be carried on during air raids and games are played on the paddock. At Bettws-y-Coed, a complete new school has had to be formed where no school was before. The Prep has lived up to its tradition and the flag is still flying in Bettws and London.

At the same time, in an article entitled *A Voice from the Burrow*, the Revd W R M Leake wrote:

> *Yes - we few, some fifty in all, are holding the fort and playing, not unhappily, a game of rabbits. We ought soon to be growing 'scuts', for - it's a nibble above - then a wail and a dive below - we have had as many as seven dives a day. So we are fortunate in our shelter, though we like it not; yet it enables us to carry on, when otherwise we might be carried off. Football, when our RAF allows, is on the paddock, and Mr Planner is the happy mentor, and all are learning eagerly under him. We play both Rugger and Soccer. In spite of the loss of some 200 panes of glass, on November 11ᵗʰ our Union Jack flaunted a brave defiance to the skies - for, are we downhearted? We send you a loud-voiced 'No', with every good wish and blessing on our more than better (?) half at Bettws . . . We, the small tail that still wags the Dulwich end. Au Revoir.*
>
> *W. R. M. L.*

I joined the school in 1942 when I was five, when the main blitz was over. My mother took me to Beckenham Junction on the 54 bus, and by the time I was six I was travelling from there to Sydenham Hill on the train - on my own! I remember, and still have, one of my school reports from the Annexe saying that there had been 'some poor behaviour to and from the station', although I cannot remember what I had been up to. From the station, we were privileged to walk through a gate and up a zig-zag path through the grounds of Lord Vestey's estate at Kingswood House. There was a cinder track leading to it which is now Bowen Drive. If we misbehaved, Lord Vestey expressed his displeasure and we had to use West Dulwich Station for a while until he relented. Although there was little heavy bombing at that time there were occasional air raids, mainly at night, and bombs did drop. The fashion of the day was to collect shrapnel on the way to school and any with writing on it was a real prize. I still have a piece. Memories of the teaching I received are rather more hazy. I remember being taught by an elderly, and no doubt sagacious, man who had been brought out of retirement to teach Maths. Rather unkindly we called him 'Post' because he was as deaf as one. His real name was Green, and the Green Maths Prize is named after him. Boys can be so unkind.

One of the boys who went to the Cranbrook Camp in 1939 but returned to London for the spring term in 1940 was John Rowe. Many years later his own son Julian would be a Prep boy, but under very different circumstances from those of his father. Of 1940 John Rowe wrote:

> *At Christmas (1939) the expected rain of bombs in London had not happened and in January No. 42 Alleyn Park opened its doors again to my profound relief for I could go home. There were 35 boys under the headmastership of the Revd W R M Leake who had retired in 1934 and had returned to take up the reins again. The months following seemed quite normal to me. I recall the exact location of the tuck shop under the staircase, the buzz bars in yellow wrappers we could buy for 2d which gave way to the coarse dark Cadbury's 'Ration' chocolate in plain transparent wrapper. The tuck shop closed as the sweet allowance became very small, 2oz. per week. The chemist in Gipsy Road complained that Prep*

boys were buying all his cough sweets which were unrationed. Numbers of boys built up to 120, but when the blitz came they dwindled to 40. The siren sounded after boys had left the school and I was walking along Alleyn Park which in those days was long, leafy and lonely for many houses were unoccupied. I reached the bottom of Dulwich Wood Avenue and aircraft were very close. I heard a whistle and got down in the gutter with my satchel over my head. The bomb landed behind the houses in Gipsy Hill and others farther away. Petrified I fled up the hill to join a distracted mother.

Collecting shrapnel became a popular pastime. It rusted very quickly so the fresh and large pieces were collector's items. The occasional fins, nose cones from anti-aircraft shells and other bits were greatly prized. Schoolboys have a great affinity for Spitfires so there was compensation in the general excitement and success of these machines. A barrage balloon on the stretch of green in Dulwich Wood Avenue provided an unforgettable spectacle which enlivened the journey to school. Constant interruptions of lessons to visit the air raid shelters were most welcome.

By the autumn term daylight raids had become night raids. The school was unoccupied at night, so a firewatching rota was quickly organised manned by Prep fathers, including mine, who used to remain there all night on watch. At home beds were rigged up under the stairs and during heavy raids stories and cocoa kept up morale. There was a substantial ack ack gun battery on Dulwich Golf Course and many guns firing continuously convinced us that no German plane could survive long in such a heartening and splendid barrage. When raids were distant we were allowed to watch the searchlights. Although disrupted, I don't believe a day's school was missed. Our sizeable garden at home, 13 Dulwich Wood Avenue, was full of hens and the production of eggs, cabbages, potatoes, etc. was substantial at the price of grossly overworked parents.

Angus Greig too remembered his journeys to school:

> *... being punctuated by stopping to collect the previous night's shrapnel, most of which came from the anti-aircraft guns which were sited on the Dulwich and Sydenham Golf Course. These were also responsible for most of the noise and I think their chief benefit was as a morale booster.*

Angus also remembered a German fighter plane being shot down and its pilot landing by parachute near the tollgate, and a small Italian prisoner of war camp being set up in Croxted Road near its junction with Park Hall Road. Later a flying bomb would fall at the crossroads and destroy the shops. He recalled listening to a lady called Theodora singing *Land of Hope and Glory* during the height of an air raid and thought this must have been an even greater morale booster than the sounds of the guns.

After the severe bombing of London during the Christmas holidays in 1940, the boys began to play their part in the war effort in all sorts of ways. They were taught how to use stirrup pumps in the event of fire and first aid instruction was also given. As well as high explosive bombs being dropped at that stage of the war, incendiary bombs were also extensively used. These were quite small and burst into flames on contact, thus causing fires rather than major structural damage. Parents, friends, boys and staff all volunteered to sleep on the premises each night and deal with any incendiary bombs which fell on the school. To help extinguish fires which could start, large amounts of ashes were carried up and placed in containers under the roof. It must have been a considerable effort to transport such a large quantity of heavy material upstairs, so much so that when the war ended no one saw any need to bring it down again and one such container of ashes remains in the roof of 42 Alleyn Park to this very day. While all this was going on, to say nothing of lessons, exams and all the normal demands of school, the boys raised £3 to maintain the bed at King's College Hospital. There were also some staff changes. Russell Taylor, who had done so much, especially in the field of music, decided to leave London to take his newly-wedded wife to the comparative safety of Dorset. An arrival was Astrid Pehrson, who joined the staff initially to teach Art, but by the end of the war had become Head of the Nursery School.

While the main school was flourishing in Wales and the London section continued to operate, somewhat haphazardly it must be added, former pupils were playing their part too. The First World War had produced five awards of the Victoria Cross to former pupils and two more were added in the Second. The first was awarded to Captain Philip Gardner of the Royal Tank Regiment in November 1941 while in the North African desert at Tobruk. There he went to the rescue of a fellow officer who was trapped in an armoured car and although wounded himself and under heavy fire, he managed to lift the officer out of the car and back to safety. When Captain Gardner returned to DCPS to give away the prizes on Sports Day in 1986, he commented that he could remember little about the event and that he was just lucky to be noticed as similar acts of bravery were going on all around him. He died in 2003. The second VC was awarded to Brigadier Lorne Campbell in April 1943, also in North Africa. By coincidence, he was the nephew of Vice Admiral Gordon Campbell mentioned earlier for his award of the VC with his Q-ships in the 1914-1918 war, so bravery ran in his family. At Wadi Akarit in Tunisia Brigadier Lorne Campbell's unit came under heavy fire. His citation reads that '*his personality dominated the battlefield*' and with total disregard for his own safety and already wounded in the neck, he went on alone and was able to regain and reorganise his position. Of equal significance was the awarding of the George Cross to Captain (as he then was) Herbert Barefoot who had left DCPS in 1900. Originally intended to be an award for civilian bravery, there have been circumstances when it has been appropriate to award the George Cross to members of the armed services and Captain Barefoot was one such example. On 1st September 1940 a number of unexploded bombs had fallen on the railway line between Brentwood and Shenfield in Essex. There was little technical knowledge about the bombs being dropped at that time and time-delayed fused bombs were being used. Not only did Captain Barefoot ignore the usual safety period of four days by defusing the bombs and clearing the line in a single day, but he was also able to provide useful and detailed information about the bombs being used. As a result Captain Barefoot was awarded the George Cross and his medal is now on display at the Imperial War Museum in London. Obviously there were many other former pupils who distinguished themselves during the war as well.

An interesting insight into the school's priorities appeared in the special prospectus prepared for the London section in 1940. Under the heading 'Air Raid Precautions' parents were advised that '*the school has available both an outside and inside shelter as well as a gas-proof room. Boys are frequently exercised in gas mask and fire drill, and the condition and fitting of masks is frequently checked*'. Under 'Clothing', a regulation school cap and tie were essential but '*boys can wait until they have worn out existing clothing before buying school uniform*'. However the school took no responsibility for clothing which was inadequately marked. Some things don't change!

The outdoor shelter to which Leakey referred was a rectangular brick structure near the Annexe. It had a thick concrete roof and a small iron door and it would have protected anyone inside from the blast from a bomb falling nearby. Inside it was dark and smelly and would not have accommodated all the boys in the school at any one time. It was not used a great deal, so far as I remember, and was still in place in 1950 when Leakey had the roof removed, using the hollow inside as a swimming pool. It was not very practical for that use either. The alternative shelters were the cellars of 42 and 44 Alleyn Park. These were

Wartime entrance to the cellar still in place in 2004

more spacious and lessons were conducted down there sometimes. The cellar of 44 had another purpose. As well as being used as a shelter and makeshift classrooms during the day, it was used by Air Raid Wardens during the night. These were local volunteers who patrolled the streets ensuring that no lights were visible and who gave help and assistance in the event of a bomb falling. In order that these wardens could gain direct access to the cellar and so that no light appeared when they did so, a concrete entrance was built over where the coalhole had once been. This odd little structure, just under the windows of the present kitchen, is still in place in 2004. Boys and parents pass it each day without having any idea of its former use and the words 'A R P Exit' can still be deciphered, just, on the outside. Inside, the steps leading up to it are still in place. Fees for the Upper School at this time were £12 per term but there was an extra charge of two shillings and sixpence for stationery and the use of text books and equipment. As well as the usual Common Entrance and Scholarship examinations, boys were prepared for the navy and entry to the Royal Naval College at Dartmouth at the age of 13.

As the war progressed the school became better organised and the number of pupils attending gradually increased. Heavy bombing moved away from London in May 1941 as Hitler intensified his preparations for the invasion of Russia and although there were air raids, they were generally far less severe than they had been earlier on. The number of boys grew, Leake continued as Headmaster and Leakey himself made periodic visits from Wales despite the difficulties of transport at the time. Among the many problems which Leakey had on his plate was the question of the relationship with Dulwich College which was not at its best. Pupil numbers at the College had been maintained during the war, but academic standards had not and when C H Gilkes succeeded W R Booth as Master in 1941, one of the first things he did was to approach Leake with a view to taking over Dulwich Preparatory School, the word 'College' being deliberately omitted from correspondence[1]. Leake refused to entertain the Master's suggestion whereupon Leakey himself was approached. The response from him was even more vociferous, but it was the beginning of a rift between the two schools. In 1942 the College complained about the standard of work and the small number of boys being sent there from the Prep and in 1943 there were further complaints, although later it was conceded that war conditions accounted for the irregularity. Then, on 23rd March 1944, as if the problems of war were not enough, Leakey received this harsh criticism from the College Governors:

> *We find a steady deterioration in the standard of work in the scholarship examination both in boys from Bettws-y-Coed and the boys from Dulwich. It is suggested that although the school at Bettws-y-Coed is adequately staffed and supervised, the school at Dulwich suffers from understaffing, an inadequate salary scale and the absence of a Headmaster. The quality of boys admitted to the school at Dulwich is not good enough, probably owing to the absence of a proper entrance test.*

1 Courtesy Dulwich College Archives

Undaunted, and despite problems building up behind the scenes, Leakey carried on as best he could and both staff and boys were encouraged to play their part in the war effort in some way. The school magazine for the summer of 1943 shows how the boys did their bit: *'the older boys very manfully and energetically formed a Cadet Corps. In this sphere they found scope for leadership and discipline, both to maintain and receive'.* Just what they got up to is not recorded very fully, but they were loaned rifles and some basic training in their use was given. In complete contrast, the same magazine goes on to say that membership of the model railway club had gone down in number, which was rather a pity as track laying, we were led to believe, was almost complete.

As John Rowe commented, lessons were frequently disrupted, but neither he nor I can remember a single day of school ever being totally lost. To our young schoolboy minds, the war was some kind of adventure and I cannot remember ever being fearful of it. Bombs always fell on someone else: they never fell on you. On 14th November 1942 the school learnt the sad news that Leake had died and this was a big blow, not only to the school and his family but also to the hundreds of former pupils who had passed through his hands and who held him in such affection. So that the Dulwich section could continue uninterrupted while the main part was in Wales, Leakey appointed O E Watson to be Master-in-Charge. A distinguished scholar and a former pupil of the Prep himself, Watson was a teacher of some substance who must have enjoyed coming back to his old school for he remained on the teaching staff for some years after the whole school resumed in Dulwich. He retired in 1958 after leading the Ojibwas tribe to victory on numerous occasions. Tragedy struck the Leake family again a few months later when Philip was killed in the Middle East early in 1943. He had been joint headmaster with Leakey when his father moved into semi-retirement in 1934, and in 1938 had decided that he wanted a change and secured a post as Inspector for Education in Southampton. He was transferred to the War Office in 1940, went to South Africa in 1942 and then to Cairo, and while stationed there he was killed on active service.

Air raids during the spring term in 1944 and early in the summer were mainly at night and, when D-Day and the invasion of Normandy came on 6th June, it brought about an air of optimism that the war was drawing to a close. Hopes were dashed just a few days later when suddenly on 13th June the first flying bomb (pilotless planes known as 'doodlebugs' or V1s) fell at Gravesend. The V1s were part of Hitler's final attempts to turn the tide of war in his favour and South East London bore the brunt of the onslaught.

In Wales, news of the flying bomb raids caused consternation. Betws was full and no more boys could be accommodated there, and of course boys there became worried about their families in London. The flying bombs made life at school difficult and work was not very profitable as frequent retreats to the shelters made concentration impossible. It was also considered unwise for boys to congregate anywhere near glass windows. By early July the situation had become intolerable so Leakey came to London from Wales to assess the situation and decided that there was only one thing for it. The school would have to close. Of his visit, Leakey wrote:

> *As 'warnings' were going on all day long, it was impossible to do any prolonged work, so we arranged for a master to be continually on duty on the playground and to ring a bell whenever he heard a flying bomb approaching, with its characteristic sound. This gave us plenty of time to get the children to the shelters and we were able to do a certain amount of work at the school, although some days we were dashing into the shelters fourteen or fifteen times. The numbers dwindled every day, bombs had been falling in the playing fields and within three hundred yards of the school, and we had no windows left. That, if anything, was an advantage. At last, after three weeks, the school numbers had fallen to eighty-eight and it was obvious that only the fact that we were open was keeping the children in London. They themselves were strained and overtired, so we decided to close the school, and should things become better, as we hoped they would if France were overrun by the Allies, to start again at the beginning of September. Correspondence lessons were set for the children and we had a rota of staff on duty in the school.*

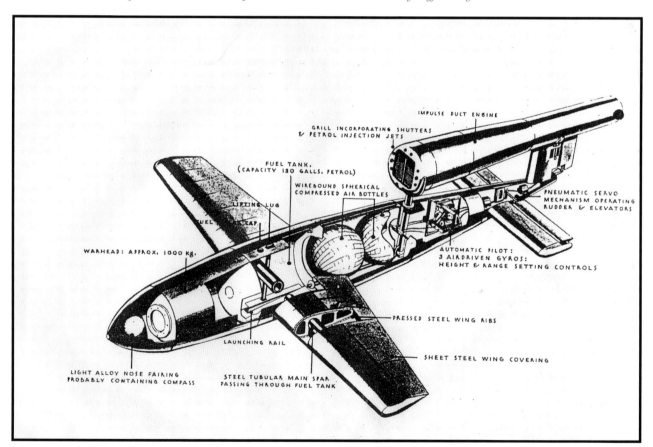

Diagram of a Flying Bomb - Doodlebug or V1 (Courtesy Imperial War Museum)

So for a second time, DCPS in Alleyn Park closed its doors to boys during term time, the first occasion being from September 1939 to January 1940 at the start of the war. Dulwich College fared even worse for during the night of 10th July a direct hit from a V1 totally destroyed the science block and caused severe damage to other buildings. After the fall of France in 1940, the College had returned to its London site and there were over 200 boarders sleeping in nearby shelters at the time. Thankfully there were no casualties but the College decided it was time to start the summer holidays early too. A flying bomb had fallen near the tollgate and another fell at the Park Hall Road shops near Lloyds Bank. These were less than a quarter of a mile from both schools, so the decision to keep the boys away was obvious and wise.

John Rowe remembered the period of flying bombs in Dulwich:

> *During the Summer term of 1944, the V1 flying bomb offensive began and the school was damaged so badly it had to close. I had been appointed Tribe Leader of the Deerfeet and one of the duties was to hoist the Union Jack up the flagpole that used to stand just inside the gate each morning. It was a wonderful year in the sixth form with more freedom and responsibility than would be possible today. I used to mow the tennis court alongside the hall with the motor mower. The school had a very rural aspect at the back, for after the chestnut trees and the field outside the old Annexe where we had the sports, there were trees and the park land of Kingswood House. I remember a trip out to Shirley Hills with my family on bicycles and from that vantage point seeing a flying bomb quite low with the flame from its early jet engine. The engine stopped, the flame went out and we were able to watch its full trajectory onto Croydon and the truly enormous bang. It was the very first jet engine we had heard. A grating, pulsating roar was unlike the whine and whistle of the modern jet. For some it was also the last jet engine they ever heard. Children were sent out of London again and I arrived in Taunton, Somerset packed with our own and American troops. There were endless convoys of every kind of military equipment a school boy could wish for to watch.*

Damage to buildings at Dulwich College by a flying bomb 10th July 1944 (Courtesy Dulwich College Archives)

The autumn term recommenced in 1944 with 177 boys, in the hope that following the success of the Allied landings in France, peace would come sooner rather than later. The school had not received a direct hit during the long summer break, but the buildings had been damaged. Leakey estimated that seventy-two windows needed to be replaced, fifteen ceilings were down, the roof was damaged and many doors were shattered, all resulting from the blast of flying bombs which had fallen nearby. Surely the flying bomb menace would end when the launching sites in Northern France were overrun by the Allies, but portable sites were quickly assembled in their place and these were more difficult to locate and destroy. One flying bomb which reached its target fell dangerously close to home on 15th October when the building next to Brightlands received a direct hit. Even closer was the one which destroyed 6 Alleyn Park where Rouse Gardens now are. Directly opposite was Number 5 which had once been the home of W W Butler where some boarders had once been housed. In 1940 it was the home of Angus Greig who complained that the flying bomb opposite damaged his home and brought down the ceiling in his bedroom.

Despite all these set-backs on his doorstep, Leakey wrote optimistically in November: '*Should no further interference on the part of Hitler come into our daily life, we ought to get back quickly into top gear again.*' His optimism, shared by others, resulted in school numbers increasing to 285 by the time term ended. What Leakey did not know when the autumn term had started in September was that Hitler would interfere again for he had one last weapon to unleash - the rocket, or V2. The first had already fallen in Chiswick eleven days earlier but the cause of the explosion there was kept secret for some while to prevent panic. The V2 rocket was far more sophisticated than the V1 and gave no warning of its arrival or subsequent devastation. Travelling at 3,000 miles per hour, at a height of fifty miles above the earth, there was no protection from the damage it could cause. The first supersonic rocket had arrived but it was not until November that the first fell in Dulwich and that some distance from the school. Much closer was one which fell in Court Lane near Dulwich Village in January. Mercifully, no V2 rocket bombs fell in close proximity to the school, but as usual, one of the boys had something to say about them:

DOODLE TIME
When we had warnings every day
We knew V1s were on the way,
No sirens now we hear at all -
Big bangs just tell when V2s fall.

The plan to drop thousands of these supersonic rockets on London in a single day did not materialise because the launching sites in France were eventually overrun by the Allies. A major disaster had been averted, but it had been a close run thing. Time was running out and the last rocket fell at Orpington on 27th March 1945. By this time it was clear that the war would soon be over and when Leakey heard that the threat from V2 rockets was at an end, he began to make arrangements to bring the main part of school back to Dulwich from Wales There was still some work to be done but the end inevitably came and peace arrived in Europe on 8th May. At last the time had come to pick up the pieces and return to some kind of normality at DCPS, as well as elsewhere. Some of the older boys came back to Dulwich from Betws at half-term in June to take summer exams and the two schools finally joined as one for the autumn term in 1945, by which time Japan had surrendered and the war was truly at an end. In the school magazine for that term Leakey declared that it was his ambition for DCPS '*to become the finest preparatory school in England*.' One wonders what he and Leake would make of it now.

War-time Britain was not an easy period for anyone and it was recognised that young people had borne the strain as much as anyone else. Long periods of separation for those who had been evacuated away from home had caused many problems and those who had stayed in the areas which were bombed suffered stress of a different kind. Although hostilities ceased formally in Europe in May 1945, there were massive peace celebrations a year later and on 8th June 1946, King George VI conveyed this message to every child who '*had shared in the hardships and dangers of a total war*'.

8th June, 1946

To-day, as we celebrate victory, I send this personal message to you and all other boys and girls at school. For you have shared in the hardships and dangers of a total war and you have shared no less in the triumph of the Allied Nations.

I know you will always feel proud to belong to a country which was capable of such supreme effort; proud, too, of parents and elder brothers and sisters who by their courage, endurance and enterprise brought victory. May these qualities be yours as you grow up and join in the common effort to establish among the nations of the world unity and peace.

George R.I

Message from King George VI to schoolchildren who had endured the war
(June 1946)
(Courtesy Imperial War Museum)

7   Post-war recovery

*I*n all our long history, we have never seen a greater day than this - so spoke Winston Churchill to the crowds in Whitehall on 8th May 1945 just after peace had been declared in Europe. Although Japan had yet to be overcome, there was a feeling of optimism and relief that after the darkness of war, things could only improve. At DCPS Leakey shared this optimism and, looking forward to the future, he said that at last school work could resume uninterrupted by the extraneous events of recent times. That was true, but soon there were other problems and the first school year after the war was one of harshness, severity and queuing. Clothing and food were both rationed and nearly everything was in short supply. Although confident that life would improve eventually, Leakey had to share the same problems as everyone else and when the school re-assembled as one again in September 1945 for the first time in five years, his problems were far from over. Clearly

---

Dulwich College Preparatory School, 42 Alleyn Park, S.E.21

25th July 1945

Dear Parents,

As the whole school will be working together again the timetable will go back to its pre-war form, i.e. the school will work on Saturday morning and there will be a half holiday on Wednesday. Games will be on Wednesday and Saturday afternoon. The Annexe and Nursery School will not work on Saturdays.

<u>SCHOOL UNIFORM</u> During the war we have not insisted on boys wearing this but we feel the time has now come when we should return to our pre-war uniform of grey flannel suit, grey shirt and stockings and the school tie.

<u>LETTERS</u> As I am very busy re-organising the school following our return from Wales I should be most grateful if parents would refrain from writing to me during the month of August.

<u>DINNER & MILK</u> In future dinners and milk will be put on the account instead of being paid weekly by cash.

<u>WEDNESDAY, September 19</u>th The main School opens from 9-11.45 a.m., but not the Annexe and Nursery School. There will be milk but no dinners.

<u>THURSDAY, September 20</u>th The Annexe and Nursery School open with whole day milk and dinners.

Wishing you all a happy holiday,

Yours sincerely,

---

he had every intention of carrying on where he had left off, as the circular to parents for the end of the summer term in 1945 showed.

By the time that September term started, Leakey had problems coming to him from all directions. To start with he had to find enough teachers but to some extent he was in luck. Taylor, Sheppard and Meyrat, his stalwarts from Wales, were all able to continue in London, Sheppard formally becoming his Second Master. Barbara Herbertson was able to manage the Lower School and Astrid Pehrson, who had joined the staff before the war but had not gone to Wales, was proving her worth at the Nursery School. But they were not enough. Several others from the school's original staff, including Maclean and Chapman, were still in military service and when Hamilton returned he had reached retirement age. Philip Leake had been killed in the war, which meant that Leakey had become sole owner and the school's future rested in his hands alone. O E Watson, who had managed the London section after the Revd W R M Leake had died in 1942, was immediately invited to stay on. A former Prep pupil, he was a distinguished scholar and a competent teacher, but fast approaching retirement age. To complicate matters, the man earmarked to be in charge of the newly formed school at Coursehorn in Cranbrook, Edward Gardner, had recently died as a result of a fishing incident. In desperation Leakey sent Freddie Taylor, who could hardly be spared from Dulwich itself, to Coursehorn in October 1945 for half a term until a successor could be found.

W A Sheppard. DCPS Staff 1924 – 1965

David Livingston, who had joined the staff in 1929 but had not accompanied the school either to Cranbrook or to Wales, had thought that DCPS would not return to London after the war and had opened his own school in Dulwich - Oakfield - for boys and girls up to the age of 11. He hoped some of his former colleagues from DCPS would join him, a situation which had not exactly found favour with Leakey. By relying on luck to some extent, and using his usual skill and art of persuasion, Leakey somehow managed to recruit sufficient teachers and the reunited school opened in September 1945 with a full complement of staff. Some were not properly qualified and others were not ideal for a number of reasons, but he never forgot those who had helped him out at a difficult time, and one or two of them were allowed to stay on for longer than was perhaps desirable.

That said there were some very sound post-war appointments. These included Elsie Smith, who became the Director of Music, L H Green (who had already retired as Headmaster of Brockley Central School) to teach Maths, and Dorothy Kay, also to teach Maths. Gavin Doig Gibb and Keith Bantoft joined the school in May 1945 before the Betws section returned, both having obtained early release from service, Gibb from the Special Police in London and Bantoft from the Royal Air Force. Gibb had been on the staff before the war and did much to resurrect sport on his return until ill health forced him to retire prematurely in 1950. He was an ardent Chippeway and led that tribe to victory for nine

O E Watson (centre) – Sports Day 1946

consecutive terms. Bantoft was also a sportsman and worked with Gibb, and for much of his time was in charge of soccer and cricket. He was also a keen entomologist and the nature club he established was popular and continued long after him. He left in 1952 to become Senior Master of a preparatory school in Southern Rhodesia, now Zimbabwe. Mention must also be made of H E Cousens, a gifted classicist, who joined the London staff in 1941. Cousens had formerly had his own prep school in Sheringham before the war, but when the East Coast was evacuated, his school was forced to close. After a short spell in the Isle of Wight, he approached Leakey for a job, who quickly appointed him. When the two schools reunited, he became Head of Classics and for sixteen years was a most successful form master for scholarship boys in their final year, at one stage becoming very elite when he and they were elevated to become 'Form 7'. Cousens retired in 1960 by which time his potential scholars had resumed their Sixth Form status.

Another successful post-war appointment was that of Terence Kelly. He taught English for many years, was librarian, editor of the magazine and tribe master of the Ojibwas. In those days, parents had far less contact with the school than they do now, and Leakey and his staff kept them, wisely some might say, at arm's length. They were invited to attend the annual spring concerts, Sports Days and that most important of all dates in the school calendar - Hobbies Day. Hobbies Day, or the Hobbies Exhibition as it was originally called, had been started by Leake as long ago as 1911. This was a day when boys brought their hobbies to school where they were placed on tables in the hall and judged competitively, later on a tribe basis. Examples of school work achieved during the year, especially artwork which then had no place in the timetable, were also brought along and admired. Hobbies Day quickly became an established and popular event and was keenly revived after a gap during the war years in December 1946. By this time it had become more sophisticated. Marks were given for innovation and originality so that stamp collecting and other very genuine hobbies were looked upon as being dull and unimaginative, and it was the unusual entries which gained marks. The result was that fathers made intricate wooden cranes, often still glistening with wet paint when brought into the hall, and mothers baked exotic cakes. Somehow this aspect of the competition was overlooked. In 1952 Kelly took up a post at Brentwood School, but was invited back to DCPS for many years to judge the hobbies, a task he took very seriously and much enjoyed. At this time Hobbies Day was still the only day in the year when parents could come face to face with those who taught their children, but times were beginning to change. Boys' out-of-school interests were moving towards football, television and the making of model kits and by the 1970s the number of hobbies on display each year had dwindled. Parents' consultation evenings had been introduced so Hobbies Day began to lose its impetus and appeal and steadily evolved into the Open Day of today, still held in early December as it has always been.

To add to the staffing difficulties, the buildings were in a poor state having received a battering during the war and money was needed to repair them. The 1937 Nursery was particularly in need of attention, so much so that in 1950 it was necessary to close it for a term while essential renovation was carried out. Although there was some government remuneration for war-damaged buildings, it was not immediately forthcoming. Text books were worn and, because many had been taken first to the camp and then to Wales, were well travelled and in urgent need of update and replacement. Food was severely rationed, and generally was less plentiful than it had been in Wales, and the first few winters after the war were colder than usual, causing problems of heating and shortages of fuel. For a short while there was some continuity with the Leake family. Philip had been killed but Leake's youngest son, Kenneth, joined the staff in 1945 on his demobilisation from the Royal Navy. After only one term he went to Coursehorn as Second Master to the new school which was growing there, but in 1950 he decided to take up a teaching post with older children, so with his departure a traditional Prep name finally came to an end.

The 1945 autumn term had not been under way for long when a far greater problem arose, which at the start posed a real threat to the future of the school. It came not from a hostile country but from an unexpected neighbour and former Prep pupil – Christopher Gilkes, the Master of Dulwich College. The College had remained open during the war and after an unsuccessful evacuation at the start had returned to its site in Dulwich and remained there for the duration. Extensive damage was done to some of its buildings, but proper and adequate precautions were taken and fortunately there had been no casualties. There were many interruptions of course, just as there were to those who had remained at the Prep up the road. Gilkes was under mandate from his Governors to raise standards and numbers as soon as he could. Like DCPS, Dulwich College was also experiencing financial difficulties and it was important to recruit the right number of able boys in order to maintain its reputation. Gilkes saw that his problems could be solved by interpreting the 1944 Education Act to his advantage. It is interesting to note that while war was still raging in Europe and elsewhere, the British National Government was able to devote some of its time to the restructuring of Britain in the peace which seemed certain to follow, and radical changes were planned in the world of education.

> *At the heart of the 1944 Act was the principle that no child should be prevented by poverty from having an education at secondary level which would best suit his (or her) aptitude and ability. Under the terms of the Act, any child who passed a Common Entrance exam of his local authority qualified for a free place at a secondary school, the fees being paid by the authority concerned.*[1]

This exam became known as the 'Eleven Plus'. It had already been anticipated that there would be insufficient places within the maintained sector for those who reached the necessary standard for a place at a grammar school, so a number of independent schools, principally those with a large number of day pupils, were invited to join the scheme, a measure which was not too popular among the left wing of the Labour party. As well as

1 *God's Gift: A History of Dulwich College* by Sheila Hodges (1986)

satisfying his own political and philanthropic beliefs, Gilkes saw the real advantages for his school in becoming part of the scheme. This became known as the 'Dulwich Experiment', and the question inevitably arose as to how it affected DCPS. The answer was the age of entry. Up until then most boys had entered Dulwich College at 13, but the age of transfer from primary schools, under the 1944 Act, would be at 11. In order to attract more pupils, Gilkes had already lowered the age of entry to the College to 10 and 11 in 1943, so an influx of boys from local authority primary schools would not be a problem, and the first intake of boys from the London County Council (LCC) arrived for the 1946 autumn term. It was not only from the LCC that Dulwich College received boys from primary schools, and a smaller number came from areas such as Croydon and Kent as well. Initially, from the viewpoint of the College, the scheme was a great success and later Gilkes claimed that he was getting the cream from all the local primary schools, a claim which presumably did not go down too well with other secondary schools in the area.

At DCPS Leakey was not at all happy at the prospect of losing so many boys at 11, and he vehemently encouraged parents to keep their boys at DCPS until they were 13, urging them, if need be, to go to schools other than Dulwich, a recommendation not appreciated by the College. But the offer of a free education at 11 was an attractive one and many boys left to go there. It had always been the tradition for the majority of boys to leave DCPS at 13, as it is now, and Leakey had emphasised this in a circular to parents of the London section in July 1942:

> On an understanding with the College Governors, boys proceeding there, unless they are sitting for a scholarship, automatically take the Entrance Examination between the ages of 13 and 13.6. We do not expect boys to leave at an earlier age.

Later on he reiterates the point:

> Boys proceeding to the College do not sit for the Entrance Examination before they are 13.

This change of policy by Gilkes went right against the grain of everything that Leakey had stood for, and Leake too it may be said. Leakey himself was undaunted and showed the same tenacity with this problem as he had with the others during the war. He managed to maintain a section at DCPS for 11 to 13 years old, greatly assisted by boys who came up from Cranbrook for two years boarding at Brightlands. Cranbrook School also operated an 11 year-old entry at that time, so boys at Coursehorn who wished to become boarders at their next schools came to Brightlands as I myself did.

Although the school had only just returned from Wales, a re-arrangement as to how it should operate for boys aged 10-13 became necessary, especially in the light of what was happening at the College. These extracts from a circular to parents dated 29th November 1945 show to some extent how Leakey set about the problem. Although he describes it as being 'clear cut', it was a complex issue and a major decision for parents to take. Leakey, as autocratic as ever, declined to offer any help whatsoever! He chose to divide the upper part of the school into sides, and it would be for parents to decide which side their boy would enter.

Dulwich College Preparatory School
42, Alleyn Park S.E.21
29th November 1945

Dear Parents,

As many of you may know, for the last few months the College Authorities have wished to lower the Age limit for Entry into the College from Preparatory Schools. For many reasons I am opposed to this, most especially since my experience convinces me that boys, as a whole, are not ready to go on to Public Schools before the age of 13 plus and I have made every effort to prevent the change. However, last week I received notification that our boys must enter the College at 10 plus except for a small proportion, covered by our Scholars and boarders, and that the College has offered to take 50 percent of its entries from L.C.C. scholars at 11 plus.

You will appreciate that this means a radical re-organisation of the Prep: and I would ask you to read the following with great care.

After next term a small new side will be started for scholars and boys wishing to remain until 13 plus and go on to schools other than the College. All other boys will be entered by us for the College examination at 10 plus. Should the Parents of these boys wish them to change to the new side in the event of failure in the College examination their acceptance cannot be guaranteed, and the decision must be left in my hands according to the number of vacancies in the new side.

In connection with the new side I have seen the Headmasters of St. Paul's, Westminster, Alleyn's, Whitgift and City of London Schools, and they have assured me that they will have vacancies for our boys at 13 plus given that they reach the required standard, a matter about which I am in no doubt. The same applies to the boarding Public Schools.

I must ask Parents to make their own decisions and regret I cannot see them nor answer letters on this matter since the matter is quite clear cut. The total re-organisation of a school containing just over 500 boys means a great deal of very hard work, especially coming just after a return from Evacuation. If the re-organisation is to be successful I must give it, and the day to day running of the School, my whole attention . . .

After giving details about each side, Leakey concluded:

Since we shall be losing the greater number of our boys over 10 it will be necessary to raise the fees of the younger age groups to meet the loss.

Although Leakey referred above to entry to the College being at 10+, the actual age of transfer was at 11, at the end of what were then the Fourth Forms (now Year 6). It is hardly surprising that relations with Dulwich College at the time were strained to say the least. The matter was compounded by the fact that Livingston at nearby Oakfield School only took boys to the age of 11, and he actively encouraged them to go to the College, so he was working closely with Gilkes. The new system of 'sides' worked reasonably well but Leakey was still not entirely happy. It was not in the Prep's interests to be at loggerheads with Dulwich College, nor had Gilkes any great desire to show antipathy towards the Prep. Earlier, in April 1945 with the war in its last throes, the College minuted the fact that '*it was obviously unsatisfactory for both schools that there should be so much sparring between them*'.[2]

Later, in a circular to parents at the end of the Summer Term in 1946, Leakey wrote:

Since our return from evacuation there have been many unpleasant and untrue rumours about us. I am the first to admit that, in common with all schools in danger areas, we suffered from the war. Again, in common with most schools, we have taken boys whose education has been retarded by the war since we conceived this to be our duty as an educational establishment. Nevertheless we have maintained our standing and our name has never been higher among the Public Schools to which we send our boys. In order to stop the rumours I asked for help from the Master and the Governors of the College and am very pleased to quote to you out of a letter received from the Chairman of the Governors on May 22nd 1946:-

> *'I am very sorry you have been caused so much anxiety, but you will be pleased to know that at the last meeting of the Governors the Master stated he was quite satisfied with the present standard and running of your school and had no criticisms to make. He has no objection to your using this statement in any way you desire'.*

I am most grateful to the Master for his helpful statement which will re-assure any of you who may have been worried by the rumours. In addition I have asked for a full inspection by the Ministry of Education which, at the present time, is quite voluntary. I am told by the Ministry that I may have to wait for this owing to pressure of work.

I am very pleased to let you know that our months of uncertainty are over and do hope you will understand how difficult this transition period has been for all of us. I fully understand how worried many of you have been and much regret having had to add to your burdens. I think I should re-iterate that any boy who fails to qualify for the College will be able to join the side for boys staying to 13 plus by which he will have a further 2 years, approximately, in which to prepare for a Public School.

> *Yours sincerely,*
>
> J. H. Leakey

Some kind of a truce had been established. Leakey and Gilkes were both men of outstanding determination and it was inevitable that they would clash as both tried to do the best for their respective schools as they saw it. The letter which Gilkes sent to Leakey, part of which is quoted above, did much to heal the rift and when Gilkes died in 1953 Leakey described him as '*a distinguished old boy who has done much for the Prep*'.

Leakey must have felt he had accomplished much in the school year ending July 1946, for he concluded his circular by taking a most unusual step for him, which was to invite parents to write to him if they were not clear on any point. He would have to wait just a year for the Ministry of Education to take action. Despite the hardships of the time, the boys who joined from Betws quickly combined with those who had remained in Dulwich and a pattern of near normal school life soon returned. As an example, when Freddie Taylor returned from Cranbrook in January 1946, he resumed Wednesday afternoon trips which had been so popular before the war, the first being to the United Dairies Bottling Depot in Streatham in March.

The autumn term of 1947 had been under way for under a month when His Majesty's Inspectors arrived on 30th September. They stayed for four days and, although there were critical aspects to the report which followed, much of it was complimentary. Despite the problems which Leakey had encountered recruiting staff, the report said that numerically staffing was extremely generous in proportion to the number of boys attending the school. At the time there were 644 pupils on the roll and 42 full-time teaching staff, including the Headmaster himself. The report went on to say that two of the best and most sympathetic teachers had no paper qualifications! One particular subject is worthy of mention. The school had always maintained high levels of drill and physical training and inter-tribe drill competitions had continued after the war. In charge of Drill and PT in 1947 was Captain Fleming, a former pupil with a distinguished military career, who had a glass eye and who was an eccentric in every sense of the word. When told by the Inspectors that his methods were not only out of date by the 1944 Education Act, but by the 1933 one also, he was asked if he had read either. His reply, roughly speaking, was that he considered both to be complete nonsense! The subsequent report stated that Captain Fleming '*should model his lessons on the recommendations of the 1933 syllabus and his work should be re-inspected at an early date*'. It is highly unlikely that Leakey ever pursued this and it is fair to say that Captain Fleming, despite the rigidity of his ways, was thought of highly by the boys and he remained on the staff for a further ten years.

As well as teaching Latin in the school by somewhat draconian methods, Captain Fleming also introduced a photographic club after school, and an archery club too, which was quite an achievement for someone with a glass eye. Although he was not a senior or long-standing member of staff, the name of Captain Fleming stands out in the minds of many. Mike Service (DCPS 1943-1945), for example, remembers him above all others for his teaching of Latin and PT, and his involvement with Punishment Drill. In his autobiography[3] the BBC correspondent John Simpson, who was at DCPS at the time, spoke highly and at some length about Captain Fleming, an accolade he did not give to many of the others:

> *... he was a heavily built old boy with a hook nose, a glass eye and a limp. If you failed to translate a*
> *passage of Latin correctly, or made some grammatical solecism, Capt Fleming would roar, "Shake him up"*
> *and the boy sitting next to you would have to grab you by the hair and start to pull your head around.*

Captain Fleming retired at the end of the summer in 1957, the same term as Simpson went on to St Paul's. Not all the staff were as eccentric as he was, but his techniques give an insight into an age long gone, and which no one, pupil or colleague, ever questioned. That was simply the way it was. The Inspectors' Report concluded by commenting that they had been impressed by the good discipline of the school, the happy, homely and friendly atmosphere, and by the devotion of the staff to their work, to the Headmaster and to the School.

So Leakey gained the favourable report he was looking for, and although many boys continued to leave for the College at the age of 11, at least his school was shown to be a worthy alternative for boys of that age. After Captain Fleming retired, PT continued as part of break, and when the whistle went it was a case of 'Coats off and fall in for PT' which lasted for about ten minutes and latterly was supervised by the older boys. When

Breaktime PT - 1960

3 Strange Places: Questionable People by John Simpson (Macmillan 1998). Quoted with the author's permission.

Leakey retired, it was one of the first things to disappear. An alternative to break, and thus PT each morning, was orchestra practice, one reason no doubt why Elsie Smith had so many budding musicians on her hands.

Despite the eccentricity of some of his staff, Leakey generally had a team who were extremely loyal to him. A major set back occurred in 1949 when the death suddenly occurred of Paul Meyrat – the dashing Frenchman who was actually Swiss. He was my form teacher at the time and I remember how subdued we all were. Earlier, one of the boys in my form, P L Warner, had written a pen portrait of Meyrat for the school magazine, the current copy of which had just been published. With a degree of temerity, I asked Meyrat if he would autograph the article for me. Being somewhat flattered by it, he agreed to do so and only a few months later he died. The article, which gives an interesting insight into the man himself, is reproduced with its authentic signature:

Funny Pieces
PEN PORTRAIT

He is a very jovial person of a healthy complexion. His face is cheerful, if not handsome, and always carries a hidden smile. Not tall, but well-built, he gets around extremely well for his age. He is very witty and finds a joke in practically everything one says.

In lessons he makes you work hard and acquaints you with punishment, detention and corrections at the slightest disturbance. He is very noisy and possesses a whistle of the loudest quality, using it passionately to bring all traffic to an abrupt halt down the stairs for one foolhardy boy who has broken his regulations.

He is an old member of the staff (and enjoys saying so). Minuses are one of his weaknesses and he gives three or four of these without the slightest hesitation.

Most boys like him because of his sense of humour. He has a rather red face, a slightly exaggerated nose and hair of the greatest profoundness. His clothes are plain and of not much variety, although on Hobbies Day he wore a smart grey tailored suit.

P. L. WARNER (13.0), O

Pen Portrait of Paul Meyrat (DCPS Staff 1915 – 1949)
Written by Paul Warner (DCPS pupil 1949). Autographed by Paul Meyrat

The problems with Dulwich College were a set-back for Leakey but the Inspectors' Report gave him respectability and there is no doubt that he was very proud of all he had achieved. He was a great showman, seeking and enjoying publicity for himself and his school from any quarter. No better were these qualities evident than in a message he wrote somewhat jingoistically to the boys in the school magazine for the spring issue in 1947:

> *Remember that the Prep is one of the best-known schools in Britain and wherever you go people will recognise your cap. Each one of you is a part of the school and it is on your behaviour that the school will be judged. Don't let your school down. Good manners and a cheerful face are worth such a lot in these drab days. If you behave as a Prep boy should, you will not only uphold the honour of the school, but you will also make a great deal of difference to your parents' happiness.[4]*

Meyrat's death was a great loss but life continued at the school, as of course it had to, and despite losing boys to the College at 11, Leakey steadily maintained his standards and his numbers. In the summer of 1949, there were 593 pupils in the school, of whom 42 were boarders. In 1950, the Sixth Form boys (now Year 8) had a weekly timetable which had been formulated after the war and, with only a few minor changes, was to stand in place for almost a decade. There was a period of Latin and Maths at least once a day, plenty of French and English, two periods of History and Geography and one for Scripture, Art and Music. Science functioned as a club during the lunch hour, but there was one period a week for Nature Study. There were four periods of 45 minutes in the morning, separated by break from 10.45 until 11.15, and two in the afternoon from 2 until 3.30. Games were held on Monday and Wednesday afternoons and there were five shorter periods on Saturday mornings. By the mid 1950s Leakey felt that Science should be introduced more widely into the school's syllabus. Joan Little was not only the wife of the Vicar of St Stephen's, the school's local church, but also a Science teacher, so when she brought her son to Leakey as a possible entrant to the school, he seized the opportunity as he was wont to do and offered her a job on the spot. One period a week of Science was then given to boys in their last two years, these taking place near the Annexe in an old wooden hut which had originally come from the camp at Cranbrook. The hut was used principally for Geography which was thus the first academic subject to have a room to itself, this being provided, it was suggested, because Leakey was a Fellow of the Royal Geographic Society (FRGS). Science was therefore an intruder, and as the hut was some distance from the main part of the school and using it meant a long trek, lessons in both subjects were correspondingly shorter.

The immediate post-war period proved to be a difficult time for Leakey and despite his great energy he was compelled, for health reasons, to take what would today be called a sabbatical term away from school. There had been no break between leaving Betws in June 1945 and preparing the school in London for the following September and since then he had devoted much of his time establishing both the London school and the one in Cranbrook. Time was beginning to take its toll. The result was that for the spring term in 1952, the school was in the hands of its Second Master, W A Sheppard. Christopher

4 It was the habit of the day for boys to wear school uniform, including caps, when out and about during school holidays.

Gilkes died in the following year and it was then up to his successor, Ronald Groves, to continue with the Dulwich Experiment, but by then the relationship with the College had begun to improve. In due course it conceded that boys aged 13+ could enter by way of a separate examination offering attractive scholarships as incentives, but large numbers of boys still left the Prep at 11+ when the possibility of a free education was on offer. Change came in 1961 when the LCC announced that it was reducing the number of free places it was providing at the College as by then it could provide enough schools of its own, and in 1963 the figure was reduced still further. This was not the case with authorities outside London who continued to offer free places at the College for some years more, some of these coming from the Prep.

As the story of DCPS unfolds, so the problem of space, or a lack of it, recurs over and over again. In 1954, the school was able to negotiate for the lease of 40 Alleyn Park, which had become available. As Leakey pointed out:

> *The Prep has been direly short of accommodation for all our many out-of-school activities, and we are delighted that we have been able to obtain 40 Alleyn Park. This will not only give us more playground space, but will also provide the school with many more amenities, the first of which will be a separate library for the Lower School.*

He was at pains to stress that:

> *We are not going to use the increased accommodation for more pupils, rather we may reduce our numbers.*

If this did happen, it was not because of gaining Number 40. The top floor was converted for staff accommodation and Leakey lived there himself from 1954 until 1962. The ground and first floors were converted to classrooms for the then Middle School (boys aged 9 – 11, now Years 5 and 6). Although Leakey had gained some extra space, by the mid 1950s he had other problems on his mind, some of them of a personal nature. He was devastated when his marriage broke up and Muff, who had achieved so much before, during, and to some extent after the war, was no longer on the scene. Whether she had had enough of school life, or of Leakey himself, for his autocratic nature meant that he could not always have been the easiest person to live with, was left to supposition and never openly revealed, but for Leakey it was a great personal loss. The outcome was that he had a successful and flourishing school on his hands but no wife, no children and no heir, although there would be a second wife and a daughter, Diana, later on. Lurking in the back of Leakey's mind was the possibility that a successor might purchase the school and be tempted to sell the site for development at a great profit, even though the school at the time was on land leased from the Dulwich College Estate. This, Leakey contemplated, must never be allowed to happen, so he made a major decision which was to alter the complexion of the school for ever. That decision was to establish both schools, the one in Dulwich and the growing one in Cranbrook, as a charitable Educational Trust. This would be incorporated by a company limited by guarantee but having no share capital, which would acquire the business from the proprietor – John Leakey. This is the status it holds today, the change taking place on 1stMay 1957.

To ensure perpetuity, a number of eminent people were approached to create a Board of Governors, the majority of whom came from the world of education. The remainder were influential parents of past or current pupils at the time. It was a most impressive list. There were five Headmasters, one former Headmaster, and one of His Majesty's Inspectors from the 1947 inspection whom Leakey had befriended and who had kept in contact with the school. The original Board members were:

Sir William Penney, KBE (Atomic Scientist and First Chairman)

R. Allison (Headmaster, Brentwood School)

A N Gilkes (High Master of St. Paul's)

C R Scott (Headmaster, Cranbrook School)

Dr R L James (Headmaster of Harrow)

G Stanforth (Master of Wellington)

Rt Revd D G Loveday (Bishop of Dorchester, former Headmaster of Cranleigh)

Mrs M Falconer (HMI – Retired)

D F Ellison Nash FRCS (Dean of St Bartholomew's Hospital)

C Madden MBA (Assistant Director of BBC Television)

Rear Admiral F Goodwin DSO

(parent with long-standing family associations with DCPS)

James Fitton, RA

Revd M B Dewey

(Dean of Pembroke College, Cambridge, which Leakey attended as an undergraduate)

The Trust had a Registered Office at Lincoln's Inn with the school's solicitors, one of whom, S E Penhallow, became Secretary to the Trust. There was already a Bursar in place, Miss Dorothy Lightley, who was given greater authority to manage the school's finances and Prince, Simon and Company, the school's accountants, were engaged to oversee them. Michael Prince became a Governor in 1971 and subsequently a chairman.

The school's leases were valued at £11,275, the furniture and fittings at £5,000 and the goodwill at £15,000, making the total value of the school at the time to be £31,275. Leakey generously agreed to accept payment of £30,000 payable by the issue of debentures with an interest rate of 4% per annum payable over a ten year period. One of the first announcements made by the new Board of Governors was that there would be an increase in fees in the imminent future. Of the original governors, Sir William Penney (later Lord Penney of East Hendred) and Denis Ellison Nash, both became chairmen and honorary presidents, the latter serving the board for many years. The Governors were empowered to appoint other governors in co-operation with the Headmasters at Dulwich and Cranbrook.

The main item of expenditure from 1957 was to establish the Trust and to pay Leakey his debentures. This was done fairly quickly and certainly well within the ten years allowed. As the years progressed after Leakey's departure, the Governing Body established itself and a broader range of experience among the governors was sought. Initially governors were appointed principally from the Dulwich school only, but as Cranbrook grew in size and influence governors were chosen from there also. There was, and still is, only one governing body for the two schools. Each school has its own Bursar and the Bursar in Dulwich is also Secretary to the Trust.

The structure of the Governing Body still looks for experience and wisdom from the world of education, but it soon became apparent that there would be advantages if the Trust widened its scope and looked for expertise from the legal profession and from the world of finance, for sound management and good housekeeping are essential to the success of any business. As both schools grew and new facilities were planned and built, so representation from the spheres of engineering and construction was considered necessary. The influence of Denis Ellison Nash meant that the medical profession was not neglected, and another long-standing governor was Lord McColl of Dulwich, a former parent, also from the medical profession, who expressed a keen interest in the school's well being for many years. The school has gained much benefit from the expertise and erudition of many people over the years who have served as governors, all giving their time amidst heavy professional commitments without fee. Initially there were governors' meetings each term, but these have become fewer with sub-committees such as Finance and General Purposes meeting either in London or in Cranbrook more frequently. Efforts have always been made to establish links between the Governing Body, the staff and the pupils and there are social gatherings from time to time.

Although the administration of both the London school and the one in Cranbrook changed with the creation of a Board of Governors in 1957, Leakey continued as headmaster and the day-to-day life for pupils and staff continued much as it had before. The school did not suffer unduly as a result of the outflow of cash being made to Leakey and one of the early decisions taken by the Board was to extend the size of the school hall which was much too small. Morning Prayers had become claustrophobic and although there were three sittings for lunch (including a separate one for the Lower School as now) boys who lived locally were still encouraged to go home for lunch, receiving a reduced fee for doing so. An extension to the hall was completed in 1959 and was formally opened by Sir William Penney, Chairman of Governors. This was the first new construction to the School since the Nursery in 1937, and the architect was Russell Vernon from Austin Vernon and Partners. These were architects to the College Estate, through whom all plans for construction had to be passed, and with whom a close relationship with the school developed as further constructions were made. The hall was extended with further development in mind and recesses were built into the rear walls for sliding doors which would follow later.

The 1959 hall extension shortly after construction.
Note recesses for sliding doors which would be added later.

Reporting boys' progress to parents during the post-war years changed little during Leakey's time. There was a report at the end of each term on a single sheet on which a phrase or a short sentence for each subject sufficed. A summarised counterfoil was also written and detached for school records, but sadly none has survived. In addition there were monthly reports on an ABC basis and an order for each subject based on marks achieved, which were scaled. These were added together to give a combined order for the form so there was a top and bottom boy for each. As well as these, a boy who was considered to be underachieving was placed on a Work Report. This meant that at the end of each lesson a letter A, B or C was given and the report had to be shown to Leakey after Prayers each morning. It also had to be countersigned by parents each evening. Cs were common and three of these in one week meant a caning as Jonathan Bosher (DCPS 1948-1955) remembered only too well.

> *I have to admit now that I did not always work as hard as I might have done while I was at DCPS and it is not surprising that on several occasions I found myself on a work report. I remember one occasion when I was given my third C at the end of last period on a Friday. I did not think that I had been particularly bad but I think the master concerned saw I had accumulated two Cs during the week and maybe it was his way of expressing his displeasure with me. To get the caning over with I went down to Mr Leakey's study as soon as school ended only to find that he had already left. As a result I had a miserable weekend knowing what was going to happen on Monday morning. When Monday arrived I*

told my mother that I felt unwell and persuaded her to keep me at home. This only postponed the day of reckoning for she was not taken in on Tuesday, not knowing what trouble I was in. To give Leakey eternal credit, he realised that I had been waiting a long time for the sentence to be carried out and he administered just one light stroke only, saying that he thought I had suffered enough already.

No other masters were permitted to cane boys as had been the case before the war, except the Second Master (Sheppard) who sometimes undertook this task, somewhat unwillingly it was generally thought, in the Headmaster's absence. Goodness knows how many boys Leakey must have caned during his thirty-two years as headmaster, but there is no evidence to suggest that he was excessive with it. On the contrary, he just took it in his stride as part of the day's work. That was the way schools were administered at the time and it was the usual way by which miscreants were dealt with. Staff and boys alike just accepted caning as part of school life and rarely did anyone complain. John Greenland (DCPS 1947-1953) remembered being sent to stand outside the headmaster's study for some misdemeanour and hearing the awesome grandfather clock ticking its slow and sombre progress towards his sentence and eventual release.

Dulwich College Preparatory School

..........Monthly Report   Term, 196...

Name............

Form.............   No. of Boys...............

No. of days late...........   Average Age..............

" " " absent.......   Boy's Age....

Place in Form (Combined Order)...............

Subject	Place	Letter	Symbol
English	....	....	....
History			
Geography			
French			
Latin			
Greek/German			
Mathematics			

General Remarks :—

These letters are awarded as an indication of effort :—

A—Good

B—Satisfactory

C—Poor

The symbols indicate the boy's standard of work having regard to his age :—

+ Good

= Average

O Below average

A Boy failing to bring back his report on the morning after its issue loses a point for his tribe.

[P.T.O.

Monthly reports like these continued until the late 1960s

By 1960, relations with Dulwich College had become more cordial and the Dulwich Experiment was in the process of being phased out, certainly so far as free places from the LCC area were concerned. Before it ended boys continued to leave at 11 either for the College, or for other independent schools in order to take advantage of free places being offered by authorities other than the LCC. Leakey did not generally hold group meetings with parents, but one occasion when he did was at the start of every school year when he gathered the parents of Fourth Form boys together (now Year 6) to inform them of the school's forecast for their son's future schooling. Those who had already decided to send their boys to schools at 13+ through the Common Entrance or Scholarship exams, were not involved and their boys automatically stayed on for a further two years. It had also become possible for boys to enter the College at 13+ either as fee payers or by scholarship. For the rest, information was placed in a sealed envelope and inside was the letter G (Grammar), T (Technical) or SM (Secondary Modern). In effect this was the school's forecast for the forthcoming Eleven Plus Examination for each boy and the occasion became known as the Betting Slip Evening. Parents then had a choice. Those with G slips were lucky and had the likelihood of a free education at the College, a local Grammar School or an independent day school offering places through the scheme. Unless considered ideally suited for the alternatives, the rest were encouraged to stay on at DCPS and go to a fee-paying school at 13+. This was all very trying for parents, boys and the school alike, and the placing of boys was not always easy.

Early in 1960, the school was able to secure the lease on 38 Alleyn Park and the adjacent garage which Leakey referred to somewhat grandly as a coach house. The ground floor of the house became an extension of the Nursery, admission for which had become increasingly popular, and the room over the garage was used for Art for a time. As well as the additional buildings, the gardens behind provided much needed space for an extra playground and grass area. During the spring term, and always on the look-out to promote his school, Leakey attended the Tenth World Conference of the New Education Fellowship in Delhi, India. While there he met India's then Prime Minister (Jawaharlal Nehru) and managed to be photographed with him. A few months later at the end of the summer term, Leakey told parents that he had been headmaster for thirty-one years and it was time to move on. Actually it was twenty-eight because he had been an assistant master for three years before becoming co-headmaster; but that aside, he had seen the school through some very difficult times, he had secured its future and he had missed a term as the result of ill health. Furthermore, the school in Cranbrook was growing rapidly, and commuting between the two and trying to be an effective headmaster of two schools forty miles or so apart no longer seemed a feasible or a sensible proposition. So Leakey made another big decision. He had fulfilled his obligation to be Headmaster of both schools for five years after the Trust had been formed, and announced that from the summer term in 1962 he would be the Head solely at Cranbrook and finish his school days there. In Dulwich, the Board was faced with the daunting prospect of appointing someone to succeed him.

Leakey with Jawaharlal Nehru, Prime Minister of India (January 1960)

Elsie Smith, Director of Music, made it known that with Leakey's anticipated departure the school, certainly as she had known it, was finished and there was much wailing and gnashing of teeth from those who could see the comfort of their lives being suddenly disrupted by the sweep of a new broom. Leakey was given a great send-off and there was a large gathering of former pupils and staff at his farewell party at the end of March in 1962. There was an appraisal of his career in the *School and College Magazine,* and an article in *The Guardian* newspaper said that his time at the School was 'remarkable and complicated'. As Leakey had always said that his was the largest Preparatory School in the Empire, latterly amended to 'the World', perhaps this was deserved. His greatest tribute came many years later at his Memorial Service in St. Stephen's Church on 12th November 1976, when Meredith Dewey, formerly Dean of Pembroke College, said:

> *Leakey had many talents beside his rare understanding of boys and their deft management. He was fluent in French, an ingenious amateur architect, and clearly an adventurous administrator. As a wise schoolmaster he knew his first duty was to implant and cultivate the seeds of a disciplined and trained mind in his boys. He had a shrewd judgement for art and music, a veneration for learning and scholarship and an engaging regard for academics. Though not a scientist himself, he was resolved that science should be taught at an early age. In a word, he was cultured without being affected and critical without being disaffected, and so was able to evoke and foster in boys a genuine love of knowledge.*

One wonders what thoughts went through the minds of the Governors as they sat round a table in September 1961 to set about appointing a replacement to the man who had originally invited most of them to be governors in the first place. There was a strong field of applicants, and by October 1961 the appointment had been made. Boys, staff and parents together had their first glimpse of the new order when Hugh Woodcock, Headmaster elect, read one of the lessons at the Carol Service later in the term. Leakey's departure at the end of the following term marked the end of an era for Dulwich Prep. A new one was about to begin.

Portrait of John Leakey by Brenda Bury (1961)

(photo: Courtesy David Whytehead)

8 Woodcock and a Wind of Change

So it was that in April 1962, Hugh Woodcock became the Prep's sixth headmaster and the first to be salaried and not the owner/proprietor. He was educated at The Dragon School and St Edward's, both in Oxford, before going up to Trinity to read History. He arrived in Dulwich at the relatively young age of 37 having spent nine years as Master-in-Charge of the Lower School of Portsmouth Grammar School. Years later he w rote that the prospect of living in London had never really appealed to him but he soon overcame any misgivings he may have had and quickly settled down to manage the school in his own characteristic way, a period which was to last for just over 29 years. He brought with him his wife Bridget, a son, Christopher aged 4, who joined the Nursery School, and a three month old daughter, Jennifer. Two more children, David and Katie, were to follow and the family soon became an integral part of DCPS.

Woodcock and his predecessor could not have been more different. Although the school had earlier become a Trust, no great change had resulted from it and Sir William Penney and his Board of Governors had had the task of finding a person who would have the strength and resolve to bring the school in line with what was then current practice, and implement fundamental change from top to bottom. At the same time there was a real need not to destroy the many

H E P Woodcock Headmaster 1962 - 1991

traditions which had been established over the years. At a cricket practice during the holidays preceding his first term, Woodcock commented that the guy ropes to the nets were slack and he would be having nothing slack in his school! In later years he regretted the remark considering it to have sounded very arrogant, but far from showing weakness it showed strength, and a determination to get things done properly from the start. Sir William Penney had found his man!

Metaphorically Woodcock was right, for within the school there were many guy ropes which needed tightening. One of the first things he did was to put the school on a more orderly and professional footing by ensuring that salaries were paid on a recognised scale, not only for the teaching staff but for the ancillary and domestic staff as well. Leakey, with all his charisma, had run the place rather like a gentlemen's club. Salaries had been at his discretion and he advised that at no time should they ever be discussed openly in the Common Room. A man of high standards and professional integrity, Woodcock was not afraid to speak his mind and do what he considered best for the school. Many beneficial transformations lay ahead, but this trait in his nature was to cause him problems from time to time.

All new headmasters have to prove themselves in the eyes of the staff they inherit and this is never easy. At Dulwich there was an 'old guard', those who had worked for many years in the school under Leakey, and in some cases Leake before him. The last thing they wanted was too much change. Among them were W A Sheppard ('Shep') who had been Leakey's Second Master and since 1945 had often been in charge of the school while Leakey was spending half the week in Cranbrook. 'Shep' had seen the school through thick and thin during the war years, as had F N (Freddie) Taylor. There was also the volatile Director of Music, Elsie Smith, the formidable Barbara Herbertson in charge of the Lower School and to a lesser extent Hamish Maclean who had just returned from Cranbrook to be the Housemaster at Brightlands and who had been on the staff in Dulwich before the war. A different approach was adopted by Dorothy Kay, an inspired teacher of Maths and much respected by generations of boys. She did not seem to notice that there was a new Head, and just went on with her life much as she had always done. Woodcock developed a high regard for her and she continued teaching Maths until her retirement in 1976. Barbara Herbertson continued to exercise considerable authority and influence in the Lower School and, whatever Woodcock's thoughts may have been, he decided to go along with her needs and her methods and by and large the Lower School continued to flourish in its own little domain in the way it had always done. Even so, Woodcock's first few years at DCPS presented him with quite a challenge, to say the least.

These senior staff had considerable influence in the school and Hugh Woodcock had to gain their co-operation if he were to succeed. It would not be easy. One of them remarked one day that the Prep, as it had become known, was finished and another said that he was just an upstart. The feathers were ruffled. In 1964 James Wood, an academic and a former Housemaster from Brightlands, chose to resign over a matter of principle, feeling aggrieved by the way one of his colleagues was being handled and over whom he and Woodcock strongly disagreed. In consequence the staff room lost a brilliant and scholastic offbeat character. A year later the outspoken Elsie Smith, whose habits were not always musical or professional, decided that she too would depart, taking all the violins with her. Whether they belonged to her or the school was never established, but it was considered best to let them go. Woodcock, no doubt, heaved a sigh of relief at her departure and was probably not alone in doing so. In 1964, Sheppard announced that he would be retiring at the end of the following spring term. Originally employed to teach Latin and French, he was a man of many parts who had seen the school through some of its most difficult times. His skill at teaching Mathematics gave many boys a love for the subject which they retained all their lives and his efficiency at organising Sports Day year after year, in his own methodical way, will long be remembered by those who took part. He was a tolerant and kind schoolmaster and, although philosophically they were poles apart, Woodcock needed his support and co-operation and without doubt he gained both.

On Sheppard's retirement, Woodcock wrote:

> *I shall always be grateful to Mr Sheppard. No headmaster taking up a new post can ever have received kinder help, greater consideration or wiser advice. His knowledge of the school is unrivalled; his understanding of school problems, and boys themselves, the result of a lifetime of experience. In a quiet model way everything was done on time, the timetable ready for a new term, staff meetings arranged and lists provided. Nothing was ever too much trouble.*

Chief Executives invariably have their admirers and their critics. In the case of a headmaster, these come from four sources: governors, parents, pupils and colleagues. Radical changes often bring criticism as well as praise and, by being adamant in what he believed in, Woodcock had his fair share of both. Day-to-day problems were not within the domain of the governors who set the fees from behind the scenes and generally gave the Headmaster all the support he needed. Approval and acclaim soon came from parents who were generally unaware of any internal problems that there might have been, although inevitably there were a few who found Woodcock's manner brash when differences of opinion arose. '*I can understand your falling out with me,*' he once said to a parent, '*people do. But you are very foolish to fall out with my school*'. That simple statement sums up the man he was, for he considered that the school and its reputation were both far more important than the opinions people may have had of him personally. He was not afraid of confrontation and he knew how to handle it. This open frankness soon gained him the respect of parents although there are a few, even today, who hold him in trepidation. The opinion was generally formed that he knew what he was doing, he had the well being of each boy at heart, and he was not a man to be trifled with.

Former pupils from the time have differing views. A few considered that their Headmaster appeared distant to them, yet he knew almost each one by name and carried in his head what each had achieved, even in the Annexe and Lower School. He also put an early stop to caning which he had never felt happy about and long before there were national cries for its abolition. There was no place for 'Tolly' in Woodcock's school! Stephen Robinson (DCPS 1967-75) later recalled:

> *The school was dominated by a series of colourful figures. Woodcock, aloof and scary, ruled supreme and, as far as we boys were concerned, without question. I don't recall discipline being oppressively strict. We wore uniform of course, including caps which would occasionally be pinched from us - sometimes with low level violence – by the Kingsdale boys who would throw them over the railway bridge at Hunt's Slip Road. The presence of a comprehensive school next door gave us, I suppose, a sense that we were privileged, but most parents were solidly middle class and not too flashy. There was an effort to instil in us a sense that others were less privileged than we were: each boy had a plastic blue money box issued in favour of the NSPCC and boys who collected the most were rewarded with different badges. The slip system was taken seriously by the boys and we assiduously sought honours certificates.*

So far as colleagues were concerned mention has already been made of 'the old guard', those whom Woodcock had inherited. Steadily these either retired, moved on or accepted the changes as inevitable signs of progress. There were skirmishes with colleagues from time to time when beliefs and principles were at variance, but as new staff were appointed, so the new regime settled down. Written reports about boys to parents and to headmasters of other schools were always honest, and to the point, and these gained for him the reputation that his word was his bond. When staff applied for other jobs, it was jokingly said that it was because his references were so honest that few moved on. Perhaps he wanted to keep the best for himself! In 1963, the Newsom Report on Education was published by the government and among its many recommendations was that Science be taught universally from the age of nine. Woodcock urged staff, parents and boys to prepare for change, for new techniques and for fresh ideas. How could they all be achieved? When the Governors, through the Headmaster, came to realise just how much needed to be done to improve the teaching accommodation and the facilities generally, they agreed to do all they could, provided the money could be found. Reluctant to raise fees too sharply, it was decided that wherever possible, two extra pupils should be added to each class throughout the school.

Apart from obtaining 40 Alleyn Park in 1955, the extension to the hall in 1959 and the purchase of 38 Alleyn Park in 1960, many of the buildings were the originals and in urgent need of repair and/or redecoration. Yet again there was a shortage of the teaching space needed to implement the changes which had to come. The greatest problem was Science. Leakey had taken the hut near the Annexe, which had been used for Science and Geography, back to Cranbrook in 1961 and a room on the ground floor of Number 40 had been provided instead. This was supposed to be a Geography Room, but it was not a very satisfactory arrangement for either subject. Seeing the problem as a priority, Woodcock made available for Science an adjacent room with a water supply, but the whole arrangement was soon inadequate. Placed in charge of Science was Joan Little, who endeavoured to establish Science throughout the school, her part-time job quickly becoming almost full-time, and the number of periods per week given to the subject greatly increased. It is to her credit that she implemented the Nuffield Science Scheme as best she could under very limited conditions and clearly a specialist room for Science was an urgent necessity. There were also pressing demands at the same time to teach French differently, using oral and conversational methods, as opposed to learning lists of vocabularies and translating sentences and exercises from text books. The Head of French was Ron Ferris, another Leakey employee, whose skills at wizardry and electronics, to say nothing of his persuasiveness, demanded that a specialist room second to none should be set aside for the teaching of French as well. Physical Education was also in a bad way. The old corrugated iron gymnasium by the paddock was on the verge of collapse and in 1960 the subject did not have a Head of Department. Woodcock made a radical decision in 1964 by appointing ex-Royal Marine QMS Harry Hubbold to be the first Head of PE although, with his military background, it was more akin to Physical Training. Elsie Smith's sudden departure in 1965 had left music in limbo and that too needed room to expand.

Ron Ferris in the Language Laboratory. A short lived experiment. (1966)

The 1966 building extension under construction

During the early 1960s, the school was paying off its debt to Leakey after the formation of the Trust and by 1964 this had been done. A limited amount of money was therefore available for expansion and, aided by further resources after raising an appeal, Woodcock decided to provide the school with facilities which were most needed. As a result, the first of what were to become many building programmes was set in place and two new rooms were created over the old hall, one for Geography, the room in Number 40 having proved inadequate, and the other for French. This was the domain of Ron Ferris who taught the subject in a 'language laboratory' using tape recorders and earphones for each boy, all operated from a central console. Although very popular with the boys at the time, and rather less so with members of the French staff who were longer in the tooth, the language laboratory concept was a nine-day wonder and it has not stood the test of time.

Over the 1959 extension to the hall, two new classrooms were created on one side, using very conventional furniture it may be added. Within a few years these became a room for History, while on the other side a much needed new Science Room enabled Joan Little to develop her subject more effectively accompanied by a small preparation room where chemicals were kept. Behind the hall, a new gymnasium was built with large glass windows at each end and this was a great improvement on what had gone before, even though it may be inadequate by today's standards.

Above the new gymnasium, there was space for two new large rooms. One was provided for Music, with three small adjoining practice rooms for individual tuition, and the other was given to Art with a kiln and facilities for making pottery. The school had never seen such days and the whole new extension complex was opened in November 1966 by Denis Ellison Nash, acting Chairman of Governors, replacing Sir William Penney who by then had become President of Governors. It was a great occasion and Woodcock was very proud of what had been achieved. The local press was invited and some coverage was given, the most eye-catching being photographs of the language laboratory.

But it was Science which was to see the greatest and lasting changes. Before long, it became compulsory for the Common Entrance Examination, single periods became doubles, the ages at which it was taught became lower and before long a second science laboratory was added. Joan Little saw the subject mushroom around her and coped admirably with the speed with which it changed. By 1979, there were four staff teaching Science in the upper part of the school and she decided that it was time to revert to part-time teaching again, which she accomplished for a further five years. Her successor was Brian Chaplin who was thus the first Head of Science to inherit an up-and-running department. As the needs for Science increased, there were timetable problems as to where all the extra periods should come from but somehow this was achieved. Chaplin developed the subject still further,

Joan Little in the school's first purpose-built Science laboratory

always keeping abreast of the changes and needs of a growing subject. Woodcock liked to consult those who were to use the rooms and did not rely solely on the advice of architects. As a result, Ron Ferris planned his language laboratory, Joan Little had considerable input as to how the first science room should be laid out and Harry Hubbold designed the gymnasium to his own specifications based on his military experience.

There were changes on the political front too. Free places at the College for boys aged 11 had already been declining when Woodcock arrived in 1962 and within three years they had almost disappeared altogether, although some boys continued to leave at that age as fee payers. More stayed on until they were 13, but in 1965 the newly elected Labour government was hostile to the whole concept of independent education and this posed a far greater threat than the Dulwich Experiment had ever done. In the summer of 1966, Woodcock wrote:

> *Can such a system and a school such as ours really be in danger from an educational revolution? Surely no one can willingly damage such priceless assets. The years ahead will tell, but for the moment every independent school must guard and fight for its independence. To ensure success in this, a school must be progressive and look to the future, not rest on its laurels but seek ways of being and doing better.*

So while DCPS was growing, expanding and recovering from the disruption of the war years, a threat to its very existence lurked in the background, a threat which was to last for several decades and one of which Woodcock was ever mindful.

In 1967 it was Freddie Taylor's turn to retire having been Second Master for just two years. Like Sheppard before him, Taylor was given a great send-off and many tributes were paid at the end of the summer term to his integrity,

Harry Hubbold in the 1966 gym, still in use in 2004

his modesty and his devoted loyalty to the school. Nowhere had this been more apparent than in Wales where he had shown great dexterity in constantly being able to make something out of nothing. Taylor, and Sheppard before him, had devoted their working lives to the Prep and with Woodcock's arrival in 1962, everything had become very different for them. Both showed that great quality called loyalty and both accepted the new regime as best they could, but their influence, and probably their happiness too, was never quite the same. Both had given devoted service to the school, especially at the time of its greatest need, and had it not been for them, and a few others like them, there may well not have been a DCPS for Woodcock to come to.

From the 1967 autumn term H J Finn became Second Master, a position he would hold until his untimely death in 1992. Bert Finn was soon playing a new and important role within the school and, although originally employed by Leakey on a short term basis, he soon became a part of the Prep, married and raised a family within its confines. A great committee man, Finn generally worked well with Woodcock and, although committees and associations within organisations come and go, Woodcock, aided and abetted by his enthusiastic new Second Master, must be given credit for creating a part of the Prep which seems set to last - the PTA. In 1969, they realised that there was a lot of goodwill being generated by parents who were eager to assist the school in any way they could, and how better to achieve this than by the formation of a Parent Teachers' Association. Opinions that this was a sensible idea were not universal for there had been examples at other schools where parents had become too influential, so from the start it was agreed that the PTA should be for the staff and the parents to work together in the best interests of the school, and not just be an association solely for parents. Generally, there was a groundswell of enthusiasm for the idea, both from staff and parents, so an *ad hoc* committee was set up composed of the Headmaster as President, eleven parents and six members of staff each representing different parts of the school. The chairman was, and still is, a parent and at the outset there were two vice-chairmen, Finn and a parent. From this, four sub-committees were formed, each chaired by a parent from the main committee and each being given a specific task.

The first was to draft a constitution, and in this several parents from the legal profession gave invaluable assistance. The second was to prepare a programme of events for the year, the third was to circulate all PTA members seeking ways by which assistance might be given to help the school with extra-curricular activities and the fourth was to establish ways of improving and developing relationships with the local community. Initially membership was open to parents who paid a fee and, after only a few months, membership extended to 340 households. This was later changed so that any parent with a child currently in the school automatically became eligible to be a PTA member and the fee was dropped. Within a year, the various committees had achieved their objectives and the PTA, as we know it today, had been born. The first PTA secretary was Amanda Osmond who remembered that there was apprehension on both sides at the early committee meetings but it did not last long, for she wrote later '*it was really good to get parents and staff working together for the benefit of the school*'. The first treasurer was Roger Shakeshaft from the Maths staff. How rewarding for those early PTA pioneers that this genial atmosphere between parents and staff has prospered ever since.

As the fledgling PTA grew and flourished, so did the school, despite periodic political threats to the whole independent sector of education. In 1968 Expedition Day was started, although its origins went back to pre-war days, and in 1969 the school contained 693 pupils - a new record. All too quickly, limitations of space became a problem yet again. The 1966 extension soon proved inadequate for an ever-growing school wishing to implement the changes being recommended and encouraged. Teaching specialist subjects in what had once been Victorian bedrooms simply would not do. More space was needed, so in 1968 the decision was taken to demolish the Nursery, which had been opened with such acclaim thirty years earlier, and to create a spacious new Nursery in the grounds at Brightlands.

The remains of the old swimming pool, once an air raid shelter, some playground lavatories and the old gymnasium were subsequently demolished and in the space provided new changing rooms were built in 1972, with modern classrooms above. That was not all. Other buildings were demolished, the most significant among them being the old Annexe building and its motley collection of outhouses. Nearby was an old brick building which had latterly been the base for the maintenance staff, but during its day had seen all kinds of other uses, including teaching space for Art, a room for Carpentry and the beginnings of Science. It had never been very well heated and was not the most attractive part of the school. The construction of the new Annexe building, and later the swimming pool, encroached still further onto the small area of grass known from Leake's day as 'The Paddock'. Virtually no trace of this remains today, and only a few of the horse chestnut trees which overlooked the paddock still rise defiantly to the sky. If only they could talk.

All this building meant that there was a considerable re-arrangement of rooms and buildings within the school itself, far too numerous to detail as many have changed several times since. The kitchen and toilets were modernised, new fire escapes were installed and an English Department was established on the ground floor of 40 Alleyn Park. Started by the then Head of English, Charles Guttmann, and extended enthusiastically by his successor, Carl Gilbey-McKenzie, a paperback bookshop was instigated in one of the rooms and this proved to be very popular. Although it has changed locations many times since, the bookshop is still a successful and integral part of DCPS. Woodcock was the catalyst behind all these developments and constructions, and he was proud of all he had achieved. In 1972, after he had been in harness for a decade, he wrote:

> *What of the future? Various ideas will doubtless soon be formulated, and thus the school will develop and continue to produce such facilities as no other prep school can rival.*

New facilities cost money, and other than adding a few extra boys to the roll, where did it come from? First and foremost it came from good housekeeping - the efficient management of the school's finances, overseen by the Governors led enthusiastically by their then Chairman, Denis Ellison Nash. It was fashionable then to raise money by appeals and they were an effective method of raising additional funds. Woodcock realised that he had inherited a school where there was considerable goodwill, not only among the parents at the time, but also from those who had gone before. Over the years money was raised on several occasions from appeals, each time using a specialist firm which set up an office in the school and which then approached as many people as it could for donations, usually from Deeds of Covenant. Woodcock was keen to explore every avenue in order to raise as much money as possible, spending many hours referencing and cross-referencing the files of old boys and anyone else connected with the school whom he could find, to this end. At the end of 1972, £111,728 had been raised by appeal, not a small sum even by today's standards, and although this included money which had been used towards the new Nursery in 1969, there was sufficient available to make the dream of a new Annexe become a reality in 1974. The Headmaster's enthusiasm for the school was apparently matched by some of the boys, for in 1973 one of them wrote: '*It is a great privilege to be at a school where you can learn Latin before you are ten*!' Latin was the reason that brought Woodcock into the classroom on a regular basis and Ben Weston (DCPS 1977-1982) remembered him as a fine teacher of the subject and '*that he was genial but not a man you wished to cross.*'

The old brick building which had so many uses. It was demolished in 1972 to make way for the Annexe. Houses beyond in Bowen Drive give an indication as to where it once stood.

No sooner had the Annexe been opened when Woodcock was setting his sights on his next project. In 1975 he noted that the school was badly in need of a swimming pool to save the endless journeys endured by staff and boys as they made their way day by day to and from the 50 metre pool at the recently opened Crystal Palace National Recreation Centre. '*How wonderful*,' he wrote, '*if one day that could become a reality*'. By 1977 it would be, and with hindsight it is clear what was going through his mind at the time. Buildings, their improvement and construction, though important, are not the only aspects of school life, although changes are always disruptive at the time. Day by day, month by month and year by year, there are all the usual routines which have to be followed, some like Sports Day, Open Day, Parents' Evenings and report writing coming round with constant regularity. The Honours Boards in the hall show that the seventies and eighties were times of growing success, with top scholarships being gained to prestigious schools and numbers on the roll steadily rising. In 1978 there were 751 children in the school.

Every now and then there is a break in the routine when one-off events occur which are usually pleasant to remember, and there are several from the Woodcock era worthy of recall. In 1977, Hugh Woodcock was appointed Chairman of the Incorporated Association of Preparatory Schools (IAPS) for a year. That was an honour for him and an honour for the school, but it meant that he spent long periods away from Dulwich. An Association of Preparatory Schools, later to become IAPS, was originally formed by a group of headmasters in 1892 who gathered together to discuss the size and weight of cricket balls to be used in inter-school matches. IAPS records go back to 1897, at which time the then Headmaster, J H Mallinson, had already been elected, so it is therefore possible, and indeed probable, that he was a founder member[1]. However for a long time, and during the whole period when the school was privately owned, its influence was slight and there is no mention anywhere of the part it played, if any, in the well being of DCPS during the first half of the last century. When the school ceased to be proprietorily owned and became a Trust, the role of IAPS became more important and Woodcock soon became a dedicated and determined member within it. Today IAPS unites preparatory schools and sets standards which must be followed by its members. Its principal objective is '*to encourage and promote the interchange of experience and ideas on education between the Headmasters and Headmistresses of Preparatory Schools and to organise their collaboration in establishing their collective views on all matters relevant to their work and in the promotion of such views*'. It also aims to protect and improve the status, character and interests of persons engaged in the profession of teaching, and it provides a recognised channel of communication with senior independent schools. There are over five hundred member schools in the UK, but it is the Head who is the member of IAPS, not the school, so when a school appoints a new Head, that person is elected to IAPS subject to accreditation. The Chairman of IAPS is elected annually by members of Council, and automatically becomes a council member for his or her year of

1 Courtesy of IAPS records

office. In view of his contributions and enthusiasm for the prep school world generally, it was hardly surprising that Woodcock was elected to be its Chairman, first in 1977 and then again in 1982. One of the Chairman's many tasks is to arrange the annual conference which is attended by a representative from a similar organisation in the United States. The Elementary Schools' Association, in return, invites the retiring Chairman of IAPS to address their own conference and visit some of their schools. Not all IAPS Chairmen follow this up, but twice Hugh Woodcock, accompanied by his wife, visited schools all over the United States following his tenure as Chairman of IAPS. This in turn led to several Heads from America visiting DCPS.

There were two royal events during the Woodcock era: the first was in 1977 when HM The Queen celebrated her Silver Jubilee and later, in 1985, when the school commemorated its centenary which was marked by a visit from HRH the Duke of Gloucester. Celebrations for the Queen's Silver Jubilee on 8th June 1977 were held throughout the country and DCPS was not backward in playing its part. It was one of those rare days when the complete school was present on one site so it was very much a corporate celebration.

The boys arrived in the late morning and there were two services of Thanksgiving, one in the school hall and the other in the Annexe hall for Annexe and Nursery children. This

Denis Ellison Nash (Chairman of the Governors 1962- 1986) and his wife Joan
flanked by Hugh and Bridget Woodcock.

The fancy dress parade on the lawn behind Block 42

The Duke of Gloucester arrives in pouring rain to mark the school's Centenary in June 1985

was followed by a series of festive picnics on the lawns within the school. After lunch, the Chairman of Governors, Denis Ellison Nash, planted a silver birch in front of the school and this was followed by a spectacular and colourful fancy dress parade involving every child. The day concluded with a Jubilee Concert in the evening, again in the school hall. This contemporary account, written by two Middle School boys (now Year 5) at the time, set the scene:

> *On June 8th the whole school arrived late to have a day of fun and enjoyment and to celebrate the Queen's Silver Jubilee. The day started at midday with two services, one for the Main School and the other for the Annexe and Nursery. After a splendid introduction by prefects, there were readings, prayers and hymns of joy. The National Anthem, played on the organ and sung by the boys, rounded off the Jubilee service. We next paraded up to our form rooms and were told what was next, although we already knew because we had been given a splendid souvenir programme with all the day's events on it. We all helped to carry the food down to the lawn where we were to have our Jubilee picnic. The food had been given by many grateful mothers who wanted their sons to enjoy this special day. Spread out on the three lawns, we began to tuck in. After that, we went to see our Jubilee tree being planted by the car park. We crowded round while Mr Ellison Nash planted a fine Silver Jubilee tree which just happened to be a silver birch. After the tree had been planted, we went up to our form rooms to put on our fancy dress costumes - all hoping that we would win a prize. We went downstairs to the lawn and had about ten minutes to look at the costumes being worn by all the other boys. We then walked past a couple of judges who (and I wish I had known earlier) gave prizes to people whose costumes had some connection with the Silver Jubilee. After judging we sat in rows on the cricket lawn and listened to Mr Smith who read out in his loudest voice the names of all the winners. The winners stood up on a raised platform and were awarded Jubilee mugs. A splendid celebration concert ended the most enjoyable school day we have ever attended.*
>
> S J Davis (10.7) and F D T Cornish (10.8)

Eight years later there was an even happier occasion so far as the school was concerned. In 1885 the school had opened quietly with a handful of boys at a house at the lower end of Alleyn Park. A hundred years later, activities to mark the event were anything but quiet. A sub-committee of senior staff was set up to arrange and organise a programme of events which involved every child in the school and spanned much of the summer term in 1985. Woodcock himself spent considerable time tracing former pupils and staff and the centenary as a whole must surely be the peak of his time as Headmaster.

Celebrations started in March when there was a Centenary Concert in the Fairfield Hall in Croydon. Centenary Day proper was Friday 7th June, the climax coming at 11 a.m. on that day when HRH The Duke of Gloucester arrived in pouring rain to visit the school. After a well rehearsed programme, the Duke toured various parts of the school and then attended a service in the hall where he addressed the boys and afterwards unveiled a plaque to commemorate his visit. He went on to the Annexe hall where he met boys from there and the Lower School. In the afternoon, a festive picnic was planned along the same lines as for the Jubilee, but wet weather sent this indoors although no one's spirits were dampened. After the picnic a grand fancy dress parade was arranged for every child, the theme being the last one hundred years, and it was another of those rare occasions when the whole school, Nursery included, gathered as one. In the evening there was a celebratory Summer Serenade in the Annexe hall. The following Saturday was Old Boys' Day when several hundred, from various decades, either attended a buffet lunch or a dinner in the evening. Such was the enthusiasm for the occasion that some even attended both!

On Sunday there was a Centenary Thanksgiving Service at St Stephen's Church when the preacher was the Revd Austen Williams, former vicar of St Martins-in-the-Fields and former pupil of DCPS. This was followed by a buffet lunch at school for staff, former staff and invited guests. There was a particular welcome for Mallinson's two surviving sons, one of whom had gone with a scholarship from DCPS to Fettes many years earlier. On the following weekend the PTA arranged a magnificent Grand Centenary Ball and towards the end of term former pupils, who had played key parts in the school's drama productions, were invited back to provide an evening of informal drama. Prominent among them was Max Hudd who had made a mark for himself on the DCPS stage several years earlier, and who came to entertain, bringing with him the famous Max Miller coat which he had borrowed from his father, Roy Hudd.

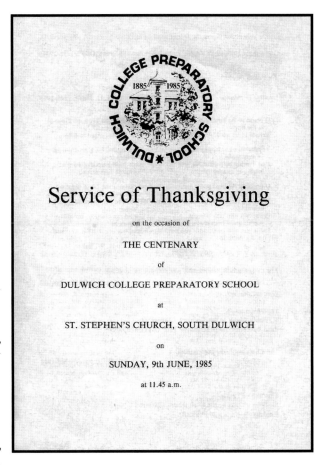

Service of Thanksgiving

on the occasion of

THE CENTENARY

of

DULWICH COLLEGE PREPARATORY SCHOOL

at

ST. STEPHEN'S CHURCH, SOUTH DULWICH

on

SUNDAY, 9th JUNE, 1985

at 11.45 a.m.

All who were involved with it will long remember Centenary Day and although it was a big event for the older boys, the younger ones were not forgotten. Here, slightly abridged, is what Richard Amlot had to say about the day's events. He was in the Annexe, aged 6, at the time:

> *I went to school very happy because it was Centenary Day and that was very important because the Duke of Gloucester was coming. I got to school and coloured in some pictures of Queen Victoria and Prince Albert. Then Miss Harcombe said, 'The Duke of Gloucester will be coming here soon but it is still raining outside. I will go and ask Mrs Cole to see if we are going outside to wait in the rain to see the Duke'. She then came back and said 'We are!' We clapped when the Duke arrived and then went*

back to the Annexe to wait for him to come there. When he arrived, we stood up and clapped like Mrs Cownie had shown us. We all had a wonderful time in the hall and then we sang a lot of songs. Then it was lunchtime. We didn't have it in the big tent but in the classroom because it was raining. I had two things but others had seven things and that was a lot. We had our fancy dress. Thomas and Patrick were chimney sweeps but they did not get a prize. I was Mrs Thatcher. I won a prize.

The Silver Jubilee and the school's Centenary were times of celebration. Two other major events, one in 1980 and the other in 1982, were not.

At the end of the autumn term in 1980, just after the boys had broken up and had gone home, and with the turmoil of the end of term behind them, the staff were settling down to their Christmas lunch in the hall. Outside the school in Alleyn Park, a drama was unfurling which in the end involved eleven vehicles. At about 1 p.m., a Securicor van was forced to stop directly outside the school and was then rammed from behind by a giant crane which was following. The jib of the crane forced its way through the roof of the Securicor van in an attempt to relieve it of several million pounds. But it was not a surprise. A full dress rehearsal involving the police had been held a week earlier and when the day came the police were ready with video cameras in the first floor bedroom of the Headmaster's house ready to provide evidence. A number of unmarked vehicles sprang into action when the robbery actually took place and a parent, who had just collected her boy from the school in a car, was caught up in the mêlée. Some of the criminals ran through the school grounds and there was a shoot-out along the path to the Annexe. More gunshots in the front of the school punctured the radiator of a staff car, making an interesting claim form for insurance! The road was closed for the rest of the day and the criminals concerned, part of a gang known well to the police, received long prison sentences. For a short time, those who were caught immediately were handcuffed to the railings outside Kingsdale School. No one knew who had given them away, but the boys were sorry to have missed the excitement when they heard about it. Since firearms were involved, it is just as well that they had. Insult was added to injury in the evening when the *Evening Standard*, reporting the incident, quoted Hugh Woodcock as being the Headmaster of Kingsdale School!

The other event, which was far more serious so far as the school was concerned, occurred in 1982 on the evening of Sunday 7th November when the resources of the school and of the Headmaster in particular, were stretched to the limit. At the end of half-term, intruders gained access to the Lower School through the new part which was then under construction and started a fire under a chair in the office of its Head, at that time Jill Caster. It was a windy evening and the fire spread rapidly to a paper store in a room above gaining a considerable hold before it was noticed.

By the time the fire brigade arrived, and they were on the scene within five minutes of being called, the Lower School was well alight and considerable damage was done. Fortunately

DCPS ablaze -
November 1982

. . . the morning after

the wind was blowing away from the school, towards Alleyn Park, for had it been in the other direction the damage would have been far greater. It was not until after midnight before the fire was under control and at first light the next day, that part of the school was a sorry sight. The Nursery and Annexe were able to continue school as usual, but boys in the rest of the school were told to stay at home and extend their half-term. There followed an amazing show of unity and camaraderie among the staff, the kind of thing that only happens in a crisis. Smoke had damaged many parts of the building away from the fire itself and teaching, administrative and domestic staff all joined together with mops, buckets and brooms in an attempt to clean up the place and make it fit to work in again, but it was all too much. As luck would have it, a parent who managed a firm of industrial cleaners, sent virtually his entire workforce and within a week school was able to resume, although boys in their last year had been able to return a few days earlier. Portacabins, as before, were brought in at a moment's notice and the whole business of reconstruction began. The new Lower School building was well advanced, so advantage was taken to reconstruct the inside of the old Lower School, while maintaining its Victorian façade. As a result, ceilings were lowered and an extra floor put in, so some good did come from the fire although it had been a wretched experience and the fact that the school had been targeted by an arsonist was not pleasant to live with.

Although there will always be 'one-off' events worthy of mention, it is the day-to-day curriculum which school is all about and DCPS has always tried to offer a broad, sound, and hopefully happy, education. The schools to which boys go after they leave DCPS have not greatly changed, the principal leaving age steadily becoming 13+ with a few going earlier. After the Dulwich Experiment and later the Assisted Places Scheme, both of which made it attractive for boys to leave at the age of 11, the College began to accept more boys at 13+ as did other day schools in the area such as Alleyn's and St Dunstan's, each using its own entrance examination. For the majority of others leaving at 13+, the main course of entry to the next school was, and still is, by way of the Common Entrance Examination, so called because it is an exam accepted by nearly all public schools and so is common to most. Schools also offer scholarships and the examinations for these are set by individual schools, each determining its own standard. David Emms became the Master at the College in 1975 and in 1978, for the first time since 1946, no new boy had gone there as a local authority scholar[2]. The College actively encouraged boys from the Prep to enter at 13+, offering further scholarships as an incentive and while Emms was at the College, relations with the Prep were at their closest for many years. This was marked symbolically in 1985 when the Master presented DCPS with a magnificent pewter salver, suitably engraved, to mark its centenary, a year also when the number of boys going to the College at 11+ was down to single figures.

2 *God's Gift:* A History of Dulwich College by Sheila Hodges (1986)

At the same time there were far reaching changes to the breadth and extent of the work to be covered. In 1961 the Common Entrance Exam was not greatly different from what it had been forty years earlier, but within three decades it had changed beyond all recognition and a far more extensive syllabus was required for each subject. Many of these changes occurred during Woodcock's time and as each subject required a greater share of the timetable cake, the big question arose as to where the extra time would come from and how it would be allocated. The problem was not made any easier in 1972 when five periods a week were lost when Saturday morning school was discontinued. Shorter, but more, periods per day was one option. Another was to start the school day earlier and/or finish it later. There was room also for some manoeuvring within the timetable. As the number of periods given to Science especially increased still further, so there were fewer lessons for Latin and to a lesser extent for French.

As in all cases, compromise was the answer and in the end some lessons were made shorter thus enabling more to be fitted into a day. The school day was made longer and on Thursdays an extra period was added so that school ended at 4 p.m. On other days it finished at 3.30 although later this became 3.40. A great deal of discussion took place in the 1970s about the best way to use Wednesday afternoons. Some felt that the demands of the timetable could be eased by making Wednesday a full school day like any other, but this was resisted strongly by the PE staff and by Woodcock himself, who felt that such a move would be detrimental to matches and physical activities generally. Other schools faced the same problems and subject meetings were arranged, often by IAPS, between the heads of departments and subject teachers from different schools.

Throughout the 1970s, there was a constant threat to the future of independent schooling from the Labour party, particularly when it was in government, and the anxieties which Woodcock had expressed in 1966 were by no means minimised in the years which followed. Even by 1981, when Margaret Thatcher's Conservative government held a large majority in parliament, the threat remained from the opposition. Stung by a statement made by the then shadow spokesman for education, Neil Kinnock, Woodcock, somewhat uncharacteristically, turned his end of year prize-giving speech in 1981 into a rallying call:

> *Will a future Labour government outlaw us? Will the charging of fees for education become illegal? Will we be taken over along with others for community purposes? While it is not fitting for a headmaster of an independent school to become political, we must nevertheless ask these questions if our future is threatened. Will we be outlawed because we are the 'cement in the wall which divides British society'? These are the words of Neil Kinnock, who also wrote that 'the existence of private schools with all its increments of status and complementary paraphernalia, of quaint uniforms and traditions, language and accent, is among the most effective means of perpetually imposing these divisions'. Well, we have faced these threats before. It is nothing new, but I sense now a new and evil tone about the latest attacks. They will be opposed all the way by the independent schools, but I do believe that it is time for all supporters of the private system to stand up and be counted. Let us not leave it too late.*

In the following year Woodcock was elected Chairman of IAPS for the second time, so he was able to be in the front line for any battle that might have ensued so far as the preparatory school world was concerned. He concluded his speech with fighting words:

> *For the moment we will continue with our paraphernalia of quaint uniforms and traditions and prize givings and Latin and Greek and good old fashioned hard work, and here at DCPS we shall strive harder than ever for academic excellence and success in every field.*

So concerned were the Independent Schools by threats from the Labour party in 1981 that an action committee was set up to discover ways by which their interests might be protected and Hugh Woodcock was chosen to represent prep schools on this committee. In 1982 the Independent Schools Information Service (ISIS) published a booklet called *Freedom Under Fire* so the whole matter was being taken very seriously. Little did Woodcock or anyone else know then that such thoughts were unfounded and that two decades later a Labour government would be far more sympathetic to the whole concept of independent education. Although political principles may have changed, the aspirations towards excellence to which Woodcock referred have not, and the academic standards and goals which the school sets today are as high now as they have always been. The school's 'academic excellence and success' were certainly evident in 1986 when no less than five boys gained scholarships to Winchester, and there were other years too when numbers of prestigious scholarships were gained to leading public schools.

Although computers, design technology and music are not skills for which Woodcock will best be remembered, all are examples of how enthusiastic he was to promote the name of DCPS and to establish it as a leader in the prep school world. At the beginning of his last decade at the school, what is now standard global equipment, the computer, made its first appearance. A ZX81 Sinclair computer arrived in 1981 and Ann Revell, who had

The ICT room, converted from a language lab. By 2004 this had become the carpenters' workshop

originally been employed to teach Maths and Science, started a computer club. After its first year this is how the club was described by Sacha Wheeler (DCPS 1974-1982):

> *The club is supervised by Mrs Revell who gives the members a simple problem to solve in a BASIC program and then, after thirty minutes, she chooses the best of them. She tells us about techniques, short-cuts and new facilities which can be used in a single program. The best aspect of the club is that at current prices of micro-computers, many children will never get the chance to work on or understand computers, but now some of those children may get the chance.*

Woodcock knew a new age was dawning and he encouraged Ann Revell to visit other prep schools to promote the use of computers and to offer advice about setting them up. From tiny acorns mighty oak trees grow, and within a few years a room with twelve networked Acorn Archimedes computers was being used once a week by boys in the Upper and Middle Schools (Years 5, 6, 7, 8). This system was introduced because it was relatively inexpensive and particularly suitable for use in schools. While Ann was busy with the boys, computers were introduced into the Bursary, and Brian Chaplin, Head of Science, superintended the single Archimedes (later to become two) which was installed in the staff room. Another subject to make an appearance during the 1980s was Craft, Design and Technology (CDT) as it was then called, and Woodcock, not wishing to be left behind in any new venture, gave his full support to that too. The new subject incorporated what had once been clubs for carpentry and metalwork, but a significant difference was that design, as well as the uses of those materials, was a major integral part. In 1987 he appointed Elaine Vestey to teach Science and within a

H J Finn, from a painting by Ken Richards

year a CDT department had been set up in a room which quickly became woefully inadequate. Initially, provision was made for one double period per week for boys in the Third and Fourth forms (Years 5 and 6), but when the Music School opened, its former room over the gymnasium was vacated and CDT moved there. Double periods were extended to include what are now Years 7 and 8 and that has been the timetable pattern ever since. As with IT, Elaine Vestey began spreading the word among other prep schools about what was possible within limited resources, at the same time ensuring that DCPS was a leader in that field too.

While the use of computers and design technology were still in their infancy, Music had been an established part of DCPS for almost a century, but until 1988 there was no music school. Even without one, the school had gained an enviable reputation for music, and like Ann Revell and Elaine Vestey, the Director of Music was encouraged to visit other prep schools in the same way. Because DCPS is large with a sizeable staff, and by leaving his deputy, Adrian Adams, to support his home base, Michael Spencer was able to attend conferences, gave lectures, wrote reports and sat on numerous committees all over the country, banging the drum and showing schools what could be done musically. Woodcock gave his wholehearted support to all these ventures, much enjoying the fact that at the time the reputation of his school was such that it was being held as a leader and innovator.

When a Headmaster stays in office for as long as twenty-nine years, thousands of pupils pass through his hands and a considerable number of staff as well. Not for every boy are the days at DCPS the happiest in his life, although most speak with affection and gratitude of the time spent there. It is neither possible nor practicable to keep in touch with them all and reflections from a few give an overall picture. Similarly it is not possible to mention every member of staff who passed through the school in Woodcock's time. Some came for a short time, others for longer. Some made their mark, others moved on like ships in the night. A few, like myself, stayed the course and remained at the school for the full twenty-nine years. Of these, by far the most significant was Bert Finn.

Finn arrived from New Zealand in 1955 with less than a pound in his pocket and had been approached by Leakey to take the place for a year of another New Zealander, with whom he was acquainted and who had recommended him. Finn lived at Brightlands for a short while, but soon met a teacher from Sydenham High School whom he subsequently married. They obviously liked DCPS, for with their growing family they decided to stay in London. That was a beneficial decision for the school, for not long after their fifth son was born, Jean Finn, a dedicated teacher in her own right, joined the Lower School staff and there remained until her premature death in 1982. Finn's early loyalty and dedication had impressed Woodcock so that when Taylor retired as Second Master in 1967, he was offered the job and moved into a flat which was then at the top of 40 Alleyn Park. Years later, Woodcock was to say of him:

A Second Master must get on well with his staff. He must be firm and, when necessary, be prepared to reprimand a colleague who is unpunctual or dilatory; he must be a source of wise counsel and be ready to give advice on any number of things, both personal and professional, especially to newly recruited teachers; he must be an enthusiast and enjoy his work, he must set high standards for others to follow; his interest must reach out to all staff, not only those who teach, for it will embrace the office and secretarial staff, it will include those who work in the kitchen, in the workshop or in the grounds, those who serve lunch and who clean the school – it must indeed embrace everyone. He must be all things to all people and Bert Finn made sure he was.

Not many staff employed by Leakey were still in post when Woodcock retired, but a few continued with him for quite a while. Geoffrey Close-Brooks was one of those and remained at DCPS until he retired in 1976. He superintended the library for many years and continued the practice of arranging trips for 'non sporty' boys on Wednesday afternoons. He was a schoolmaster of the old school, gentle and modest in the extreme and the boys loved him. He found Woodcock's regime somewhat harsh at times, but happily worked within it, and is on record as saying once to a class of bright nine-year-olds, *'I think the Headmaster is going to come into this lesson so I am going to give you each a sweet and ask you to be good'.* They were of course as good as gold, but he just thought that his lessons and way of doing things were a bit noisier and more relaxed than the Headmaster might have wanted.

Another master taken on by Leakey was Xavier Piazza, the boys being constantly puzzled as to how anyone could have a forename beginning with 'X'! He taught French consistently and meticulously until he retired in 1988, at times seemingly unaware of changes happening around him. Not so Charles Guttmann, who was employed by Leakey in 1960 at the same time as Close-Brooks. Both men taught English, but they could not have been more different. Guttmann either created or sought confrontation and invariably found both. One of his main gripes was the indifference given to football at the time, as in those days the game was only played by Middle School boys (Years 5 and 6). Guttmann must be given credit for establishing the practice of an annual school play held at the end of each Summer Term for many years. His first production, *The Happiest Days of Your Life*, in 1966 set new standards and was a great success. Despite his volatile nature, Guttmann generally worked well with Woodcock and his departure from the school in 1972 came as a result of confrontation, not with his Headmaster, but with a newcomer who had been appointed by Woodcock principally to teach French. The newcomer was Carl Gilbey-McKenzie, who as well as teaching French also taught English and had considerable talent in the production of school plays and drama generally. Gilbey-McKenzie had high standards and ideals and would not be trampled on by anybody, be it Headmaster, colleague, parent or pupil, and certainly not by Guttmann whose ideas on school drama were at variance with his own. It was an explosive mixture which ultimately resulted in Guttmann seeking a post elsewhere. Another early Woodcock appointment was that of Michael Rowett, a brilliant classicist who as Head of Classics stayed for fifteen years. Described as a man of scholarly tastes with a quiet sense of humour, none of his colleagues was ever asked to cover work for him, for in those fifteen years he never missed a day at school. He also took parties of boys to Greece for the first time and led many other school journeys to the classical world.

Not so much to the fore in the daily life of the school as parents, pupils or staff at all levels is the Governing Body, a group of talented people who give their time on an unpaid basis to the well being of the school. Rarely seen or recognised by the boys, the Governors rely almost entirely on the Headmaster to ensure the sound day-to-day management of the school, it is them to whom he is ultimately answerable. Michael Prince was Chairman of Governors when Hugh Woodcock retired, and was well aware of the contribution he had made when he wrote:

> *He was never afraid to do what he thought was right and best. If impulsive at times, he was quick to see this and to acknowledge it and make amends. He set himself a hard task: he worked hard and never turned his back on difficulties. He was heard to say once: 'I wish we did not have this problem, but then we are not paid to run away from problems'. Nothing escaped his attention. He set the example; he read everything in every room and every notice board. He knew every boy, he knew his fellow prep schools, he knew all his senior schools and this has been so valuable to the advice he has been able to give to parents. He has a photographic memory – a very challenging one. All boys, members of staff and parents have been aware of his thoughts and standards.*

Woodcock's remarkable memory meant that invariably he knew the name and face of each boy. By 1987 he had completed twenty-five years as Headmaster, by then exceeding those of Leake, and like Leake at a similar stage, he was beginning to think about retirement which he eventually announced would be at the end of the summer term in 1990. Principally because the Governors were unable to find a suitable successor, Woodcock agreed to continue for a further year. During his time at DCPS he had fought many battles, he had enjoyed many successes, he had put the school on a sound financial footing and he had secured for it a reputation second to none. He had also been the instigator of numerous structural changes, the Music School being the greatest of them and which is named after him. The appeal for money to build it greatly exceeded expectations and was the result of long hours seeking out former parents, former pupils and well-wishers to contribute towards its cost. As he approached retirement he said that it was his intention, not to hand over the best school within IAPS to his successor, but the Flagship of its Fleet.

It was therefore not surprising that on the occasion of his retirement towards the end of the summer term in 1991, the staff gave him a farewell dinner, the like of which has not been matched before or since. Proceedings began at 6.30 p.m. followed by a dinner and dancing, and although the principal guests had retired long before, there were still signs of merriment at 6.30 the next morning. Many appreciative speeches were made during the dinner, not least to Bridget Woodcock. When she had been interviewed by the Governors twenty-nine years earlier, she had been asked what she considered to be the role of a headmaster's wife.

She replied simply by saying that it was to support the Headmaster and that she certainly did. At one time she took on the duties of Domestic Bursar and was more than a worthy successor to Mrs Mallinson or Mrs Leake, although she was never asked to carve joints of meat at lunch! She was a frequent visitor to the Nursery and emptied and counted the NSPCC boxes with monotonous reliability. She started the *Prep Advertiser* where parents and boys exchange goods within the school and she was the hostess at countless school functions even if sometimes hidden behind the scenes. For the grand farewell occasion, at which all the family were present, the hall was superbly decorated by Ken Richards, the then Head of Art, and reflected a dazzling cricketing theme. After an emotional prize giving at the end of the term, Woodcock's headmastership came to an end. Another era was about to begin and soon another wind would blow.

'Out with the old and in with the new'
tailpiece to the school magazine - Summer 1991

(George Marsh (L) with Hugh Woodcock at the cricket ground in Longparish in Hampshire, Hugh Woodcock's family home, where the two headmasters played cricket together on several occasions)

9   Cranbrook

People often ask, and indeed become confused about, the two Dulwich Preps. Are there really two schools called Dulwich Prep? The answer is yes, DCPS Dulwich and Dulwich Prep Cranbrook. Some parents and pupils at Cranbrook know about the school in London because of its name, but it takes a while for the school in Cranbrook to become known to parents and pupils in London, and some pass through barely knowing of its existence. This is a pity, since the schools began as one, with a similar if not identical uniform and despite subsequent differences, they still have the same Board of Governors. So how did this come about?

It has already been established that the London school, under the inspiration and foresight of its then headmaster/owner John Leakey, set up a camp near Cranbrook in 1938 in the grounds of a house which he had purchased from his wife's parents. This camp was used for a short time in 1938 and then again when war was declared in September 1939. Through the autumn of that year and the spring of 1940, the Prep was based there. After the evacuation of the British army from Dunkirk later in May, it was impossible for the school to remain in Cranbrook and, as established in Chapter 5, it settled eventually in Snowdonia for the duration of the war.

John Leakey always had it in mind to open a school at Cranbrook as soon as he could once war had ended. His original idea was to refurbish the camp and start a small day school which would be additional to the school in London. This extract from a letter which Leakey sent to parents towards the end of the war gives an idea of what he had in mind:

> *A number of parents will remember the camp which we used throughout the first year of the war, and where we would still be had not the fear of invasion in 1940 forced us to move. As well as the camp, there is a small Georgian House with large airy rooms which would also be available for use by the school. Both the camp and house are, at present, occupied by the military, and many improvements, which we began during our stay at the camp, have been completed by them.*

> *We propose to utilise the camp and house in two ways, the first of which has been reached as a result of our experiences which have convinced us that a knowledge of communal country life, as well as town life, is beneficial to everyone. We intend therefore to take all boys from Dulwich, both day and boarding, over the approximate age of 11, to spend the whole summer term at the camp, accompanied by their usual staff.*

The second way in which we propose to use Coursehorn, ultimately, is by running a permanent boarding branch for those boys who will develop better, both physically and mentally, in the country. These boys will be able to help in growing their own vegetables and flowers, and as we know most of the local farmers, will be able to take a practical interest in farming. There will, of course, be full facilities for the usual games and work, the latter being correlated with Dulwich. This school will be in the hands of staff who have been with us through the war, under my, and domestically my wife's, supervision, the journey between the two schools being one and half hours by car, they will be kept in close touch.

We realise that the above is a very large, and to some people a revolutionary, undertaking but we feel sure that it will be of enormous help to the boys. They will benefit not only from the point of view of health but also by learning to mix with others in a different type of life from their usual environment. They will thereby acquire both self-reliance and, we hope, a permanent love of the country. We may add that the Summer Camp will be part of the normal school curriculum in which all boys in the Upper School will be expected to join.

These grandiose plans did not materialise in full and one wonders in hindsight how parents of pupils who had been through so much during the war, and had already spent a lot of time separated from their families, would have reacted. The idea to have all boys over the age of 11 away from home for a whole summer term was like evacuation all over again. However Leakey never had to face this problem. As early as 1944, and thus before the war had ended, he took out a lease on two houses on Dulwich Common half a mile or so from the main school in Alleyn Park. His plan was that Brightlands and the neighbouring house called Tiverton were to house the school's boarders after the war, Brightlands being for the 11-13 year olds and Tiverton for the 9-11 year olds. That did not work out because late in the war, as we have seen, a flying bomb fell on Tiverton and destroyed it, and Brightlands was shaken and damaged. A change of plan was therefore necessary, so Leakey decided to house the younger boarders at Cranbrook who would then move up to Brightlands for their last two years. The idea of the summer camp was dropped and although the site is now a part of Dulwich Prep Cranbrook, the original camp was never used by boys again. But even at this last stage, Leakey was thwarted again. When war ended in May 1945 he wanted to open a school in Cranbrook as a junior boarding house, with a few day boys, in September for the start of the new school year. The army had left the house fairly quickly, but late in the day the Ministry of Health informed the school that they were taking over a part of the camp for temporary housing. Not only that, but a neighbour had lodged a complaint against the main house being used as a school. Fortunately, from the school's point of view, this was overruled and Kent County Council granted a licence.

Although the war had ended in May and the school had vacated Wales by June, these set-backs meant that the Cranbrook school was not ready until October 1945, although Alleyn Park had managed to open at the usual time in September. As the camp could not be used that only left the main house itself, and that too needed a lot of attention. A number of people set about the task of preparing it for habitation. Among them was Phyllis Glazier (Bones), who was to play a big part later on in looking after early generations of Coursehorn boys, and another stalwart from those early days, Helen Dickson. With others, Helen Dickson and 'Bones' returned to Cranbrook in June 1945 to receive furniture and other equipment from Wales.

Although steps had been taken to protect the mantlepieces and stair treads, the house was in quite a state. Windows were covered with brown paint, which had been put there as war camouflage, and there were greasy marks on the walls everywhere. Problems with the plumbing and the installation of bathrooms meant that there was no hot water. Finally, and with the help of a Mrs Farmer from the village, the house was able to receive its first post-war pupils in October 1945, after half-term. There were thirty-nine boarders, of whom I was one, and to start with just six day boys.

In 1945 the buildings consisted of the original Georgian house itself, a few huts brought over from the camp in the orchard which had been released by the Army, a two-storey oast house in a dilapidated condition, and a garage, long since gone, opposite the house. The boys were accommodated in the house itself. Upstairs were dormitories and downstairs

there was sufficient space for a dining room, a common room for the boys to play in, a bathroom and rooms for the staff. How well I remember listening to *Children's Favourites* and Uncle Mac in Helen Dickson's room in the evenings. No television or videos in those days! The small entrance hall was the focal point, and a seasonal play was performed there in that first post-war Christmas. The small garage opposite had a few desks placed in it with a small electric fire and there I

Helen Dickson – tragically killed in 1981 after she had retired

The author with Phyllis Glazier ('Bones') enjoying her retirement in 2001

learned my first words of Latin: maturo=I hasten, and of course the evergreen 'amo' from Kennedy's *Latin Primer*. The oast house was used mainly as classrooms during the early years, both upstairs and at ground level, and the upper level continued to be used in that capacity for some time. Today part of the ground level area is the headmaster's garage and the rest is his private accommodation.

As 1945 gave way to 1946 huts at the camp began to be vacated and were available, but as the whole site was not yet in the school's possession Leakey decided to bring huts over to be near the main house at Coursehorn. Initially two huts were brought across, one as a classroom and the other for recreational purposes, and as the school grew in size so the number of huts increased. Leakey's idea of planning seemed to be to find a position where a lorry could get a hut into a place and off-load it there and then. Nor was the weather helpful as 1946/7 was one of the coldest winters on record. To our delight, we boys were sometimes excused lessons and told to play outside in the garden, where there was a large amount of snow which had drifted in places and was well above our heads. When I spoke to Leakey about this years later, he asked if I had ever complained about this to my parents. Of course I had not, but I enquired why he had asked. 'Because,' he said, 'there was no electricity and no heating at times to keep you warm, and sending you outside was the only option'. I do remember the heat in the huts being barely adequate.

Coursehorn Dormitory in 1946

In due course an old stable, which had once been part of the adjacent farm by the main entrance, was reconstructed as a cottage for Helen Dickson and staff accommodation steadily improved. As the school grew in size, so more and more huts appeared from the camp, but to start with there was no covered way between them. 'Bones' remembered walking among the classrooms in the rain, turning on heaters and noticing frozen ink in the ink wells. Games days were hectic, with no proper changing facilities. She said her life became heaven when new changing rooms were built.

Leakey himself wanted to be in London to put his energies into revitalising the war-battered school in Alleyn Park. To administer Coursehorn, he had earmarked Edward Gardner who had been on the staff in London before the war and who had gone to Wales before being called up in 1941. He was unable to take up his post for a rather unusual reason. Gardner's war service had taken him to India and, not long before he was due to return to the UK to be demobilised, he took a short fishing holiday there. He was a keen fisherman and although his boots were later found, no trace of him ever was and it was even rumoured that he might have been attacked by a crocodile. This was a tragic end for a man who was clearly able and much liked, and his unexpected death presented Leakey with yet another problem. Who was to be in charge at Coursehorn? He turned to his trusted and loyal friend Freddie Taylor, who had joined the staff in 1925 and had done so much to keep the school alive in Wales. Would he agree to supervise Coursehorn until a housemaster could be appointed? Having stood by Leakey through thick and thin, Taylor agreed to do this, though how willingly is not known, but Leakey always had a persuasive way with him.

Huts from the camp being used as classrooms – 1946

H W A Lewis was appointed to be in charge at Coursehorn from January 1946, and after staying on for a few weeks to see the new man in, Taylor returned to London. Lewis was there for just three years and his period of tenure almost coincided with my own as a pupil. As well as Lewis, teaching was mainly in the hands of Helen Dickson and Elaine Barnett, both of whom had been with the evacuated school in Wales. Elaine Barnett, a violinist, established music at the school from the very start although at that time it was limited mainly to piano and recorder playing.

With the departure of Lewis, a new regime began – that of Hamish and Olivia Maclean. They were at Coursehorn from 1949 to 1961, and a very successful period of growth it proved to be. Hamish Maclean had joined the staff at DCPS in London in September 1938 and had been involved in the camp following the Munich Crisis of that year. He married Olivia in the following year but did not go with the school to Cranbrook in September. Instead, he left the Prep and went to Maidenhead where his father owned a factory which, amongst other things, designed refuelling systems for aeroplanes. He soon joined the London Scottish Regiment and Olivia took a job in Bedford where she had first met Leakey when Hamish had been on the staff at Bedford School. After distinguished war service, Maclean was demobilised in September 1946 and returned almost immediately to teaching at DCPS in London. When Lewis departed from Coursehorn in December 1948, Leakey invited Maclean to become Master-in-Charge there from the following term. By this time Leakey was the sole owner and Headmaster of both the London school and the ever-growing one at Cranbrook. He travelled to Cranbrook on Friday afternoons, remained there until Sunday evening and was usually back in Dulwich early on Monday morning. During the 1950s numbers at Cranbrook steadily rose, mainly from day boys. The Leakeys occupied part of the oast house during their weekend visits and the boarders continued to be accommodated in the house itself. Classrooms were still huts brought across from the former camp in the orchard, but passageways between them were built so the school resembled something akin to a rabbit warren. Apart from the house itself and the oasthouse, there were no other substantial buildings.

Apart from Leakey's weekly commuting, the two schools were closely tied and in the early days the Cranbrook section was heavily subsidised from Dulwich. Nowhere was this more apparent than by the school magazine which was shared by both schools. In 1953, with numbers still growing, a house known as The Lodge was built for the Macleans by the entrance in the lane near where the camp had been. By this time, the number of boarders exceeded the space available in the original house so another hut was attached to The Lodge for these extra boarders. At times the Macleans also had two or three boys in The Lodge itself. A major development in the school's history at this time was Leakey's decision (referred to earlier) to sell the school to a Trust, thus ensuring its future. At Cranbrook, the school was growing and a neighbouring farm with some adjacent land was purchased. Once owned by the Luck family, whose boys passed through the school,

Stream Farm was at the edge of where the camp had been. Access to the school then became possible from the Sissinghurst Road, although the roadway through to the main house was not built until later. The farm house was adapted for school use and became a department for girls aged five to seven, generally siblings of boys already at the school. This sub-section of the school grew rapidly as well and became known as Little Stream. Today it is the Lower School of Dulwich Prep, Cranbrook. In charge at Little Stream was Elizabeth Morrison, the sister of Leakey's second wife, so the school was still very much a part of the family. This account about life at Little Stream in the early years was written by Jill Standen, then aged 11.2.

MY LIFE AT LITTLE STREAM

Little Stream started seven years ago on 8th May 1956. There were fourteen boys and five girls. The numbers have gradually increased to one hundred and fifteen. Little Stream was formed because Dulwich was evacuated here during the war and parents wanted a school near to Coursehorn where they could send their girls. Little Stream was at first a chicken farm (the old incubating room is now the present kitchen and dining-room), but in 1956 was opened as a school so that parents of Coursehorn boys could send their daughters to Little Stream.

As a result many more buildings have had to be added to the house as the numbers have grown. Now we have six classrooms, four added to the original building, plus an extension on the dining-room. It has been great fun seeing these buildings put up. The two newest attract all the sun, which enables us to have blue and white striped sunblinds. A great achievement was when a swimming pool was built in 1969. It is very good for the younger children and helps them to learn to swim, but the Upper School still goes to Coursehorn to swim in the big pool. In the Summer Term of 1962 we had our first swimming sports. A cup was kindly presented by Miss Morrison. Other outdoor attractions include a netball court at Little Stream and one at Coursehorn, where we can play netball in winter and tennis in summer. There have been many interesting visits which include a visit to the Cranbrook Post Office, a tea auction in London, the Benenden School Pageant, and the Rudolf Steiner Theatre in London.

The school library, which started from almost nothing, has now become quite large with the kind help of gifts from parents and Mr Leakey's contributions and from many of the staff and children. In 1962 a Savings Group was organised by Miss Dewey and in the Summer Term of 1962 our first church service was held at Cranbrook on Ascension Day. Since then we have had several school services both at Cranbrook and Staplehurst. The school plays have always been a great thrill and we certainly owe a great deal to the staff for helping to produce them. We started with two Houses, Effra and Crane, the first being the name of a river at Dulwich in London and the other a river at Cranbrook. Now we have Stream House as well. We were pleased to receive cups for House Competitions and Sports. For example, two Victors Ludorum, the Marriot and the Harding Cup. There is also a Music Cup presented by Mrs Walkey. As I have been here for just over seven years, I shall be very sad to leave at the end of this term. And I certainly have enjoyed 'My life at Little Stream'.

By the time this article was written in 1963, big changes had occurred. Numbers at Little Stream had grown to 66 girls, most of whom moved up to the main school when they were seven and there were 25 younger boys there as well. Numbers of boys at Coursehorn itself were growing too, and the school as a whole was gaining an enviable reputation in the area. By 1960 Leakey was finding it an increasing strain to be the Headmaster of two schools some fifty miles apart, so he made a decision which was to affect the lives of everyone both at Dulwich and at Cranbrook. He decided that he would devote all his energies to the Cranbrook section alone, and so from the summer term of 1962 he became the sole Headmaster there, and in Dulwich a new Headmaster was appointed.

The Macleans moved to London and Hamish became the Housemaster of Brightlands. In Cranbrook, Leakey had quite a team. Jack Guy, a cousin of Katherine Leakey and thus another member of the family, had joined the staff in 1955 and was appointed Senior Master and for a while occupied The Lodge which became the senior boarding house. Its impeccable state of cleanliness was maintained by Mrs Farmer, who was one of the originals from 1945. Peter Parker-Smith was appointed to be in charge of the Middle School (now Year 5) as well as being Head of History and in charge of games. Peter's wife Mary was Deputy Head at Little Stream for a while and he and Jack Guy formed a partnership which lasted for some years. Helen Dickson was responsible for the younger boys, by now all in the Coursehorn Lower School, and 'Bones' Glazier, who had played such a large part in the early days simply went on and on looking after the well being of one generation of boys after another. One person who encountered Leakey's 'bonhomie' and unique way of running a school, was Jill Tingley. Jill approached Leakey in 1964 with a view to discussing her son's future and she made an appointment to see him:

> *He was about twenty minutes late and apologised saying he was having problems with one of his teachers at Little Stream. I said that I fully understood as I was a teacher myself and immediately Leakey shot back and offered me a job there and then. I explained that I had a small baby but all objections were overruled and he asked, almost in desperation, if I could help him out at Little Stream for six weeks. At that*

Jack Guy (left) and Peter Parker-Smith

time I was young and had modern ideas but, for some reason which I have never fully understood, I accepted. As soon as I arrived, I was faced with a class which used books which were at least twenty-five years old and had done the rounds. The room was exceedingly poky and for art I was allowed one quarter of a sheet of grey sugar paper per pupil per week.

At the end of the six weeks, Jill realised that she had not been paid, so she raised the matter with Leakey. He told her to go to Harrods and get some groceries and put them on his account as it would take a little while to obtain some cash. When Jill declined, saying she did not really want to go to Harrods, she was offered a four-poster bed instead. This she accepted and it remained in her possession. Such were Leakey's persuasive and unorthodox ways! Needless to say, the DCPS bug had been caught and Jill agreed to stay on, as she saw that many things needed to be changed. She felt strongly that there was a need for a Nursery and Kindergarten section, as had been established in Dulwich, and Leakey was far from hostile to the idea. So before long a small building was constructed nearby, which was named Nash House after the then Chairman of Governors, Denis Ellison Nash. It opened in 1965 with three rooms and Jill became its first headmistress. Nash House was an instant success and a further room was soon added. Little Stream had originally opened in 1956 for girls aged 5 to 7, but with the arrival of Nash House it began accepting girls from there, at the same time extending the upper age to 11. Elizabeth Morrison remained in charge and it too began to expand. Little Stream was in membership of the Association of Headmistresses in Preparatory Schools (AHMPS), whereas the boys' section at Coursehorn

The beginnings of Little Stream in 1956 - now the Lower School at Cranbrook

itself was in membership of the Incorporated Association of Preparatory Schools (IAPS). The school thus accommodated boys and girls to the age of 11 at that time, but they were not taught together and the school was not co-educational.

When boys left Nash House they went to the junior section of Coursehorn where they were looked after first by Helen Dickson, until she retired in 1973, and then by Rita Bennett. Jill Tingley stayed at Nash House for nine years and then, seeking a new challenge as Jill Day, she became Headmistress of the DCPS Nursery and Kindergarten at Gallery Road in Dulwich. Her place as Head of Nash House was taken by Caroline Salmon who had a long stay, eventually retiring in 2001.

Leakey's decision to be at Cranbrook on a full-time basis from April 1962 made a considerable impact. Buildings began to appear, more permanent ones this time, although this did not prevent him from taking back to Cranbrook a hut from Dulwich (which to be fair had originated from the camp) and numerous other bits and pieces of furniture as well. These included some fine wrought iron gates which once graced the entrance to the garden at Brightlands.

One of the first changes which Leakey made was that the magazine for the school in Cranbrook should be a separate entity. Although a start had been made for Coursehorn to have its own magazine in 1945 this only lasted for a few issues and, thereafter, news about Coursehorn appeared in the DCPS London magazine as a supplement. The new magazine first appeared in the summer of 1962 and was printed by Battley Brothers, who at that time were printing the Dulwich magazine. Battley Brothers had a long association with DCPS over three generations. An early *School Notes* section written by Leakey in one of the first magazines shows that, while having considerable persuasive charm, his enthusiasm was not always matched by his organisation:

> *I rang up Messrs Battley Brothers a few days after half-term to ask when they wanted copy for the School Magazine. A charming young lady on the telephone said, 'Oh, tomorrow if possible' and I was completely taken by surprise. She went on to say that the Dulwich copy was already in, which shook us still further. Having been involved with the DCPS magazine since 1930 and knowing all the ropes, I managed to get a stay of execution but, if by any chance this seems rather a hurried production, you will know the reason why! Incidentally, while I am writing about Messrs Battley Brothers, I think Coursehorn readers might be interested to know about the Queensgate Press which was started by two brothers, one of whom became a Member of Parliament and whose son was at the Prep. Battleys have served us long and faithfully, not only in the publishing of a great deal of school books such as the first Prep Registers, but also with SCHOOL ERRANT. They have always been most helpful, and I would like to take this opportunity of thanking them for all they do for us.*

History does not relate how long a stay of execution Leakey received for his late copy of the school magazine, but it does reveal his way of solving problems. He was clearly a dynamic man who made a tremendous impact wherever he went, and the Editorial in the first Coursehorn magazine described him thus:

> *For many years Mr Leakey used to arrive at Coursehorn on Friday evenings, and leave for London on the Sunday evening, or very early on Monday morning, but during these brief visits his presence here always invigorated us like a gust of fresh air. Now these gusts are with us permanently, and the resultant breeze blows steadily and forcefully into every corner of the school as a real wind of change.*

And changes there most certainly were. Two new classrooms, a much needed changing room and a new dormitory appeared within a couple of years, as did a covered way at the front of the school. 'Bones' at last received a laundry room in the autumn of 1963 and with a new convalescent room this made an enormous difference to the efficiency of the school and work generally. Another classroom was added at Little Stream and a Medical Room as well, and not long after that a new classroom appeared at the growing Lower School which was then near the original house. Nothing, it seemed, could curb the Leakey bandwagon. Scouts and clubs grew in number as did the size of the choir and the orchestra and a golf club was started, but it was limited to boarders as the only available time to play was in the evening. In 1962 Coursehorn held a carol service in Cranbrook Church, the first time it had done so since 1939. The Revd Trevor Vickery, whom Leakey had already appointed as School Chaplain and who was the Rector of Staplehurst, conducted the service. Vickery's flamboyant and generous nature won him many friends at the school and he became associated with it for over forty years. His three sons were educated at Coursehorn and his wife was Head of Science there for a while. Although matches continued to be played between Cranbrook and Dulwich, the two schools, although united by a common Board of Governors, began to drift apart slightly as the two Headmasters had their own ideas and ways of doing things.

A big event occurred in September 1964 when there was a Jubilee dinner to commemorate the 1939 evacuation and to celebrate the 25th anniversary of Coursehorn as a school. To be strictly accurate the school was not actually at Cranbrook from 1940 to 1945, but this did not detract from a momentous evening when many of the original staff gathered together again. Sheppard (WAS) was unable to attend, so the toast to absent friends was given by Taylor (FNT), most appropriately as it happened because he had been in charge at Coursehorn for a few months in 1945 as we have seen. Describing himself as 'Shep's shadow', he spoke warmly of those early difficult months in 1939 which, he said, would not have been as successful as they were had not everyone, boys and staff alike, worked as a team. As ebullient as ever, Leakey replied with some pride that from a total of 44 boys in 1945, numbers in 1964 had grown to 50 boarders, 130 day boys and a further 118 girls at Little Stream.

Two years later in the autumn term 1966, the school was given a full inspection by the Ministry of Education. The subsequent report was commendatory on the whole, the main criticism being the lack of a school hall, a situation of which Leakey was well aware and which would be remedied before too long. As with the 1948 inspection at Dulwich, the inspectors commented on the happy atmosphere prevailing in the school which was achieved, they said, by showing 'love without sentimentality'.

What did not change during the 1960s was the age at which boys, and girls, left Coursehorn which had always been at 11. Girls went to local schools and many boys went on to Cranbrook School, but those boys who wished to stay at DCPS until they were 13, in order to take scholarship and Common Entrance to other public schools, went on to Brightlands in Dulwich where the Macleans were only too pleased to receive them. This arrangement continued until 1969, when Cranbrook School introduced a 13+ entry, and from then onwards Coursehorn became a school for boys to the age of 13. This had an effect on Brightlands, which began to take in boys from 9 at the same time.

Leakey, with his second wife Katherine, enjoyed nine happy years at Cranbrook and much was achieved during that time. He had seen the benefits which new buildings had brought to the school in Dulwich and, with the Trust firmly established, he realised that the life of the huts which had come across from the camp could not go on for ever. Money at that time was not freely available for reconstruction on a major scale so, for reasons of economy, the new buildings which appeared were generally semi-permanent pre-fabricated ones and it would be some time before the school was in a position to build substantially in brick. Following the 1966 inspection a new hall was built a year later and Leakey, as resourceful as ever, converted the room which had once been the hall into a new classroom, with improved space for the teaching of Art and Music. At the same time another hut was converted to become a science laboratory. By 1970, Coursehorn, with its 'satellites' at The Lodge, Little Stream and Nash House, had become a thriving and successful school in its own right and sound foundations had been laid to secure its future. Even Leakey could not maintain the momentum for ever. He moved to the nearby village of Rolvenden in 1968, announcing at the same time, and after much heart searching, that he would finally retire from school life at the end of 1970. So for a second time he received a grand send-off, when numerous former pupils, parents and friends of the school came to bid him farewell. This time it really was farewell and a special edition of the school magazine was produced to mark the occasion.

Helen Dickson, who had been at the school for almost forty years, said she had always felt she had worked WITH Leakey and not FOR him, and the Chairman of Governors, Denis Ellison Nash, spoke of his generosity, his great foresight and eternal optimism often in the light of hopeless odds. Leakey chose to retire to Argyll, an area of which he was particularly fond, so close links with both schools were well and truly severed. As a memento of his time at Dulwich and at Cranbrook he took with him to Argyll those selfsame gates which had once graced the entrance to the garden at Brightlands. He died just six years later, so had only a comparatively short time in retirement to enjoy the fruits of his labours – not that he was a person ideally suited to a leisurely retirement.

Many tributes have been written about John Leakey, none better than that by Peter Fairley, former journalist and science correspondent to ITV. Peter was an old boy of the school who was at Betws during the war, and who had his own sons educated at DCPS. It is a great sadness that Peter himself died in 1998 and so has not been able to see these words in print. Of Leakey he wrote:

> As a formal teacher of subjects, he was lousy. As an educator, in the full sense of the word, he was superb. Into the dusty scriptures and pages of history and literature he would breathe a fire that set the imagination alight. Out of the window would go the curriculum – indeed, out of the window would frequently go Leakey and his pupils – as some practical demonstration or way of illustrating a point occurred to him. John Leakey's qualities as a headmaster were legion. His kindness and understanding meant that his staff always worked with him and his enthusiasm and tremendous energy also meant that they worked very hard! He was a sincere Christian and boys learnt to trust each other because he trusted them. Whenever a prospective parent arrived who needed help, the staff all knew that the child would be accepted. It did not matter that there was no vacancy. A vacancy would be made. Although he had little patience with red tape and had a healthy contempt for Common Entrance phobia, unbeaten teams and social or academic snobbery, his mind was always receptive to new ideas. He was preaching the liberal curriculum, the need for music, the importance of the happiness of the child, long before such ideas were fashionable, and his stress on oral French, the acceptance of girls and the financial disadvantages of small schools have all become recent talking points.

Jack Guy was to write some years later that the word 'crisis' had no place in the Leakey vocabulary and in view of all the hardships which the school had endured, especially during the war years, that was a concise summary of Leakey's philosophy.

Leakey thus laid the foundations on which the present Dulwich Prep in Cranbrook has been built, and many of its idiosyncrasies, such as the unique tradition of houses, which DCPS calls tribes, were brought to Cranbrook from Dulwich and continue to this day. In 1964, he appointed Robin Peverett to his staff who, with his wife, became the Housemaster at The Lodge, with 28 boys. Peverett soon became fully involved with the school and Leakey was impressed by his enthusiasm and methodical manner, so much so that for the last two years after Leakey had moved to live in Rolvenden, Peverett was groomed to be his successor. So, from the autumn term in 1970, Peverett became Headmaster and Jack Guy continued as Second Master.

A new regime began and, as at Dulwich, things were going to be very different. Woodcock was already well established in Dulwich when Peverett took up the reins at Cranbrook, but a rivalry quickly grew between them. Both brought changes which were badly needed and both were single-minded and autocratic by nature. Woodcock, perhaps with tongue in cheek, considered Coursehorn to be an inferior country cousin and Peverett ensured that however things were done at Dulwich, his way would be different. As a result the two schools drifted apart socially, matches ceased between them and there was little contact between staff. This is not something that Leakey would have wanted and, although relationships between the two schools are now more cordial, the distance alone between them means that each is still very separate from the other.

Although the school had become a Trust in 1956, Leakey's influence at Cranbrook in the 1960s continued much as it had before and generally he was known simply as 'The Boss'. As we have seen, his methods and his style were not always conventional and there were many loose ends which needed to be tightened up. The improvement of buildings continued, principally those nearest the main house which had been erected first and which had originated at the 1939 camp. In 1973 a new dining room and kitchen were built, but by far the greatest change, and perhaps Peverett's most far-reaching one, came in the autumn term in 1975.

Until 1975, the school had accepted boys at Coursehorn, as it was then known, and girls at Little Stream, but they had worked as separate units. Peverett considered that the time had come for the two schools to merge as one and become fully co-educational for all year groups. There were a number of reasons. The first was Peverett's own philosophy that this was the right thing to do. Secondly, Cranbrook School announced that it was becoming co-educational, so the time seemed right to make the change. Thirdly, and not insignificantly, it would make the school different from Dulwich. Not all members of staff were entirely happy about the change, although most were. Elizabeth Morrison, Head of Little Stream, considered that it might be difficult for the girls from there to integrate and mix with the tougher older boys and she decided that it was time for her to retire. This she did in April 1975, although her fears were proved to be ill-founded. Peverett decided to ease the change in gently by not mixing all the boys and girls classes immediately. At the end of the summer term in 1976, a year after co-education had been in existence, he wrote:

> ... *the change went so smoothly that most people, parents, teachers and children, forgot about it after a very short time. Perhaps it was because it seemed academically and administratively right; perhaps it was because the boys and girls accepted it as natural. But for whatever reason, few parents noticed that the Sports Day and the Swimming Sports were quite different from anything we had organised before and that in everything we undertook, the division was now by age and not by sex. Problems we had worried about did not materialise, and within a very short time all the staff were immersed in the normal problems of school life dealing with children instead of boys or girls.*

Initially, there were two classes of boys and one of girls in each of the Upper School year groups, and for one year only they were taught separately but within the same buildings. Then after a year the classes were mixed. The old Little Stream became the new Lower School for boys and girls aged 6-9, its new head being Rita Bennett, and Nash House continued in much the same way as it had before. As a result of co-education, a degree of reorganisation within the school was necessary. Iain Clarke became the Senior Master and Jack Guy was promoted to the new position of Deputy Head. When Guy retired in 1984, Clarke became

The entrance to the original house in 1946

Although altered, much of the original has been preserved - 2003

Deputy Head, and for a time his wife Jean was the school's registrar. For the first year of co-education Peter Parker-Smith continued as Head of the Middle School.

As Leakey had only recently died, it was said by some that Peverett had pushed through his ideas with indecent haste, but this was not the case. Leakey was not opposed to the principle of co-education, but he had never reached the point of putting it into practice except with very young children. As long ago as 1966 he had written:

> *I am not qualified to say how it [co-education] would work with teenagers, but with present trends in education it should prove to be an exciting and interesting thing to do which may prove of benefit to education.*

The 1980s were years of growth. In 1982 the school was able to purchase an adjacent eight-acre field adding to the thirty-two acres it already owned, and in 1984 the school received more registrations for pupils than ever before. Stalwarts from Leakey's time steadily retired and Peverett created a new team around him. Helen Dickson, who was subsequently killed in a tragic road accident in 1981, retired in 1973 and 'Bones' Glazier followed five years later in 1978. Jack Guy retired in 1984 after almost thirty years and during that time had done almost every job within the school, including a term in 1974 when he acted as headmaster. Known for his dashing bachelor image and his love for fast cars, he surprised everyone by marrying in 1968 and admitted that his new wife was even better value than his Aston Martin! Peter Parker-Smith retired in 1976 to continue his love of gardening in Cornwall, but sadly without his wife Mary, who had died earlier. Other newcomers who were to stay for many years included Maggie Wright, John Hendy, Ross Settles, Caroline Salmon, Simon Montgomery and Lynda Fisher from the Matron's Department.

One of the last appointments made by Leakey before he retired in 1970 was that of Maggie Wright, initially to teach PE at Little Stream. She moved on to the Middle School and became its Head in 1980, later being appointed as Deputy Head to the whole school in 1993, a position she held until she retired in 2001. John Hendy joined the school in 1974 and in 1976 became Head of the Middle School, known simply as the Fourth Year from 1988. Subsequently he played many roles within the school, not least being editor of the magazine for a long stretch and Head of Geography. His wife Stella is currently Director of Pastoral Care within the school. Special mention must also be made of Ian Larkin, who was employed by Leakey as a lad of 16 in the maintenance department. He remained until 2003, retiring at the age of sixty. By the time he left, he knew every nook and cranny of the place and had seen many structural changes. He recalled that one of the highlights of his time was early in 1970, when he was able to keep generators functioning while there were power cuts. Thanks to him, school life was not disrupted. During the 1980s there were still buildings which had originated at the camp and these were rapidly becoming in need of replacement. A number were swept aside in 1985 when a new Music School, with teaching and practice rooms, was built thus creating greater scope for a wider range of instruments to be taught. In consequence, the school's reputation for music, already well established, was enhanced still further.

Peverett had progressive ideas. He wanted every child to become involved in some aspect of school life both inside and outside the classroom. He wanted the school to progress and be the best in the area, intending for it to move with the times and not be regarded as a traditional prep school. Music had been taught in the school from the very start but he was keen to see it develop and he pioneered drama, producing many of the plays himself, involving as many children as he could in his productions. He improved sport and believed everybody should have a chance to take part. His philosophy was best summed up by John Hendy, who considered that Leakey founded the school but it was his successor who established it. Although there were subsequent events which clouded Peverett's career, and which are not worthy of further mention, much was achieved during his twenty years of headship and he must be given credit for that. When he arrived many of the buildings had either originated at the camp or had been replaced by others of lightweight structure. There were not many solid brick buildings. The school was also being heavily subsidised from Dulwich. Leakey had performed miracles since the start in 1945, but much still needed to be done. By the time Peverett retired most, but not quite all, of the original buildings at the main school had been replaced by more substantial ones, and, most important of all, the school was more than adequately self-supporting financially.

In 1989 Peverett announced his anticipated retirement, and the search was on to seek a new Headmaster. As a result Mike Wagstaffe, with his wife Helen, was appointed thus becoming the third Headmaster at DCPS Cranbrook from the summer term in 1990. Very quickly he was accepted by staff and children alike, although he did not get by totally unscathed in his first term, when one of the younger children was overheard to say that he had very curly hair for a headmaster. Wagstaffe's style of management was very different from that of his predecessor. For the first time staff were consulted over decision making and there was a more open atmosphere within the school which was welcomed generally. In his first term, Phase 1 of

Mike Wagstaffe Headmaster DPS Cranbrook 1990-2004

a building development plan was set in place, this being the construction of a new swimming pool, and a sports and gymnastic hall with changing rooms attached, all of which opened in April 1991. Two further phases would follow, and Wagstaffe was keen to emphasise that the school was not expanding but that existing buildings were being upgraded or replaced.

Recent changes in organisation left confusion in the names of the buildings, so these were simplified. The original Georgian house had been called Coursehorn and that was the name the school acquired, later to become DCPS Coursehorn. The school thus became established in the vicinity of the original house and adjacent oast house. Some distance away, and later on, Little Stream as it was first called, had been built as a school for girls, and a house with huts surrounding it, known as The Lodge was created for boy boarders. Not far away, Nash House was built as a Nursery school. Near the original house another building had been added in 1981. This was called The Moat and was built to accommodate an increasing number of girl boarders at the time. By 1990 the whole campus had become known as Coursehorn and the original school area around the house was the Upper School. Pupils going there from the Lower School said they were going to 'The House' and colloquially that is how that part of the school became known. In 1999, when further reorganisation was necessary, The Moat was converted to become the school's administrative centre and the bursary moved there from the oast house. All girl boarders were then accommodated in the original house, which was given the more dignified name of Manor and boys who had been accommodated in the main house up to then, moved to The Lodge which became the boarding house for junior and senior boys.

These changes in nomenclature seemed logical but they were not the only ones. Wagstaffe, strongly backed by his colleagues, considered that the association with Dulwich College had become irrelevant, so from 1995 the word *College* was dropped, the formal title of the school becoming *Dulwich Preparatory School Cranbrook*. By chance, the words Cranbrook and Coursehorn both started with the letter C, so the logo legitimately stayed as DCPS.

In 1990, Wagstaffe said that he was fortunate to be following two visionary headmasters who had established the school as one of the leaders within IAPS. Initially he felt that no radical changes in administration were called for, and variations would be in style rather than in substance. He introduced weekly management meetings, and believed strongly in delegation and consultation. The building and refurbishment programme continued in the 1990s. In September 2000, the old hall was demolished, as were other buildings from the 1970s which latterly had been used for the teaching of French and Art. All this was done to make way for new classrooms and a new hall, and building soon commenced. At the same time, in January 2001, a further ten acres of land were purchased for more playing fields. By 2002 all was ready and the new complex, which included a multi-purpose theatre named appropriately the John Leakey Hall, was opened by his daughter Diana and is now the centre for major school activities including morning assemblies. A pupil from just a decade earlier might be excused for not recognising a great deal of his/her former school.

The John Leakey Hall - opened 2002

Prospects for the future are bright and with its new buildings and spacious campus, the school has gained an enviable reputation in Kent and Sussex, thus fulfilling expectations from the 1970s. Registrations far exceed the number of places available, but no organisation, let alone a school with its responsibilities to the young, can rest on its laurels and be complacent. A great deal has been achieved, particularly at the Main School, but the Lower School, the former Little Stream, although adequate, is a rabbit warren of different flat roofed buildings most of which are in need of replacement. There are future plans for the construction of a new Lower School in modern buildings with standards to match those already in place at the Main School. It is at the Lower School where one of the huts from the 1939 camp still survives sixty years on but little of the original remains as Ian Larkin testified from his experience of make do and mend over the years. In 2002 this hut was in use as a computer room, hardly a requisite for 1939! Plans are also afoot to add another classroom to the Nursery, not to increase the number of children in the school, but to provide smaller classes for those in attendance already. There are also plans to encourage greater use of the school's facilities by the local community and to develop stronger links with former pupils.

Although DCPS London and DPS Cranbrook have strong links and much in common, and no great change is envisaged in that direction, there is little interchange between the staff, many of whom have never visited the other. One occasion when the two schools were

One of the original camp huts in 2002 . . .

. . . being used as a computer room. Such things were unknown in 1946.

brought together was for a Millennium Service at the chapel of Tonbridge School in June 2000, but such events are rare. The two schools are not the same, nor can they be and nor was it Leakey's intention that they ever should be. Achieving the highest standards in all fields of endeavour was his simple common goal. There are variations in uniform but the four tribes and the school crest are common to both. There are bound to be differences as each headmaster is given the freedom by the Board of Governors, common to both schools, to administer their schools in the way they feel best. As examples, Dulwich Prep Cranbrook has become fully co-educational and this has not happened in London. The school in Cranbrook has also always been non-selective. In London, Saturday morning school was abolished as long ago as 1973, yet in 2004 it survived for the older children in Kent. Urban and rural demands from parents, and indeed from staff also, may well be different, but the five day working week is now expected by many. As with the school in London, there will always be sporting activities at weekends, but a shorter working week may well mean a longer working day and when children travel long distances to school, that may

Stephen Rigby
Headmaster 2004 –

not be so acceptable. These are the sorts of decisions which headmasters, in full conjunction with their staff these days, have to make. However they will not be taken by Mike Wagstaffe as he announced that his turn for retirement had come from the end of the spring term in 2004. His successor, Stephen Rigby, came from Westbourne House near Chichester and thus became Coursehorn's fourth headmaster in almost fifty years.

Whatever the outcome of working hours, Dulwich Prep Cranbrook has made a great name for itself since those early days of thirty-nine boys in 1945 and seems set to remain a leader in its field. Plans for expansion and improvement are always in the pipeline, as facilities which are acceptable now, may well be obsolete thirty years hence.

10 Away from Home

From early days there has always been a small percentage of boys who have been boarders although only since 1945 have they been housed at Brightlands in Gallery Road. The first boys to board were in Mallinson's time not long after he became headmaster in 1887, when half a dozen or so lived with him and his family at their home at Whitfield Lodge. When 42 Alleyn Park became the family home in 1897, Mallinson was able to house a greater number of boys there (about a dozen) and they began to have a more corporate existence than being extensions to his family.

The school had already leased 44 Alleyn Park for teaching purposes and not long after 42 was acquired, the hall with a large room above was built between them. This room became a dormitory for boarders so Mallinson was able to increase their number to about fifteen. To assist Mrs Mallinson, a matron was employed whose sitting room was on the first floor at the top of the stairs in Number 42 overlooking the garden[1]. A boarder's day usually started with a cold bath followed by a run to the tollgate after which matron gave each boy an apple. In those days it was medical practice to isolate boys with complaints such as measles, mumps or even 'flu to prevent the spread of an epidemic, and for this purpose a sanatorium was built at the rear of the premises overlooking the drive which led to Lord Vestey's Estate (now Bowen Drive). Opened during the summer in 1897, it was principally single storeyed but still large and not very cost effective in terms of its use, for if there were no boarders who were ill, it was largely vacant. By December of the first year it had not seen a single overnight patient.

When Leake succeeded Mallinson in 1910, the pattern of life for boarders remained much the same, and such was his fatherly care for them that they soon became known as 'Leake's Boarders'. 44 Alleyn Park (the old part of the present Lower School) continued to be used as classrooms and most of 42 was the residence of Leake and his family, with the hall and the boarders above sandwiched between them. By 1922 the school was growing in size and Leake was anxious to find more classroom space. He achieved this by moving his boarders away from the main school buildings to join those who had already formed an overflow at the home of A E J Inglis and his family at 28 Alleyn Park. This was a large Victorian building similar in size to the present Number 38 and which at the time had room to accommodate them, but before long this too proved inadequate. Two years later when W A Sheppard joined the staff, he made mention[2] of there being four housemasters, but they were not true

1 In 2004 this was the PE department's office
2 *41 Years at The Prep* by W A Sheppard (DCPS magazines 1969-1974)

An early photograph of 'Leake's boarders'. Leake with his family and staff - 1910

housemasters in the accepted sense and DCPS never had four boarding houses. They were senior members of staff who lived locally and who accommodated a few boys in their homes, but they clearly had some influence in school affairs. Most of the boys in the school wore Eton collars during the 1920s and on Sundays the boarders wore Eton suits. For church some even wore top hats or bowlers which Matron brushed on Monday mornings before returning each to its box. Church meant the College Chapel where the boys sat in the gallery, one of them invariably being asked to pump the organ to provide air for the pipes. When Inglis left DCPS in 1929, his house was taken over by C P Hamilton, who had previously housed boarders at his home at 32 Croxted Road. Nearby, at 5 Alleyn Park, more boarders were housed under the stewardship of W W Butler, who was the first editor of the school magazine. There were yet more with W H Walker at 6 South Croxted Road for a time. By 1938, when the fees for boarders were £38 per term, their principal home had become 28 Alleyn Park under the care of Mr and Mrs Hamilton and a resident matron. Robert Guttman (DCPS 1935-1940) remembered the matron as a forbidding person who strictly enforced the rule about no talking after lights out and who administered a weekly bath for each boy. He remembered disliking Fridays because there was always fish for tea, but commented that the most dramatic moment of his time as a boarder was watching in awe the destruction of the Crystal Palace in 1936 which he could see, with others, from his dormitory window. He was also slightly envious of those few boys who went home at weekends, a practice which was not continued after the war for a long time. When war was declared, Hamilton was soon called into military service and most of his boys at Number 28, including Robert Guttman, went to the evacuated camp at Cranbrook and later to Wales. The house was severely damaged by a bomb in 1940 and when Major Hamilton, as he had by that time become, returned in 1945, he was nearing retirement age. If the school were to continue taking boarders after the war, different arrangements would have to be made.

The new home for boarders, which opened at the start of the autumn term in 1945, was at Brightlands in Gallery Road and the background to the house and how it got its name is of interest. It was built in 1864 to the designs of Charles Barry Junior for the solicitor of the Dulwich College Estate, Alexander Druce. Dr. Jan Piggott[3] described it as:

> *...a handsome house which would not look out of place in Kensington Palace Gardens. The building, originally externally more decorated than it is now, also alludes at the rear (facing Dulwich Common) to the elder Barry's 'Travellers' Club' in Pall Mall, with its shell motif in the lunettes above the windows.*

An early picture of Brightlands taken in 1905, before the chimneys and decorative ballustrades were removed

The Druce family had secured the building on a twenty-eight year lease, but by 1892 it had been vacated and was empty and in need of attention. The cottage and other outbuildings had been the stables to a former building, a house having been on the site since the eighteenth century.

So far as the name of the house is concerned, reference must again be made to Miss Elizabeth Shorter, who in 1874 had opened a small school in a house called Brightlands in Rosendale Road. No trace of this house exists today. Assisted by her sister, Mrs Annie Growse, the

3 *Charles Barry Junior and the Dulwich College Estate* (Dr J Piggott 1986 - Dulwich College Archivist)

*The view into the grounds at Brightlands in 1905, with the kitchen
garden and greenhouse on the right*

*A similar view into the grounds at Brightlands in 2004, with the Nursery
School standing on the site of the kitchen garden and greenhouse*

school grew so that by 1883 there were about 40 boys in attendance. Soon after, they moved to larger premises to what is now 71 Alleyn Park and for a short while this was called Brightlands as well. The school was successful and there are records of many boys entering Dulwich College during the 1880s. Miss Shorter died in 1893 and the school was taken over by Archibald Collins, who was one of the teachers, in partnership with Leonard Worth. For a short while they acquired Whitfield Lodge just four houses down when it was vacated by the Prep, but this proved inadequate so in 1895, and by then calling themselves 'Joint Principals', they secured a three-year lease on a building on Dulwich Common taking the name of Brightlands with them, the name it has kept ever since. Whereas Whitfield Lodge was destroyed in the war, Number 71 survived and is one of the few remaining Victorian houses in Alleyn Park. It is currently occupied by Chris and Charlotte King whose three sons subsequently became boarders at DCPS Brightlands, almost a hundred years after their own home had been the original house of that name for a short while.

There was a small fire in 1899 which fortunately did little damage, and in 1902 the school was taken over by Vivian McLaughlin. During his time many improvements were made, and Brightlands became a well organised and successful prep school. Then in 1907 he made a major decision - he wanted to move his school away from Dulwich to a large house at Newnham-on-Severn in Herefordshire. Just why he wanted to do this after he had worked so hard during the previous six years to build up his school is not clear. Maybe the locality did not suit him in that there were too many rival schools nearby; perhaps it was the climate, the size of the premises or even some unmentioned personality clash. Whatever the reason, McLaughlin had his heart set on moving. But not all of his parents wanted their sons to be transported to Newnham-on-Severn - indeed over half of them (about 24 boys in all) said they wanted their sons to remain in London. So a deal was struck. McLaughlin sold the goodwill and the remaining lease for £1500 to Leonard Frances Duckworth, who became the Headmaster, and the name of Brightlands in Dulwich was retained. McLaughlin took 25 boys, two masters and a Matron to Newnham-on-Severn and called his new school Brightlands as well - so there were then two schools called Brightlands. The one at Newnham flourished and only closed in 1996.

When Duckworth arrived to start his first term in Dulwich for the summer term in 1908, he was dismayed to discover that more boys had gone to Newnham than he had thought, and several others, whose parents were not happy with the disruption, had removed their sons to other schools, DCPS no doubt receiving a few of them. Duckworth only had 19 boys at the first roll call, but by 1913 this had gone up to 60 and by 1920 numbers had reached about a hundred. The grounds were extended and during the 1920s Duckworth obtained a reputation as a firm disciplinarian and an excellent headmaster. During his time the large Victorian house next door had been one of the boarding houses for the College called Ivyholme and when it became vacant, Duckworth acquired the lease on that as well and used it as classrooms. Because he had been born in Tiverton in Devon, this was the name he gave it. It was destroyed in the Second War, but its modern replacement, Tiverton Lodge and now privately owned, carries that name to this day. Duckworth's reign came to an abrupt end during the summer term in 1935, when on 7th July at the age of 62 he died of a heart attack on Dulwich and Sydenham Golf Course. After that unhappy event the school then passed to a Mr S de Moyse Bucknall for the princely sum of £6000 and that is when DCPS began to become involved.

In the late 1930s, DCPS was growing in size and eager to find more space. Bucknall, down the road, was a close rival, his school having several attractive buildings and, at the time, about nine acres of land. In consequence DCPS made overtures to Bucknall in an attempt to buy him out. Brightlands was not as prosperous nor as large in terms of numbers as its neighbour in Alleyn Park but it was by no means insolvent, and Bucknall resisted any such offers. Indeed so confident was he of his school's survival and reputation, that a new sports pavilion was built in the grounds in 1937, although no trace of it remains today as the DCPS Nursery occupies its site. Records show that the school was totally redecorated in 1937 and the fees were increased from £10 to 10 guineas (£10.50) per term to cover the cost.[4] For the next couple of years Bucknall and Brightlands School continued as rivals to DCPS, and then came the war.

By chance both schools, DCPS and Brightlands, moved out of London on 1st September 1939 and finished up near each other again. While DCPS went to Cranbrook, Brightlands moved initially to Lenham in Kent and shortly after to Heathfield in Sussex. By then, Bucknall was in financial difficulties and he asked the Dulwich College Estate Governors if they would cancel his lease on Brightlands and Tiverton. They at first refused, but when they discovered in October that the premises were empty, the furniture all removed and the doors and windows open, they relented and a Deed of Surrender was agreed on 7th December 1939. By this time, Bucknall had been called up for military service and his school was taken over by his cousin, Harold Bucknall, who invited Malcolm Tattershall to assist him. Both had been masters at the Dulwich school. They became joint headmasters and the school became known as Tavistock Hall, the sole pupils at the beginning being boys from Brightlands School. It prospered until 1973 when Jack Bucknall, Harold's son, sold the site to property developers. It is a coincidence that Peter Ashenhurst, who became the Housemaster of DCPS Brightlands in 1966, was a master at Tavistock Hall in 1944/1945.

At the outbreak of war, Belair in Gallery Road was used as an Army Ordnance Depot and about 70 men from the Royal Army Service Corps were billeted there. Gallery Road was closed off and used as an army lorry park and it is probable that Brightlands remained empty until being occupied by No 3 Company, 6th Battalion Home Guard in August 1940. Three

---

4 *Brightlands School A Brief History* 1995 (Bob Foskett: a Brightlands School pupil 1930 to 1936)

months later, in November, Tiverton was also requisitioned by the army. The Home Guard did not stay long and by December 1940 both Brightlands and Tiverton were occupied by the Royal Observer Corps and there is one lasting relic from their occupation. In order for personnel to move from one building to the other in total safety, and without producing any light during blackout time, an underground concrete tube way was built to link the two buildings. Its entrance, though now bricked over, is visible in the basement of Brightlands and a section of the outside can be seen as it crosses the subterranean passage, so cleverly designed to give light to the basement of the building. In October 1944, Tiverton received a direct hit from a flying bomb and was destroyed, and the accompanying blast caused structural damage inside Brightlands, a few traces of which are still visible. The army by this time had only a minimal presence.

At DCPS, Leakey never lost sight of the enormous advantages which the acquisition of the former Brightlands School could bring and he had been the prime mover in trying to secure it for DCPS in 1937. With the Bucknalls out of the way and the army not likely to have occupancy for ever, Leakey saw his chance. There was even talk that he had his eye on neighbouring Belair and its grounds should Brightlands not be available. Belair had been the home of the Spicer family of notepaper fame, but structurally its condition was far worse than Brightlands. So, in the middle of 1944 while the flying bombs were falling and the war not yet ended and his foremost attention was with the school in Wales, Leakey approached the College Estate Governors with a view to gaining a lease on both Brightlands and Tiverton. Once hostilities were over, his plan[5] was to make Brightlands the school's senior boarding house for 11-13 year olds, whereas Tiverton would be for 9-11 year olds. The October flying bomb put an end to that idea as Tiverton could no longer be used, but the lease on Brightlands was secured and it became the school's only boarding house from 1945, the role it has played ever since.

The army left the building in a sorry state at the end of the war, and considerable refurbishment was necessary, in stringent times it should be added, before it could be occupied by boys. DCPS took possession during the summer of 1945 in readiness for the September term. The first housemaster was G T H Hammerton, who had been in Wales and who brought with him a number of the traditions and habits gained there. As an example, the linen room at the camp had been in a long passage nicknamed 'The Tunnel', and this name continued to be used at the Royal Oak. So well established was it, that the basement room at Brightlands used for the same purpose carried that name for a long time. For almost twenty years, the boys' clothes were looked after in 'The Tunnel' by Maggie Glenn, whose father had been on the staff earlier, and Joan Taylor who had been with her husband Freddie (FNT) in Wales. Taylor also came to take prep at Brightlands twice a week for many years. Hammerton ran

5 See Chapter 9

Brightlands on very militaristic lines and an experiment was introduced whereby the boys were divided into six orderly squads, each squad having a duty day. To use Hammerton's own words *'it was a hybrid between the Scouts, the Tribes and a pinch of the OTC [Officers' Training Corps]'*. The experiment did not last long. He must have been an innovative person for, in the summer of 1946, he introduced a zoo consisting of mice, caterpillars, newts, frogs, stag beetles and a grass snake. That experiment did not last long either! Chris Holloway (DCPS Brightlands 1945-1946), who was thus one of the first post-war boarders, remembered the spaciousness of the garden, climbing trees and hurrying to and from school for lunch at Brightlands each day, crossing what is now the South Circular Road when it was virtually devoid of traffic. He also remembered watching steam trains going under the Hunts Slip Road bridge and passing by the postal sorting office in Alleyn Park.

One year later in 1946, a new Housemaster, H F Harley, was appointed and it was under his jurisdiction that I was to enter Brightlands as a boy in September 1948. The house was divided into four sub-divisions, a bit like tribes, for which points were awarded - Nelson, Collingwood, Marlborough and Wellington - and these survived for a long time after him. Numerous outings were arranged at weekends, and the dormitories were named after famous

A house photograph taken at Brightlands in 1948
Staff (L to R): Sister Dawes, H F Harley (Housemaster), Maggie Glenn, A C D Clelland
The author is in the bottom row, second from the left.

ships, *HMS Black Prince*, *Cutty Sark*, *HMS King George V* and so on. Annual house plays were introduced and in them he was aided by the Assistant Housemaster, A C D Clelland. Harley died unexpectedly in the middle of the spring term in 1949 so Clelland took control for a short while at a moment's notice until a new housemaster was appointed. This was Charles Hesketh, who arrived for the autumn term. Of his first term he wrote that to arrive at Dulwich from Victoria, and then to discover the seclusion of the Brightlands grounds, was an unexpected charm.

Brightlands could not have been charmed by Hesketh to any great extent, for he only lasted one year and, by the autumn term 1950, Clelland was back in charge again. In my two years at Brightlands I thus had three housemasters. By and large I look back on my own days there with a degree of happiness, although by modern standards I don't know why. The inside of the building was spartan to say the least. There was no central heating and only one gas fire on each floor, which burnt your hands if you touched it but left everywhere else freezing cold, especially in the severe winter of 1947/48 when I can remember water freezing in the dormitories overnight. The kitchen was in the same place as now, but from it a dumb waiter lift remained in place, having originally been designed to convey food from the kitchen below to the dining room above when it had been part of Bucknall's private house. Despite the hardships of the time, I remember being well fed and Mabel Drewry, the house cook for many years, and who had been in Wales and earlier at the camp before the war, performed miracles to feed us within the restraints of post war-rationing. We were given good marks for being good, which was rare, and bad marks for the slightest offence. For every nine bad marks a boy received he was caned and talking in prep could gain nine bad marks in a single go! Many boys queued at the top of the front stairs each morning to be caned before going off to school, but we were always excused if it was our birthday. Since no check was ever made of the exact date of a boy's birthday, some boys must have been ninety years of age when they left!

There was no television and I can remember evenings huddled round a small gas fire in the main room reading books. Members of staff came down to entertain us, and there was a basketry club as well as billiards and table tennis - or ping-pong as it was then called. The trees and the woods were always fun in summer, as indeed they are now. Mumps, measles and chicken pox were all frequent visitors, as was influenza, and a full-time State Registered Nurse lived in and went to the school for a few hours each day to administer to day boys. The 1947 Inspectors' Report for the Ministry of Education said, amongst other things, that there was no adequate provision for a fire escape from the top floor, but the manners of the boys were delightful and their health was good. Despite being told in the spring 1949 School Magazine that Brightlands had a new look with the common room and dormitories *'following the example of spring with green and pink everywhere'*, the place was still drab. There were no curtains, no carpets, and in most cases one single light bulb in each room - two in the larger rooms. Yet despite the hardships and the eccentricities of the various housemasters, no

Posed photograph for a post-war prospectus showing boarders during their leisure time.
(The author is sitting by the fireplace, sideways on, making a basket.)

Boarders in 2004 enjoying their leisure time in the same place as in the photograph above

one ever complained. This account, written by a boy at the time, gives an interesting insight into life at Brightlands from a boarder's point of view:

A DAY AT BRIGHTLANDS

On getting up at a quarter past seven we shake our arms about vigorously for five minutes and that is called PT. We then go and wash and go downstairs and wait for the gong. After breakfast we make our beds and then the microphone is switched on and a loud voice bellows out "Get ready for School". After morning school we come back to Brightlands and have dinner. After dinner we have a reading period of about a quarter of an hour and then go off to school again. Then after school between four o'clock and five o'clock we are free to do anything we like within reason. At a quarter past five we have tea and after tea comes prep. After prep we have prayers and then we are free until we go to bed.

The entertainments at Brightlands are table tennis, billiards and the field and woods to play in. Indoors there is a quiet room for reading and other quiet things and in the billiard room you can play table tennis, billiards or any other game you like. Outside you can play rugger or soccer, climb trees or do anything else you feel inclined. You are allowed two weekends a term. On Saturday we go shopping and on Sunday we go to church. The rest of the time is free. On the whole we get quite a lot of free time. We have patrols and good and bad marks, bad ones more frequent than good, unfortunately. But I still like Brightlands and will be sorry to leave.

S Garland (12.1) Christmas 1950

ORDER OF EVENTS

1. **100 yards. (Senior)**
   1. Bartlett 3. Epps R. 5. Johnstone-Hall
   2. Dawson 4. Jackson M. 6. Young

   1st....... 2nd....... 3rd....... 4th....... 5th....... 6th.......

2. **100 yards. (Junior)**
   1. Clarke A. J. 3. Garland S. 5. Stormer
   2. Epps J. 4. Robertson 6. Wandless

   1st....... 2nd....... 3rd....... 4th....... 5th....... 6th.......

3. **Throwing Cricket Ball (Senior)**
   1. Garland R. 3. Hosie 5. Rogers
   2. Glover 4. Jackson M. 6. Ward

   1st....... 2nd....... 3rd....... 4th....... 5th....... 6th.......

4. **Throwing Cricket Ball (Junior)**
   1. Clarke A. J. 4. Garland S. 7. Smith B.H.
   2. Epps J. 5. Lawrence 8. Stormer
   3. Friedenheim 6. Rust 9. Wright

   1st....... 2nd....... 3rd....... 4th....... 5th....... 6th.......

5. **440 yards. (Senior)**
   1. Bartlett 3. Hosie 5. Johnstone-Hall
   2. Garland R. 4. Jackson 6. Young

   1st....... 2nd....... 3rd....... 4th....... 5th....... 6th.......

6. **Egg and Spoon Race (Junior)**
   1. Drew 5. Machray 9. Singleton
   2. Epps J. 6. Mitchley 10. Stormer
   3. Garland S. 7. Robertson 11. Wandless
   4. Gibbard 8. Rust 12. Wright

   1st....... 2nd....... 3rd....... 4th....... 5th....... 6th.......

7. **Egg and Spoon Race (Senior)**
   1. Dawson 5. Gibson 9. Knight D.
   2. Donovan 6. Glover 10. Smith N.
   3. Clein 7. Jackson M. 11. Treves-Brown
   4. Epps R. 8. Johnstone-Hall 12. Tyzack

   1st....... 2nd....... 3rd....... 4th....... 5th....... 6th.......

8. **High Jump (Junior)**
   1. Clarke A. J. 3. Garland S. 5. Robertson
   2. Epps J. 4. Machray 6. Stormer
   7. Wright

   1st....... 2nd....... 3rd....... 4th....... 5th....... 6th.......

9. **High Jump (Senior)**

   1st....... 2nd....... 3rd....... 4th....... 5th....... 6th.......

10. **Three-Legged Race (Patrols)**

   1st................. 2nd................. 3rd.................

11. **Wheelbarrow Race (Patrols)**

   1st................. 2nd................. 3rd.................

12. **Relay Race 4 x 110. (Junior, Patrols)**

   1st................. 2nd................. 3rd.................

13. **Relay Race 4 x 110. (Senior, Patrols)**

   1st................. 2nd................. 3rd.................

14. **Chariot Race. (Patrols)**

   1st................. 2nd................. 3rd.................

15. **Obstacle Race (Junior)**

   1st....... 2nd....... 3rd....... 4th....... 5th....... 6th.......

16. **Obstacle Race (Senior)**

   1st....... 2nd....... 3rd....... 4th....... 5th....... 6th.......

SCORING: 1st—6 points. 4th—3 points
2nd—5 points. 5th—2 points.
3rd—4 points, 6th—1 point.

Programme for Brightlands Open Day in 1950

Clelland was not a very savoury character, but his period of tenure lasted for four years from the autumn of 1950 until his sudden departure from Brightlands in the middle of the autumn term 1954, although he continued to teach at the school for a further year. Despite his shortcomings, he left his mark in one important way. He was keen on drama and he instituted an annual boarders' play which continued long after his departure. So successful were these plays that they soon became known as *Brightlands Productions*. As well as the house play at Easter, there was an annual Open Day in the summer which involved a boarders versus their fathers cricket match in the morning, followed by inter-patrol sports in the afternoon. As well as the various 'in-house' clubs such as basketry and stamps, there were outings as well. In June 1953, for example, the boarders went to London one evening by train to see the lights. Floodlighting of buildings was still a novelty then, following as it did the euphoria of the Coronation after what had been an austere post-war period.

In the following year Clelland was replaced by a most remarkable Canadian called James Wood, who could not have been more different. He had only been on the staff for a few months when, in his usual persuasive way, Leakey asked him to be responsible for Brightlands for a 'short while'. Wood had been a Rhodes Scholar at Oxford and had served with distinction in the Royal Canadian Navy. Things at Brightlands became very different, as this abridged account by the House Captains for the spring term in 1955 implied:

> *One November afternoon when we arrived back at Brightlands after school we were very amazed to see Mr Wood climbing around the chimney pots. He was looking for a suitable place for a television aerial. Now, if we are quick, quiet and good we are allowed to watch television two or three times a week.*

> *The end of term found us all busily decorating Brightlands. Everywhere was transformed into a blaze of colour. Room 8A won the competition with a very artistic effort and a tidy dormitory. We had two Christmas spreads! Mabel cooked us a sumptuous dinner and there were hundreds of sixpences in the plum puddings. Miss Guest gave us a lovely tea-party, and the surprise this year was that we each had an ice-cream from Father Christmas. We said good-bye to Wilkins, who has gone to Hereford, and to Tucker, who has become a day boy. This term many of us have been victims of 'flu, but thanks to Sister we have kept very fit in spite of the cold weather. We are sorry that so many of our rugger matches have had to be cancelled, but we have had some good snowball fights. We are very lucky to have Mr Wood as our housemaster. He has an excellent collection of gramophone records, ranging from 'Hillbilly' and Doris Day to Chopin and Beethoven. If we are awakened to the strains of 'Bell Bottom Blues', 'The Naughty Lady of Shady Lane', or 'Get Up, Me Boys', we know the mood is good, but if the choice is of a more serious nature and the rising call is 'Get out of bed you bunch of savages' - we are forewarned!*

In 1955, Brightlands had a real colonial team for its housemaster was Canadian and the house tutor, Lee Stafford Bush, came from New Zealand. When Stafford Bush returned to his home country at the end of 1955, he was replaced by another New Zealander, Bert Finn, who also planned to stay in Britain for a short time but then had different ideas, ultimately settling and staying at DCPS for the rest of his working life. Brightlands ticked over happily under James Wood. The plays and the patrols continued, as did the annual Fathers' cricket match and Open Day. A young house tutor to arrive at Brightlands in January 1958 was Roger Shakeshaft:

> *Coming straight from the staff of a small residential prep school, the experience of my first term at Brightlands was electric! Wood, a serving naval officer in the war, was a Newfoundlander by birth and upbringing (he told me he voted against union with Canada in the 1949 referendum) and he had no experience of English boys' boarding schools. His knowledge of procedure owed more to Frank Richards and Thomas Hughes than Doctor Arnold. His personality had magnetic appeal to the boarders. He ran Brightlands like a private club, and day staff were discouraged from making social calls. In the boys' eyes he could do no wrong. At one time, I remember, towards the end of the month when cash was short, boys were willing to lend him money to tide him over until pay day. I hasten to add that he declined this feudal offering. On the subject of money, I am reminded that an allowance of two shillings was distributed to the boys after lunch on Saturday which was then eagerly spent in the shops at Dulwich Village. What was special about Brightlands as a boarding house at that time? Simply, it was the extent of freedom offered to the boys in the grounds and around the village. Coming from a conventional boarding school this struck me as very progressive for the 1950s. By and large the boys did not abuse this privilege: they seemed very happy and as a result moved on to public school both street-wise and confident to take on authority when it came. I came across hardly any homesickness and saw no bullying.*

James Wood (left) at Brightlands on Open Day in 1954, not long after he became Housemaster. Freddie Taylor (FNT) is in the centre and on the right is Jack Guy who was visiting with some boys from Coursehorn who would be joining Brightlands the following term.

Wood remained at Brightlands until the autumn term 1959, by which time he had at last persuaded Leakey to let him stand down. His so-called short stay had lasted for five years. Brightlands then found itself with a new housemaster, and again things were different. Michael Stephenson, an old boy of the Prep, and his wife and family moved into the cottage opposite and supervised the operation of the house from there. Inside the house itself were two resident tutors and a State Registered Nurse. Shakeshaft was joined by Malcolm Curtis and, under Stephenson, the two of them had considerable influence in the day-to-day running of the house. Shakeshaft continued to produce the annual house play started a decade earlier by Clelland and which in 1960, for example, was an adaption of *Robin Hood*. He also organised the annual Brightlands Sports Day held each summer, and Malcolm Curtis started a house choir which made a contribution to the spring concert, although this did not continue after he left. His major contribution to the well being of Brightlands was that he persuaded Leakey to obtain a swimming pool for the boarders. It was constructed of wooden panels with a plastic liner and a great deal of energy was put into its construction by the boys themselves. It proved to be so popular that it was soon doubled in size and lasted for about thirty years, by which time its life had expired and it was no longer necessary as the pool at Alleyn Park was built. The arrival of the Stephensons marked a change to the more liberal attitude which was to sweep through all schools in the 1960s and beyond. Corporal punishment was phased out and boys were beginning to be called by their forenames, both amongst one another and when the moment was right, from staff as well.

Boarders giving a hand to the construction of the swimming pool in 1964

Because the water was unheated, use was limited to about six weeks a year at best.

Demise of the pool, - 1993

David Griffith-Jones and his vegetable patch where the pool once was - 2004

At the end of the summer term in 1961, there was another change. Michael Stephenson gained an appointment to be the Headteacher at a comprehensive school in Bristol, having been at Brightlands for only two years. Leakey was about to become the full-time Head at Cranbrook, having decided that being the head of two growing schools at the same time was not fair to either, and Hugh Woodcock was about to become the sole headmaster of DCPS in London. The obvious person to become the housemaster at Brightlands was the former master-in-charge at DCPS Cranbrook, J B Maclean. Hamish Maclean and his wife Olivia arrived at Brightlands for the autumn term in 1961 and Roger Shakeshaft saw in his third housemaster in five years. The Macleans were not entirely happy about leaving rural Kent and coming to the Borough of Camberwell, as it then was. They had become settled where they were and felt that Leakey could have found a place for them on his staff at Cranbrook. But Brightlands needed a housemaster, Leakey did not need a master-in-charge at Cranbrook as he was doing the job himself, and this seemed the simplest answer. He did try to make London as comfortable as he could for the Macleans. The cottage was completely refurbished and the Macleans decided to call it *The Bothie*. Other improvements were made and Messrs Curtis and Shakeshaft and Sister Sylvia Burgess continued inside the main house as they had done before. The four patrols continued and Brightlands soon settled into a new regime. Maclean was a sportsman, competent in youth and fervently enthusiastic in his later years, so the house became a place for the hale and hearty with a clear emphasis on sport. He even introduced house boxing for a while.

The Maclean era passed uneventfully by and large, the termly reports making a strong reference to the success or otherwise of boarders on the sports field. The spring terms were noted for outbreaks of influenza and sometimes chicken pox and, horror of horrors, heavy snow in the spring term of 1963 meant that virtually no rugby was played before the last few weeks of term. For the summer, Maclean instigated cricket matches with boys from The Orchard, one of the junior boarding houses of the College and almost next door to Brightlands. Open Days were held towards the end of the summer term, with a cricket match against the fathers in the morning and an athletics sports, organised by Shakeshaft in the afternoon. The four patrols, Collingwood, Marlborough, Nelson and Wellington continued, so there was a competitive spirit within the house. Afterwards, a sumptuous tea was always provided by Mabel Drewry and Hilda Ruffle. Mabel and Hilda, who had joined Brightlands after the war, lived in the cottage opposite until the Macleans arrived and gained much affection from the boys as cooks often do. They just went on and on as housemasters came and went, and Shakeshaft's spring plays became more ambitious as each year passed. The Brightlands library, organised by the boys themselves, gradually improved during the Macleans' time, one righteous librarian writing in 1964:

> *During this term, we have been all out to encourage boys to read good books, and so far we have been quite successful. Unfortunately boys read comics and annuals more than good literature, but the difficulty has been partially overcome by removing these and putting them out of sight.*

One wonders what the author, G J Reynolds, is doing now.

There was a regular pattern of boys new to Brightlands each September. A few came from the day school at Alleyn Park, but a much larger proportion came from Coursehorn (DCPS Cranbrook) which at that time was only taking boys up to the age of eleven. Local boys there went to Cranbrook School, and boys wishing to go on to public schools through scholarships and Common Entrance came to Brightlands at 13 . Conversely boys in Dulwich who wanted or needed to board between the ages of 9 and 11, as I myself did, went to Coursehorn although not a great many did so. Until the mid 1960s, Brightlands only had boarders from the ages of 11 to 13 and boarding meant full time, with boys going home during term time for the half-term break, which was for many years nothing more than a long weekend. In addition there was a weekend away at either side of half-term, these breaks being known as exeats. If boys lived abroad, or if long distances were involved, some inevitably remained at school over half-term, and various activities were laid on for them, although every effort was made for these boys to stay with friends whenever possible. From the mid 1960s, a few boys started to go home for weekends and the idea of weekly boarding was born again, although at the time it was considered the exception and not the rule.

In the spring term of 1965 Shakeshaft announced that his play *Afternoon at the Seaside* by Agatha Christie would be his last, as he intended leaving to marry the former school sister, Sylvia Burgess, although he continued on the day staff for a further eight years. One of the major improvements in the house at that time was the installation of central heating, which followed a particularly cold winter. There had still not been any heating in the dormitories and although the boys may have been 'toughened up' by the experience, this may also have been a contributing factor to the regular influenza outbreaks already referred to.

At the end of the summer term in 1966 the Macleans decided to call it a day. They had been at Brightlands for five successful years, and during their time there had been an atmosphere of discipline coupled with friendly camaraderie. Maclean had been a major in the London Scottish Regiment, and this was reflected in the way he chose to administer Brightlands – a sort of junior Army in Civvy Street. Change was on the way.

If Hugh Woodcock sought a different philosophy at Brightlands, he certainly achieved it by the appointment of Peter Ashenhurst as housemaster with his wife Denny in September 1966. Things changed overnight. Ashenhurst felt that Brightlands should be home for the boys, with a far softer and more caring atmosphere, so out went the harshness of school furniture and the formality of a school routine, and in came curtains, multi-coloured walls, attractive pictures and vases of flowers. Never known to raise his voice, Ashenhurst achieved his objectives by gentle persuasion. During his period of tenure the number of boys coming from Coursehorn grew and grew, so that there were almost sixty boys in the house at one stage. Change was not always easy to accept or to implement, and despite the good intentions, the three years the Ashenhursts spent at Brightlands were beset by problems. To start with, Mabel and Hilda, who had never been entirely happy since they had been compelled to leave the cottage to make way for the Macleans, decided that it was time to retire. They were replaced in the kitchen by Nancy Abbott, Welsh and highly volatile to say the least. In the house itself, house tutors came and went, the longest serving being Peter Cook, who had replaced Roger Shakeshaft and who, like him in due course, was to marry a member of the school staff, Ruth Green.

Peter's wife Denny was Head of Art at the main school, managing to co-ordinate a great deal of redecoration within Brightlands at the same time. Much needed to be done, including brightening up the dormitories which had again become drab, and with an ever-increasing number of boys arriving at Brightlands each term, suitable and comfortable living space somehow had to be found for them. Brightlands was bulging at the seams and at one point several boys were 'farmed out' to live with the Vicar and his wife at the Vicarage at St Stephen's Church in College Road. Although there was still school on Saturday mornings at that time, very few boarders were away for the weekend so arrangements had to be made to entertain the majority who remained. The situation was not made any easier by the fact that the Housekeeper/Matron was French and her spoken English was limited. Her remark one day that 'Go has a co', implying that a boy called Gough had a cough, is legend.

By living opposite in The Cottage, the Ashenhursts were not always on the spot when problems arose and being responsible for so many boys under a different roof was far from easy. Somehow each challenge and each problem was overcome as Brightlands steadily settled into a new regime. Ashenhurst had the strong belief that the boarders should be a united group and not be divided amongst themselves, so the four patrols were phased out and patrol leaders became house captains. The traditional offerings by the orchestra, the choir and the boarders' play continued, and it is worth mentioning that in 1967 the play (*The Haunted Barn*) was produced by David Tanner, a young student teacher fresh from school. Later he was to become the Headteacher at a large London comprehensive, so he must have learnt something from his time at Brightlands. The concerts continued for a few more years, but music and drama were growing rapidly at the school as a whole and before long the boarders became fully involved with them.

The Ashenhursts agreed to be at Brightlands for three years, and in the spring of 1969 they announced that they had done their time and wished to move on. Again there was to be a change. A consideration in Hugh Woodcock's mind must have been that the housemaster-in-the-cottage arrangement was not a good one, and there was not enough space in the house itself for a family unless major alterations were made. No one was more surprised in the summer of that year than I was when Woodcock invited me to be the Housemaster. In the interests of continuity, he hoped that I too would accept the post for a minimum of three years. I would have a housekeeper/matron living in, and in the cottage opposite would be an assistant housemaster with his wife and family. So in September 1969 I moved into Brightlands as housemaster, and David Whytehead and Anne moved into the cottage. We were to be there for twenty-five years.

Our years at Brightlands were happy ones by and large, and although there were the occasional set-backs, our time was generally successful and well spent. Things started very differently in that first autumn term for although there was some domestic continuity, there were far fewer boys. The Ashenhursts had employed Nancy Goldberg to superintend the boys' clothes after Maggie Glenn and Joan Taylor had retired and she was happy to continue, as was the temperamental cook, Nancy Abbott. I also inherited in the kitchen someone called Winnie, who must have been nearly eighty years of age and who had been slaving away there since I had been a boy at Brightlands, and of course she remembered me. She told me that she had seen housemasters come and go, she would see me out and then call it a day. She stayed for a few years but did not fulfil her promise!

Lois Stebbing-Allen was my first matron/housekeeper. Intelligent, alert, and the daughter of a prep school headmaster, she soon became a surrogate mother not only to the boys, but to me as well, and her wisdom and experience were invaluable. But the greatest change was with the boys. At his peak, Ashenhurst had as many as sixty boys in the house. I started with just thirty, respectable by today's standards, but a considerable shortfall then. The reason for this sudden drop in numbers was that boarders stopped coming in from Coursehorn as Cranbrook School began to accept boys at 13. Coursehorn therefore kept its boys until that age, and the automatic supply of boys from there to Brightlands at the age of 11 came to an end. At Cranbrook, Leakey considered that all boarders should go there, and the Brightlands facility was no longer necessary. I would be a caretaker housemaster who would just see out the boys currently there. In London Woodcock had different ideas. He considered that boarding was an integral part of DCPS life, making it known that boarding at Brightlands could start at the age of nine. Although there were the inevitable moments of homesickness from boys of all ages, they were generally happy in their surroundings and in consequence numbers grew steadily, reaching 45 within a couple of years.

At the time I saw my job as threefold. First I had prime responsibility for the boys and their day-to-day welfare. Although it was a twenty-four hour obligation, the well being of pupils in one's charge is the role of all teachers. Secondly there were the parents. By and large they were agreeable and co-operative although inevitably over the years, there were a few who were inclined to blame the school for their son's shortcomings, but these were in the minority. There was the added responsibility, and sometimes concern, when boys had parents living on the other side of the world. The third side of the job was the upkeep of the building and the welfare of the staff who worked within it. This resembled being a hotel manager, assisted of course by the matron of the day. I was not trained for this and learned a great deal as I went along. We employed all the domestic staff, arranged interior decoration, ordered the food and attempted to resolve domestic disputes with the staff, not always of the school's making. Amazingly, I had no budget to work towards, and was trusted to save money where I could and to spend it wisely. I remember doing some major rewiring myself, described later in a report following an inspection of the building: *some of the electrics have been installed by a competent amateur'!* I was glad to have been considered competent. Such practices are quite untenable and outside the housemaster's control today. Food is prepared by caterers, the staff employed by the school and the fabric of the building looked after by the school's maintenance staff. Budgets are strictly adhered to.

Things never stay the same and gradually there came a demand for boys to go home at weekends and be boarders just for the week. Initially, this move was frowned upon, the main reason being that just as a boy had become established in the boarding routine, he would go home for a weekend and would have to start all over again on Monday morning. Soon it became clear that the advantages of weekly boarding, as it became known, greatly outweighed the disadvantages, and by the mid 1970s it was being actively encouraged. Quite apart from anything else, it was an excellent way to 'break in' boys who were going on to board at their next schools, and more and more came in to board for their final year. A number continued the full boarding option, so for a while the house was divided between 'full boarders' and 'weekly boarders'. Gradually, the scales began to tilt in favour of weekly boarding which became more and more popular. By 1984, the number of full boarders had fallen to single figures so that from the school's point of view it was no longer viable for boys to stay on over a weekend. The end of full boarding meant that the sons of parents who were abroad with the Foreign Office, construction companies or with the Armed Services, could no longer be accepted and that was a disadvantage. When this change came about, I had been the Housemaster for fifteen years, the normal period of tenure, but it meant that I too became a 'weekly' which made a big difference, so much so that I continued at Brightlands with the Whyteheads for a further decade.

When the school had 'full boarders', there was the question of how they should be occupied over a weekend. After all, this was home of a kind and not school. There was always plenty of activity on Saturdays when there were school matches in which boarders were invariably involved. When it was fine, the grounds were a great area to let off steam, especially in the summer when the pool was an added attraction. However it was unheated and relied on warmth from the sun only, so if the weather was cool, so was the water. Visits to Dulwich Village and other local places were permitted by boys in groups on their own as long as it was established where they were going and that they signed a book indicating their time of departure and return. Permission was sometimes granted for the older boys to visit Central London on their own either by bus or train, although not many took advantage of this concession. Today such ventures are out of the question. In the evenings, there was television to fall back on, and in the closing years a video was acquired through the generosity of the PTA and video films were hired, the boys taking it in turns to choose which film was seen whilst I, sometimes less successfully than others, did the vetting. A popular evening activity for a long time (strictly at weekends only) was when boys went off to one of the dormitories to play a sort of hide-and-seek game called 'Colditz'. I always felt that entertainment which the boys devised for themselves was preferable to television or videos. Boys could also go out with parents or friends for the day so long as prior notice was given and, although exceptions were made, the normal time of return was 7.30 p.m.

Sundays were the domain of David Whytehead. The boys had a 'lie-in' and were encouraged not to cause a disturbance before 8 a.m. Nancy Abbott provided an enormous high cholesterol breakfast and then there was a period when boys wrote letters home. Church going followed and every effort was made to make these visits as varied and as interesting as possible. It was compulsory unless there were genuine grounds for non-attendance. In a typical term, two visits each were made to the local parish church at St Stephen's and the Dulwich College Chapel, and twice a term the boys conducted their own services, with a visiting preacher, in the school hall. Allowing for half-term and the two exeat weekends, for the remaining two weekends visits were made to churches away from Dulwich, these sometimes being followed by a picnic and a visit to a place of interest. Examples were many and varied but among them were the Guards' Chapel in London, St Clement Danes and the parish church at Westerham with a visit to Chartwell afterwards. I especially remember being made welcome at Canterbury Cathedral, where we were invited to sit in the choir for the service, and afterwards a visit was made, with a picnic, to Howlett's Zoo nearby. Sunday afternoons were normally not organised, and the weekly boarders returned in the evenings, although later on some came back on Monday mornings. The normal weekday programme was then adopted for Sunday evenings, and the times at which boys went to bed depended upon their age.

As well as weekend visits, other outings were arranged during the year from time to time. At Christmas there was a lunch followed by party games which seemed to become better year by year, and more often than not the boarders were taken to a London theatre in December,

The Housemaster with three of his matrons -
from L to R: Eileen Shepherd, Lydia Spurrier and Lois Stebbing-Allen
(Nancy Abbott, cook for many years, is extreme right)

assuming something suitable could be found. The last night of the summer term was usually spent at the Royal Tournament and when the boys returned at about 11 p.m. there was a final dip in the Brightlands pool before bed. This was always a moment of reflection because it occurred to me each year that boys who had worked and played together as an integral group for months, or even years, would never gather together again.

On the domestic front, Lois Stebbing-Allen, the first matron, was succeeded by Eileen Sheppard, who also stayed for five years. Different, but efficient, she won the hearts of all by becoming fully involved in the house and accepting no nonsense from anyone. In 1981 she was succeeded by Lydia Spurrier who stayed for a further five years. She had the distinction of being in Brightlands when we had two diabetic boys, Alexis Pavlou and Andrew Curley. David Mann, the school doctor, said that the chances of having two diabetics out of forty in the house at the same time were unusual to say the least and we soon became experts at detecting the various aspects of insulin-dependent diabetes. Lydia Spurrier was followed by Ann Webb, whose stay was not as long as the others, and in 1988 Mary Royall appeared, by which time the job had changed as weekly boarding had become established. No longer did I have to make arrangements for matron's day off, a duty more often than not performed by Anne Whytehead. Mary Royall was the only one of my matrons to be a State Registered Nurse, and although it was not a necessity for the job, she certainly proved her worth when it came to giving the boarders their 'flu jabs.

My last matron was Heather Phillips, who left Brightlands when I did. Her previous experience as an air hostess meant that she could handle almost any situation, bearing in mind that apart from caring for the boys, the role of matron also included ordering the food, preparing menus and looking after the domestic staff with their periodic problems. From time to time, a boy would ask as he hurried off to school in the morning, '*What do you do all day matron?*' Little did he know. From the mid-1980s the school began to accommodate day boys who came into Brightlands for a week, sometimes for less, if there was room. There were many reasons why this happened and it proved to be very popular. Maybe day-boy parents chose to take a short holiday or there may have been work obligations away from home. Sometimes the boys themselves just wanted to try boarding to see if they liked it. No special arrangements were made for these 'short stay' boarders as they became known, and I often used to refer to them as our Country Club members. Invariably some did return as boarders later on, and just occasionally a boy chose to stay on as a boarder once his time was up simply because he had found that being with his friends was fun.

In 1992, Hugh Woodcock was succeeded as headmaster by George Marsh, and it was a time of social change. Marsh continued to show the same enthusiasm for boarding as his predecessor, but the number of boarders began to fall off again. One reason was the arrival of the Children Act 1989 which, though well intended, was introduced hurriedly and was inclined to show boarding school life in a poor light. Because Brightlands had less than fifty occupants, it was registered as a Children's Home and not a boarding school, to be inspected by the Social Services of the London Borough of Southwark like others of their homes in the area. The inspectors who came were pleasant enough, but seemingly out of their depth, in all probability having never set foot inside an independent boarding school before. They simply could not understand or accept why many of the boys were boarders because they wanted to be, and were happy to be there. In due course the procedure changed. Brightlands was registered as part of a school and the inspections became less social towards the problems of Southwark and more practical towards a school like DCPS. In 1994, David Whytehead and the matron (Heather Phillips) reached retirement age so we agreed to finish together at the end of the summer term of that year and hand the house over to a new team which would introduce fresh ideas and innovations. We had done our stint, so from the autumn term of that year 'Bunky' Symmes and his wife Lindsay and family arrived to start another era.

Almost immediately life at Brightlands was different again. Bunky, who came originally from the United States, had his own ideas about how a boarding house should be run and organised. Sensibly it was decided that, with his family, he should live in the house and not be detached from it as had been the case with previous housemasters in a similar situation. Extensive structural alterations within the building were made and the opportunity was taken at the same time to update the fire regulations and make other changes. All this resulted in there being less space available for the boys. Bunky's wife Lindsay undertook a programme of making the rooms more cheerful, especially the dormitories which, with fewer boys, appeared more spacious. With a husband and wife team at the helm the house became more family orientated, this reflecting the general emphasis towards pastoral care, now very much a part of school life. Even the rigidity of the term 'housemaster' gave way to 'houseparents' in certain circumstances and administratively there were changes too. The provision of food was put into the hands of the school caterers, and the upkeep of the building was no longer a part of the housemaster's responsibility. To some extent the role of housemaster became less autonomous, but it is still very much a twenty-four hour job. At the end of July 2002, Bunky and his wife completed five years at Brightlands and the call to retirement came to them too, certainly so far as boarding school life was concerned. Sadly the retirement which Bunky had planned and had anticipated was not to be for he died in February 2003 and his illness cast a shadow over the change at Brightlands which had already been planned. From September 2002, the new enthusiastic houseparents were Jeremy and Sophie Banks who brought with them their infant daughter, Emily. Very quickly she became the house mascot and a different and more youthful regime began. Before long, Emily was joined by sister Isobel and a scattering of cuddly toys and infant impedimenta created an atmosphere whereby the boarders began to find themselves becoming part of an extended family. Although there were more boys and the regime of discipline was different, this close association with a young family was not dissimilar from the way boarding had started with Mallinson in 1887.

Bunky Symmes (centre) at a Brightlands supper with his successor, Jeremy Banks - 2000

The 1990s were lean times for boarding schools generally, brought about partly by adverse publicity in the wake of the Children Act and spiralling costs resulting from the enforcement of new fire alarm systems and other mandatory regulations. No one doubts that boarding schools are better and safer now than they were, and gone are the days of Tom Brown. As the new millennium got under way so the face of boarding became brighter. The Boarding Schools' Association publicised an extensive campaign to show boarding in a better light, not only at the traditional boarding schools, but at state boarding schools as well, details of which are less known. More and more boarding schools introduced weekly boarding, and in this DCPS may be considered a pioneer. This provides the best of both worlds - a routine and an ordered life to be followed during the week, followed by the comforts of family life at weekends. Another option is 'flexi-boarding' which is being adopted by some schools and has been introduced at Brightlands. By this arrangement, boys come in for a few days or weeks, or maybe for two days or so in every week, depending on their commitments. They thus gain the flavour of boarding for a short time and this can be advantageous given the right circumstances, but a school boarding house can never become a hotel. Finally more and more boarding schools, both at primary and secondary level, have become co-educational. There is no scope for this at Brightlands at present, but who knows what the future holds? New ideas and new challenges need a new approach, and the appointment of a young vigorous and enthusiastic family at Brightlands has unquestionably provided it.

Boarding has been an integral part of DCPS almost from the start and headmasters through the years have actively encouraged and supported it. Boys who board at DCPS live in a magnificent building away from the school campus and experience a camaraderie not enjoyed by their day-boy counterparts. The future looks bright and it is to be hoped that the facilities and opportunities which Brightlands offers will continue for many years and that boarding will not be strangled by spiralling costs or social change.

Sophie Banks with Emily, Isobel and some of the boys from Brightlands (2004)

Into the 21st Century: boarders busy with computers

11 Puppies and Bulldogs

When DCPS started in 1885, it did not offer the age range to pupils that it does now, and gradually the age of entry came down as space became available and as the demand for places grew. Until 1922, boys entered the school between the ages of 7 to 13 and classes were numbered by years from First Forms at 7+ to Sixth Forms at 12+. The qualifying date was and has always been 1st September, and from 1893 all year groups worked together in the somewhat cramped conditions of 44 Alleyn Park. Boys had most of their lessons in their own classrooms, the staff teaching them going from room to room at the end of each period. The only place where boys could go to play at break times was part of what is now the Lower School playground. No attempt was made to segregate the age groups, although Leake referred to the 7 year olds as 'Puppies' and that was the name by which they were generally known.

By 1922 there was a need, as well as a demand, for boys to come to DCPS at an earlier age than 7 and Number 44 was clearly not large enough. To create the space needed, Leake decided to move the boarders away from the main school site so that the building which had been their sanatorium was no longer required by them. It must be remembered that in 1922 the school possessed only 42 and 44 Alleyn Park, with the playground behind 44 and a large lawn behind 42. Beyond the lawn, which also served as a tennis court in the summer, was an area of grass the size of a small football pitch known as 'The Paddock'. This paddock had a long line of chestnuts to one side but only four remain today to give some idea as to where it once was. On the other side of the paddock in a more isolated position and facing the drive which led to Lord Vestey's Estate at Kingswood House, was this sanatorium building. Leake decided that he could provide more teaching space by converting it into a new junior school for boys from the age of 5 to 7. As they would be taught in a separate building away from the main school facing Alleyn Park, it would thus be an Annexe to it, and this was the name it quickly gained and has kept ever since. It was principally single storeyed with two large rooms and two smaller ones at ground level, and a small room at the top of a flight of stairs which became a staff room. One of the large rooms was big enough to be used as an assembly hall where concerts were sometimes held, but during school hours it could be partitioned into two smaller classrooms. Placed in charge of the new Annexe was Miss G A Osborne upon whom Leake conferred the grand title of 'Headmistress'. She had formerly been on the staff of Dulwich High School, a local girls' school which has long since disappeared. Later described as a woman of great

The old Annexe and the Paddock.
Only the overhanging leaves of the horse chestnut tree (top right) remain today.

charm and a genius at handling young children, she won the hearts of many, and under her direction the Annexe flourished. Within a year of its opening, it was home to nearly 70 boys *'all doing their best'* she wrote, *'and eager to get into 'The Big School' as soon as possible.'* Although Leake remained as overall headmaster, the Annexe developed a degree of autonomy with its own library, its own sports day which was always held on the adjacent paddock, and its own open day, then known as Hobbies Day. From time to time there were lantern slide lectures for Annexe boys in the main school hall and most important of all, the tribe system was moved down to include the Annexe boys as well, including the award of good and bad slips. Such was their enthusiasm that we read of 7 year olds taking their tribe duties very seriously. Miss Osborne must have had considerable influence over the editor of the magazines in the late 1920s because news about Annexe activities is often greater than that from the main school itself. Of work in the Annexe a boy called Lloyd, who was just seven, wrote in 1926 about one of his history lessons:

> *My best lesson is History, all about Alfred the Great and Hereward the Wake. Small children nearly always think of Alfred and the burning of cakes, but we cannot be sure this is true. He did a lot for England; he built churches and he gave his soldiers better armour. I am afraid I have no time left to tell you about Hereward the Wake.*

But what of 'The Puppies'? Since Leake himself had introduced that endearing name to the younger boys, one wonders why it disappeared while he was still headmaster. The arrival in 1922 of boys in the Annexe who were aged 5 – 7 meant that they were younger than the 'puppies' who were over in the main school, so there was a misnomer. For a while the Annexe boys became known as 'Annexe Puppies' and the boys in the their first year of 'Big School' were promoted to 'Bulldogs', but clearly there was confusion about who was who, and the terms began to be used less often. This reference from 1923 shows how the tribe system was well established, and it also gives an insight into boys' interests at the time:

> *It may console Mohican puppies to know that although they failed to distinguish themselves on the sports field, in the matter of good slips for work, they easily outdistanced their fellows. This term the craze has been for collecting cigarette card pictures. Some of us remember last summer when newts and tadpoles were the rage. At least cigarette cards do not escape and wriggle.*

Things could have been a great deal worse!

As early as 1927, there was a sign of things to come. The Annexe, still numbering about 70, began to take in boys aged 4 or 5 mainly, but not exclusively, the siblings of older boys already in the school. For the next decade it flourished, maintaining numbers and steadily feeding boys through to the main school, sometimes in mid-year, but more generally at the end of each academic year as now. Teaching in the Annexe in the 1930s was a Miss Loveridge and more than a few former pupils have made mention of her. She can perhaps be best summed up by John Bazalgette (DCPS 1930-1936):

> *Miss Loveridge was a very pretty lady with whom we were all in love. I do not know how good a teacher she was, as I never had anything to do with her, but if she smiled at you as you went by, your day was made!*

In 1932 there was a small re-organisation within the school. The 11 to 13 year olds became known as Upper School, the 9 to 11 year olds were Middle School and the 7 to 9 years olds were Lower School, but these were divisions by name and age only and there was no autonomy between the groups. The Annexe, with its own headmistress, provided for the 5 to 7 year olds with a few younger ones, and the terms 'Puppies' and 'Bulldogs' were finally dropped. Such was the demand at the time that Leake wanted to extend the school still further by offering a section for boys aged 3 to 5. This was a major step forward as nursery education was in its infancy and it was practically unknown for a prep school to have such a facility. A hut, which was in effect a revolving summer house, was acquired and was placed on the playground next to the Annexe where it became home for a dozen or so small boys. Initially they were under the care of a Miss Gray and a Miss Hudson. The idea caught on and soon there was a demand for more to be admitted, but the recurring question of space and where to put them had yet to be resolved. In 1935, and as a short-term measure, DCPS obtained a wooden pavilion from Dulwich College when a large brick one was built there to replace it. This pavilion was placed at the back of the garden of 42 Alleyn Park and accommodated a small number of infants some as young as two. In charge was Miss Helen Dickson, who had joined the Annexe staff in 1932 and who was to play a large part in the life of DCPS in the years to come, principally at Cranbrook.

By this time, Leake was playing a lesser part and Leakey was having a much greater influence in school affairs. The wooden pavilion soon became inadequate and a site for a new nursery and kindergarten would have to be found if the school were to achieve its objective. When it was clear that Brightlands School could not be obtained[1] Leake, with Leakey's encouragement (and probably his financial backing as well), decided to replace the pavilion at the back of 42 Alleyn Park with something new, other sites including one in Dulwich Village having been considered first. This 'something new' was not going to be just any old building. It was to be a single storeyed nursery and kindergarten of revolutionary design for children aged 3 to 5. Buildings of striking design were not new to Leakey. He had already had built a spacious and most unusual home for himself on Sydenham Hill (Six Pillars) and so pleased was he with it that he approached the same architect, Val Harding, to design a new nursery school for him.

Inside the 1937 Nursery.
Although not very complimentary, the picture shows how spacious it was – a rarity for DCPS at the time.

1 see Chapter 10

Before construction could begin, the old wooden pavilion was dismantled and taken to the school field in Grange Lane where it remained for many years until eventually it was destroyed by arson. The former summer house hut was then used by the Annexe for class 1E, its occupants otherwise being known as 'The Hut Boys'. David Mann (DCPS 1935-1939) remembered his first encounter with Miss Osborne and his experiences of the hut:

> *I first met Miss Osborne through my brother's attendance. I was four and he was nearly seven. He took me into the Annexe and said to Miss Osborne, 'You needn't put him into 1E because he knows his two times table'. I was put into 1D. 1E was an open glass-fronted wooden hut which could be turned to face the sun. It was invariably too hot in summer and too cold in winter.*

DCPS was thus one of the first, if not *the* first, private school in Britain to have a nursery department and it was not only the building which was revolutionary. Girls, albeit aged 3-5, were also admitted for the first time, and the magazine of the day proclaimed that there were several cries of 'things aren't what they used to be'. Things calmed down when it was realized that the new building was entirely separate from the main school itself. Although boys aged 3 to 5 had been accommodated at DCPS from as early as 1927 their departure, first to the old pavilion and then to the new building, meant that the Annexe was able to expand and reorganise.

This article appeared in the *Croydon Times* in June 1937.

NEW NURSERY SCHOOL AT DULWICH
Aims and Ideals
A well-attended meeting of parents and friends was held on the evening of June 23rd at the Dulwich College Preparatory School to mark the opening of the new Nursery School. The object of the meeting was to explain the aims and ideals of the Nursery School movement.

School Welcomed
Miss de Lissa, the chairman of the Nursery School Association of Great Britain gave a general account of the movement and especially welcomed this school as one of the very few private nursery schools opened for children of the professional classes. Dr Elder pointed out that nursery school was designed to teach children to help themselves and to look after themselves.

The New Building
After the meeting, the new building was open for inspection, and the clever and attractive design of the architect, Mr Val Harding, was very highly praised. The school consists of two large rooms, painted in bright and lively colours, well furnished with toys and apparatus and provided with separate washing and lavatory accommodation. Both rooms open onto the paved playground, which is equipped with sand pit, paddling pool and climbing frame. The school has its own kitchen where the children's special meals are prepared. Although the building has only recently been completed, there are already over 30 children in attendance.

It is a pity that a building of such striking design should only have a life span of some thirty years. The bomb which fell in 1940 and which destroyed or damaged neighbouring houses in Alleyn Park sealed its fate. Although much repair work was done after the war, the single storey building had suffered foundation damage which meant that it could not be built over so was wasteful in terms of space, for DCPS that most precious of all commodities. As a result it was demolished in 1969 and the present changing rooms and rooms above stand now where the old Nursery once was. Had it survived, it would probably have become a listed building.

In 1938, a combined prospectus for the Annexe and Nursery was produced for the first time, but nothing untoward was in anyone's mind when it appeared and events for the summer term in 1939 seemed to be a case of business as usual.

These excerpts from the prospectus convey an impression of life for the younger boys at the time.

Nursery

Nursery children are accepted from 2 years old in a modern building where they are prepared by free and organised work and play, to take their part in school life. Children pass into the Kindergarten when they are ready for more formal work and remain there until ready for the Annexe.

Hours: 9.30 to 12 (morning) and 2 to 3.20 (afternoon)

No school on Saturdays.

Uniform is not compulsory but children must keep an overall, preferably of school pattern, and spare shoes at school.

Annexe

Monday to Fridays only: Saturday is a whole holiday

Morning school: Opens at 9 o'clock. Formal lessons do not begin until car boys arrive. Boys leave from 12 o'clock depending on form. Dinner can be taken at school at a cost of 1 shilling per day

Afternoon school: 2 till 3.20. The usual subjects are extra reading and writing, handwork, gardening, speech training, drill, organised games (football or cricket).

School uniform is not immediately compulsory in the Annexe apart from school cap, but in winter we prefer grey shorts and shirts with school ties, and grey pullovers rather than suits.

FEES PER TERM (for Annexe, Kindergarten and Nursery)

Entrance fee £1.00

From 2 years old until term in which 6th birthday occurs:

£5.10 shillings for whole day and £4.10 shillings for half a day.

From 6 years old until term in which 8th birthday occurs:

£7.10 shillings for whole day and £5.10 shillings for half a day

There is a reduction for brothers of £1.

No charge is made for Handwork, Stationery and Games. A health certificate must be presented on the first day of each term. Boys suffering from colds must not come to school.

When war came in September and the school evacuated to Cranbrook, most Annexe boys and all nursery children stayed with their families in London. Just 28 Annexe boys went to the camp but Miss Osborne did not go with them. For the boys who did go the harshness of the camp environment was not considered suitable for them so arrangements were made for them to stay at the Old Parsonage in Benenden where they were looked after by Helen Dickson. From all accounts, they were very comfortable there and again boys of Annexe age were housed away from the main school itself. When the move to Betws came the following May, rather more boys from the Annexe were evacuated and yet again they were housed in a building away from the main school at the Royal Oak Hotel because it was not big enough. Instead, Leakey was able to secure the lease on the nearby Llugwy Tea Rooms and the small hotel which accompanied them, so that was where the Annexe boys lived, although they did most of their lessons over the road in the former stables with the older boys. This time Miss Osborne was at Betws for a short time, but soon after the school in London reopened, she returned and looked after the boys of Annexe age there for much of the war-time period. Helen Dickson stayed on in Wales, soon accompanied by Barbara Herbertson, who also began to play a major role with the younger boys.

Barbara Herbertson was a formidable person but much respected and indeed revered by those who passed through her hands. 'Herbie', as she was almost universally known, joined the staff in 1934 and quickly gained a reputation as a gifted and devoted teacher. She came to teach Maths to boys of the 7 to 9 age range, although her influence over them quickly extended beyond Maths. When war came, she went to the Cranbrook camp and then to the evacuated school in Wales where she came into her own, taking on the responsibility for those boys who were above Annexe age (who were under the care of Helen Dickson) but who needed more care and attention than the older boys. So successful was this in Wales that when the school returned to London in 1945, Leakey decided to give the Lower School the same autonomy as had been given to the Annexe. As a result a headmistress was appointed there too and Barbara Herbertson was the obvious choice. Plays had been produced and performed separately by boys of Lower School age from the days when they were 'puppies', but not until 1945 did the Lower School become a separate department within the school as it is now.

In 1945, only a part of the original school in 44 Alleyn Park was available for the Lower School, but as new buildings appeared or were acquired, including in due course Numbers 40 and 38, so the Lower School was able to expand. Herbie was a progressive teacher for her time and new methods and subjects were investigated fully and put into practice if of any real value. She was always seeking better conditions for the Lower School and her 'girls', as she always called her staff, and boys and colleagues alike approached her with a degree of temerity. One short sharp shrill from her whistle when she was supervising lunch in the school hall, brought complete silence in a matter of seconds and no one spoke again until she said so.

Although the main part of the school was in Wales for the duration of the war, the London section managed to re-open a nursery section, albeit with fluctuating numbers, in the fine building which had been opened with such grandeur less than a decade earlier. Helen Dickson was in Wales so in 1941 Leakey employed another gifted and much loved teacher to administer the Nursery School. How fortunate he was to find Astrid Pehrson who became an indispensable part of the DCPS team, devoting the rest of her working life to the school. For almost thirty years Astrid Pehrson and the 1937 nursery were inseparable and I had the unusual but great privilege of being a boy under her care in the Nursery and then a colleague at the school many years later. Although I was very small at the time, she had not forgotten me, nor the many generations of boys who passed through after me. As a teacher of young children she had that remarkable skill of remaining fresh week after week, term after term and year after year. Eric Hamilton, a former parent, wrote of her:

> *Astrid Pehrson had a very special and unique quality that one rarely encounters. It is the quality of zest for life or aliveness. One that is almost magical, of wonder at being alive and of intensely enjoying the present. She was able to give her undivided attention to each child under her care and they responded to her genuine interest and love, as she saw the world through their eyes.*

Astrid Pehrson addressing nursery children on road safety in 1948 following the introduction outside the school of a 'Belisha Crossing'. Later these became 'Zebra Crossings'.

Her successor likened her to the kind lady in the 'Barbar' books who was always bursting with energy and ideas and ready for any fun that came along. Latterly she was accompanied by her black poodle 'Jet' and the two became inseparable.

The Nursery School at Gallery Road shortly after its opening in 1969

Apart from the early days with Helen Dickson, Astrid Pehrson was at the old building for most of its existence until its subsequent demise. One of the benefits of gaining 38 Alleyn Park in 1960 was that the ground floor was converted as an 'overflow' for the Nursery and although this was beneficial and created more space for nursery children, being in two places was not always convenient. By 1967, with a new classroom extension for the older boys already one year old, thoughts turned to modernising both the Nursery School and the Annexe in phases as money became available. In both cases the decisions taken were far reaching. The existing Nursery building was war-damaged and occupying space urgently needed, so once again a building of totally new design was planned, not this time at Alleyn Park, but in the grounds of the school's boarding house at Brightlands in Gallery Road in what had once been the kitchen garden. Planning permission was not immediately forthcoming from the Estate Governors, but eventually it was granted on the clear understanding that like its predecessor it must be a single storey building. Money was raised as a direct result of an organised appeal to parents, former parents and friends of the school, a common way of raising money in those days, often by Deed of Covenant. As a result a new Nursery came to be built and was opened in September 1969. Astrid

Pehrson took charge for the first four years and, although sad to see the end of the building where she had worked for so long, she said once that going into the spacious new nursery at Brightlands was the next best thing to paradise. Not everything from the past was left behind. Several items of equipment were dear to the hearts of Nursery children and Astrid did not want to abandon them. One was a homemade climbing frame in the shape of a boat called *Captain Pugwash*. This was meticulously dismantled piece by piece and re-erected at its new home. There was also an old hand-drawn delivery cart which had been donated years earlier by Slatters Bakery and this too found its way to Brightlands. Very quickly, the Nursery grew and prospered and as usual demand far exceeded the number of places available.

The Annexe too continued in London during the war. When Miss Osborne was forced to retire through ill health in 1945, she was succeeded by Muriel Spokes. Miss Spokes had joined the Middle School staff in London in 1943 and taught the youngest form under the most difficult war-time conditions. Her task of being in charge of the Annexe when the school returned from Wales proved to be very demanding as she had to deal with large numbers of parents whose children had returned to London and were seeking admission to schools. She only had limited places available and found it exceedingly difficult to turn away so many potentially sound boys. Ill health caused her to leave the Annexe in June 1948 before the end of term, but after a spell of sick leave she returned to teach the younger boys in the Middle School where she felt more at home and where she had started. She finally retired from DCPS in 1963.

Muriel Spokes was succeeded at the Annexe by Victoria Copley who had joined the school in 1945 as one of Leakey's immediate post-war appointments, initially to teach in the Middle School. An experienced teacher with traditional values, she was just the person needed to fill the breach at a moment's notice. She completed the summer term, and the autumn term had only just started when HM Inspectors arrived at the end of September. Their report was not too generous so far as the Annexe was concerned. It stated that basic work at that level was too formal and there was insufficient correlation between one subject and another. The classrooms were also far too small. Victoria Copley began to remedy some of these shortcomings and it soon became apparent that Leakey had made a sound appointment. She is remembered for her demand for high standards of work and behaviour and although she had considerable patience and a sense of humour, she was not a woman to be trifled with. She stayed at the Annexe for twenty years during which time almost a thousand boys had passed through her hands. In 1948, there were still about 70 boys in the Annexe, divided into four classes.

In 1952, to provide more accommodation for the Annexe, Leakey brought to Dulwich another glass hut which had once been a conservatory at his family home in Devon. The original revolving summer house had not survived the war and its replacement was more

The 'Gazebo' or 'Glasshouse' brought from Devon as an addition to the Annexe in 1952

The long hut on the paddock, brought from the camp in Cranbrook in 1950, originally an extension to the Nursery

The small paddling pool shared by Annexe and Nursery children, with the old gymnasium behind

or less where the original one had been. This enabled the Annexe to have an extra class, the total number of boys by this time creeping up to almost a hundred. Because of its peculiar shape, the new glass hut was quickly nicknamed 'The Gazebo' by some or simply 'The Glasshouse' by others. Like its predecessor, it was not ideal and was again cold in winter and far too hot in summer. At this same time, there were spare huts available from the former camp at Cranbrook which by then had been fully vacated, so Leakey brought another one of these to Dulwich. At sixty feet in length it was one of the larger ones and was placed at the side of the paddock where the swimming pool now stands. The hut was divided into two sections and was first used as an overflow for the Nursery. A smaller hut had already been brought from Cranbrook and placed near the Annexe, but this was used by the older boys for Geography and a little Science. When the Nursery was able to use the ground floor of Number 38 in 1961, the hut on the paddock was released to the Annexe which was then able to increase its size to 120 boys. Victoria Copley saw the Annexe through all these changes and it is to her credit that despite the limitations of space, her standards and reputation were such that the increase in demand for places made expansion necessary. Constant high standards of school work were achieved, proving the point that it does not have to be fine buildings which produce the best results.

The Nursery and Annexe were near neighbours at this time and both shared amenities such as the paddock, the old gymnasium, when it was not required by the older boys, and a small paddling pool built at the side of the paddock. There were no changing facilities and as the pool could only be used on warm days, it became the practice for whole classes of naked children to run around the paddock to get dry. This they apparently enjoyed in the innocence of the time, although it would not be acceptable today.

Whereas Astrid Pehrson had been able to enjoy a few years at the new Nursery, this was not something to be shared at the Annexe by Victoria Copley who retired in 1968. Her successor from the following January was Sue Cownie who had joined the Annexe staff two years earlier as a class teacher. Before long she had her first crisis. During the October half-term in 1972 she received a message at her home informing her that the hut on the paddock had been destroyed by fire, almost certainly the result of arson. The Headmaster was in Cornwall and asked Sue to go out and obtain two temporary classrooms, not exactly a straightforward task. The Bursar of the day, Douglas Ardron, came to the rescue and organised two portacabins which were hauled over the fence from Bowen Drive by crane and placed on the Annexe playground. Books and furniture were quickly organised and the boys concerned were able to return to school by the following Wednesday, only missing two days of school in the process. They were shown the burnt out shell of what had once been their classrooms and some were traumatised by it.

The hut after its destruction by fire in 1972 with the 'glasshouse' beyond (left centre). This survived the fire but was demolished soon after.

After a successful appeal for money to build a new Nursery, the decision was taken by the Board of Governors to implement the next phase of development: the construction of a new building for the Annexe. By 1972 this had become a ramshackle collection of buildings, including two portacabins, none of which had been designed for school use and most of which had outlived their usefulness. The cost of constructing a new Annexe, which would bear no resemblance to the one it replaced, was again supplemented by money raised from an organised appeal and construction began. Initially planned to be single storey, permission was granted for a small upper level as well. It was built on land slightly to the north of the old building which continued in use, so through 1973 disruption to school work was kept to a minimum. At the same time the paddling pool, the gymnasium, the gazebo and several other buildings were demolished and the adjacent paddock was much reduced in size. It would disappear altogether later when the swimming pool was built. The old Annexe had no hall, and morning assemblies and plays took place in the old gymnasium nearby. This was the old corrugated iron building from 1910 which had somehow survived the war and was basic to say the least.

When the new Annexe opened in September 1974 there was a great improvement in facilities all round, and with larger rooms class sizes were increased slightly so that the number of boys rose from 120 to 132. The greatest improvement was the hall at its centre which could be used for assemblies, a dining area, and with a stage at one end, a place for drama as well. Sue Cownie produced the Annexe play each year and the new hall gave her far greater scope. Not only had she been given considerable influence in the design of the new building, but she determined the syllabus to be followed, based on her own experience. Those were the days before a National Curriculum. There was a stock room for materials, and one of the strengths coming from that was that creative work could be displayed more readily. Lunch was transformed as well. Before 1974, Annexe boys used to eat in the main school hall having a very early lunch at 12 noon and it was often difficult to be finished before the Lower School arrived at 12.30 for theirs. Although the new building was luxury after the old huts, not everything that glittered was gold. To everyone's surprise, one of the flat roofs was not as sound as it should have been and in the early days there were a series of floods after heavy rain. With the disappearance of most of the paddock, the Annexe sports were held initially in the grounds of the Nursery School at Brightlands in Gallery Road, and crossing the South Circular Road with so many young children for this annual event was a nightmare. Within a few years the location moved again, this time to the school field in Grange Lane, which proved to be much easier.

As the Annexe settled down to a regular routine in its new home, changes were happening at the Nursery. After three years at Gallery Road, Astrid Pehrson announced her retirement. Her successor in 1973 was Fen Palmer who had been on the Nursery staff earlier, and after a short time working at sea, had returned to Dulwich. She had a daunting prospect on her hands. Although able to enjoy the spacious surroundings and the atmosphere of the new building, taking over from someone who had almost become an institution in her own right was not easy. Full of charm and poise, Fen soon had the parents and the children on her side and the happy atmosphere which had prevailed at the Nursery for so long continued, but her time was beset with problems. One was an invasion of Rottweiler dogs in January 1978 from a neighbouring garden early one morning resulting in the Nursery being under siege for a few hours. This was a terrifying experience for all concerned and for a short time the police themselves had difficulty approaching the building. After nine years, Fen decided that the lure of her Cotswold home was very strong and she decided to leave London, its problems and its Rottweiler dogs to other hands. In December 1979, she wrote:

> *There is so much that I shall miss at DCPS but the yearning for country life has become so overwhelming in the last few years that I have taken the plunge, admittedly with many a second thought.*

Jill Tingley, who had started the Nursery at Nash House at Dulwich Prep Cranbrook, saw that the job in Dulwich was in the offing, so seeking a new challenge, she applied. Woodcock was delighted and from January 1980 Jill Day, as she was soon to become, became the Headmistress of the Nursery at DCPS in London. It must have been interesting for her to compare the two. She continued to commute from her home in Kent and quickly brought in a whole lot of new ideas and innovations. Quite early on she remembered hearing the word 'dyslexia' mentioned on a course she was attending and she quickly became interested in the problems it created for young children. A lending library was introduced and emphasis was placed on the importance of starting children to read at a very early age. During the early 1980s, more children were entering the school from different ethnic backgrounds and Jill considered it important that they should learn from early on about festivals and religions other than their own. Parents were sometimes invited to visit the school in national costume and these became memorable events for the children concerned. Sports days at the spacious grounds at Brightlands took on themes such as 'Cowboys and Indians' and Jill remembered a great ethos and enthusiasm among the staff at the time. Just as Fen Palmer had found London a strain six years earlier, so Jill found the commuting to and from Kent each day more and more demanding and Kent was where she felt she really belonged. To there she returned in 1986, setting up a special needs department at Bedgebury School which was much nearer to her home. Once again DCPS needed a new headmistress for its Nursery department.

In September 1986, Jill Day was replaced by Helen Allan, a committed teacher who was eager to improve standards still further. She had been on the Nursery staff since 1976 and had been deputy there for a year. High standards were maintained, but soon there were more problems. The Nursery was broken into and severely vandalised on two occasions and this was very demoralising for the staff there. As it happened, her stay was short lived for after only three years she decided to leave teaching in order to raise a family. One happy event during Helen's time was a big reunion and display of photographs in June 1987 to mark the Nursery's fiftieth anniversary.

From the summer in 1989 Helen Allan was succeeded by Susan Metzner who was favoured by glorious weather for much of her first term. She adored young children and loved working with them, her philosophy being that they learnt through play, and that formal school should come a little later, a view which was not universally shared by all with whom she came in contact. More welcome was her decision that the children no longer needed an enforced rest after lunch each day. She felt that it was being done simply because it always had been and that it was not a good idea for over-active children to arrive home after sleeping at school, so the practice was dropped. Otherwise Susan described her time at the Nursery as being profitable and uneventful, but there was a gathering there to mark Hugh Woodcock's retirement in 1991 at which a very frail Astrid Pehrson made her last visit to the school. Happily a photograph recorded the event.

In September 1996 Helen Strange, who had taught at the Nursery under three previous heads there since 1983, became Head herself in a seamless transfer. She made it her mission to preserve the existing traditions of excellence, while continuing to develop the Nursery into a vibrant, happy and exciting environment. During her tenure, the school expanded to six classes with a huge increase in resources enabling both indoor and outdoor activities to reflect all areas of the curriculum. Information Communication Technology (ICT) was introduced with computers in every classroom, and opportunities were provided in the expressive arts, virtually unique for children of this age. Promotion of the Nursery's extended family was actively encouraged with parents welcome at all times, and a partnership between parents and staff steadily grew. One such highlight was

Four generations of Nursery Heads in 1991.
From left to right - Bridget Woodcock, Millie Herbert (who worked at the Nursery with all four
of them), Astrid Pehrson, Hugh Woodcock, Jill Day, Susan Metzner and Fen Palmer

Grandparents' Day celebrating the Queen's Golden Jubilee in June 2002. Involvement with the local community also became a priority with visits, as a public relations exercise, from organisations such as the Fire Service.

Links with the community - an aspect of modern Nursery school life.

In 1997 the government introduced Foundation Stage Curriculum Guidelines for children aged 3 to the end of the Reception year, and the Nursery was visited as exemplar before consultative documents were produced by the Department for Education and Employment (DfEE). In the same year the school became involved in the government's Nursery Voucher Scheme, the purpose of which was to provide greater educational opportunities for children of that age. This was beneficial financially to parents and as public money was involved, the Nursery became subject to periodic inspections by Ofsted. After one such visit in 2000 the report which followed simply stated that there were no weaknesses and nothing needed to be improved, an accolade in itself. As all these beneficial changes were taking place, it was never overlooked that the independence of the Nursery should not be lost and that the demands made upon it should not interfere with the opportunities which had evolved over the years. DCPS led the way in 1937 as being one of the first prep schools anywhere to offer nursery education. As the new millennium began, it clearly remained a leader in its field, thanks largely to a dedicated staff led by Helen Strange.

Having settled the Annexe into its new home in 1974, Sue Cownie quickly introduced an ordered and purposeful atmosphere which has continued ever since. For many years she taught almost all of the music and masterminded the annual Christmas concerts, somehow managing to involve each child every time in some way. As building programmes took shape in other parts of the school, so the spotlight moved away from the Annexe and memories of how life had once been, began to fade. One person who never forgot was Linda Stickney who described herself as the 'Annexe dogsbody'. From 1964 until 1982 Linda had an instant remedy for everything, from mending a fuse to dealing with cuts and bruises, and she became an integral part of Annexe life upon whom everyone could rely. Sue Cownie enjoyed fourteen years in the new Annexe setting high standards and preparing boys each year for the Lower School. With the satisfaction of a job well done no doubt, she announced that she would be retiring at the end of the summer term in 1986. At her final assembly she presented a silver cup to the Annexe called the Good Behaviour Cup which is still presented to a class or classes each Friday morning. Ruth Cole (DCPS Annexe Staff 1983-2002) considered it to be a great idea and a most engaging carrot to encourage young boys to work and behave within a group. She recalled:

It is amazing to see the children suddenly sit up straight and listen eagerly when comments made by teachers about how classes have behaved that week are read out at assembly. Then the children are asked if they really have behaved and which class they think deserves the cup. After further loaded questions and answers, the cup is presented with a flourish and is taken back to the classroom where it is put in a prominent place and proudly displayed for the whole week. At the end of the day it was wonderful to hear the boys proclaim to their parents that they had won the cup.

Sheila Meadows with a group of Annexe boys in 2004

Former pupils also remembered Sue Cownie with affection. Andrew Slatter (DCPS 1968-1978) wrote of her:

> *My teacher in the Annexe was Mrs Cownie, a very kind lady who was responsible for my knowledge of my times-tables. I remember cutting from card our own hot air balloons which would progress over a wall chart over various obstacles, higher and higher as one recited to the class, the tables. The pinnacle was when one's balloon arrived at the top of Everest. I have never reached that peak and to this day can be caught out on my twelve times table.*

By 1986 the Annexe, like the Nursery, had changed beyond all recognition and the hunt was on to find a successor for Sue Cownie. This time Woodcock chose to make the appointment from outside and Sheila Meadows was selected from a shortlist in December 1985. With broad experience gained in schools for all ages, the DCPS Annexe was a new venture for Sheila Meadows but from the start she knew it was where she wanted to be. Following a six-month period of familiarisation, boys greeted their new Head of Section, as she was later to become, at the start of the autumn term in September 1986. Being a traditional teacher, she soon realised that she had inherited a school within a school, where there were already high values and high expectations. She reassured her staff that in due course there would be changes, but they would be ones of progression of what was already in place rather than changes in direction. So without reducing the importance of the basic subjects, horizons were broadened by the introduction of new equipment,

The first Annexe carol service at St Stephen's Church - December 1999

especially for the teaching of Maths, as well as new and more interesting books. Within a few years greater time was being given to activities such as History, Geography, Art and Crafts and, most importantly, to Science. Music was extended too, with a new specialist teacher, to include instrumental lessons and music appreciation as well as singing and recorder playing which had generally gone before. Concerts involved all the arts: poetry, drama and music, and since 1999 the Annexe has had its own carol service in St Stephen's, the local parish church.

During the 1990s, physical activity took on a greater role with boys having their own PE kit and tracksuits at school with at least four periods per week being devoted to games or PE – a far cry from the old music-and-movement activities. With the availability of the former Mary Datchelor playing fields which are nearby, the Annexe sports were then held there each year, thus avoiding the need to cross the South Circular Road en route to Brightlands, so much dreaded by Sue Cownie. As well as appreciating the need for these developments, the introduction of the National Curriculum made them necessary and that, in conjunction with other obligations, led to a great increase in documentation as has been the case in schools everywhere. Unlike her predecessor, Sheila Meadows had no fires or structural alterations to contend with and no major events to celebrate, except possibly the Millennium activities and the Golden Jubilee in 2002. The changes she had

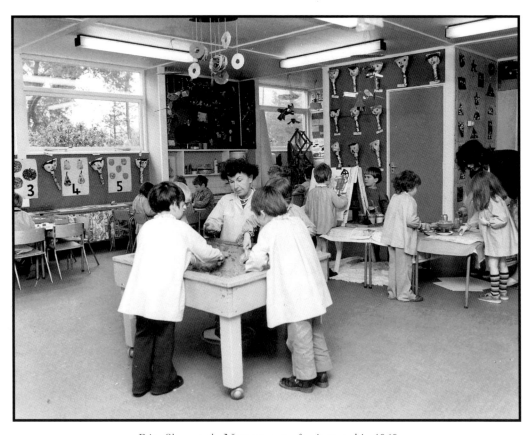

Rita Shaw at the Nursery soon after it opened in 1969

to implement were far-reaching in their own way, though perhaps not as sensational, as those that had gone before and she had the reward, with her staff, of seeing many happy and successful boys pass through her hands into the Lower School to start what is now Year 3. Sheila Meadows retired from the Annexe at the end of the summer term in 2004 and was succeeded by Emma Adriano. Future plans may one day see boys of Annexe age being housed elsewhere, but the traditional name will almost certainly follow it wherever it goes. It is a strange name for this important part of school, but it is in as much demand now as it has ever been, and it is as well to remember how it gained its name.

Although the Annexe and the Nursery have always been autonomous within the DCPS framework, there was for many years a link between them. Mention must be made of two sisters, Rita Shaw and Jose Dobson. Rita Shaw joined the Nursery staff in 1967 and remained for eighteen years offering stability, and doubtless sound advice, to three headmistresses. Her sister Jose was at the Annexe for almost as long from 1972 until 1988, thus providing a link for children moving from one part of the school to another. She too played an important part in the change from the old buildings to the new and for her last two years was deputy to Sheila Meadows, to whom like her sister, she was able to provide words of wisdom from her long association with the school. Moving from the Nursery to the Annexe sometimes caused problems for the boys too, some of them not anticipated

44 Alleyn Park, the original school building leased by Mallinson in 1893. This picture was taken in 1980 shortly before the addition of the new building and before the fire which destroyed much of its upper part.
(Courtesy Pat Soan)

as Gareth Rhys (DCPS 1993-2002) remembered only too well:

> *Before the Annexe I had not really learnt what school was about. Before then there were no uniforms or text books, and the step from Blue Class to Miss Costaras' class was a huge one. One of the major new problems was unforeseen and involved two lengths of cotton and a piece of cloth – yes, the dreaded shoelaces and tie syndrome. It took me for ever to learn how to tie up my laces and produce a neat knot for my tie without garrotting myself. Fortunately my friend Barnabas Purbrook was an expert at both so helped me to avoid serious embarrassment on more than one occasion.*

While the Annexe was enjoying a spacious new building and the Nursery was happily settled at Brightlands, the Lower School soldiered on at 44 Alleyn Park in the original building which Mallinson had obtained in 1893. It had suffered war damage, the rooms were far too small and a gully at the top of the building had a drain which was frequently blocked by tennis balls which had somehow reached that high from the playground far below. In consequence, floods after heavy rain were commonplace. From 1945 each class in the Lower School had its own mistress who taught most subjects as now, but a few masters went to the Lower School to take specialist lessons, such as Physical Education, or Physical Training as it was then. Captain Fleming's drill and influence even extended to the 7 to 9 year olds. Jill Caster, who joined the Lower School as a class teacher in 1953, remembered that school work was very formal at that time. There were no expeditions outside the classroom, there were weekly marks and reports and boys and staff referred to each other by their surnames

Barbara Herbertson in the Lower School Maths Workshop (1970)

only. Conditions were basic. There were three classrooms on the ground floor, three on the next floor and one half way up which was no more than a cubby hole. Soccer and sports kit stayed at school all term and was kept in string bags in the cellar. Changes did come but very slowly. A room in the loft which has now totally disappeared, had been used for a model railway club and this was converted as a place for handwork. Art took on greater importance and clubs were introduced during the lunch hour. When Hugh Woodcock arrived in 1962, Herbie still had considerable influence and although she was a traditionalist, she was not opposed to new methods and when it was decided to teach maths by a workshop method, she approved wholeheartedly.

Gradually as the school gained the use of other buildings more space became available for the Lower School again. A large room was made available for puppets, a popular club for Lower School boys, and for the first time the Lower School had a proper library to itself. Herbie made her mark on generations of boys, many of whom held her in high regard, even though a little fearful of her, and the Lower School was her domain until she retired in 1972. By this time, Jill Caster had been on the Lower School staff for almost twenty years and as it was the practice at the time to promote from within, she was the logical successor.

Different in manner and outlook but expressive in her ideas, Jill Caster, as the new Headmistress, achieved a more relaxed atmosphere without lowering standards. She introduced simple outings during class time to local places of interest and her annual

Jill Caster on one of her pond-dipping expeditions to Golden Staple Wood, near Tonbridge

pond-dipping trip became a firm favourite. For three or four weeks every spring term the Lower School entrance lobby became an entanglement of buckets, fish tanks, specimen glasses, magnifying glasses and fishing nets, these being made by each boy under her precise instructions. Payment for trips and outings made during school hours became an issue at this time, the question arising as to whether parents or the school should pay for them. Woodcock chose to increase fees to include payment for outings, not only in the Lower School but generally, and lunch, medicines and text books, which up to that time had been paid for by parents separately, were included in the termly fee. This, he considered, would reduce administration and make the overall cost simpler for parents. Jill's interests went well beyond occasional visits to local ponds. As well as being a formal classroom teacher, she created much enthusiasm for weaving and handwork and boys made letter racks, woven pot stands and table-mats during the lunch break. She was a great exponent of topic work, whereby boys learnt about a set subject for themselves through their own enquiry. Quite often these topics led to whole families becoming engrossed for days. One of her passions was Egypt and many of her colleagues will remember when she appeared one morning at break wearing her Egyptian jellaba, this being a gentle hint to her superiors that it was time to turn on the central heating! As she did not live too near the school, winter brought other problems. When snow and ice were forecast, she kept an 'overnight' case under her desk in case conditions became too inclement for her trusty Ford to get her back to Carshalton where she lived. Then she would stay with a local member of the Lower School staff and such was her standing with them, that she was always welcome wherever she went.

The highlight of Jill Caster's time as Head of the Lower School was undoubtedly the day in July 1983 when at last the boys were able to move into the spacious new building which was adjacent to the old. Yet it was ironic that although the boys with their teachers moved into new classrooms just as the school year was ending, her office remained where it had always been, but earlier on it had played a far bigger part in her life than she had first envisaged. It was here that a fire was started on the evening of Sunday 7th November 1982. Mention has already been made of the fire and the way the school reacted to it, but it was the Lower School which bore the brunt and where there was the most disruption. Throughout the previous summer, school life had been interrupted by bulldozers, bricklayers and bangs and bumps from all directions coming from the construction of the new building nearby. By the autumn term, the structure was approaching completion and thoughts were moving towards colour schemes and the types of furniture to be used. The Nursery and the Annexe had both been transformed by the luxury of modern buildings and now it was the turn of the Lower School to have a change in lifestyle. And a change it most certainly had – but not one which was anticipated. Anyone who witnessed the awesome sight of the fire that November night will testify to that. The result was utter confusion for a while as the whole of the Lower School was rendered unusable and the boys were sent home for a week. The week which followed was one of salvaging, cleaning, improvising and rescheduling. Pat Stallard (Lower School staff 1980-1999, later Pat Soan) remembered the fire and Jill Caster's reaction to it:

> *She was devastated by the loss, not only of the boys' possessions, but also many of her own personal artefacts collected from trips overseas. Gone too were her beloved woodwork and handwork tools and materials. However she rolled up her sleeves, donned a safety helmet and as soon as it was safe to do so, sorted through great heaps of charred remains. She salvaged many treasured books, and their smoky mustiness tainted the freshness of the new Lower School building for many years.*

As with the fire at the Annexe hut in 1972, portacabins came to the rescue, one of them even being placed on the sacred cricket lawn. When the boys returned, they were totally disorientated, but quickly a new pattern of school life emerged and whereas the old building had seemed so inconvenient and cumbersome, it now seemed compact and homely by comparison. The outer fabric of the old building was not damaged by the fire, and when reconstruction commenced the opportunity was taken to make changes and improvements, one of which included the addition of a new room over Jill Caster's office. DCPS has never lost a moment when it comes to finding a bit more space. The fire delayed the opening of the new building by a few months, but all was virtually ready by July of the following year when the boys packed up their books, vacated the temporary rooms and enjoyed just a week in the new accommodation before the school year came to a close. First impressions were somewhat mixed as Paul Chapman, who was a Lower School boy at the time, remembered:

> *To get in, we have to go through the old school. The new school is bright and colourful, it has taps with running water in each classroom, a whiteboard that you write on with felt tips instead of chalk, flowers, double glazing and carpets. The classrooms are big and roomy and easy to work in. It is very nice and I like it. But there is one problem: your voice bounces up so the teacher can hear you even when you whisper.*

The Lower School soon found its feet in its new home and Jill Caster remained at its head until she retired at the end of the summer term in 1989. In over forty years, there had only been two people who had been responsible for leading and managing it. Jane Maynard joined the Lower School staff in 1985 and within a couple of years had become Jill Caster's deputy. Twenty years later she was still there, by that time having served three Heads of Section, each having different qualities and each adjusting to the demands of the time. She considered that boys of Lower School age were at an endearing stage of their lives and of whom she wrote:

> *Their energy and enthusiasm, their curiosity and character make work in the Lower School fun and rewarding. We may now have computers and climbing frames, but conkers still refuse to fall from the trees sufficiently quickly and their appeal remains undiminished.*

Such are the qualities of a dedicated teacher. Jane mentions the appeal of conkers. They may not be quite so popular with the older boys now as they used to be, but conkers have a long tradition at DCPS. Maybe the horse chestnut trees by what was once the paddock have something to do with it.

When Woodcock chose to find a new Head for the Lower School, he again looked outside as he had done with the Annexe three years earlier, and Christine Radcliffe was appointed to that position from the start of the autumn in 1989. In many ways, there were similarities between those two sections of the school with the problems and complexities of one being shared by the other. Both were housed in purpose built buildings, and both Sheila Meadows at the Annexe and Christine Radcliffe at the Lower School inherited organised and effective departments which only needed fine tuning. Neither was in need of any major change of direction and it was the introduction and implementation of the National Curriculum which brought about the greatest challenges to all sections of the school during the 1990s. So far as the Lower School was concerned, the practice hitherto had been to study the Annexe syllabus, and then the Main School syllabus and try to plan a continuous programme with the Lower School in the middle.

The National Curriculum set out schemes of work for each subject from Years 1 to 8, with Keystages at the various levels which were often at variance with what had been done before. The whole timetable needed restructuring and for a newcomer this was a mammoth task. Woodcock retired in 1991 just as the changes were developing and it was up to his successor, George Marsh, to set the school as a whole on the right footing. One of the first things he decided was that some of the classes in the Lower School were too large, there being four classes of 24 boys in the First Forms (Year 3). The Second Forms (Year 4) had five classes of 20 boys each so they were acceptable. An extra room had to be found and despite all the enlargement to the Lower School which had occurred after the fire and with the building of the new teaching block, the old problem raised its head again. Where was the space for this extra room to come from? Marsh was in luck. The school had adopted outside caterers and he felt that it would be more convenient to them and desirable socially if the staff ate lunch with the boys in the school hall and not in their own dining room as had been the case until then, a decision which was not universally appreciated at the time. The room in question was in the Lower School and had been a part of it from the start, so the room was found and in a convenient place. The number of boys stayed the same, but both year groups then had five classes of approximately twenty boys in each.

The National Curriculum brought other changes to the Lower School. In 1990 Science was not timetabled and there was no provision for computer work, later to become ICT, but in due course these were introduced and more French was taught. Christine Radcliffe also decided that the system of rewards and sanctions within the Lower School was outdated. 'Detention' for poor behaviour and 'Corrections' for work which was not of the standard expected, were phased out and greater emphasis was placed on work and behaviour being good rather than bad. A sticker system of rewards was introduced and a boy whose work reached a creditable level was invited to take it along to the headmaster who gave him what is known in DCPS jargon as a 'Good Show-Up'. This system extended to upper levels of the school as well. Boys are allocated into tribes in the Lower School but these are used mainly for sports, although they do provide a sense of belonging when they move up into the main school after Year 4.

Another change affecting the Lower School of which Christine Radcliffe was for ever mindful concerned Year 3 – the old First Form boys at age 7. About a third of the boys entering Year 3 arrive as new boys, the rest coming through from the Annexe. Until recently DCPS was the only local school with an intake for 7-year-old boys. Now Alleyn's and Dulwich College offer this facility giving parents a much wider choice of either co-education, a single sex school through from 7 until 18, or DCPS itself, a dedicated prep school with the choice for boys leaving principally at 13. Although entry into the Lower School remains as popular as ever, DCPS has no time to rest on its laurels. Christine Radcliffe retired at the end of the summer term in 2003 and her successor, Kathryn Wilkins, had a challenging task to ensure that the decision to enter a boy into the Lower School was not only a wise one, but also an appealing one.

When Leakey chose to instigate a Lower School in 1945, he did so because separating the older boys from the younger ones while the school had been evacuated to Wales had worked so well, and this had happened largely because there was insufficient space for them all to work together. Call them what you will – infant, pre-prep, primary – the three sections of DCPS known as Nursery, Annexe and Lower School are the foundations upon which the success of boys at a later age are laid.

Lower School Basketry Club on the front lawn - June 1959

Winter at the Nursery - 2003

Morning break at the Annexe - 2004

12   The Arts

Aglance at a class timetable for 1888 shows that there was precious little classroom time allocated to what could loosely be called The Arts. Singing was the first musical activity and a Christmas concert, which incorporated a little drama, was given in a hall in West Norwood on 18th December 1895. The singing was led by E D Rendall, then an assistant master at the College, later to become Director of Music there. Rendall wrote music prolifically and among his repertoire were songs written specifically for the College. Alleynians will recognize *Pueri Alleyniensis* which has been passed down through the years and is still frequently sung.

Music for *The Preparatory School Song* was written by H W Russell, who was also on the music staff at the College, but this has been lost in obscurity. The words have survived and were written by P N Pocock, who was one of Mallinson's staff, and convey a jingoistic view of school life at the time. Pocock was not at the school for very long, but he seems to have gained an intimate knowledge of it. The song was given an airing in 1980 at an evening of informal drama when it was set to lively music written by Robin Whitcomb, a member of DCPS Staff, and sung lustily by a group of boys. The song was popular during Mallinson's time and was often sung at the end of concerts. In 1897 the school hall was opened and this gave greater scope for Music and Drama, and a farce called *Tweedleton's Tail Coat*, with some musical accompaniment, was performed there in December. At that time the stage, or the platform as it was then called, was where the servery is now and although there were fewer boys in the school, it must be remembered that the hall was then half its present size. Soon it was not large enough and it became necessary to have two performances. In 1899 the St Barnabas church hall in Dulwich Village was used instead and this remained the venue for the school's concerts for many years. In the summer of 1905 another farce called *Taming The Tiger* caused much amusement and was well received, and a separate concert of music was given in the hall in December. A clear raising of standards occurred in the summer of 1906 when Shakespeare's *As You Like It* was performed on the lawn behind the Headmaster's house and so successful was this that a rendering of *The Tempest* was offered in 1908. Still eager for Shakespeare, *The Merchant of Venice* was performed in December 1909.

When Leake became Headmaster in 1910, he knew H W Russell from the College and invited him to become more involved with music at the Prep. Russell had already made his mark with the School Song, and he soon co-ordinated the St Barnabas concerts taking over from Rendall. It was not a full-time appointment and Russell was still employed by the College

Dulwich College Preparatory School   - School Song

Words by P N Pocock Esq ., B.A
Music by H W Russell Esq.

We all of us love to remember
How blushing and blatantly new,
On that red letter day in September
We first wore the Black and the Blue.
Forsaken by friends and relations
Left stranded alone and in tears,
We quiver and quake and shiver and shake
At the thought of the forthcoming years.

CHORUS:
When they've Gone! Gone! Gone!
We'll remember the days that have been
As the babe in 1C, as the boy in IVb, as the autocrat in the Fifteen;
And where'er we may be, ashore or at sea:
We'll endeavour with main and with might
In the days that will come, to shove hard in the scrum
PACK TIGHT, Dulwich Prep! PACK TIGHT!

In a blur of strange featureless faces,
We take our first plunge into life,
And we find we must carve our own places,
For the fittest survive in the strife.
Though the climb be a long and a hard one,
To the sixth from the depth of 1C,
If through foul and fair weather, we struggle together,
We'll all reach the top of the tree.
(Chorus)

We remember our first game of cricket,
The terrific applause for each run,
The tropical growth at the wicket,
And our own dashing drive for a "one".
Till at length in Fifteen and Eleven,
In the "vulgaris profanum" no more,
We mortals are given a first glimpse of heaven
While piling on runs to the score.
(Chorus)

When we've passed from the Prep to the College
That last unavoidable step,
We will always take pride in the knowledge
That we have been part of the Prep.
And at last when we're aged and hoary,
When the span of our years is thirteen,
We'll shove hard in the scrum in the days that will come
For the love of the days that have been.
(Chorus)

Programme for a performance of The Tempest at DCPS in July 1908

> The Tempest (without scenery)
> Presented by forms VI & Va Dulwich Coll: Prep: Sch:
>
> DRAMATIS PERSONÆ.
>
> Alonso — King of Naples — Claridge-Grey
> Sebastian — His brother — Beer
> Prospero — Duke of Milan — Wann
> Antonio — His brother — Gropius
> Gonzalo — A Counsellor — Tenkin (ma)
> Francisco — A Courtier — Dykes
> Caliban — A deformed Savage — Mallinson (ma)
> Trinculo — A Jester — Jacob
> Stephano — A Buffoon — Bamber
> Master — Macdonald (ma)
> Boatswain — Attwater
> Ariel — An Airy Spirit — Fagge-Reiche
> Miranda — Daughter to Prospero — Miss M. Mallinson
> Mariners — Grey, Lambert, Dawson, Hooker, Russell.
>
> Choir — Apergis Claridge, Ellis, Hooker, Lambert,
> Violin — Russell.
> Music — Where the Bee Sucks — Purcell.
>   Come unto these
>   Yellow sands   A.F.
>   The Cuckoo.   Anon.
> Scenes 1 a Shipwreck; other scenes - the Island.
> Stage manager & prompter — E.C. Clark Esq.
>
>   Epilogue will be spoken by
>   Bernard.
>
> July 25 - 1908.

although as the years went by he spent more and more time at the Prep. Singing was the major musical activity in the early years, and senior and junior choirs were supported by members of staff. Just how willingly the staff were co-opted is not known, but it is clear that the concerts were popular and went down well. Russell had his own band outside school and this often came and gave musical support for the concerts. The 1915 concert was simply called *An Entertainment* and is of interest as it took place six months before the slaughter on the Somme during the First World War. As well as including in the repertoire of songs *Till the Boys come Home*, the National Anthem was accompanied at the end of the programme by those of our French and Russian allies. This type of programme set the scene for many years and, although the plays and the music varied, the general pattern remained the same. These concerts were always well received as this critique for the 1925 concert shows:

> Owing to the very many people who wished to attend, two performances were held this year, one in the afternoon and one in the evening. The chief feature of the afternoon performance was a dramatic recital of 'The Pied Piper of Hamelin' by the Annexe. Afterwards the players returned to school for tea although some embarrassment was felt by the wooden soldiers owing to their inability to sit down. The evening performance seemed more vigorous than that of the afternoon, though some of the actors were beginning to get a little hoarse. Thanks are due to Mr Russell who provided such excellent music, and to all the many friends and parents who helped to make the costumes.

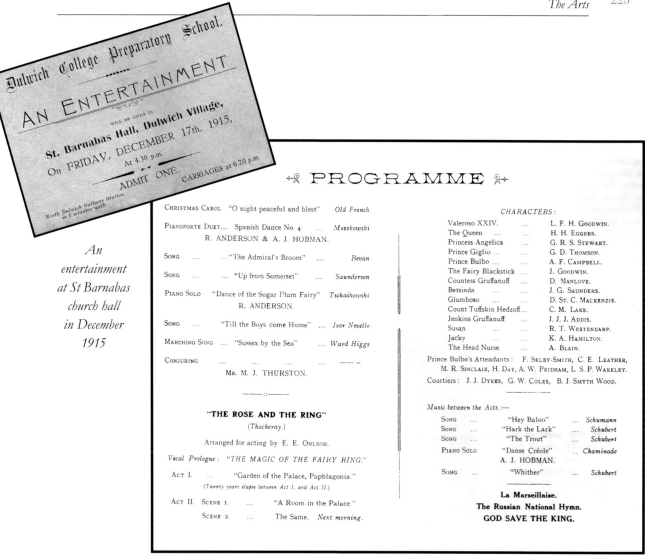

An entertainment at St Barnabas church hall in December 1915

Dulwich College Preparatory School.

AN ENTERTAINMENT

WILL BE GIVEN IN

St. Barnabas Hall, Dulwich Village,

On FRIDAY, DECEMBER 17th, 1915,

At 4.30 p.m.

ADMIT ONE.   CARRIAGES at 6.20 p.m.

North Dulwich Railway Station is 5 minutes south.

⁂ PROGRAMME ⁂

CHRISTMAS CAROL	"O night peaceful and blest"	*Old French*
PIANOFORTE DUET...	Spanish Dance No. 4	*Moszkowski*
	R. ANDERSON & A. J. HOBMAN.	
SONG	... "The Admiral's Broom" ...	*Bevan*
SONG	... "Up from Somerset" ...	*Saunderson*
PIANO SOLO	"Dance of the Sugar Plum Fairy"	*Tschaikowski*
	R. ANDERSON.	
SONG	... "Till the Boys come Home" ...	*Ivor Novello*
MARCHING SONG	... "Sussex by the Sea" ...	*Ward Higgs*
CONJURING	... ...	————
	MR. M. J. THURSTON.	

"THE ROSE AND THE RING"

(*Thackeray.*)

Arranged for acting by E. E. OHLSON.

Vocal Prologue : "*THE MAGIC OF THE FAIRY RING.*"

ACT I.   ...   "Garden of the Palace, Paphlagonia."

(*Twenty years elapse between Act I. and Act II.*)

ACT II. SCENE 1.   ...   "A Room in the Palace."

SCENE 2.   ...   The Same. *Next morning.*

CHARACTERS :

Valeroso XXIV.	...	L. F. H. GOODWIN.
The Queen	...	H. H. EGGERS.
Princess Angelica	...	G. R. S. STEWART.
Prince Giglio ...	...	G. D. THOMSON.
Prince Bulbo ...	...	A. F. CAMPBELL..
The Fairy Blackstick	...	J. GOODWIN.
Countess Gruffanuff	...	D. MANLOVE.
Betsinda	...	J. G. SAUNDERS.
Glumboso	...	D. ST. C. MACKENZIE.
Count Tuffskin Hedzoff...		C. M. LAKE.
Jenkins Gruffanuff	...	J. J. J. ADDIS.
Susan	...	R. T. WESTENDARP.
Jacky	...	K. A. HAMILTON.
The Head Nurse	...	A. BLAIN.

Prince Bulbo's Attendants : F. SELBY-SMITH, C. E. LEATHER, M. R. SINCLAIR, H. DAY, A. W. PRIDHAM, L. S. P. WAKELEY.

Courtiers : J. J. DYKES, G. W. COLES, B. J. SMYTH WOOD.

Music between the Acts :—

SONG	...	"Hey Baloo"	... *Schumann*
SONG	...	"Hark the Lark"	... *Schubert*
SONG	...	"The Trout"	... *Schubert*
PIANO SOLO		"Danse Créole"	... *Chaminade*
		A. J. HOBMAN.	
SONG		"Whither"	... *Schubert*

La Marseillaise.
The Russian National Hymn.
GOD SAVE THE KING.

Russell's influence was not limited to the older boys and R E Jackson (DCPS 1926-1933) remembered a band flourishing in Miss Osborne's Annexe in 1927. A picture taken in the main school hall in March of that year showed that over fifty boys were involved and drums, recorders and tambourines were to the fore. What a noise they must have made! The critique in the magazine related that the theme of the play was Hiawatha and:

> . . . *it was most kind of Mr Russell to compose such thrilling Red Indian music for us and we much appreciate the difference it made to the play. Mr Pitt's dead deer thoroughly deserved the applause with which it was received and his wigwam was much admired.*

Russell fell ill in the summer of 1928, and was compelled to stand down. He was succeeded by Mr Russell Taylor who became the school's first full-time Head of Music and under his direction Music was put firmly on the map. He had many innovative ideas about the importance of music in a school like DCPS, and he set in place a number of musical activities which continue to the present day. 1928 was a big year for the Arts, for it also saw the arrival of David Livingston to the staff. He was not employed to undertake Drama on a full-time basis, as had been the case with Music, but he became much involved with it and for the next ten years both Livingston and Russell Taylor worked together on the annual

The Annexe production of Hiawatha *in 1927*

Christmas concerts and they became firm friends. Russell Taylor subsequently became the best man at Livingston's wedding. Nor was music with the younger boys forgotten for, during the 1930s, the Annexe had its own orchestra which was conducted by one of the boys and although the accompanying photograph was posed for the 1938 prospectus, it does give some idea as to the calibre of music reached by boys of Annexe age at the time.

But what of Creative Art? Magazines and other documents show that this was the Cinderella of the art scene at the time. No art lessons as such appeared in any of the school's timetables in the 1920s for the Upper and Middle school (Years 5 to 8), although prizes were given for drawing. The best of these were shown at the annual Hobbies Day (as Open Day was then known) and budding artists pursued their interest as a hobby. There were art lessons for the younger boys though. Mention is made of a Miss Cane who gave excellent training in drawing and brushwork to boys in the Annexe in 1927 and this may well have been one of the reasons why an art club was introduced in 1930 for older boys and as a class subject for some age groups. An interesting reference to Art was made in a letter sent to David Livingston (in 1989) by John Shaw, who was one of his former pupils. The year is 1934:

> *Mr Russell Taylor dismissed me from the singing class, saying that I was flat and did not have a true note in my head. I had to make my way crestfallen to the Art class, only to realise on arrival that the*

laugh was on him. The gorgeous blonde Miss Loveridge, and what an appropriate name, took me under her wing and I set to with a will to draw for her my best battleships and scenes of violence.

The Annexe Band - 1938

This is the same Miss Loveridge from the Annexe to whom John Bazalgette made reference earlier. She must have made a big impression to be remembered so vividly so many years later. The theme of art lessons in those days was principally based upon drawing. It is interesting to note that John Shaw made reference to singing. When Russell Taylor arrived, music playing and music appreciation had less emphasis than singing, so he instigated a tribe singing competition which continued long after his departure and disappeared only in the 1960s. However, the singing was not always to his liking, for in the same year he wrote:

> *If a vote were taken, it is almost certain that 'Marching through Georgia' and 'Old Folks At Home' would take their place in popularity. It is regrettable that this should be the case as it seems only right that our British songs should take pride of place. There are quite a number of boys who are not able to sing the National Anthem without the words in front of them.*

A year earlier, the reviewer of the magazine had commented that the words of the songs sung by the boys were woolly and indistinct … *'not so much because of the laziness of the singers as the laziness of the singers' mouths and throats'.*

At the end of the summer term in 1933 Russell Taylor announced that he intended to launch out into three new areas so far uncharted. These were to hold a carol service for the first time, which would be held in the Dulwich College Chapel, start a gramophone club in the 'dinner' hour, membership for which would be limited to those willing to pay a nominal subscription, and perhaps most importantly of all, to form a school string orchestra. The first carol service was clearly a success even though *'the persistent drilling of pneumatic drills outside the Chapel ruined the singing of the choir'*. The orchestra soon became well established, with assistance coming from A W P Gayford, who was then Director of Music at the College, and Jack Chapman, teacher of French at the school, who gave the orchestra body by playing the viola. Russell Taylor himself played the 'cello, and the conducting appears to have been done by one of the boys.

The magazine describes the 1934 concert, which involved boys from the Lower School upwards, as *'being a success'*. Livingston was congratulated upon the excellent production of the plays while the choir, trained by Russell Taylor, and the orchestra, under Chapman's direction, rendered selections between the plays. Livingston and Russell Taylor also made much of the scenery. In his review of the year Russell Taylor made reference to the Dulwich College concert held in the Great Hall in 1934 when he wrote:

> *Out of 72 First Trebles, 38 came from the Prep, as did 16 of the 34 Second Trebles. This is a gratifying aspect of the School's music, and we hope that such a splendid percentage may long continue.*

Russell Taylor's wishes have certainly been fulfilled and many DCPS boys continue with their music to a high level

Russell Taylor - 1934

at Dulwich College. In 1934 the matter of a School Song arose again, this time more eruditely than the previous effort. Russell Taylor found some words by Rudyard Kipling, no less, and set them to music. This time the music (and the original score) has survived and this too receives an airing from time to time.

DCPS School Song

Words by Rudyard Kipling : Music by Russell W K Taylor

Verse One

Land of our Birth, we pledge to thee,
Our love a toil in the years to be;
When we are grown and take our place,
As men and women with our race.
Father in Heav'n who lovest all,
Oh help thy children when they call;
That they may build from age to age,
An undefiled heritage.

Part of the score for the 1934 School Song.
Music by Russell Taylor, the school's first Director of Music.

Of this, many years later, Russell Taylor himself wrote:

We started off by using the song as the test piece for the Tribe Singing Competition and it soon became well known. I well remember how pleased I was when there was a general inspection of the school (in 1933) and Geoffrey Shaw, who inspected the music, wrote glowingly about it. He was particularly impressed with the key change in the middle.

By 1934 the Art Club was also growing. In addition to drawing, painting and poster work, lino cutting had been introduced. So ambitious were some of the posters that there was hope of some of them appearing on the walls of railway stations. The Art Club had plenty of enthusiastic members, for in that same year visits were made by budding artists to sketch the buildings and grounds of the Crystal Palace. This was only two years before the fire which destroyed it, and by that time the whole area had become run down. How wonderful it would have been had some of those schoolboy sketches of the erstwhile Crystal Palace survived. On 4th July there was a trip to the Royal Academy.

Not to be outdone by the Art Club, Livingston established a Drama Club in 1935. This involved play reading and, in the autumn terms, devoting time for rehearsing for the 'School Dramatic and Orchestral Concert', as it had become grandly known. Chapman, with the colourful Meyrat, produced a small play in French called *La Valise de Papa*, set in a railway carriage. The magazine referred to a stout man entering the carriage played by Silkin, later to become an eminent politician. As usual the plays and the concert met with much acclaim. In 1936, mention is made of '*Swann's valuable contribution on the piano to the orchestra*'. This was Donald Swann, later to make a name as a pianist and composer, including two West End shows with Michael Flanders whom he subsequently met at Westminster School. The music concert held in the school hall on 1st April 1937 included *Land of Hope and Glory* sung by Madge, with orchestra and choir. Frank Madge had an outstanding voice but died a few months later in June of that year. His family created a prize to his memory and the Madge Memorial Singing Prize is still awarded each year.

Music grew and grew and the number of boys involved with it steadily increased. By 1937 one tenth of the school was learning to play the piano, although it had to be admitted that not all of those were being taught at school. Boys were even turning up for choir practices in the lunch hour dressed in rugby football clothes - a sure sign of things to come. The carol service, still held in the College Chapel at that time, was becoming more and more popular and also, in 1937, the choir outshone all previous efforts to good effect with '*Ding Dong Merrily on High*'. Music was flourishing in the summer of 1939 and seemed prepared to continue into the autumn by which time, without any great comment, the school found itself at Cranbrook. That year a carol service was arranged in Cranbrook church, assisted by a 'special choir'. When a small part of the school re-opened in Dulwich on 15th January 1940, Russell Taylor was already in London. During the war, the orchestra never regained its pre-war strength and as the number of boys fluctuated so did the quality of the music. In 1940 it was noted that:

> *… hymn singing at Prayers has been extremely poor, but by keeping to one hymn for each day of the week, the singing has improved and by the end of the term, the school was able to produce a lusty sound.*

In 1937 the Art Club was meeting four times a week instead of two, the chief interest in the summer of that year being design, '*with white wood articles being painted and varnished, many showing forethought and originality*'. As a further extension of the Arts, a Drama Club competition was held in July, when the whole school had the opportunity of hearing the winners and judging the standard of eloquence of the budding actors.

While the school was evacuated to Wales none of the Arts came to the fore as other activities were considered to be of greater importance. There were no heads of Art, Drama or Music in Wales where teachers at the time were in short supply. Music tuition and appreciation was given by Elaine Barnett, who returned to Cranbrook after the war, and who started music there when Coursehorn opened in October 1945. By the time the school returned to Dulwich from Betws, Russell Taylor had moved to Dorset and from the autumn of 1945 Miss Elsie Smith was appointed Director of Music. She continued the good work of her predecessor and did much pioneer work in the field of class string teaching, publishing several books on the subject and encouraging teachers' training colleges to take string teaching seriously. Although corporate music in the school was limited to choral singing, and string and recorder playing, high standards were reached and music scholarships began to be gained. The orchestra was thus principally of strings and an array of instruments hung gracefully from the music room wall.

The array of stringed instruments in the Music Room in 1950

Elsie Smith was a remarkable person and one of the great characters to have passed through the doors of DCPS. The favoured few of her orchestra thought highly of her and treated her with respect and caution. But to those whom she considered better suited to *'agriculture than culture'* (her words) she was a formidable person both in manner and appearance. Her penchant for keeping gin, Martini and Campari in the grand piano inevitably meant that eventually she fell foul of the system, but she achieved much musically and the part she

Miss Elsie Smith, Director of Music 1945-1963

played in the development of the school's music should not be underestimated. The carol services continued and after the war moved to the local parish church at St Stephen's, where they have been ever since. The quality and ambitions of the carol services grew each year and it was not unusual for a collection of 'cellos and violins to be carried to St Stephen's by their players to become a part of the service. In 1950, I played the double bass at one such service - a skill I have since totally lost, casting doubt as to whether I had any in the first place. I well remember how important it was to avoid Miss Smith's wrath by not getting the spike of our instruments stuck in the church grating and clearly this was far more important than the quality of the music we may have produced. The tribe singing competition continued, but when regular music lessons found their way into the school timetable, the music club and the appreciation of music through gramophone records did not continue.

Unquestionably, Leakey had appointed an extremely talented but volatile person to direct the school's music. Probably by chance rather than by design, the person appointed to teach Art in 1946 was also a musician, an organist and a Fellow of the Royal College of Organists (FRCO) no less, and the two characters were about as different as chalk from cheese. He was Charles Hambleton. Hambleton was equally talented but modest in the extreme. As well as being an organist, he was a draughtsman and a brilliant teacher who had a great gift of imparting knowledge to both young and old alike. Under his direction, Art flourished, both as a club activity and in lessons, now introduced into the timetable on a regular basis for boys from the age of 11 (Year 6). He was full of new ideas. He introduced the basic skill of draughtsmanship, termly art shows and set about a study of heraldry. The art room was a mine of information. Art in those days was in a room at the top of 44 Alleyn Park, now a part of the old Lower School, although it was destroyed by the 1981 fire and the place where it once was has totally disappeared. The room contained a little cuckoo clock which fascinated the boys and also, it was said, had the hottest radiator in the school, making the art room a very snug place to be in the cold winter of 1947. Hambleton was a man of many parts, for as well as Art and Music, he was also in charge of swimming for a long time and later on he introduced folk dancing into the school, which proved to be remarkably, and perhaps surprisingly, popular. Art grew and grew and became ever more popular with new ideas and new enthusiasms being introduced all the time. Other activities which come under the umbrella of 'The Arts' were being introduced too as members of staff with new interests came and went. There was a pottery club and a most successful photographic club organised by Captain Fleming, who managed this as well as his archery.

The one activity which did not fare as well after the war was Drama, and little mention is made of it in school magazines of the day. Plays and play acting were generally in the hands of the boarders who presented an annual play in conjunction with a music concert. These started in 1947 when A C D Clelland, who subsequently became the Housemaster at Brightlands, had a personal enthusiasm for acting and plays began to develop again. Each spring term there was a boarders' play coupled with a concert of singing and instrumental music. These continued for many years and were the main cultural event in the school's calendar for a long time. I recall being involved in *Scuttleboom's Treasure* in 1950, so the plays were not very challenging by today's standards and using make-up and dressing up were both far more fun than acting. Whether on grounds of cost or convenience is not known, but the school never returned to St Barnabas Hall in Dulwich Village after the war and the plays were performed in the school hall thereafter.

In 1949 the art room moved to part of a ramshackle brick building, long since demolished, approximately where the Annexe kitchen is now and which had once been the school's first science room. The other part was the carpenter's shop and maintenance area. Art was growing as a class subject and needed a full-time teacher, so Hambleton turned his attention to other activities in the school, principally swimming. He continued with the handwork club, taking his little cuckoo clock with him.

The new Head of Art was Mary Thwaites, the wife of Bryan Thwaites (later Sir Bryan Thwaites) who had been a musical and talented boy at DCPS in the 1930s and who subsequently became a Governor. Mary Thwaites was the first true artist as such and gave the subject a new emphasis. In 1950 she wrote: '*The club gives its members an opportunity to develop the techniques, which is very valuable when the time spent in class is necessarily so limited*'. She stayed for a couple of years and when the old brick building became totally unsuitable for teaching, Art took up residence in a room on the ground floor of 40 Alleyn Park which had recently been purchased. There followed a series of art teachers, Miss Beevers and Peter Sumsion being among them, each offering their talents in different ways. In charge of Art from 1958 to 1966 was Roger Warren, an old boy of the school, who put his mark on

Art in his own characteristic way. In 1960 the subject moved again and took up residence in a room which was almost as eccentric as its teacher. This was over a garage next to 38 Alleyn Park which by then had been acquired. The room itself was reached by a small external staircase and was barely capable of accommodating a single class. Later it was given over to Latin and gained the name 'ad pontem'. When it was subsequently demolished it was replaced by a modern version, strangely also with an external staircase, doubtless the result of protracted planning permission. Today it is the school's maintenance area. Warren achieved much in his little domain and it was a pity that by being so secluded, the work the boys achieved was seen by relatively few. He was responsible for Art throughout the school, including the Lower School and the Annexe and, despite the limitations of space, much was achieved. Warren had all sorts of innovative ideas such as the re-introduction of lino cutting, the design of book jackets and the creation of friezes, each term having a different theme. He extended the Art Club during out of school hours so he could cater for different boys on different days. By 1966 the subject was bulging at the seams and when new rooms were created over the hall in 1966, one was devoted exclusively for Art, but Warren did not go with it.

The new room saw the arrival of Denny Ashenhurst as Head of Art, wife of the then Housemaster at Brightlands. With much improved facilities she had the scope to broaden the subject considerably and it gained a higher status with more classes timetabled for a double lesson each week. The room included a kiln, so pottery became an integral part of artwork and generally there was greater space to display boys' work in a more central part of the school. Although there had been pottery of sorts before, there had never been the scope or the equipment to develop it. As well as lessons, Denny Ashenhurst extended the existing art clubs at lunch-time and after school still further, and being enthusiastic to promote a wider interest and awareness of Art, she took groups to exhibitions in London such as the Royal Academy and Hayward Gallery. Rather less grand were the visits to Peckham Town Hall when boys who had entered the Southwark Arts and Crafts Exhibitions each year received their prizes. Knowing that she had considerable artistic talent within her ranks, Denny Ashenhurst was keen to maintain links with local art competitions.

1971 was an exciting year as in that year DCPS was invited to create a picture to mark the life of Cecil King who had become seventy years of age and was then Chairman of Mirror Group Newspapers. As a result, a large mural was painted and when it was presented at Claridges two boys, Jonathan Flint and Edward Heinemann, met Edward Heath, the then Prime Minister who was present, as well as Cecil King himself. Art became actively involved in school plays and, as a result of lessons and clubs, there were few who did not contribute to the sets or costumes in some way. More boys entered competitions each year, both locally and at national level, art scholarships began to be gained and each display on Open Day seemed grander than the year before. When the changing room block was built in 1972, part of the area above was given to Art so the subject moved again, by then the original 1966 room having proved inadequate for the needs of an expanding department. By the time Denny Ashenhurst moved to pastures new with her husband in March 1975, sound foundations had been laid for her successor.

Ken Richards became Head of Art in the summer of 1975 and, by being trained as a potter, his approach was different. When two new kilns arrived, the result was that piggy-banks, ceramic pies, puddings, and slices of gateaux were soon being produced in profusion by boys of all ages. His previous experience had been with older pupils so he had high expectations of what could be achieved and he introduced many new ideas, not only for the boys in his charge but for adults too. Saturday and evening classes for parents, members of staff and governors were held for ten years or so and they became popular social occasions. Richards had the knack of being able to make something out of nothing and he never threw anything away. The art room became a grotto of discarded gadgets and, in addition to water colours, boys used a wide range of materials and techniques, conventionally and experimentally, so that by example they were often able to achieve the seemingly impossible. The Christmas decorations in the hall each year, often made from nothing more than items of rubbish such as old plastic bottles or umbrellas, were a treat to behold. In 1985 there was an autumn project on Sir Christopher Wren which led to the mural in the hall that year. As well as the annual displays on Open Days, the boys in their art lessons became involved in decorations for functions at other times such as PTA theme nights.

The influence and needs of the subject continued to grow so that by 1985 the two adjacent classrooms had been added, giving the department the whole floor above the changing rooms. Currently this area is the domain of Design and Technolgy (DT). Part of the new space became a projection room with slides showing the history of art and architecture. 1984 was an exceptional year for the school's budding artists. In that year entry was made to the National Sir Charles Wheeler Art Awards and drawings from Patrick Bateman, Julian Rowe and Simon Rucker led to the following comments from the adjudicators:

> *Technically the best all-round entry by any school in the Preparatory and Junior Divisions, DCPS is the only school from which all candidates have won awards. The three candidates each have a particularly sound draughtsmanship base, from which to branch out into greater creativity.*

Three years later the art department gained £500 for itself. This was achieved as a prize for the Best School in a self portrait competition organized by *The Independent* newspaper. Several hundred schools entered a total of six thousand paintings from which three were chosen from DCPS for inclusion in an exhibition held in the foyer of the National Theatre. Not only did the achievements of pupils increase but so did the number of staff. It became virtually essential for Richards to have an assistant and more often than not these were young ladies who came in for a year or so. Inevitably they made a big impression on the boys. This is how Andrew Slatter (DCPS 1968-1978) remembered one of his art lessons:

Ken Richards was a most creative and inspiring teacher who devised all sorts of strange and interesting activities in the name of art. One week we would be sent out to find a brick wall to draw. Another we would be creating copies of famous masterpieces out of offcuts of carpet. One morning he explained that we would be drawing woodscrews. His mistake was to announce that accordingly Miss Turner, his not unattractive young assistant, would come round and give each one of us a screw. For twenty thirteen-year-olds that prospect caused some degree of hilarity and, ultimately, a block detention for the whole class.

An art assistant to make an even greater mark was Shelley Sutton who worked with Richards in 1995. She helped to paint the mural on the exterior wall of the gymnasium, which in 2004 is still in place, and so taken was she by DCPS that she joined the permanent Annexe teaching staff in 2001. Ken Richards had a moment of great personal achievement in 1991 when his portrait of the outgoing headmaster, Hugh Woodcock, was unveiled at the final assembly. Now in the hall, it drew gasps from those present, such was the likeness. In 1995, four boys achieved art scholarships in a single year which was a new record at the time and by the time Richards himself retired two years later, the subject

A drawing of the screw for which Andrew Slatter and his class received a block detention

Christmas decorations for the hall based on the theme 'Homage to Sir Christopher Wren'

Boys working on the mural in the Art room - autumn 1985

had reached a peak hitherto undreamt of. His successor was to show that in Art there is no such thing as a peak. The new Head of Art from September 1997 was Glenn Smart. Much as he respected the achievements and methods of his predecessor, he set about developing additional, as well as existing, skills among the boys in his own way. His philosophy was that art is for everyone and that it was up to him and his department to find something which every boy could achieve and be happy about. He recognised that not all his pupils might be skilled in drawing or painting but that they might have other talents which were more mechanical such as ceramics and sculpture. New equipment would be necessary to put Smart's ambitions into practice and within a year of his arrival it became clear that the existing art facilities, although much enlarged from the original, were not adequate. The room was dark, the ceiling low and pressing noises were coming from the nearby DT department which also needed more space. So the decision was taken to move yet again and no subject has had more locations within the school than Art. This time the subject was to have a new fully equipped purpose built facility. Plans had been in the pipeline for decades to build a link between 40 and 42 Alleyn Park but it had never been done and when the decision was taken in 1998 fill the gap, Art was given a new home on the top floor of this link building. Opened in December 2000 by Dr Stephen Deuchar, Director of Tate Britain and former DCPS pupil, the new department is bright and spacious. There is a large studio with top north light and a smaller studio for ceramic work and display. There is also a gallery-cum-resources centre with computers, a digital camera, a library and space for special exhibitions. The computers were for boys to become familiar with computer-generated art as an extension to their work, and the camera has been used extensively, particularly with boys' art based on the self portrait and still life. These installations enabled new aspects of art to be introduced and incorporated multimedia activities such as PowerPoint, African masks, printing and music together, or as digitised images run on computer screens reflected into mirrors looking at the manipulation of landscape. Other equipment was needed to enable boys to develop their various talents in the ways Smart envisaged. This included two new

An after school life-drawing class in the new Art room in 2004
(Courtesy Ann Revell)

kilns, two printmaking tables and two precision presses. Silk screen printing, drypoint onto perspex and aluminium, and monoprinting were among the new activities which were introduced with the new building.

The practice of employing a full-time gap student as an art assistant has continued and there have been part-time teachers in addition. In 2004, this was Jo de Pear, a specialist printmaker who thus gave strength to that area. On an *ad hoc* basis professional artists have come to the school for a few days to share their talents and to offer guidance from their own experiences, and visits to museums and galleries have been made from time to time for those who are interested. There is no art club as such and the department is open all day for boys to visit as and when they can. Art is a timetabled subject for all year groups. Not surprisingly, standards have been elevated with no less than six art scholarships being gained in 2004. Soon after the new art department opened a parent said to Glenn Smart *'Look at the Art Department and Library within a school; it will reveal a great deal about the ethos of that school'*. DCPS scores highly on both counts - with more, much more, beside.

In 1966 drama too was on the threshold of major change which would evolve in the years to come. Post-war plays had been started by A C D Clelland and the boarders at Brightlands. When he left in 1954 there was a short gap before Roger Shakeshaft resurrected them and they prospered under his direction, carrying on for a short while after he left. For almost fifteen years nearly all the drama in the upper part of the school was performed by boarders, principally because interest for it came from staff there.

The absence of drama in the school generally did not go by unnoticed. In 1962 Dolly Wraight, later to become Dolly Walker, joined the Lower School staff. She was wildly enthusiastic about all forms of theatre and had considerable knowledge about it. Although principally working within the Lower School, one of the first things she did was to create a Drama Club for the older boys. It met with instant enthusiasm, as this account for the summer of 1962 shows:

> *We decided to start a light-hearted drama club which was made up of the boys themselves. The subject of 'Holidays Abroad' was agreed upon and we thought in terms of a series of scenes loosely connected by a story involving a family trip to the continent. Each scene was given to a member of the club to produce and write a script for. Enthusiasm was overwhelming and the main problem was to keep the production within the limits of time at our disposal and the producers were soon clamouring for more rehearsal time.*

In 1963, the Drama Club produced excerpts from *A Midsummer Night's Dream* on the lawn behind Number 42, evoking memories of the Shakespearian plays performed there in Mallinson's time. These fledgling ideas soon led to greater things and before long Dolly Wraight was producing plays exclusively for Lower School boys. The annual boarders' play, with a concert, continued each spring for a while but there was a need and an impetus for drama to spread its wings. The Head of English at the time was Charles Guttmann who worked closely with Dolly Wraight and was impressed by her enthusiasm. Encouraged by her and not without the necessary ability himself, Guttmann announced that there would be a school play at the end of the summer term in 1965. The play he chose was *The Guinea Pig* by W Chetham Strode. It was an outstanding success and nothing on such a large scale had ever been performed at the school before. In his critique, Peter Ashenhurst wrote:

> *Some came to bury Caesar and stayed to praise him. Such is the nature of drama, that all is lost or won in one swift parting of the curtains: the producer, his play, his actors stand or fall in one brief flicker. So was there ever a more apt title for a new surge of drama in the school? 'The Guinea Pig', tautly laid before us for vivisection, revealing all, or nearly all, of a long summer's spurge of nervous activity. New curtains, new cast and a new producer were all arraigned before us for cross-examination.*

Fired and encouraged by his success and given all the encouragement he needed, the end of term play in the summer quickly became an established part of the school's calendar. The following year saw *The Happiest Days of Your Life* being performed on the DCPS stage; in 1969 it was the turn of Shakespeare to appear again when Guttmann chose to perform *The Merchant of Venice*. In 1971 he went even further by selecting the challenging, and for a prep school astonishing, Wilde's *The Importance of Being Earnest*. How could a boy possibly play the part of Lady Bracknell? Yet Tom Gardom and Richard O'Flynn achieved the impossible and each gave stunning performances of the part. Despite rising so high, this was to be Guttmann's last play at DCPS. There were two reasons: he found it difficult to cope with the tremendous pressure put on boys at the end of the school year and his own temperament. Perceptively, he had become aware of the problem of timing himself after his first play when he wrote of *The Guinea Pig*:

> *There are obvious difficulties to be overcome: the lack of both time and availability due to the large number of school and out-of-school activities which have claims on most boys: the fact that type-casting prevents open volunteering - for certain characters can only be played by certain boys and it would be pointless to extend invitations for volunteers to members of the school generally.*

At the same time, Ashenhurst also foresaw problems after *The Guinea Pig*:

> *For Charles Guttmann, the producer, who could so easily have been buried by the many trials and tribulations, there came that moment of praise, always well deserved, and not unnaturally relief at curtain's fall*

After *The Importance of Being Earnest* in 1971, Guttmann deserved all the praise he received, but it had not been an easy term and there had been far too many 'trials and tribulations'. There had been conflicts and differing demands made upon the boys which put them into a difficult position, so much so that Guttmann sometimes interpreted the request for a boy to miss a rehearsal, either from staff or parent, as being a personal slight. Seeing a crisis in the wind, and at the time with Guttmann's approval, the Headmaster invited Carl Gilbey-McKenzie, who had recently arrived and was teaching French at the time, to undertake the school play for the following year. Gilbey-McKenzie, an amateur actor himself, who was not without the skill and the ability to produce school plays, accepted the challenge and presented *The Thwarting of Baron Bollingrew* in 1972. It was totally different from anything that had gone before and was a remarkable success, having been chosen as a result of a reading and improvisation session at the recently formed Drama Club. One person who remembered that play well was Richard Hodder (DCPS 1967–1972):

> *On the last night I let myself go and it was perhaps the only one I really enjoyed. As I walked on, those on stage already looked at me and seemed to say 'It's all OK tonight'. The performance went all too quickly and as the curtain closed for the last time I was hit by a wave of tiredness.*

Seeds were sown that night, for Richard Hodder became a successful actor in adult life, as have several others who have been involved with drama at DCPS. The play had been produced with relatively less confrontation, but Guttmann took what must loosely be called 'umbridge' at G-M's success and within a year had chosen a post at a school elsewhere. But Gilbey-McKenzie was not exactly easy-going himself and although he put a degree of calm on troubled waters so far as the plays were concerned, his time at DCPS was colourful and not without incident. Stephen Robinson (DCPS 1967-1975) remembered him:

> *He was a young firebrand, both inspirational and alarming. He had a genuine temper, not one just for show. For boys aged 11 to 13, there were two key defining aspects to his personality – his toupee and his BMW, both then rarities, certainly in South East London.*

The problems of producing plays at the end of each summer term did not go away with a new producer, but Gilbey-McKenzie sought ways of trying to overcome them. First he set about having two casts for each play. This had the advantage of involving more boys and also produced an alternative if a boy was unable to perform at the last minute. This was far more satisfactory than having under-studies. He also needed the co-operation of parents so that dental appointments were not made at times of a crucial rehearsal. He devised a kind of contract with them, setting out times well in advance when boys were needed so that parents could plan accordingly. The co-operation of the various sports departments also had to be considered so that rehearsals did not take place when essential actors were required for matches. By and large it worked and some colourful and spectacular plays were produced. These always involved many people behind the scenes, not least the painting and preparation of the set by the Art department. It might be said that the standard of drama at the school at this time reached peaks which have not been matched before or since and there were some very talented performances. There are two worthy of mention and both occurred during the production of *The Royal Hunt of the Sun* by Peter Shaffer in 1974. Roland Keating (DCPS 1967-1974) played the part of Pizarro and this may have been the sign of things to come for by 2002 he had become responsible for the digital television channel BBC4, moving up to Controller of BBC2 in 2004. Even more stunning was the part of Atahuallpa, Sovereign Inca, played by Nicholas Langford (DCPS 1970-1974). To this day, Gilbey-McKenzie considers these to be the finest schoolboy acting performances he has ever seen, but it takes talent to spot and develop talent. In 1987 Gilbey-McKenzie produced *Billy Budd* and it was to be his last play at DCPS. Again two talented boys, Andrew Green and Noel Casey, played the part of Billy at separate performances. Gilbey-McKenzie and his play went out in a blaze of glory to the extent that he turned the producer's nightmare of a large pillar in the middle of the audience to great advantage by placing scaffolding around it and using the top as the crow's nest for his play. Much discussion had taken place earlier as to whether the school should provide a music school or a theatre. When this eventually came down in favour of the former, Gilbey-McKenzie realised that without the resources he would find it difficult to match music so far as standards were concerned while the school dining hall doubled up as an auditorium. With this die cast, he decided that it was time to move on, having accomplished for himself, he said, all that there was at the school for him to accomplish.

His achievements at DCPS can best be summed up by Ben Weston (DCPS 1977-1982):

His school plays were seriously ambitious affairs, mounted in a style that gave a real insight into how professional productions were put together. Shows like 'Macbeth' and 'Oh What a Lovely War!' are not for the faint-hearted and I can imagine many schools balking at the prospect of mounting them with a cast of boys aged between ten and thirteen. Gilbey, in contrast, seemed to relish the challenge. He was an all-rounder; someone who understood not only the principles of acting and the language brilliantly, but theatre lighting and design as well.

In 1973 Gilbey-McKenzie inaugurated what was initially called a Drama Festival, but this soon developed into several evenings of informal drama at the end of each spring term. Boys wrote their own plays, selected their own characters and arranged their own rehearsal times, overall guidance being given by English teachers. Auditions then took place and the most suitable sketches were put together to create an evening of entertainment. For many boys, this was their first opportunity of appearing on a stage and it was also useful for talented boys to be spotted.

Thanks to Dolly Wraight, by then Dolly Walker, who had encouraged Guttmann and later Gilbey-McKenzie to produce high calibre plays for the older boys each year in the first place, Drama was flourishing in the Lower School. There in 1973 she produced *St George and the Dragon* and in 1978 she wrote the words and directed a play which she simply called *Tutankhamun*. She actively encouraged form drama and, with Pat Stallard, form plays became regular events. When the Annexe had a hall of its own from 1974, Sue Cownie was able to develop drama in that part of the school as well. She too had a personal interest and as well as producing Annexe plays each year, she sometimes took an active part herself as in 1974 when she presented a play called *A Thousand Years of History* providing sound effects on the cymbals herself. For the younger boys, the Annexe hall was more suitable than the main school hall and was sometimes used by the Lower School as well. Although lacking theatrical trimmings, its comparative informality gave greater scope to these boys and extracts from *The Hobbit* and *Goldilocks* in 1986 by Annexe boys were notable examples.

For the summer production in 1988 the new Head of English and Drama, Ian Kendrick, wanted to present something different but ambitious. He was well aware of the legacy of his predecessor and his own preference was for linguistic versatility involving pupils in the transfer of text to stage rather than pageant. As a result, his first production, *Crouchback*, was a play which he wrote himself and was essentially Shakespeare's *Richard III* interspersed with original commentary from the two murderers of Clarence, which sought to clarify whether Richard was really as wicked as Shakespeare had portrayed him. The play was written by the preceding Christmas, parts were cast and boys began learning their lines before the end of the spring term. In 1993, Wilde's *The Importance of Being Earnest* was presented again, being equal to if not better than the production of two decades earlier. Again two talented boys, Thomas Wood and Jonathan Munroe, were chosen to play the demanding part of Lady Bracknell on different nights, and the standard of acting generally reached a high standard. Kendrick considered that his greatest highlight at DCPS was the production of *Hamlet* in 1990 which was favourably reviewed by *The Times Educational Supplement*. The title role was played by Miles Kemp who revealed that he had a remarkable understanding of the character for a boy of his age.

Kendrick's final production in 1996 was Stoppard's *The Real Inspector Hound*, after which he returned to his old school, Cabin Hill in Belfast, as headmaster. As well as the annual plays,

Ian Kendrick's production of Hamlet *- 1990*

Kendrick developed the evenings of informal drama into what he called 'fully blown annual revues' which were more structured and involved slick backstage work. These evenings always brought a large number boys onto the stage for the first time and that called for a high degree of organization, especially at the auditions when the boys often became over excited. The patience and calming influences of both Ann Earle and Richard Witts were vital cogs within the drama wheel at these times, but the revue evenings were always much enjoyed and were clear evidence of the way drama had progressed since the immediate post-war years when only a few boarders had been involved in an annual production.

Elsie Smith's successor as Director of Music in 1965 was Roy Thackray, and he could not have been more different. To start with he was a professional oboist and, not until then, a schoolmaster. Although the school orchestra continued to have a strong string contingent under his direction, he broadened its scope and encouraged boys to start playing brass and woodwind instruments. It quickly became apparent that there was not the musical capacity within the full-time music staff for tuition to be given to a wider range of instruments, so teachers were brought in from outside. The days of the peripatetic music teacher had arrived. Soon it was evident that facilities for music in the school were hopelessly inadequate. More and more boys required tuition with an ever-increasing range of instruments, and every spare room, nook and cranny in the school became the home of yet another peripatetic music teacher. When the area over the school hall was built in 1966, part of the space was dedicated to Music with adjacent small teaching rooms, and this eased the situation for a while.

Just as 1928 can be regarded as a milestone in the school's music-making with the arrival of Russell Taylor, so another milestone was reached forty years later by the arrival of Michael Spencer. Already on the music staff, albeit in a part-time capacity, his first concert on 10th December in 1968 surpassed anything that had gone before. Vivaldi's *Gloria* was the major work of the evening and performers included a large number of parents, guests and boys. Roy Thackray played the oboe and, at the end, the concert was met with thunderous applause. A further boost came a few months later when on 5th March 1969 London Weekend Television filmed the choir for a programme which was subsequently shown on all Independent Television channels. Thackray and Spencer worked together for a while, but Thackray began to realise that schoolmastering was not quite his line and so decided to return to the world of professional music. Before he left, he wrote a musical called *Joseph* which was a light opera on the life of Joseph Haydn and this was performed as the school play in July 1970. The Art Department made the set so, with music and drama, the Arts were together as a team, a scenario which was to be followed many times in later years. As an opera, *Joseph* was an artistic first for DCPS.

In 1970 another musical first was reached when boys from the Lower, Middle and Upper Schools combined with parents and friends to form a much larger choir, later to become the DCPS Choral Society. Their first major rendition later that year was Haydn's *Nelson Mass*. In May 1974, *Noye's Fludde* by Benjamin Britten set the pattern for many concerts to follow and not for the first time was the school hall considered too small and acoustically unsound. Gilbey-McKenzie, the new Head of English, directed the work and Adrian Adams, recently appointed to the full-time music staff, played the organ. The organ itself, which came from Dulwich College, was also a new acquisition. *Noye's Fludde* was not just another milestone in the history of music-making at Dulwich Prep. One of the boys to sing at that concert was Ian Bostridge, who must be regarded as one of the greatest tenors of our time. When he and Michael Spencer gave interviews to Emily Moore from *The Guardian* in November 1999, both made reference to it and to each other in glowing terms. Ian Bostridge said: [1]

> I was about seven when I first met Michael Spencer. I sang in one of his concerts before he even became my music teacher. Michael was quite young, quite plump and very jolly and I really looked forward to his lessons as he was a very kind, funny, inspiring man. He was incredibly enthusiastic and very ambitious for us, in the best sense of the word. He put on operas and concerts. I sang Schubert's Shepherd on the Rock *with him for the first time when I was only twelve and I really benefited from Benjamin Britten's wonderful music for children. Michael also sent me off to audition at the English National Opera for a child's part in Massenet's opera* Werther. *That was my first proper audition – and at the Coliseum! I got the part and sang with one of the singers I now most admire, the great Janet Baker. If I hadn't met Michael I can't see how I would have ended up singing. I don't know that making people into professional musicians is really Michael's thing. He wanted to give us preparation for the things that are wonderful in life and to me that's what education is all about.*

In his reply to Ian Bostridge, Michael Spencer outlined his whole philosophy:

> Ian did a lot of singing at school. We introduced him to three or four pieces for which he has become known including work by Schubert. I think his introduction to Britten was singing one of the animal parts in Noye's Fludde *when he was about seven. For me, being director of music was more about being an enabler. I enabled children to fulfil their potential by providing them with opportunities. We set very high standards and that paid off. The music profession is full of disappointed people who have a lot of talent but who have not made the big time. It's a difficult career and I never thought it was my job to persuade people to become professional musicians. Despite this we have produced many talented pupils and many have become professional performers or composers.*

As a result of Spencer's endeavours and that of others, notably Derek Herdman the Director of Music at Downside Prep School in Purley, an orchestra was set up by IAPS whereby boys and girls from prep schools were auditioned to take part in an annual music course culminating in a concert. The first, in 1972, was held at the Snape Maltings near Aldeburgh in Suffolk, the venue it has used almost every year since. Seventy pupils from prep schools throughout Britain took part in that first concert and so successful was it

1 Both these extracts from an article by Emma Moore are reproduced by kind permission of Guardian Newspapers Ltd.

that within twenty years the number of auditions alone each year had reached almost a thousand. Over 200 boys from DCPS have benefited from these music courses since they started, giving each the opportunity of playing in a great concert hall. Spencer believed that children could sing at almost any age and could therefore sing great music such as *The Messiah* even as young as seven or eight, without necessarily being able to read music. He gave them support by having parents, staff and professional musicians performing with them thus elevating their standards well above what they would otherwise be able to achieve. He was of the opinion that music was not an esoteric pursuit for the few, but should involve as many children as possible. He considered too that it was not only important to cater for boys of scholarship ability, and all the prestige which came from it, but also for those who just wanted to be involved. As a result, works such as *The Christmas Oratorio, Verdi's Requiem*, and *The St Matthew Passion* were performed over the years, either in the Great Hall at Dulwich College or at St John's Church in Upper Norwood. In 1985, the school celebrated its centenary and in the following year a grand concert was held at the Fairfield Hall in Croydon for the first time. This was an overwhelming success when the challenging *Belshazzar's Feast* was performed. This was a great achievement for boys of prep school age and the culmination of years of endeavour. As if that were not enough, 120 boys also played *The 1812 Overture* by Tchaikovsky at the same concert. Spencer regarded this as his greatest musical achievement which set the standard for many concerts to follow. Cramped and overflowing conditions came to an end when the Hugh Woodcock Music School was opened on 14th October 1989 by John Amis, musician and former pupil. DCPS was not the first prep school to have such a facility and the school in Cranbrook

Michael Spencer with his orchestra in the then new music room, which opened in 1966

had built one there several years earlier as had schools elsewhere. Music at Cranbrook too had flourished from the start, John Leakey being the catalyst for both.

The spacious new music school did not improve the quality of music to any great extent, but it did make much easier the way by which it was taught and performed. It also set a standard which all subsequent building developments would have to match. Spencer and Donald Sillett, one of the Governors at the time, spent many hours planning its design and although there have been minor modifications since, it continues to fulfil admirably the purpose for which it was built. The concert hall proved to be a better setting for morning assemblies in place of the original hall, and with its seating retracted it was an ideal examination room for Common Entrance exams and sometimes for other functions. The new music school gave Spencer a reason to celebrate in style and within a month there was another concert at the Fairfield Hall in Croydon to mark its opening. Over 120 boys were involved, the programme including Handel's *Music for the Royal Fireworks* and Britten's *St Nicholas*. Spencer's contribution to the world of prep school music did not go by unnoticed. In 1987 he was elected President of the Music Masters and Mistresses Association (MMA), the first ever to come from a preparatory school, and in 1990 the annual MMA Conference was hosted by DCPS, when 170 music teachers from all over Britain came and saw what Dulwich had to offer. Never before had the Conference been held at an IAPS school. Successive years saw concerts of one form or another take place in almost every term and if the concert hall was not large enough other venues such as St

The Hugh Woodcock Music School opened by John Amis on 14th October 1989

John's Church were chosen instead. More and more boys gained music scholarships and in 1993 the Fairfield Hall was the setting again to mark Spencer's twenty-fifth major concert since becoming Director of Music. This time the principal work was *The Creation* by Haydn and Ian Bostridge returned to sing a tenor part to pay a personal tribute to his old school in general and to Michael Spencer in particular. When Spencer retired in 1997 he was able to hand over a flourishing department, commenting at the time that his greatest rewards had been the broadening of musical interest to so many others, and making music in prep schools something vibrant, exciting and, most important of all, recognised.

The new Director of Music was Philip Brooke who thus inherited a well established department. He had been attracted to DCPS because of the size and reputation of its music department and his challenge was to maintain it, extend it wherever he could and adapt it to his own beliefs and needs. The Christmas and spring concerts continued, invariably at St John's Church, but new and different venues were often chosen for concerts in the summer. Spencer's belief that the performance of children could be enhanced by participating adults, either as individuals or as members of a choir, was shared by Brooke but when Spencer retired, many former members of his choral society had been with him for a long time, their sons having become adults, and they chose to move on with him.

A new influx of parents was eager to take their place and the DCPS Choral Society quickly began to flourish again, culminating in 2002 when over 100 adults joined a large boys' choir at the Theatre Royal Drury Lane in Central London, the major work being Mozart's

The DCPS orchestra, choir and choral society in the Fairfield Hall, Croydon (1985)

Coronation Mass. This was held on a Sunday in March when the theatre would otherwise have been dark. Another highlight, two years earlier, was the Millennium concert at the Fairfield Hall. This was a celebration of English music and included Handel's *Zadok the Priest* and Elgar's *Pomp and Circumstance March No 1*. A light-hearted addition was Michael Hurd's *Hip Hip Horatio*, an inventive mock oratorio about aspects of the life of Horatio Nelson. Ideally suited for young people, there were 380 voices in all of whom almost 300 were boys from Years 2 to 8. The dressing rooms were clearly inadequate for such numbers and the Year 2 boys from the Annexe, when not performing, were supervised in the boxes where they were as good as gold. The atmosphere of this part of the concert was best summed up by Purav Patel who was in Year 3 at the time:

> *Concert 2000! This was a smashing hit. The audience loved it, I loved it, everyone loved it. We sang thirteen songs and through the concert Mr Brooke conducted. The first song was called* Hip Hip Horatio *and then* When There's Hunger in the House. *My favourite songs were* Cor blimey Admiral Nelson *and* Blast of Gun. *Concert 2000 was the best I have ever been to. Our bit was after the interval and my mum said I could not stay quiet for two hours, but I did.*

In recent years choirs were invited to take part in concerts for charity, notable among these being the involvement of a DCPS choir in 2000, and each subsequent year, at the carol service at St James' Piccadilly for The Dementia Relief Trust. On another occasion a choir took part in a Thanksgiving Service for the sponsors of the children's charity The Story of Christmas which was held at St Paul's Church, Covent Garden. Going further afield, and

Philip Brooke offering advice to the trumpeters in the Music School - 2002

in collaboration with the modern languages department, 80 boys, principally musicians, went on a tour in 2001 to Strasbourg where a concert was given at the Pavillon Josephine, a splendid Georgian concert hall seating 400 and directly opposite the European Parliament Building. Concerts were also given at Baden Baden and Colmar. Originally planned as a one-off, similar tours took place in 2002 and 2004 to the same region and more are planned. The breadth and depth of Music has steadily increased so that by the summer of 2004, 587 boys received individual music lessons covering a wide range of instruments, a record which was broadened still further after the school was approached to provide tuition for the bagpipes. A great deal of organisation is required to cater for such numbers as well as the employment of many peripatetic music staff. In addition to the Director, there are three full-time members of the music staff who become involved in all aspects of school life. Notable among these has been Adrian Adams who joined the staff in 1968 and has given profound advice to both Spencer and Brooke over the years and also Barbara Dalton who left the school as Head of Wind in 2000 after more than twenty years. The number of boys gaining music scholarships has increased steadily, the school continues to be well represented at the Snape Maltings each year, concerts proliferate often in new and grand surroundings and the subject, it appears, has no bounds.

Although there had been a degree of co-operation between the Arts prior to 1970, the appointment of Spencer (1968), Gilbey-McKenzie (1972) and Richards (1975) resulted in many ventures which brought the three disciplines of Creative Art, Drama and Music closely together for over a decade. Richards involved as many boys as he could both in club and class time to create scenery and costumes for all of Gilbey-McKenzie's plays as soon as he arrived. His art assistant was always kept busy and Christine Riley from the book room gave a willing hand towards making the costumes. Music also often played a major part in main school plays, at that time always held at the end of the summer term. 1975, the first year when the three worked together, was an example when almost everyone was involved. The production, *The Ever Popular Fall and Redemption Show*, was a musical adaptation of the fall

Max Hudd (left) as Huck and Andrew Savege as Tom in Tom Sawyer (1977)

and redemption of Man. Richards and his team provided the set and costumes, the latter being made extensively out of plastic bags and off-cuts from bins outside a plastics factory! Whitcomb, from the PE staff, wrote the songs and played the drums, Spencer arranged the songs and produced some energetic and lively piano music, boys from the orchestra provided musical accompaniment and the student of the day, John Ratcliff, played the guitar. Among other productions to include music extensively were *The Rise and Fall of Arturo Ui* (1979) and *Oh! What a Lovely War* (1980). In 1977 *Tom Sawyer* involved the whole school orchestra, the boys wearing white shirts and neat bow ties for the occasion, and there were so many boys involved as actors or musicians that there was hardly enough room in the hall for the audience. A rugged Huckleberry Finn was played by Max Hudd, son of Roy Hudd the comedian, broadcaster and entertainer. Now following in his father's footsteps, this was Max's first major stage performance. The peak of artistic co-operation came with *Adventure Story* in 1985, the year of the school's centenary. This involved a dance-mimed battle scene with a large cast and two talented boys, Nick Rucker and Tom Amlot played key roles. Adrian Adams was the Deputy Director of Music during the entire period and of this co-operation he wrote:

> *Gilbey-McKenzie's stage productions, and especially the musicals, were hard work but enormous fun. He was a hard taskmaster but he knew exactly what he wanted and he was always grateful for the musical input from Spencer and his team, especially the boy musicians, instrumentalists and singers. G-M's productions were, and still are, unique not just in the prep school world, but in the various theatrical groups with which he has been involved.*

This cultural activity was not restricted to the older boys. Sue Cownie presented *Pooh* for the benefit of parents and boys at the Annexe, and at the Nursery there was an adaptation of *Cinderella* for children as young as three. It must not be assumed that this was the only time in the school's history when the three arts have worked together, but it was a time when the links were close and continuous. It is logical for Art and Drama to come together and there have been productions before and since when this has been the case. Music and Drama have always co-operated as those early concerts at St Barnabas Church Hall have shown, and if a producer wishes to involve music in a school play it is logical that the talents of both should be brought together.

When Kendrick left the school in 1996 responsibility for the annual school play fell to his successor Jonathan Kreeger, but he was to produce just three. He continued with the revue evenings, and his love for music and drama meant that his productions involved both. Like his predecessor, he wrote his first play himself and *The Government Inspector* in 1997 was based on an original work by Gogol. Of his involvement, Edwin Morgan (DCPS 1993-1999) wrote:

> *The rehearsals are great fun as I enjoy singing and acting. Mr Kreeger is a perfectionist which is good because without him the play would fall apart.*

The play did not fall apart and Kreeger's first received wide acclaim. His second was also home produced for although *The Frog* was based on Aristophanes, he wrote the play and the lyrics for it. This time the music was provided by the school band led by Adrian Adams and an imaginative set was created by the then recently appointed Head of Art, Glenn Smart. Of this a former parent (Fiona Holman) wrote:

> *The whole hall seemed to be filled with scenery and staging cleverly creating London at one end, Paris at the other and the entire English Channel and Tunnel between, with of course Eurostar travelling from one to the other.*

For his third and final play in 1999 Kreeger wrote the lyrics for a musical adaptation of *Toad of Toad Hall* based on Kenneth Grahame's *Wind in the Willows*. He played the piano himself as well as directing and producing, and again many boys were involved, the play being much enjoyed by all who watched or performed in it. But there were to be no more Kreeger productions for the school was saddened to hear of his unexpected death in March 2001. Many tributes were paid to a talented man and a 'JSK' Memorial Prize for Drama was created to his memory.

In 2000 the school was treated to two one act plays instead of the usual one. The first, *Good Morning and Welcome to the Last Day at the Berlin Oval* was the bizarre title of a well performed play by Years 5 and 6. This was produced by Alex Woodard from the English staff. The other, for Years 7 and 8, was *Ernie's Incredible Illucinations* produced by Richard Aitchison. As usual the boys became wildly enthusiastic and gained much pleasure from being involved. In 2001 the play was produced by Richard Aitchison who had been appointed Head of English. He chose Lionel Bart's *Oliver!*, always a favourite because much of the music is familiar and the play involves a large number of participants. Senior and junior drama clubs were resurrected in 2002 and Aitchison brought Shakespeare to the fore again with an outstanding production of Macbeth, the *Good Schools Guide for 2003* describing it as 'breathtaking'. In a totally different vein, Woodard presented the *Demon Headmaster* in 2003 and with schoolboys playing the part of schoolboys, it could hardly fail.

Two years earlier, Aitchison, ever mindful of the need to involve more boys in drama, decided to make some changes. Producing high calibre plays at the end of each summer term had always presented problems, so much so that by 2001 calendar demands and ever-increasing commitments for boys and staff alike, made it almost impossible to continue at this time. As a result the annual production was switched to the end of the spring term with auditions taking place early in the preceding autumn. The slot thus vacated meant that the revue could be resumed at the end of the summer term and could involve more boys offering a greater degree of flexibility. Known as *Stuff and Nonsense*, this revue takes place each year in the studio theatre in the Betws building, this being better suited to informal drama. As before, members of staff offer guidance, but the material is original and auditioned, and the revue often gives boys the opportunity and pleasure of appearing on a stage for the first time. In 2004 the main production was *The Devil and His Boy,* adapted from the novel of the same name by Anthony Horowitz. Produced, directed and adapted by James Carroll from the English staff, the first performance was attended by Anthony Horowitz himself, who kindly popped backstage after the performance to congratulate the actors and all involved for their efforts.

By 1930, Drama and Music were working closely together and there were many productions, usually at Christmas, involving both. It was Creative Art at that time which was lagging behind with few lessons devoted to it, and most art work being done after school as a club. Seventy years on the situation has changed. Both Art and Music have spacious facilities, with a nominated Head for each, and it is Drama which has become the 'Cinderella' of the arts scene. In the Main School, more lessons

'A boy - boy for sale'
Mr Bumble (Dominic Hodson) offers Oliver (Richard Southgate) for sale in the school production of Oliver! *- 2001*

were devoted to it after 2004 and the subject comes under the umbrella of the English Department. There are plans, tentative ones, to broaden the scope for drama in the future and to give it greater status. On the serrated edge of the £2 coin are the words 'Standing on the Shoulders of Giants'. The giant has been firmly in place for Music and Art for some time and upon the shoulders of both, achievements each year have stood higher and higher, with facilities for both being second to none. The shoulders for Drama are still in the making.

A constant recurring theme over the years has been a lack of space, although DCPS is better off in this respect than many other Inner London schools, and headmasters (or since 1957 the school's governors), have bought or leased further property whenever opportunities have arisen. Facilities for Art and Music in the twenty-first century are beyond the dreams of those who pioneered those subjects so long ago. The problem of finding space for a theatre has yet to be solved and the magnificent John Leakey Theatre at the school in Cranbrook is the envy of all in Dulwich. Maybe the dream of a theatre on site will one day become a reality.

. . . music has no bounds!

Sam Williamson (DCPS 1987- 1996) with instrument

13 Physical Challenges

When the school opened in 1885, the only space available for any kind of physical activity was the garden behind Whitfield Lodge, the headmaster's house at the foot of Alleyn Park where the Alleyn's Head now stands. Within a short time, the Master of the College, Dr Welldon, permitted 'The Preparatory School' to make use of some of the College grounds, but it would be several years before the school was large enough for matches to be played.

Within ten years, Mallinson, who had succeeded Mason as headmaster, managed to secure a ten year lease from the Estate Governors of a field by the side of what is now Grange Lane. A field it most certainly was for Mallinson immediately had to set about the task of levelling and draining it. This was an expensive business and in 1896 parents were invited to contribute towards the cost. By the following summer enough ground had been levelled for six games of cricket to be played in front of where the pavilion now stands. The area behind had yet to be leased. Known still as the 'School Field' the heavy London clay has always caused problems and there have been several attempts at drainage since, none of them being particularly successful. When the lease was renewed in 1915, the cost was £68 per annum[1].

Notes from *The Alleynian* provide information about the schools with which the Prep had fixtures in the early days, many of them now just memories. There was a school for the Sons of Missionaries in Blackheath and schools such as The Abbey in Beckenham, Royston House in Lewisham and St Winifred's in Kenley have long since disappeared. Most reports give detail of the prowess of the 1st XV and the 1st XI although a cricket 2nd XI had been formed by 1909. Weather and illness often played a part and in 1905, for example, several rugby matches were cancelled because of measles on one side or the other and in the summer cricket suffered in a similar way. The fielding of the 1st XI that year was poor because '*players were slow to back up and were uncertain of catching*'. Prolonged poor weather was also a problem. 1909 was a disappointing season for the rugby players with no matches won at all, the one against The Orchard boarding house of Dulwich College being lost 30 points to nil. It was not all doom and gloom and there were some successful matches, but reports were generally more critical than commendatory. Some of the matches were to distant destinations such as The Bengeo School in Hertford and Hillside School in Godalming. No mention is made as to how the boys travelled to these

---

1 Minutes of the Estate Governors (Courtesy Dulwich College Archives)

destinations, how long they took, who paid for them and whether they were full day fixtures or not. As well as fixtures with other schools, inter-form matches in both rugby and cricket were played in the days before tribes and although some games were voluntary not all were. Years later Mallinson's daughter Muriel wrote how her father was very strict about games and frequently took a roll-call himself at the school field to make sure that everybody was present.

Mallinson's successor, Revd W R M Leake, made an enormous impact on the school as we have seen. He distinguished himself both academically and on the sports field whilst a boy at the College and by playing rugby for England on three subsequent occasions, enthusiasm for sport was very much in his blood. Such was his reputation that, even before he became headmaster in 1910, Mallinson had invited him on several occasions to judge competitions in Drill which had been established. The 1st XV and 1st XI continued to dominate the sports scene but by 1915 the school was able to field three cricket teams against the College. In the following year there were 1st and 2nd XV teams, both of whom played successfully against Dulwich College, King's Wimbledon and Bickley Hall, a prep school which closed in the 1960s.

With the arrival of its own magazine in 1919, news about The Prep's sporting achievements became more detailed. The 1st XV was in the hands of A E J Inglis, who had left briefly in 1920 but was soon back again. Before his sojourn, a report about two matches played away at King's Wimbledon on 12th November 1919 is of interest. By this time a 2nd XV was being fielded and C W Hamilton was in charge of this. As the boys left the school on foot for Gipsy Hill Station *'whispered murmurs of admiration could be heard emanating from the various houses en route'*. On arrival at Wimbledon the two teams played close to each other and *'Mr Inglis and Mr Hamilton distinguished themselves by producing the most wonderful volume of sound ever heard on this continent and have been reduced lately to speaking in a hoarse and weird whisper'*. After a game which was described as magnificent, the 1st XV was beaten by a narrow margin of three points and a similar defeat befell the 2nd XV. At the end of the day *'The whole party arrived back at The Prep battered and bruised but intact, at about 6.15pm. Thoroughly happy and not a little tired, all having had a first class game and a most enjoyable outing'*.

As well as the results of matches, the annual reviews often gave advice and criticism as to how the games should be played. In the spring of 1920 for example, Inglis exhorted his players to *'Play hard, run hard and tackle hard'*. 1924 was an exceptional year for the 1st XV and the team photograph for that year, with a triumphant Leake seated in the middle, proudly proclaimed that six matches had been played and there had been 156 points for and only 5 against. Leake invariably appeared in team photographs and always took a keen interest. On 25th October 1925 two teams ventured to St John's, Leatherhead, their mode of transport this time being a small charabanc. Inglis was invited to referee and not long after the game had started, the boys were delighted to see Leake at the touchline, for as soon as school had ended he had

A proud Leake with the 1924 1st XV whose season ended with 156 points for and 5 against

grabbed his bicycle and cycled there to watch them. The result was a draw, six points being scored by each side. As the years went by more matches were played and by 1930 a team for the younger boys had been formed. Fortunes depended upon the calibre of boys in any particular year, the weather and to a lesser extent illness, at a time when epidemics were prevalent. Sometimes boys played for more than one season, but more often than not teams were brought together each year from scratch. The school teams were the elite. Other boys played games at lower levels but without the cutting edge of a match with another school. There was never any shortage of enthusiasm and boys who showed promise were moved up to the Second or First team, no doubt at the expense of some unfortunate who was moved down. There was clearly much talent around for in 1935 a 3rd XV was formed. They only had one match against the 2nd XV which, not surprisingly, they lost 3-15, but no doubt some talent was spotted. Boys often left the school at Christmas in those days and this had an adverse effect on rugby for the following term. For the two rugby playing terms in 1937 for example, fifteen matches were played by the 1st XV without defeat, thanks largely to a strong team captained by W J D Bradfield who played at scrum half. Without him and other outstanding players, the spring of 1938 was described as a bad patch when things went from bad to worse. Bradfield was an exceptional sportsman who also captained the 1st XI and it must have given him much pleasure when he was invited back to the Prep to give away the prizes on Sports Day in 1986. Rugby in the spring of 1939 was limited by poor weather, but it took more than a war to dampen the spirit and enthusiasm for the game and when the school found itself at Cranbrook in the autumn of that year, rugby continued almost as if nothing had happened:

> *Despite Hitler's desire to conquer Europe, the term's rugby has been reasonably successful and we have managed to play three matches.*

As the war progressed, and the school moved to Wales, matches became more difficult to arrange and play but games were played whenever it was possible to do so.

In 1937 an Under 10 soccer team was created for the first time, this being an experiment to give the younger boys a chance to play for the school and, it was said at the time, to lay foundations for rugby later on. In the first season there were seven matches, five of which were won. Soccer proved to be very popular and within two years a 2nd XI had been added so that by the time war arrived, it was well established. Some attempts were made to arrange matches on arrival at Cranbrook but with little success, and once in Wales soccer was played but it was not amongst the priorities of activities there.

No less important was the summer game - cricket. Cricket was played almost as soon as there were enough boys to create two sides and, as with rugby, games were played on ground belonging to the College until the Prep had its own field at Grange Lane. Within ten years of its founding the school was able to field a team against St Paul's Junior School (Colet Court) and a year later, in 1896, a match took place in Beckenham against a school called Merton House. Unfortunately no results were recorded. In 1907, there was a match against St Olave's School and another against Alleyn Court at Westcliff-on-Sea. In 1907 a match was played against the masters for the first time but again the result is not recorded[2]. Tribe matches were played from 1916, and in 1920 an outbreak of mumps caused problems which may have contributed towards the Prep's batting that season, which was described as 'poor'. An exciting match against the College was played at the end of June which resulted in a nail-biting tie. Leake took as much interest in cricket as he did in rugby and in 1922 was heard to murmur a piece of verse which illustrated the point:

> *Sweet is the music of the harp*
> *And sweet the song of the bird*
> *But I deem the noise of the cricket bat*
> *Is the sweetest ever heard.*

2 Information from relevant issues of *The Alleynian* (Courtesy Dulwich College Archives)

In 1924 a pavilion, which was of particular benefit to the cricketers, was built at the field in Grange Lane. On 16th July that year, the 1st XI played a match against the masters which by this time had become an annual event. The staff, captained by Hamilton himself, scored 176 and, when it was time to draw stumps, the boys had scored 100 for 3. Leake laid on a grand tea afterwards for spectators and players and so successful was the whole occasion that in the following week a match was arranged between the 2nd XI and a 2nd team from the staff. This included Marjorie, Leake's daughter, the report on the match stating that '*her hefty slogs proved that the weaker sex is the stronger as she managed the top score of 33 not out*'. In the end the boys were defeated by eight runs.

In the summer, cricket was played on what were called half holidays - Wednesday and Saturday afternoons after school which finished earlier (at 2.45 p.m.) on those days. In 1928 Hamilton recorded that no fewer than 358 boys had played cricket during the summer term and that '*no boy could complain that he has not had every chance of trying to learn more about our national game.*' Throughout the 1920s Hamilton had two constant gripes. One was that at the end of every season he lost his best players to other schools, but such is the lot of the prep school teacher. The other moan was about the weather which at the start of season after season was disappointing for cricket. In 1932 for example, it was so cold that rugby resumed until mid-May, but a reasonably successful season followed. Hamilton continued to organize the cricket throughout the 1930s and more and more boys became involved in the game. In 1933 he made an unusual entry in the cricket notes for that year. It is worth quoting, not so much because of its relevance to DCPS cricket, but because it is a social cameo of the time reflecting what were then current attitudes:

> *One of the eleven was worried because his white socks had not been returned from the laundry in time for the match, but nevertheless the player played well and scored runs although his socks were grey; and while the tennis gentlemen at Wimbledon have a decided leaning towards short knickers, the cricket gentlemen of DCPS have a strong liking for long trousers. Personal pride in appearance is right and good, but the Game's the thing.*

1934 was a particularly successful season and carrying on with the same theme, Hamilton reminded boys that cricket was a grand game because it was British! Grand it may have been but there were only five or six matches for the 1st XI each season. In 1937 games of cricket were organised on whole school days for the first time, these being for enthusiastic boys who did not quite make the grade for match teams and in 1938 all weather nets appeared on the school field. N C Blomfield became responsible for the 1st XI and in 1939 an Under 10 team was created, the cricket season generally being described as one of the best ever, with much enthusiasm being shown by boys at all levels. This came to an abrupt halt when war was declared soon after the season finished. In Wales matches were played against other schools in the area but there were transport difficulties. During the war some matches were played in Dulwich, but these depended on conditions prevailing at the time and the number of boys available to play.

The annual Sports Day which was held each summer term quickly became a major event in the school's calendar and was a grand occasion. Before the tribes were created in 1916, there was little team competitiveness and awards were based on the prowess of individuals. The oldest cup currently in circulation is the *Richmond Cup* which was given to the school in 1892 originally for the Quarter Mile (440 yards). It is still awarded each year but has since been amended to 400 metres. A cup for the *Victor Ludorum* was awarded to the boy who had displayed the greatest skill overall. In 1908, the prizes were awarded by Mrs Mallinson, the Headmaster's wife, and for Leake's second year in 1912, Sports Day was held in glorious weather. A large number of visitors showed their approval for 'The Great Day' and a relay race was introduced for the first time involving four boys from each form in the Upper School. In 1916 the annual sports would have been based on a tribe competition for the first time, but they were postponed at the last minute because of the death of Lord Kitchener the day before. In the years that followed, and especially after the First War, Leake gradually evolved Sports Day into a grand annual occasion. The tribes and boys took pride of place, but spectators were included too with races for sisters and other visitors. Sports Day in 1924 was held on 25th June and this description set the scene:

> At 1.30, the Tribes fell in on the playground, and with the Union Jack at the head, marched to the field where a good number of spectators had assembled. The marching was excellent in spite of the excitement that prevailed.

As well as the race for sisters, there were relay races for the 'puppies', an obstacle race and at the end, the pole race which in that year was won by the Ojibwas. The tribes then returned to their bases and marched past the parents before forming a square around the pavilion for the prize giving. This was done by Mrs Leake, who was given a large bouquet of flowers, and in his address Leake thanked Messrs Butler and Inglis for arranging the day so well. When Inglis left the Prep in 1929, Hamilton took over the organisation of Sports Day, as well as being responsible for the 1st XI, and throughout the 1930s it continued to provide a sense of occasion. Leake regarded it as a major event in the school's sporting calendar and it was always a grand occasion when the sun invariably shone. From the school, and dressed in their athletic gear, the boys marched down Union Road (now Hunts Slip Road) by tribes, the leader of each in front carrying a large flag of the respective colour. Once at the field, the boys formed into groups by tribes and races were run. Elimination heats had already been decided beforehand so that only the best performed on the day. Eminent people were invited to give away the cups and certificates, more often than not this being the Master of the College. Alan Wesencraft (DCPS 1921–1925) recalled a typical Sports Day:

> Four portions of the ground were allotted to the four Tribes as a kind of base from which those not involved could watch events and cheer their members. Provided the rules of good behaviour were observed, senior boys were usually allowed some freedom to stroll around and mingle with the spectators. All were expected to hear Mr Leake's closing speech, the final words of which were usually 'To your wigwams, Oh Tribes!' After the proceedings, two large barrels of ginger beer were provided for the boys.

Leake was very proud of the tribe system which he had created and Leakey carried on the tradition after him, often becoming involved in the races himself. In 1933 the results were broadcast over a loudspeaker system for the first time, and in the following year this was extended to provide music for the march past which as a result was much improved. Prizes and cups were awarded by the Master of the College, W R Booth, and when he was invited again in 1937, he said that the march past was the best he had ever seen, the Mohicans in particular marching like guardsmen! Sports continued to involve boys from the Lower School upwards, the Annexe

Programme for Sports Day 1936

Leake and his wife at Sports Day 1936. Behind him is W R Booth, Master of the College, who is about to present the cups. (Courtesy Sir Bryan Thwaites)

Dulwich College Preparatory School

ATHLETIC SPORTS

TRIBES: Chippeways, *Red.*   Ojibways, *Orange.*
         Deerfeet, *Blue.*   Mohicans, *Green.*

EVENTS:

N.B.—*Those marked with an asterisk count for the Championship Cup*

*1. 100 yards Open.
2. 100 yards under 12.
3. 100 yards under 11.
4. 100 yards under 10.
5. 100 yards under 9.
6. 220 yards handicap, Heats, by Tribes.
7. 150 yards under 10 handicap, Heats, by Tribes.
8. Balloon race.
9. Wheelbarrow race, under 11.
10. Wheelbarrow race, over 11.
11. Cricket ball race, between 10 and 11, Tribes.
*12. Quarter Mile.
13. Race for Changing Room.
14. Little Visitors, under 8, Girls.
15. Little Visitors, over 8, Girls.
16. Little Visitors, under 8, Boys.
17. Relay race, under 10, Tribes.
18. Relay race, over 12, Tribes.
19. Relay race, under 12, Tribes.
20. Ball race, under 10, Tribes.
21. 220 yards, Final.
22. 150 yards, Final.
23. Hurdles, under 12, Final Heats 1 and 2.
24. Hurdles, Open, Final Heats 1 and 2.
25. Hurdles, under 12, Final
*26. Hurdles, Open, Final.
27. Pole race, Tribes.

MARCH PAST   ::   PRESENTATION OF PRIZES

Events decided before Sports Day :
*Half Mile, Open.   ::   *High Jump, Open.
*300 Yards, Open.   ::   *Long Jump, Open.
Patrol Leaders Race.

The March Past in front of appreciative parents - Sports Day 1937

boys having their own sports on the paddock which, although they were not so grand, did prepare boys for the 'big sports' which were to follow. In 1939 Sports Day was on 1st July. Music for the march past was provided by the College band and the proceedings were rounded off with ginger beer and buns as usual. It was to be the end of an era. Two months later the country was at war and sports afterwards were never the same again. During the war years, sports of a sort were held at Betws-y-Coed but without many spectators and all the razzmatazz of pre-war days.

A sporting activity which leaned heavily on the College for support was swimming and Prep boys were able to use the College baths almost from the start. From 1905, boys were taken there after school one form at a time, thus enabling individual instruction to be given. It was a voluntary summer activity as the water was not heated, but the baths had a glass roof which helped. If there was little sunshine, the water remained cold. Despite these limitations, boys were constantly being urged to swim as this rallying call from the Preparatory Section of *The Alleynian* for 1907 recalled:

> *It is to be hoped that every boy will do his utmost to learn to swim this term. Not only will his pleasure in bathing be doubled thereby, but it may enable him in later years to save his own or his comrade's life in case of accident.*

By the end of the summer term in 1910, 83 boys could swim a length at the College baths, over a hundred could manage a width and the first swimming sports were held there on July 20th. The creation of the tribes in 1916 gave an impetus to competitive swimming as it did with other sporting activities and it became better organised. Inglis took swimming

Boys using the College swimming baths before the roof was blown off during the war. The water was unheated.

under his wing as well as rugby, constantly urging more and more boys to take part although it continued to be a summer term activity only. Some years were better than others. In 1923, for example, the weather for much of the term was cold and *'few boys were brave enough to venture into the icy water'*. In 1928, Inglis bemoaned the fact that out of 480 boys in the school, only eighty-one could swim a length and this was not a credit to the school. With biting tongue, he continued by saying *'fancy diving, splashing about and horseplay are of no practical use and do a great deal of harm at the learning stage.'* The success or otherwise of swimming each year was clearly dependant on the weather. By 1931, S F Swayne was in charge and he encouraged more of the younger boys to venture across to the College for a swim. In 1932, which was presumably a warm year, over 200 boys had swum a length and this annual count of lengths appears to be the way by which the success of swimming was judged. There were inter-tribe swimming sports at the end of each summer term and by 1937 matches against other schools were being held for Over 12 and Under 12 age groups. On 12th July 1937 a match was held at the College baths against the masters who were just beaten by the boys. Matches and sports held at the end of the summer term in 1939 were the last for a while. No swimming was possible in Dulwich during the war and in Wales occasional trips were made by train to public baths near Llandudno. Peter Vernon (DCPS Betws 1940-1944) remembered what were loosely described as swimming sports one year taking place at a still spot on the River Conway at Betws, but otherwise swimming there resorted to little more than paddling in the nearby River Llugwy.

Tennis, the Cinderella of summer sports at DCPS, was introduced in 1934. The lawn behind 42 Alleyn Park was made into a tennis court and remained so until converted into cricket nets which themselves were displaced when the 'cage' playgrounds were made. Tennis was also played on the paddock and at Hamilton's house at 28 Alleyn Park where the lawn was large enough for it to be marked out as a tennis court. As this was one of the houses where boys boarded, matches were arranged there between boarders and day boys. By 1937, matches with other schools had been arranged and in 1939 tribe tennis matches were introduced amid *'an atmosphere of determination and tribe feeling'*. Little mention is made of tennis being played either at Cranbrook, Betws or in Dulwich during the war so presumably there were other priorities.

Perhaps the severest of all physical challenges is boxing which was first introduced into the school in the spring term of 1920. It must have stopped soon after, for when introduced again in 1931, it was described as a new venture. Gibb was in charge and it proved to be very popular. Almost at once, inter-tribe boxing bouts were held and in the following year fixtures were made with other schools at what was called bantam weight. Notable among

these were the matches against the College and Colet Court. Boxing was an activity for the autumn and spring terms and took place at the College baths which were boarded over in winter and used as a gymnasium. When J B (Hamish) Maclean joined the staff in 1938, a keen and competent boxer himself, he gave boxing a brief impetus before the war took him off to fight elsewhere.

P L Amlot and G J Harper receiving instruction from Matt Wells whom Leakey described as an 'ex-Lightweight and Professional Champion of Great Britain' in 1952.

No mention is made of any boxing activity during the war either in Dulwich or in Wales. Because of damage sustained to the College baths during the war, it was not possible to use them as a gymnasium in the winter terms afterwards, so when boxing resumed at DCPS makeshift rings were made in the old corrugated iron gymnasium and also in the school hall using the two central pillars as supports. In 1946, Leakey gained the services of Matt Wells an ex-lightweight professional, who offered boxing tuition after school three times a week. Matches were held with other schools and for a short while boxing flourished. When Matt Wells retired in 1957, the whole concept of schoolboy boxing was becoming less popular with parents, not only at DCPS but generally, although there were still boys eager 'to have a go'. When Maclean returned to Dulwich in 1962, he tried to resuscitate boxing with the younger boys and it became popular again for a short while, even extending to the occasional match. The last of these, against a junior team from Dulwich College, took place on 7th   March 1967 by which time schoolboy boxing was well and truly in decline and within a year it had finished altogether.

Even before the school was fully reunited in September 1945, sporting activities resumed almost at once. The 1st XI played nine matches in the summer of that year, winning four and drawing two of them. Although there was plenty of enthusiasm at lower levels, it was only possible to play one match for the Under 11 team, that being against University College School (UCS) in Hampstead, which resulted in an easy win. The previous major Sports Day had been held in glorious sunshine just two months before war had been declared and in 1945, again on a beautiful day, it reappeared virtually two months after the signing of peace in Europe. In the autumn, rugby got off to a flying start with matches played on the new ground which had come with the acquisition of Brightlands that term. Enthusiasm was not entirely matched by success and the first post-war match for the 1st XV against the College was an overwhelming defeat, the score being 33 points to nil. Opponents in both cricket and rugby were often the junior departments of neighbouring day schools and, as well as the College, included Colfe's in Lee, St Dunstan's in Catford, UCS Hampstead, KCS Wimbledon and later King's, Rochester.

Rugby was in the hands of Gibb and in the autumn of 1946 he wrote that not only had the weather been kinder than usual, but that was small fry when compared with the return of J B Maclean to the school and the rugby field, which happened the following term. For the next few years the pair of them enthusiastically encouraged the 1st XV to play their hardest and more often than not a season which started with comparative novices ended successfully with some fine and experienced players. But the partnership did not last long. In 1948 Maclean went off to be Master-in-Charge at DCPS Coursehorn and two years later, Gibb retired prematurely as a result of ill health. After the war an afternoon of games was allocated in the school timetable and was compulsory for all, the lower games being anything but glorious. In addition, Wednesday afternoons were set aside for sporting activities of one kind or another, although there were a few other options. One such 'option' was known as 'Punishment Half Holiday Detention', which was intended for major misdemeanours. This quickly became popular with the non-sporty fraternity who would otherwise have to play games, but when this was switched to Saturday afternoons instead, it quickly lost its popularity. There was no school on Wednesday and Saturday afternoons and most matches were played on those days. There were 1st and 2nd teams for rugby and cricket, an Under 11 team for cricket in the summer, and soccer for all under 11 boys in the two winter terms. The weather caused many interruptions and during the spring term of 1947, when there was heavy snow for much of the term, and regarded as one of the severest winters of the century, virtually no outside games were played at all. Spring 1959 was also a disappointing term for rugby with no matches played at all as a result of floods, frost and 'flu, or a combination of all three. Things were no better a decade later when the pitches were unusable for much of the term. Thanks to the generosity of a parent, the school had the exclusive use of the ice rink at Streatham for several Wednesday afternoons, although how much was exercise and how much was fun was a matter of some conjecture.

Thanks to the generosity of a parent and the Mecca organisation boys were taken to the ice rink in Streatham for exercise on a series of Wednesday afternoons in February 1969 when the pitches could not be used.

With Gibb's departure in 1950, several members of staff were responsible for rugby until the arrival in 1956 of H J (Bert) Finn. Under his jurisdiction, more matches were arranged and by introducing league tribe matches, greater involvement in the game was given to boys who were not quite good enough to play in school matches. As always, some seasons were more successful than others but generally the 1st XV lost more games during a season than were won, although this was not due to any lack of enthusiasm or talent. Many matches were played against the junior departments of senior schools whose boys invariably appeared to be bigger physically, if not older, than Prep boys. When Finn had a year in New Zealand in 1962, the 1st XV was looked after by Malcolm Curtis who wrote that '*it would be nice to be able to report to Mr Finn in New Zealand that the school rugby teams were winning their matches*'. Opponents varied little from the pattern established after the war but matches with other prep schools such as Rokeby, King's House Richmond and the New Beacon in Sevenoaks began to appear. At the end of the autumn term in 1964 Finn bemoaned the fact that once again the DCPS boys that year were so much smaller in size than their opponents and during the following term the 1st XV was heavily defeated by St Dunstan's, the score being 0-37. Yet in the same term the team managed to defeat Rokeby, then a new fixture, by 14 points to 13 and the match against King's Richmond was drawn with 11 points each, thus illustrating Finn's point that matches with other prep schools were more balanced, while those with senior schools often provided the greater challenge and useful experience. The pattern for the 2nd XV in 1964 was much the same. Their match against St Dunstan's, oddly enough, produced the same result (0-37), Maclean describing it as a severe thrashing. Revenge followed in the game against a 2nd XV from Homefield a few weeks later when the score was reversed with a DCPS win by 30 points. Perhaps neither game was the most exciting to watch. Things perked up a year later when, with a new 1st XV, the City of London was defeated 9 points to 6, a season which Finn described as outstanding. The matches against Dulwich College were always the local Derby and when the 1st XV played a junior College team, it was not unusual for several opponents to have been old Prep boys who had moved on at the age of 11. In 1967 rugby began to encroach into the domain of soccer, which had always been exclusively for boys under the age of 11, when an Under 11 rugby team was introduced as an experiment. Three matches were arranged for them, two being drawn and the other lost. This was hardly surprising as David Whytehead, who had agreed to be responsible for them, wrote afterwards that several of the team players had never handled a rugby ball before the match! In 1969, the 1st XV played twelve matches and won seven of them, but the weather was so poor in the spring, that Whytehead's newly formed Under 11 team had few games and no matches, a situation which he described as being exceedingly frustrating.

C F Hamilton, who had coached the cricket XI for many years before the war, was of an age which made him eligible to serve in both wars, fortunately returning from both. Understandably he decided that he had had enough when he was demobilized in 1946 and chose to retire and not return to schoolmastering. Maclean took charge of cricket for a couple of seasons and when he went off to Cranbrook this became the responsibility of Bantoft who had joined the staff in 1945. More matches were added each year and under Bantoft's care, the 1st XI had several successful seasons. In 1951 T F Merritt took over the 1st XI and was responsible for it for a decade and, during much of this time, H E Cousens, who was Head of Classics, had a long spell in charge of the Under 11 team. Cricket had an interesting development in the 1956 season when an Under 11 boy played in the 1st XI for the first time. This was Derek Underwood, whom Merritt described as a player with considerable promise whose bowling was very fast for a boy of his age. A year later Merritt said that Underwood's bowling was fast but not very accurate, yet the team had a very successful season. In his third and final season at DCPS, Underwood was described as the strong member of the team whose bowling was hostile and whose batting had improved considerably. Merritt did not choose him to captain the team, but nor did he know that within a decade, Underwood would be playing cricket for England, his first Test being against the West Indies in 1966. Merritt's last season in 1961 appeared to have a strong team again, there being three 'colours' from the previous season, but it was slow to start. The first two matches were lost, the first to St Olave's and the second to UCS Hampstead, both senior schools. By the end of the season, things had improved and the last three matches were won, the last by 41 runs against Dulwich College. The Under 11 team did well that year too, winning four of its five matches. In some years there was a light-hearted match between the 1st XI and the staff, but Merritt considered this to be too frivolous to be worthy of mention in school magazines so no results have been recorded for posterity. Only a photograph of the staff team for 1961 remains to recall the event.

Merritt's departure at the end of the 1960 season put Maclean back in charge of the 1st XI again and, as before, the start of his first season back at the helm was slow to start. Matches

Staff cricket team v the boys - 1961. Only one person cannot be identified.
From l to r: Geoffrey Close-Brooks, Neil Smith, Roger Warren, Malcolm Curtis, Bert Finn, Student of the day,
Mark Merritt, Roger Shakeshaft, James Wood (umpire), John Hemming, Ron Ferris, Charles Guttman

were won at the end of the season, by which time the boys had learned to work together as a team. An Under 11 team was created from totally untried boys who managed to win two and lose three of their five matches. In 1965 the Headmaster, Hugh Woodcock, a man with cricket in his blood, found time in a busy life to lead the 1st XI himself. In his first season, five matches were won and four drawn out of the nine played and Maclean turned his talents to the Under 11 team which was in need of a competent coach. In 1966 Woodcock wrote that there was plenty of interest being shown in the school for cricket, especially among the younger boys, and there was no shortage of volunteers keen and eager to use the nets at school. However, 1967 was a disappointing season for all teams, Whytehead commenting (for the Under 12 team) that damp pitches and frozen fingers did not help the schoolboy cricketer. In contrast, 1971 proved to be one of the most successful cricket seasons ever for the 1st XI with nine boys remaining from the young team of a year earlier. The XI won nine of their ten matches, losing only to Reed's School in Cobham by three wickets and defeating a team from the City of London School by ten wickets. It is always a good idea to go out on a 'high' and at the end of the season Woodcock announced it would be his last. Once again responsibility for the 1st XI passed to new hands.

With rugby being played at Brightlands, most of the pitches at Grange Lane were devoted solely to soccer during the two winter terms. In 1968 the land behind the pavilion (known formerly as 'The Alps' because of its irregular terrain) was levelled and three rugby pitches were created there. Soccer at that time was played only by boys under the age of eleven, and Bantoft quickly arranged soccer matches for a 1st XI team although for the first season it was only possible to secure three. By 1950, which was not a very successful season, soccer matches were played against three prep schools which have since disappeared, Bickley Hall, Royston House in Lewisham and Carn Brae in Beckenham, now a primary school. The weather affected soccer just as much as rugby and some soccer seasons, notably 1947, suffered badly. When Bantoft left in 1952, responsibility for all the school's soccer passed on to Merritt, giving him a respite from cricket. For the next ten years the XI did well, although during his first season when there were just six matches, the result against an XI from Alleyn's was a crushing defeat, the score being eight goals to nil against, Merritt writing later that both the opponents and the pitch were far larger than the Prep boys were used to. But never again would he suffer such a defeat. By 1956 he was able to report that out of twenty-four matches played during the previous two years only one had been lost, that being against Highgate when the score was 0-1. Perhaps Merritt ensured that his players were not overpowered by stature! At that time, Highgate provided the main source of opposition and the fixture was regarded as one of great importance.

In the following year, fortunes were reversed when DCPS beat Highgate by the same result, one goal to nil. Success followed success and in 1958 the soccer team lived up to its reputation by remaining undefeated for the spring and autumn terms. In some years, there was an Under 10 team as well and each year there were tribe matches which brought many boys into competitive soccer of a kind. Charles Guttmann arrived on the staff in 1960 and immediately took charge of all Under 10 soccer, taking his influence down to the Lower School. Merritt continued with the 1st XI for a year and when he left in 1961, Guttmann took charge of soccer overall. Wildly keen to make sure that it should not be the underdog to rugby, and that its reputation should continue, he put it firmly on the map by bringing notice of its activities to readers of the school magazine during his first season:

> *Soccer is played on every afternoon of the week, with twenty-two games in all, the Lower School providing seven of them. The games are so arranged that roughly the same age group play together on any one afternoon. The exception to this is Wednesday. This is THE Games Day when matches against other schools and tribe league matches take place.*

In the spring of 1962, Guttmann introduced an Under 9 team which had just one match against DCPS Coursehorn, which they won. The 1st XI in the same term had nine matches and won six of them, the greatest victory being against Belmont School which was won four goals to nil. In the autumn a new 1st XI won all of their matches, so Guttmann was doing well. Soccer prospered under Guttmann as it had under Merritt and there were several very successful seasons. In 1967, for example, he proudly announced that in the fourteen matches played that autumn, thirteen were won, one was drawn and none were lost. However he still felt strongly that the older boys aged 11 to 13 should have a chance at playing soccer at match level.

Tennis was not neglected, and after the war became the responsibility of Bantoft for a couple of years, but when he took over cricket in 1948, tennis was passed on to Jack Chapman, who taught French. The first post-war match was in 1951 against an Under 15 team from James Allen's Girls' School. The girls won eight sets to one and for this reason or some other, the fixture was not resumed. Games were played on the single grass court at 42 Alleyn Park and the one at Brightlands. Sometimes, the school used the courts at the Old College Lawn Tennis Club in Gallery Road, especially when there was a strong showing of talent in any particular year. When Chapman died suddenly in 1958, Rex Audley, a member of staff, took over tennis for a few years until 1960 when Guttmann, already responsible for soccer, undertook summer tennis as well. Three years later, as if that were not enough, the unstoppable Guttmann re-introduced a gymnastics club. This held an annual display on Open Day, or Hobbies Day as it was then called, and highlighted the need for a proper gymnasium.

After the war, the College allowed the Prep to use the baths there again and swimming lessons for some classes were re-introduced into the timetable. As the roof had been lost during the war the baths were open and usable only on fine days and it was indeed a sorry sight. With its forlorn turrets pointing to the sky, F C Hambleton, who was in charge of swimming at the time, described it as a mixture of a Shakespearian theatre and a vision of the seaside. Extra instruction was sometimes given by the College Physical Training

Instructors (PTI's) and Hambleton took his responsibility seriously and clearly enjoyed it, winning especially the regard of boys who found swimming more challenging. 1953 was the last season for the old baths before the College decided to demolish them and build a completely new swimming complex which opened two years later. Somewhat nostalgically, Hambleton was sad to see the old baths go: *'Good bye, friendly old baths,'* he wrote. *'What years of fun we have had together within your nice tall walls'*. Two years later it was time for him to say good-bye too, certainly so far as swimming was concerned.

For a year, swimming became the responsibility of a New Zealander, L Stafford-Bush and when he returned home in 1956, his place was taken by Finn, who was thus responsible for rugby during the two winter terms and swimming in the summer. By 1957 the College wanted to make greater use themselves of the new baths they had built, so less time was made available for the Prep. This resulted in the walks to and from the College taking longer than the time boys spent in the water. To ease the pressure, Leakey decided to convert an old air raid shelter at 42 Alleyn Park into a swimming pool. This had lain empty since the war and his plan was simply to remove the roof, line the walls and make them watertight. No heating or filtration was provided and the idea was not a great success. Jeffrey Eacersall (DCPS 1953-1956) remembered it all too well. He described it as a place he never went to unless he had to, as it was small and smelt. He was under the impression that it was filled with water at the beginning of the summer and the water gradually turned green. It was not one of Leakey's best ideas. Finn organised swimming overall and despite the restrictions of time, swimming sports were held at the new College baths for some years and matches were held there. A break with long-standing tradition came in 1964 when Finn

The wartime air raid shelter with its roof removed was converted into an unfiltered swimming pool. It was not one of Leakey's best ideas.

decided that DCPS should discontinue using the College baths, principally because more boys were learning to swim and more time was needed than the College could provide. There was still Saturday morning school in those days and this was an ideal time to use the pool at the new Crystal Palace National Recreation Centre. Finn described how it was done:

> *Each Saturday morning 325 boys go by coach to Crystal Palace in groups of about sixty. The coach driver is the key man for he is moving almost the whole morning from 9.00 until 12.30. With the co-operation of all, the operation moves very smoothly and should prove a great advance for school swimming now that we hope to continue with it for every Saturday throughout the year in term time.*

However the break with the College was not total as the Crystal Palace facilities were not always available. In consequence, swimming sports were held at the College again in 1965 and Finn commented on how agreeable it was to be returning to familiar and friendly territory.

1964 saw another major change in the DCPS sporting scene. This was the appointment of ex-RSM Harry Hubbold who had just retired from the Royal Marines. He took immediate charge of Physical Education and was the first to be the Head of that department, although it was still much akin to Physical Training (PT) in those days. Hubbold helped with swimming, boxing, athletics and sport generally, and his dynamic enthusiasm with its military precision and background soon had everyone on their toes. He was skilled at fencing and introduced that activity into the school on a club basis. He quickly came to be much respected and liked by parents, boys and staff alike, and all with whom he came in

Boys in the new gymnasium in 1966. The glass windows at each end were subsequently removed.

contact. His time at DCPS proved to be all too short, for although a picture of health and fitness, he died unexpectedly during the summer term in 1969.

Sheppard resumed responsibility for Sports Day after the war and the programme of events continued much as before but without the march pasts and flag waving. The day was still a big annual event, but it resembled a gymkhana more than a display of athletic talent. A demonstration of scouting activities was included in the programme when a school sea scout group was formed and, in 1959 for example, events included a wheelbarrow race and a potato race, as well as races for old boys and visitors. The Lower School was still included and for these boys there was tunnel ball and a horse and rider race. Leakey enjoyed Sports Day even to the extent of taking part in it himself, and he regarded it as a grand public relations exercise much as Leake had done before him. He was always at his best, invariably inviting some eminent person of the day to give away the cups and certificates at the end.

Sheppard organised Sports Day with meticulous efficiency and continued to do so after Leakey left in 1961, but times were changing and the Woodcock wind of change blew towards sports too, resulting in the need for activities to take on a new direction and a new format. Sheppard retired at the end of the spring term in 1965 and responsibility for Sports Day the following term fell upon the shoulders of Roger Shakeshaft, a mathematician like his predecessor. Some changes he implemented at once. He separated the older boys from the Lower School which, from then on, held its own sports on a different day, these continuing with some of the old traditions. For boys in the Third Forms upwards (Years 5 to 8) there was a move towards athletic events. Shakeshaft felt strongly that there was need for a change and as a gesture of goodwill he invited Sheppard to return to give away the prizes at his first Sports Day. The potato race and the wheelbarrow race continued for a few years, but they soon succumbed to new events like the javelin and shot-put and

Sports Day 1946 - Leakey giving support during a race for little sisters

only the pole race remained as part of the traditional past. Shakeshaft also decided that the time had come to stop praising individuals and to concentrate more on winners from team events, so the *Victor Ludorum* cups were discontinued. Years later, he looked back:

> *I brought Athletics into the serious games sphere at DCPS. Prior to 1965 we had an annual Sports Day which was more like a carnival, and hedged with safety restrictions and rules of convenience. Soon we had exact measurements, spikes, a Star Awards System given by the Amateur Athletics Association (AAA), an expansion of field events and matches against other schools. The only relic from the past was the ludicrous pole race.*

Sports Day 1962   An enthusiastic author encouraging the Deerfeet tug-of-war team to pull a bit harder!

In 1970 further changes were made when he decided to hold Sports Day on two different days, the major field events being held separately. By this time, athletics were beginning to be taken seriously, but were still arranged on a club basis, this usually taking place after school on the school field. Of greater significance in the same term was the change to metrication. Of this he wrote:

> *The most important event of the term was the introduction of metric units for all athletic events. The boys took to the new system very easily and the greatest confusion came from the staff.*

Shakeshaft continued to be responsible for athletics and the annual Sports Day until he moved to another appointment in 1973.

In 1970 Woodcock made a decision which was to change the complexion of physical activities at the school for ever, although he may not have realised at the time what far-reaching consequences there would be. Needing a new Head of PT to replace Harry

Hubbold, he approached St Luke's College in Exeter which had a high reputation for the calibre of the Physical Education teachers it produced. As a result, Paddy Costeloe was appointed directly from there as the school's first qualified PE teacher. He introduced new and modern methods to the lessons but changes elsewhere did not come overnight. Until the arrival of Harry Hubbold and the 1966 gymnasium, physical training lessons and match teams had been administered by members of the academic teaching staff. This continued to be the case when Costeloe arrived although he took responsibility for all PT lessons which immediately became PE. Finn coached the rugby XV, Guttman the football XI, Woodcock himself continued with the cricket XI, as did Shakeshaft with athletics and the annual Sports Day. Within a year PE lessons had broadened across the timetable and such was the growth of the subject that St Luke's was approached again. From there in 1971 came Ian Martin who joined the PE staff and became responsible for a number of teams at different levels.

In the following year Finn decided to pass on the swimming which by this time was in need of a full-time teacher, so once again St Luke's was approached and Alan Friell came from there to fill the position. Friell was a rugby Scotland International Trialist at the time and his skill and tuition gave valuable assistance to Finn and the 1st XV, at the same time giving an impetus to swimming throughout the school. 1973 was a turning point. First of all it was decided that all boys in the Upper and Middle Schools (Years 5-8) should play rugby in the autumn term and football in the spring. Although Guttmann had always campaigned for this, by the time the first Under 13 football match was played in 1974, he had moved on. Playing rugby in the winter term and football in the following spring had, and still does have, disadvantages. Apart from the actual length of the terms not being equal, the days are longer in September and there is more time for practice. The spring term is short and the weather often wet and cold, so less time is given to football than to rugby, but at least all boys have an opportunity to take part in both games. As well as Guttmann and Costeloe, Shakeshaft also left the school in 1973, with all three pursuing teaching posts elsewhere.

Ian Martin immediately became Head of PE assuming responsibility for athletics, PE lessons, football and Sports Day. Having given up the 1st XI cricket in 1972, Woodcock found himself coaching it again in 1974, but it was to be his last season. At a party at Brightlands in the summer of that year, Woodcock met Robin Whitcomb whom Friell had known from St Luke's. Cricket and sport were soon on the agenda and before the day was out, Whitcomb had been offered a job, part of which was to coach the 1st XI. As a result, Whitcomb started a remarkable career with the school's cricket by coaching that team continuously for over thirty years, an achievement which cannot be matched. Put another way, he has been nurturing the DCPS 1st XI for a quarter of the school's history! By 1975 the sporting scene had changed totally. Finn was still coaching the rugby XV, aided by Friell, although within a year he too would stand down and Whitcomb assumed responsibility for that as well. The influence of St Luke's was strong and for almost twenty years the threesome of Martin, Friell and Whitcomb worked with homogenous success.

Martin's newly formed Under 13 football team had a reasonably successful first season in 1974, winning four of its seven matches, and this set the pattern of fixtures for future years although, because of poor weather and problems of drainage, not all matches were played. In 1981, for example, the season showed plenty of promise but fell away because of mud and rain in the latter part of the term, and in 1988 the pitches were so sodden that use was made of the astroturf at the Crystal Palace National Recreation Centre for a number of matches and practices. On the other hand a match in 1987 against fathers, by and large of boys in the 1st XI, produced an honourable result of three goals each. In that same season the 1st XI visited Crystal Palace Football Club at Selhurst Park as part of that club's drive to encourage a youth policy towards the game. Matches at lower age groups were arranged under Martin's stewardship and football became an established part of the sporting programme. Athletics, on the other hand, was already well established. His predecessor had already introduced athletics fixtures so he was able to build on foundations already laid. He continued to treat Sports Day as an authentic athletics meeting, the only traditional parts being that it continued to be held on a Saturday morning towards the end of the summer term and culminated with the pole race. Efforts were made to involve more participants, as the day still required a compulsory attendance from all boys. More matches were introduced, including triangular ones, and in 1975 for example, fifty boys were involved in seven athletics matches all of which were won except that against Alleyn's. Progressively boys took part in inter-schools championships, there were some remarkable performances and school records were constantly being broken. Refuting accusations that athletics were for the few Martin wrote in 1981:

> *Many genuinely believe that athletics is a sport which is best suited to the elite. By introducing a full range of events, providing opportunities to all age groups in athletics club sessions, organizing sports days and matches, athletics can reach out to a vast number of boys, providing opportunities to compete in both track and field events. However no one would deny that exposure to any sport will inevitably produce a group of boys demonstrably better than their fellows, and so it is to our school team that we look to see how our standards compare both locally and nationally.*

Martin was also responsible for a number of junior rugby teams and a potential moment of glory came for him in 1978 when he was coaching the Under 11 XV. One of his boys, who did not stay on to reach the 1st XV because his parents left the area, was Philip de Glanville, later to captain England. Of his star-to-be Martin wrote:

> *The hooker, de Glanville, had an excellent season. Apart from a very fast strike, he had the ability always to be in the right place at the right time, and his passing, kicking and tackling were all of the highest standard.*

By the time Martin left for a post at Dulwich College in 1992, much to the chagrin of DCPS, athletics and gymnastics had gained a status within the school which would not have been considered possible a decade earlier, and in the summer athletics was playing an ever-increasing role and although cricket remained the dominant sport, some boys managed to show their skills at both. He had also established football as a major sport.

From 1975 and through the 1980s a regular pattern emerged. Members of the PE staff not involved with 1st teams coached others at lower levels and gradually more teams were introduced so that a greater number of boys were able to enjoy the experience of playing in a match. Cricket started encouragingly with Whitcomb, whose sense of humour and close rapport with his players brought about many successful seasons. Of the first, he wrote in 1975 saying how much he had enjoyed being with his young cricketers who had given such a splendid account of themselves:

> *They have worked laboriously at all aspects of the game and even on stifling hot afternoons after formal school hours they have put all their energies and co-operation into pre-match fielding practices. The spirit and enthusiasm was all there and this simply had to produce results.*

Stephen Robinson (DCPS 1967-1975) was a member of that team. Years later he wrote:

> *Robin Whitcomb was our coach in 1975 and was a splendid character, never seen without his dog at his side. I was surprised to discover years later that we played eleven matches that summer and won nine of them which suggests he knew his stuff.*

Whitcomb inaugurated the first sports tour when at half-term in 1976 he took his team to the West Country where the boys were hosted by the schools they played. The following year they visited Sussex and later in 1991 there was a tour to Jersey. On average there were about a dozen matches played each season involving some very promising young cricketers who invariably continued their cricketing careers at their next school. Some seasons were more successful

Robin Whitcomb coaching boys in the nets - 2003

than others but none passed when more matches were lost than were won and there were moments to remember. In 1979 boys, and not only the 1st XI, were coached by T C ('Dickie') Dodd who had played cricket for Essex, but in 1983 disaster struck when no nets were possible because portakabins had been erected in their place. These had been necessary as a result of the fire from the previous November. Instead boys were taken either to nets at the Crystal Palace National Recreation Centre or to Dulwich College who offered a helping hand. In 1990 Derek Underwood returned to his old school and offered some sound cricketing advice to boys playing in the nets.

1990 - Derek Underwood offering advice to boys in the nets behind 42 Alleyn Park

In September 1976, Whitcomb became responsible for the 1st XV and as with cricket, his style meant that he gained the best from his boys and soon moulded them into a team, many of whom would be the same boys to form his cricket team the following summer. An average of almost a dozen rugby matches were arranged for the 1st XV each season and over the years many boys were involved. 1982 was a pleasing year when thirteen matches were played of which nine were won producing an end of season result of 291 points for and 47 against. The matches against the College were always fiercely played but King's Wimbledon and Whitgift were long-standing rivals and invariably produced strong opposition each year. The 1980s saw the introduction of Inter-Preparatory School Rugby Sevens tournaments and DCPS became involved with two of them, the Millfield Junior (Edgarley) Sevens and the National Prep Schools' Sevens. In 1992 DCPS won the Edgarley Sevens which was an appropriate year to do so as the recently appointed Headmaster, George Marsh, had just come from there. After the 1993/94 season, Whitcomb passed the rugby XV to younger hands but continued with the cricket XI.

The third of the trio from St Luke's was Alan Friell. Although a rugby player, and representing the London Scottish 1st XV for several seasons, his key role at DCPS was swimming. When he arrived, swimming lessons were still being held at Crystal Palace National Recreation Centre and soon he was making mutterings about the wisdom and need for DCPS to have a pool of its own. To emphasise his point, in 1976 and again the year after, swimming sports were held at St Joseph's College in Upper Norwood because neither the College nor the Recreation Centre could accommodate at the times required. Hugh Woodcock's dream for the school to have its own pool eventually came to fruition in September 1977 when a 25 metre swimming bath was opened by Denis Ellison Nash, then Chairman of Governors, at the edge of what had once been the paddock. In view of restrictions of space and cost, it was decided to limit spectator space and have as much width as possible for swimming itself, the result being that six lanes were squeezed in. Friell was ready. The quality of swimming improved overnight, more matches were arranged and, as no time was lost in travelling to the pool, swimming could be timetabled into a single lesson. Despite the many and obvious advantages, the new pool presented one disadvantage - diving. A diving competition had long been established but the new pool was not deep enough, sensibly for safety reasons, so diving was discontinued. In 1979 family membership was introduced whereby boys and their families could make use of the pool at weekends and, when not in regular use, it was hired out to local organisations thus bringing in extra revenue. Lower School boys were timetabled to use the pool from the start and regular lessons for Annexe boys commenced in 1980, the same year as swimming became an option for older boys on Wednesday afternoons. Friell established a programme which improved each year, with more matches being arranged, including

The swimming pool under construction in 1977

those for boys at lower age levels. The strongest opposition usually came from Highgate School which was eventually defeated in 1981 for the first time in over a decade and in 1986 a sponsored swim raised over £11,000 and led to the best season ever when all matches were won. Friell left in 1991, his last season being crowned by a most successful season when Philip Ross-Martyn not only broke several school records but made a name for himself away from Dulwich by swimming nationally within his age group.

Much mention has been made of 1st teams in cricket, rugby and football, but from early on far more boys were involved in matches at other levels with second teams, sometimes merging to become Under 12s, as well as Under 11, Under 10 and in some cases Under 9 teams in all the major sporting activities. Whenever possible members of the PE staff became responsible for different teams depending on the season, but inevitably it was necessary to bring in members of the academic staff to coach teams as well. Some stayed for long periods and with considerable success. Among those in the 1970s and 1980s were David Whytehead (Head of RS), Tony Revell and David Hughes (both Head of Maths) and Peter Evans (Head of History). Whytehead was one those people who must have been an organiser's dream for he would lead a team for a couple of seasons, then happily stand down if asked to do so, expecting to be called again, maybe in another sporting discipline if need arose as it invariably did. He had a long spell coaching the 2nd XI football, but his reports afterwards often complained of frustration from the weather, an example being the 1982 season when four matches were played, all of which were won, but two others had to be cancelled because of 'awful' weather. David Hughes, a keen sportsman himself and with rugby very much in his blood, was a vigorous coach to the 2nd XV for many years turning his hand to an Under 11 football team in the spring, and Peter Evans had a long and successful spell looking after an Under 12 XV.

When Martin left in 1992, only Whitcomb remained from the original St Luke's trio, but the link was maintained by David Adkins who had arrived from there in 1985 as a further addition to the PE staff. By 1992 athletics had become an integrated part of the PE Department so it was logical that with Martin's departure Adkins should become Head of PE, this to include athletics. At the same time a new post of Head of Games was created which was filled by Whitcomb who continued on the PE staff. This time it was a St Luke's duo. Backed by a new Headmaster, Adkins quickly made changes. On the athletics front it was decided that every boy should take part on Sports Day in at least two individual events and one tribe event. Since this would be impossible to achieve in a single day, two days were set aside, one for heats and one for finals. This had been done before to some extent but not every boy had been involved. In 1993, there was a further change when it was decided to break with tradition and hold two separate events, one for Years 7 and 8 and one for Years 5 and 6. Permission had been gained to use the College athletics track and, since it was not always possible or practical to use it on a Saturday, weekdays were chosen instead, thus bringing the great Saturday Spectacular to an end.

Parents were still invited and the events continued to be competitively organised within the tribe system, but the formality of a single occasion faded still further from 2001 when each year group had its own Sports Day making four in all. For safety reasons events involving the discus were dropped and in 2000 school athletics records were restarted because few had been broken since 1985 and converting yards to metres was not an exact comparison. Stop watches had also become more accurate. All that remained from the past was what Shakeshaft had described as the 'ludicrous' pole race which traditionally ended Sports Day, now the one involving Year 8. In 2004 Adkins announced that DCPS held the world record for this event since it was highly probable that it was the only sporting venue where it was ever held!

The pole race 2004

When Whitcomb stood down from being in charge of rugby in 1994, Adkins assumed responsibility for that as well. The number of matches for boys at different levels increased and as with all teams, some years were better than others. 2000 was a year which Adkins will long remember for in that year his team managed to achieve an unbeaten season. Eleven matches were played and all were won except that against Whitgift which was drawn. During the season, 483 points were scored for, with only 44 against.

In 1992 John Morland was appointed as the first full-time Head of Swimming, although he too worked within the PE Department and became involved in other sporting activities as well. He quickly announced:

> *The swimming curriculum is designed to develop boys' confidence, skill and stamina in the water. An extra-curricular competitive programme is also arranged to challenge and develop talented swimmers.*

As a result, even more matches with other schools were arranged, nearly all of which were won except those against Trinity in Croydon which proved to be the most challenging. In 1993 a timetabled period of swimming was allocated throughout the year for the first time for those in their final year (Year 8) and more lesson time was given to boys in other parts of the school. The annual swimming sports had always involved all year groups participating in one big event, minimising the number of boys taking part and causing congestion in the changing room and limited spectator space. In 1994 swimming galas for each year group held on different days were introduced instead and more boys took part. Matches for boys in younger age groups were extended and in 1996 Trinity was at last defeated. As well as regular matches with other schools, there were annual galas such as the London Primary Schools Championships and National Prep Schools Championships. Swimming has become a part of life at DCPS and it has become virtually unheard of for a boy to leave the school without the basic skills. As the pool is let out to adult groups in the evenings and during school holidays, the use it gets, to say nothing of the pleasure it gives, more than justifies the decision to build it in the first place. From January 2004 Morland took up a post in Queensland, Australia so swimming at DCPS became the responsibility of Andrew O'Loughlin.

While the major sports were changing hands in the early 1990s, Whitcomb continued steadfastly with the cricket XI, broadening its scope all the time. Opportunity came in 1993 when the school entered the JET(Joint Educational Trust) National Prep Schools Cricket Competition and although victory did not come that year, the Shield stood proudly in the school two years later when Edgarley was defeated in the final at Oxford. An exciting new venture occurred in 1997 when Robin Whitcomb and Craig Gordon, accompanied by a number of parents, arranged a cricket tour to Cape Town and Johannesburg. Eight matches were played in all and the tour was an overwhelming success, with three matches being drawn and one won. Although the results revealed the superior strength of the opponents, some fine cricket was played under almost perfect conditions and the hospitality offered wherever the team went was second to none. The tour was self-financing but money was raised, not only towards the actual cost of the trip, but also to provide cricketing facilities for under-privileged children in the Alexandra Township in Johannesburg. As well as cricket matches, time was given on the tour for leisure activities, the climax being the overnight visit to the Kruger National Park. So successful was this trip that DCPS established a relationship with the township and another tour took place in 2000. This time the matches were against teams from development schools in Johannesburg and Durban, including Soweto with a return visit to Alexandra. A further tour to Cape Town took place in February 2004. From Leake's enthusiasm in the early days to the long Whitcomb period of recent years, cricket has become well established at DCPS. Maybe there are more Derek Underwoods in the making.

From 1992, the Soccer 1st XI became the responsibility of different members of the PE staff notably Simon Bailey and John Morland, with matches being introduced against the neighbouring schools of Langbourne and Kingsdale. Yet despite the same number of soccer fixtures being arranged each season as for cricket or rugby, it remained the sporting poor relation at DCPS. This is partly because of the brevity of the term and the weather often associated with it, and also because rugby sevens are usually squeezed in as well. By the turn of the century, more importance was being given to the round ball game and Morland led a successful soccer tour to Italy for the first time in 2002. The school also staged a six-a-side competition for Under 11 boys which by 2004 had attracted an entry of thirty-two teams from twenty schools.

Playing against and visiting other schools at away matches is a social experience in itself, and in recent years attempts have been made to give this experience to as many boys as possible. This has steadily increased over the years and in 2000 for example, there were four rugby teams at both Under 13 and Under 12 levels, three at Under 11 and as many as five at under 10. A similar pattern was arranged for other sports with the introduction of A, B, C, D and E match teams. There may not have been more than two or three matches for some, but involving so many boys brought problems. The first and obvious one was that arranging such a large number of matches during a year needed central organisation to prevent duplication and muddle, so in 1995 Mark Mitchell of the Maths staff, himself a keen cricketer, became responsible for arranging all fixtures in the major sports, including the booking of coaches for away matches when this was necessary. He gradually found new opponents, particularly at football, in local primary schools and smaller prep schools. This was especially useful in obtaining matches for the lower (C, D or E teams) in all sports, as these were able to take on the A or B teams from these smaller establishments. A deliberate focus was placed upon the lower teams and results against level opposition became more creditworthy. The opportunities for boys to play in matches steadily grew, this being well illustrated by the number on offer for the autumn term in 2004. For that term there were 152 rugby matches arranged for 19 teams, for ages ranging between Years 5 to 8. In addition, there were 10 tournaments and A and B teams for the Under 9s – Year 4 in the Lower School. There may only have been a couple of matches available for any particular group, but nearly every boy had the opportunity of playing in a match regardless of his ability.

Traditionally the strongest sport is cricket which needs more space and for which the former Lloyd's playing fields at Gallery Road were principally obtained. With coaching being offered to boys below Game 1 standard at all ages, more boys have been eager to play in matches for that game too. With so many boys involved in matches and games, it became necessary to call upon the academic staff still further. Prominent among those has been Piers Tobenhouse, Head of History and also from St Luke's, who had a long spell looking after an Under 12 football team. Craig Gordon, also from the History department, not only coached the cricketers and went to South Africa with Whitcomb, but also coached an Under 13 rugby team in the winter as well. Richard Witts from the English department took his skill and enthusiasm to a young team of Under 10 cricketers and Glen Smart, Head of Art, turned his talents elsewhere by coaching an Under 11 cricket and football teams. Simon Severino, Head of Geography, and Bob Villars have also been responsible for match teams. Mitchell introduced a squash club in 1992 which was soon playing matches against other schools, the first against Whitgift in that year being won convincingly. By 2004, with fixtures becoming more and more secretarial, responsibility for Mitchell's squash passed to Justin Veitch. Such are the diversities of a DCPS teacher's role.

As Head of PE, David Adkins had overall responsibility for all physical activities within the school and thus implementation of the National Curriculum. Of the five disciplines, swimming, cricket, rugby, soccer and athletics, only swimming has a target which should be met, this being that all children from Year 6 should be able to swim for 25 metres unaided. At DCPS all boys reach this level from Year 3. In 2004, boys from Years 5 to 8 have one lesson each per week of PE and swimming and a further afternoon of games with an option for a second. In addition there are extra-curricular activities such as gymnastics, tennis, athletics, basketball, hockey, badminton and squash all of which are provided on an optional basis, and at an additional cost boys can take part in activities such as fencing, judo, squash or karate.

From the autumn of 2004 a break with tradition was made concerning the pattern of games days. For boys in the Main School (Years 5-8) there had never been timetabled classroom periods on Wednesday afternoons which had always been considered sacrosanct for games, although there were other options. The acquisition of more playing fields made it possible for more boys to become involved in games, which in turn placed a strain on the changing rooms and on the number of staff available. After careful thought and planning it was decided for Years 7 and 8 to continue playing games on Wednesdays (and Mondays) as they had done before, but Years 5 and 6 had their games days on Tuesdays and Fridays instead of Wednesdays and one other afternoon as previously. Non-sporting activities were no longer an option on Wednesday afternoons, but the range of activities offered was broadened to include minor sports such as basketball, fencing, 5-a-side soccer, hockey, tennis, water polo or swimming depending on the season. Some of these activities had only previously been available as clubs. The re-arrangement also meant that the Lower School could have a games afternoon on Thursday afternoons, thus making better use of the PE staff.

Mention has been made of the principal physical activities which have been provided over the years and the ways by which more and more boys have had an opportunity to become involved in teams and matches. Inter-tribe competitive games in the major sports have been played since 1916, and activities such as fencing and golf have been arranged from time to time as clubs. Physical activity has not been limited to the older boys. The Lower School and Annexe have their own sports days and PE lessons, all of which develop talent and prepare boys for the day when they too will be eligible for matches. The purchase of playing fields at Gallery Road, in addition to those at Brightlands, Grange Lane and Hunts Slip Road, provide additional space for pitches, but the condition of the London clay will not change despite periodic attempts to drain it, nor does the school have any say in the weather. The 1966 gymnasium, so splendid then, is small and inadequate for today's needs. In 1972 Hugh Woodcock was fired by the idea of providing DCPS with a proper covered 25 metre swimming pool which came to fruition before that decade was out. A covered sports hall will be a reality in 2006.

Mohicans on parade before Sports Day 1936

In 2002 Sports Day had adopted a different approach

14   Out of School

These days it is common for schoolchildren to travel together away from school to all sorts of places far and wide. Sometimes this is done in term time, but more often than not trips are arranged for leisure purposes during school holidays. Either way, children learn and benefit a great deal from travelling together outside the family unit, as long as everything is properly organised and adequately supervised. Travel opportunities offered to the boys at DCPS have steadily increased over the years. Usually the cost of these expeditions has fallen upon parents, but there are occasions when the school funds journeys as part of the overall curriculum, the cost being built into the fee structure.

The earliest 'out of school' journeys seem to have been introduced soon after the First World War. One of the earliest, on 19th February 1920, does not appear to have been a great success. It involved some of the senior boys and the tribe leaders going to Coulsdon for what would today be called a series of wide games. One game was a kind of 'Hare and Hounds' but owing to a misunderstanding as to where the starting place of the game should be, the proper trail was not followed. Some boys who were thought 'lost' returned to school early on their own whereas others reached the school much later. How they travelled back to Dulwich, and who paid the fares is not recorded, but in the end everyone seemed well pleased with the outing. Things had improved later in the year when on Wednesday 27th October more senior boys, strictly allocated by tribes, set off for Coulsdon again. The games were better organised this time, but the boys arrived late at Coulsdon because the train was delayed at Crystal Palace. Some things don't change! It is worth mentioning that there were no prefects at that time, but there were senior boys who held positions of responsibility. The four tribe system had started and for each there was a tribe leader, a second and a number of patrol leaders. Each tribe was divided into patrols, like squads in an army platoon. A year later, when the outing came round again, the railway did rather better. On 16th July 1921, this time on a Saturday, the tribe patrol leaders had an outing to Hayes Common. Catching a train from West Dulwich at 2 p.m., they went first to Kent House and then 'marched' to nearby Clock House Station. From there they caught a train to Hayes which arrived at 2.35, half an hour earlier than expected:

> On arrival at Hayes Station, they marched to a suitable place on the Common called Caesar's Camp.
> The patrol leaders were in two parties, the Chippeways and Mohicans against the Deerfeet and Ojibways
> (sic). Each party had a base at the opposite ends of Caesar's Camp. In each party's base six red flags
> were hung on some trees. Each boy had a tie or a handkerchief in his belt. If this was pulled out by one
> of the opposing side, the boy to whom it belonged was captured and sent behind the enemy's lines. The

object of the game was to capture as many flags and prisoners as possible. The Deerfeet and the Ojibways won the game having eleven flags to one. After this most exciting game the whole company marched off to the teahouse. After a huge tea, the patrol leaders, excepting Lumsden i, Hammer, Williams i and Hill i marched to a place nearby and divided into pickets of three or four. The four patrol leaders mentioned above were given postcards addressed to Mr Leake. They had to go through the pickets without being caught. If they succeeded, they were to post their cards in a letterbox. Hill i and Williams i succeeded and the other two were caught. Everybody arrived back at the station in good time for the train and reached home safely after a very enjoyable day.

These outings continued through the 1920s. The games and the locations varied – Cavaliers versus Roundheads being the theme for 1925 – but the general pattern was the same. In 1926, the boys went by train from Dulwich to Bromley from where they marched to Hayes Village, a distance of several miles, but the operation came to an abrupt end after tea when a thunderstorm caused the games to be abandoned. Records do not show how the boys returned to school, or in what condition, although the next day the patrol leaders declared that they had had a good day and were none the worse for their soaking. In 1927 the destination was Shirley Hills when, according to one of the patrol leaders of the day:

40 of us took a journey on the noble bus all the way to Shirley. Sad to relate, we were lost on the way in the wilds of Norwood, but after slipping round all the corners we could see, and dodging greengrocers' carts, we arrived at our destination without further mishap. A game of Hare and Hounds was played, and once more dodging overhanging trees from the top of our open bus, we reached school tired but happy.

1927 was a big year for DCPS for it saw the arrival of a major first – the first trip to a foreign destination. This was to Paris and was led by Monsieur Paul Meyrat, Head of French. His wife accompanied him, and an assistant member of staff called Wilson. David Marshall, who as a boy went on one of the early visits to Paris with Meyrat, describes him thus:

M Meyrat was a short voluble sandy haired blue-eyed Frenchman who usually wore blueish trousers. His teaching was memorable and left me with a very good French accent. The structure of his lessons was of the 'Plume de ma Tante' variety, always preceded by an illustrated textbook.

Since this Easter 1927 trip to Paris was such a milestone in the history of DCPS, it is worth quoting, in abridged form, from the magazine of the day:

About 11.30 am, April 14th, the crowded Continental departure platform at Victoria might have been seen dotted with lovely new Prep. caps and a few, not so new, College caps. Hither and thither they bobbed, stopping here to buy reading material of anything but classical nature, and there to lay in stores for the comfort of the "inner boy" enough to last for a trip of days instead of hours. At last under the leadership of Mr Meyrat all took their seats in a fine carriage, after having bidden 'Au Revoir' to genuinely concerned parents. Doors are locked, flags are waved and the great adventure begins.

On the way to Folkestone, the conversation is mainly about weather conditions and speculation is rife as to what the crossing of the channel will be like. Preparations are made to provide Father Neptune with the royal tribute he expects and usually gets. A roughish sea, a glorious fight with honours on the side of the boys who suffered few casualties, and France is reached. The customs presented no difficulties and a few minutes saw the invading army looking interestingly out of their carriage windows at the sight of French rural and town life. Paris at last, just as night fell and myriads of lights justify its name of 'La Ville Lumiere'. A short trip along the boulevards and the hotel is reached where ample justice is made to a really good dinner, and so to rest.

The next morning our autocar was not kept waiting very long before the start of a general visit of the town began. Stops were made to climb the Arc de Triomphe, admire the view from the Trocadero, attend service in La Madeleine and visit the Sacre Coeur. On Saturday we had a ramble in the Luxembourg Gardens, a lovely river trip to St Cloud where we had an al fresco tea, followed by a strenuous impromptu game of football. On Sunday the weather was beautiful. We had a quiet walk to Notre Dame where we arrived, unfortunately too late for Mass and then took a stroll through the bird market and a visit to the Palais de Justice and the beautiful Sainte Chapelle. After lunch we went to the Louvre followed by tea and cakes in the Jardin des Tuileries. This was followed by a race in five taxis to the hotel for a quick dinner and a change into evening dress for a remarkable visit to the Opera to see and hear Faust. Monday was still fine and more taxis took us to the Bois de Vincennes where boats were obtained for a row on the beautiful lakes there. None will easily forget the afternoon visit to the Tour Eiffel, even if some were too nervous to attempt the climb. Tuesday again broke fine and with eagerness we took our seats in our autocar taking with us a picnic lunch for a visit to Versailles. No one is likely to forget such a day. On Wednesday after a hasty breakfast we scrambled into the autocar once more, this time to Fontainebleau. One place is much like another to young boys and it was felt that the lunch at the Cadran Bleu and the al fresco tea at Brabizon, together with the drive at some 40 miles per hour, have left a greater impression than tapestries and furniture. Thursday was spent at Les Invalides with some time for shopping and on Friday we packed lemonade, biscuits and sandwiches and went off once again in our autocar this time to the Valley of Chevreuse for another picnic.

On Saturday morning, we rose early. Frantic endeavours to pack the scent, which all mothers and sisters had demanded, besides many other souvenirs, and we say goodbye to a most obliging hotel staff and leave Paris regretfully. Soon we reach Boulogne, visiting Wimereux on the way, and return on the night boat to England glad to escape a rough crossing. At Victoria, glad parents welcome the 21 pilgrims and rush them home.

Another visit to Paris is planned for Easter 1928. We cannot take everybody so apply early if you are interested.

In these days of Eurostar when Paris can be reached in less than three hours, and when travelling to France is so easy and common place, the excitement of the great adventure of 1927 makes fascinating reading compared with modern experiences. Party sizes varied from year to year. In 1930 when there were 25 boys Meyrat was accompanied by Livingston, but in 1932 when there were only 14 boys, Meyrat and his wife went unaccompanied. School trips to Paris are still arranged from time to time although in recent years there has been a move away from visiting large cities. Although some places of interest remain the same, the boys of today are not likely to be taken, as a group, to a performance of *Faust* formally dressed. The first mention of visits in term time to places of interest in London appeared in the school magazine for the summer of 1929. During this term, boys were taken to the 'Star' Newspaper offices, Prices Candle Factory and the South Metropolitan Gasworks. These trips were clearly successful and enjoyable for those who took part and were arranged by Freddie Taylor who was then a comparatively junior member of staff. Although some took place on Saturdays, as for example on Saturday 29th October 1929 when boys visited the underground Post Office Railway, most were on Wednesday afternoons and what was to become an institution in the school for many years – Wednesday Trips – was born. Boys went all over the place on Wednesday afternoons, examples including a bell foundry in Croydon, Cross & Blackwell's food factory in Bermondsey and, unheard of today, Carreras Cigarette Factory. The boys obviously appreciated these trips which Taylor arranged for them:

> *Well over a hundred boys in the Upper School have participated in these visits and their warmest thanks are due to parents and friends who have made them possible. Several industrial visits have been arranged for next term: we should appreciate any suggestions, for these excursions have a very definite educational value. Our thanks are due to Mr Taylor for the trouble he has taken in arranging these outings. He has spared neither time nor energy and we wish him to know how greatly we appreciate his efforts.*

The 1930s did not initially see any great change in these out of school excursions. The Paris trips continued regularly each year up to 1938 and were well supported. Bryan Thwaites (DCPS 1934-1936) went on one such trip with Meyrat and his wife in 1935 and was taken to task by his parents when he returned because had taken too many photographs, then an expensive item. He particularly remembered a picnic at Fontainebleau and the journey there. The Wednesday industrial visits also gathered momentum in their scope and popularity and gradually became an established part of school life each week. It is not entirely clear how boys were chosen for them but those who had a commitment to one of the major sports had an obligation to put that before any other interest they may have had. Not all the trips went to local factories as this short account recalled from 1935. The modes of transport are of interest too:

> *On July 8ᵗʰ, a party of 35 boys took a char-a-banc to Richmond and proceeded thence by steamer to Hampton Court passing through Teddington Lock. We went over the Palace and were duly thrilled by the Haunted Gallery. After an excellent tea at The Moseley Country Club, we returned to Dulwich by char-a-banc.*

Boys had already started going further afield in the mid 1930s for in August 1934 an excited amateur crew from DCPS took charge of the motor cruiser *Yvette* on the Norfolk Broads for a week. Another crew of boys took over for the following week and a few fortunate ones stayed on board for both. 1934 also saw the first of what would now be called a Geography Field Trip when Reg Hatton took a party of boys to Littlehampton for a week. Here they learned how to read the one inch Ordnance Survey map and learned

Paul Meyrat (hatless, on the right) with a group of boys in the Forest of Fontainebleau (April 1935)
(Courtesy Sir Bryan Thwaites)

about tides, the beach and the use of breakwaters. Similar visits were made in following years although not a great number of boys was involved.

A break into pastures new occurred during the summer holidays in 1935 when 35 boys went on a cruise from Liverpool on the Cunard White Star liner *Doric*. The cruise, which was led by Reg Hatton and his wife, was especially arranged for schoolchildren, and called at Gibraltar before going on to Naples where there was a two-day stopover. On the return a call was made at Malaga before returning to Tilbury. The cost was ten guineas, which included shore excursions and entry into museums, and no special adaptations were made to the ship for its young passengers who slept in cabins. This cruise is significant because it shows that although Cunard had an early interest in conveying schoolchildren on cruises, it was to be their rival company, P&O, which would eventually become the leader in this field. Two years later in the summer of 1937, a party of boys went on another cruise to waters elsewhere and with another company. The ship used this time was the troopship *Nevasa* operated by the British India Steam Navigation Company (BISN). Quite often troopships were redundant in the summer months because they lacked air conditioning, so they were used instead to convey parties of schoolchildren, with their teachers, to places where heat would not be a problem. Again no special alterations were made to the ships and the children slept in hammocks on the troopdecks and followed a somewhat military routine when on board. The ten-day cruise, which was less luxurious than the previous one, went to Scandinavia and the fare was just £6. This was to be the forerunner of regular educational cruises for boys from DCPS in later years, but there would be a gap of twenty-four years before the next one.

A group of boys with Reg Hatton (centre rear) and his wife on board Doric *at Naples - August 1935*

In 1936 a group was taken to Cologne, Heidelberg and the Rhineland, the magazine stating that *'whatever we may think of the politics of Germany, we can be in no two minds about the beauty of the Rhineland.'* The school could hardly be called unadventurous and Leakey saw many advantages being gained from boys going to foreign places and he actively encouraged it. Although the political situation had deteriorated following the Munich Crisis in 1938, neutral Switzerland was still considered a safe destination for the school's first ski-ing trip to Champery in January 1939. Undaunted by the prospects of war and travelling across northern Europe by train to reach their destination, the skiers were met by perfect weather and accounts show that a great time was had by all. One of the participants on that first trip was Kenneth Fyson (DCPS 1936-1939) who remembered little about this great expedition except that his father insisted that he attended skating lessons at Streatham ice rink before he left. Many years later Fyson commented that he enjoyed the ski-ing but was never very good at it. As with the cruises, there would be an interruption of more than a quarter of a century before DCPS took collectively to skis again.

In January 1939, over fifty boys were taken out of Dulwich for a very different venture. The school had been invited to provide pupils for the filming of *Good Bye Mr Chips* staring Robert Donat, still considered a classic today. Two coaches conveyed the boys to Denham Studios where on arrival they were told to put on Eton collars and prepare themselves for a busy day. Much fun was had by all and the day, like the film, was a great success with the added bonus that each boy was paid a small sum for his efforts. Despite the impending gloom as the year progressed, the pattern of school life continued normally including the Wednesday trips. When war arrived in September and much of the school left London for

Cranbrook, there were far more pressing things to be done than activities which involved taking the boys out of school. During the war, when much of the school was evacuated to North Wales, there was plenty of scope for boys to explore the hills around and the local area generally including places like Caernarvon Castle, but severe restraints on petrol meant that school expeditions never went very far afield. In London, the unevacuated part of the school was far too busy just surviving, and apart from visiting other schools for the occasional match, school journeys, educational or otherwise, were out of the question.

With the coming of peace school life began to return to normal again, but post-war restrictions, especially food rationing and a shortage of petrol, made life difficult for a while. Within a year Taylor managed to recommence the Wednesday afternoon trips the first being on the 30th January 1946 when a party of boys visited the United Dairies depot in Streatham. Later that year, a group was invited to the Houses of Parliament by Major Vernon, then Member of Parliament for Dulwich. A popular destination each autumn was the visit to the Schoolboys' Exhibition, now defunct, at the Central Hall Westminster and another favourite was the ascent of Big Ben, no longer possible for security reasons. These Wednesday trips gathered momentum in the 1950s and were always popular and well supported - especially by the non-rugby-playing fraternity. Taylor stood down in 1949, having arranged Wednesday visits for many years and they became the responsibility of Terence Kelly. Kelly was only on the staff for seven years but in that time he played a major part, teaching English and History and also editing the magazine. An account of a visit to the London Docks in November 1952 told of another problem prevalent at the time. A group of boys had been invited to board the S. S. *Uruguay Star* which was berthed at the Victoria Dock. *'We went to the docks by coach in thick fog and we had a job finding the right landing stage'*. Details were then given of a tour of the ship and after being provided with tea, the journey home was clearly eventful … *'on the return journey, the fog was so thick that boys took it in turns to walk in front of the coach and lead it through flare-lit streets'* .

The annual trip to Paris resumed in 1951 and went by way of Newhaven/Dieppe. By this time, Meyrat had died (in 1949) and it was led by Kelly. On their return one of the boys wrote:

> *Although the main reason for the trip is to improve the boys' knowledge of French and France, another important thing is for the boys to enjoy themselves so keep smiling, you lucky people.*[1]

By 1953, Jack Chapman had become Head of French and he decided that some variety in the destination of the French trip would be better than just going to Paris each year. In July of that year boys visited Normandy for the first time from a base at St Malo, and in subsequent years annual visits were made to other parts of Northern France, a day trip to Ostend being made from the base at Wimereux in 1954. Chapman died suddenly at the end of the spring term in 1958 and later that year H J (Bert) Finn, who had accompanied

1 'You lucky people' was a popular expression in vogue at the time

Chapman on several earlier trips, took a party of almost fifty boys to Duinbergen near Ostend for a week. In the following year he led another party to Dunkirk but stood down when R E Ferris became Head of French in 1960. Ferris was a man of grand ideas, many of which he implemented during his time at the school, and he placed greater emphasis on boys speaking French while they were away. At the same time, new opportunities for travel were appearing on the horizon which had not existed before and with lower prices and group travel, more and more boys were able to travel to places which had not previously been possible. Even so, travel to European destinations often involved long and tedious rail journeys.

In 1961 a former troopship, *Dunera,* became redundant and the British India Company (later to be absorbed into P&O) decided to convert her into a schoolship following the success of their earlier pre-war venture. As a result a programme of cruises for schoolchildren in what was virtually a school at sea started in April of that year to various ports in Europe. Always full of enthusiasm for anything different, Leakey liked the idea and asked if I would be prepared to take a party of boys to Scandinavia on *Dunera* in the following September. I jumped at the chance, so twenty-four four lucky boys were taken to Bergen, Amsterdam, Hamburg and Copenhagen for £28, including the price of shore excursions. This time the boys were accommodated in dormitories. A year later, again on *Dunera,* a larger party was taken to Leningrad to what was then a great adventure behind the shadows of the Soviet Union. In 1963, twenty boys were taken on *Dunera* on a cruise to the Holy Land for

DCPS boys relaxing at Athens while on a **Dunera** *cruise - April 1963*

Christmas and this must surely be the only occasion when a school trip has been organised at that precise time of year. Bethlehem was off-limits on that occasion, but Christmas Day in Jerusalem was an unforgettable experience. Apart from the pre-war cruises already mentioned, nothing like that had ever been done before. By this time National Service had ended, service personnel were conveyed by air and the former troopships were either broken up or new work found for them. Extensive conversions were made to four ships in all, including a new *Nevasa,* and each was equipped with classrooms, a large assembly hall and all the necessities for a school at sea.

For the next twenty years, boys from DCPS travelled to all the corners of Europe from Reykjavik in the North, to Haifa and the Mediterranean in the South. Various members of staff led these cruises, the ones to the Baltic and beyond starting from British ports while the southern ones generally started from a Mediterranean port. Initially, parties joined the ship at Venice or Genoa after a long overnight train journey across Europe, but later flights to join the ship became the norm. Each ship carried about 900 boys and girls aged 12 to 18 and these school cruises were enormously popular and not excessively expensive in view of all that was included. At sea, the day was divided into periods with plenty of activities being arranged, and ashore there was always an inclusive excursion accompanied by a local guide. Just how much the boys appreciated all they saw remained to be seen and unquestionably some got mental indigestion. A boy looking at the magnificent ruins at Byblos in Lebanon on one trip asked if he really did have to look at any more stones! School cruising came to an abrupt end in 1982 when the last surviving schoolship, *Uganda,* was requisitioned for use as a hospital ship during the Falklands war, and when that was over the ship was too old and dilapidated to continue. Without another ship readily available, P&O decided to abandon the whole idea, although the concept of taking children on school cruises was kept alive by a company called Schools Abroad, which chartered smaller ships and employed a few former P&O staff. By the mid 1980s different kinds of travel opportunities were becoming available and, with the arrival of package tours, were within financial reach of more.

During the course of 1962 Malcolm Curtis, who was a keen skier, announced that he would be taking a party of boys to Hochsölden in Austria in January the following year. He himself went out a few days earlier and in spite of lengthy preparations, things went wrong from the start. The channel crossing was rough and there was a four-hour delay in Basle because trains were running late and the party was very weary when it eventually reached Hochsölden. On arrival a sorry sight met their eyes. Curtis was on crutches to greet them, having broken his leg on his second day and, before the trip was over, one of the boys was to suffer a similar mishap. All this did not bode well for the future, but the boys enjoyed themselves regardless, ski-ing became popular and more trips followed. During the 1960s cruising and ski-ing vied with each other for the most popular school journeys and as they took place at different times of the year, some lucky boys were able to participate in both. Curtis himself managed both, eventually meeting his future wife on a school cruise in 1964. Undeterred by his previous experience, Curtis led a ski-ing trip to Königssee in Bavaria in January 1964 and was accompanied by Roger Shakeshaft and the school Sister, Sylvia Burgess, who was his wife-to-be.

When Curtis left in 1965, the ski trips were led by Ferris who chose various destinations, including Kandersteg in Switzerland and in 1968, to neighbouring Grächen. These trips were always well supported but were not without incident for in 1967 Ferris too managed to break his leg on the ski slopes, the reason being, and to quote his own words at the time *'because some tourist got in the way'*. Boys too broke limbs on the ski slopes from time to time, but despite the set-backs Ferris returned to Grächen with a school party in 1970. In the same year there was a cruise in the summer to Russia in the schoolship *Uganda*, a year which saw the arrival of Michael Rowett to the staff as Head of Classics and he was another great traveller. He broadened the scope for school journeys and although his first venture in 1973 was a school cruise on *Uganda* which included Athens and Istanbul in its itinerary, he instigated a classical tour by land for a group of boys in the following year which took the boys to Rome and Florence. Ferris accompanied him on this trip. So successful was it that classical trips of one kind or another rapidly became annual events and were strenuous and were inspiringly led by Rowett, so much so that boys and staff were often in need of a holiday when they returned! Rowett's enthusiasm and depth of knowledge about the places he visited meant that the boys learned and saw a great deal. Although Venice was visited during the October half-term in 1977, Greece was generally the most favoured destination and package tours aimed specifically for the schools market meant that schoolchildren could travel further and further away during a comparatively short time. Ski-ing to various centres, school cruising and trips to the Classical World were the major travel opportunities for much of the 1970s and early 1980s and it is clear that those boys who were lucky enough to partake, found them immensely rewarding. They were not the only opportunities on offer and Peter Ashenhurst took two parties of boys to Denmark in 1982 and 1984. Accompanied by his wife, travel was by sea and by using one of the school mini-buses he was able to offer a holiday which would be different and less expensive than most of the other trips on offer at the time. He also wanted the boys to gain the 'feel' of Denmark and this they achieved.

The trips to France, which had been passed on to Ron Ferris, continued into the 1960s but as he was soon organising the ski-ing trips, and scout camps too, school journeys to the near continent were not quite as frequent as they had been before. In April 1966 he led a group of boys to Paris which had not been visited by DCPS since before the war, and in June of the same year, and thus in term time when exams were over, twenty boys visited the 1944 landing beaches in Normandy. Normandy was particularly popular and there were further visits there in subsequent years. Many of these trips involved the use of the first school minibus, a Bedford Dormobile with sliding doors on both sides which were sometimes left open while travelling. With its characteristic numberplate of FBK 34D, it was invariably referred to as Full of Bloody Kids! By 1970 it had been joined by a new Ford Transit which had long longitudinal bench seats on each side so that boys faced each other. It was not conducive for long journeys.

The first school minibus - Bedford Dormobile FBK 34D.
Roger Shakeshaft with a group of boys in Normandy - April 1968

In 1967 there was a trip on the Dutch canals on the barge *Vrijheid*. Most of the boys flew out to join the barge at Amsterdam while a few went out in the Dormobile with all the possessions and food to last a week. It was a tense moment when the end-heavy vehicle was crane loaded at Harwich. There was a similar trip in 1973. Ferris died in February 1976 and so that boys would not be disappointed, Rowett filled the breach by taking a party to Belgium later that year in addition to his Greece trip. The new Head of French was Stuart Sharp who continued much as his predecessor had done, but varying the destinations. In 1977 he led a party of skiers to Saize d'Oulx in the Italian Alps and in 1980 his choice of destination was Verbier in the Swiss Alps which he visited again for the following two years until he left DCPS. He continued to take boys to France regularly, including Paris and to some southern destinations for the first time, one example being in August 1980 when, with plenty of staff helpers, a group of boys went on a camping holiday to the Loire Valley.

All these journeys cost the parents money, and to some extent each vied with the others for popularity. In 1969, David Whytehead, Head of Religious Knowledge, held the opinion that there was scope within the school for trips which were far less grand. By remaining in the UK he felt that the school should offer some kind of leisure activity during the holidays which would cost far less and be enjoyable as well as having some educational value. By staying at Youth Hostels, he was sure that walking holidays in Wales and the North of England would have an appeal and how right he was. His first venture to Northumberland and Hadrian's Wall was limited to Fourth Form boys (Year 6) but after a year or two, such was their popularity that they were opened to all. Destinations varied from year to year, from the Yorkshire Dales to North Wales, while Hadrian's Wall was always popular. The first trip was by coach which stayed with the party for the week, but this proved costly and more often than not school vehicles were used instead, proving on occasions to be less reliable than they are now! Always keen to do things a little differently, Peter Ashenhurst also arranged trips during school holidays. One of his ventures was almost a family affair when in 1971 with his wife he took just seven boys to Scotland for a week. Not to be outdone, the newly formed PTA was keen to be involved and for a short while several walking holidays and rambles were arranged by them, the South Downs ramble in 1971 being one such example. Members of staff accompanied these trips, notably Roger Shakeshaft who was PTA Treasurer for the first few years. Similar ventures were subsequently arranged by DCPS staff and whether at home or abroad, the opportunities for boys to travel during the school holidays was steadily broadening.

Boys on the Dutch canals - April 1973

On the home front, Wednesday trips were as popular as ever and when Terence Kelly moved on in 1951, they became the responsibility of Charles Hambleton. He obviously enjoyed his clientele of loyal supporters and his wisdom of all things mechanical and his breadth of knowledge meant that the boys gained much benefit from their Wednesday outings. All his enthusiasm and traditions continued when Geoffrey Close-Brooks took

David Whytehead and his wife with boys on a walking holiday in
Northumberland. Hamish Maclean is to the right - 1975

over in 1971. Boys were taken to all sorts of places in London including the usual attractions such as the Tower of London and the Science Museum and there were also visits to more off-beat places such as the signal box at St Pancras Station and an opportunity to see the *Daily Mirror* go to press. One appreciative Wednesday tripper was Peter Dodge (DCPS 1964-1973) who wrote:

> *All the trips are either fun or interesting. If they were not why would about twenty-five boys gather at*
> *2 o'clock outside Block 40 every Wednesday? People may prefer to go home or play games. Wednesday*
> *trips are not compulsory, but I, like many people, enjoy spending my Wednesday afternoons exploring*
> *London's wealth in museums and its history.*

The cost of Wednesday trips usually only involved a train fare and an admission charge which were paid for on the day. Coaches were rarely used. As late as 1970 attendance at school on Wednesday afternoons was not compulsory except for boys required for teams and matches. Boys could slip away home if they wanted to although this was frowned upon officially. There were simply not enough pitches available for all to play games, especially in the summer, and at that time there were not sufficient alternative activities to occupy every boy. Close-Brooks put his own stamp on these trips and magazine articles about them produced many literary gems. Here's what he wrote at the end of the autumn term in 1965:

> *The first term of 'our season' is always a little difficult because not all the newcomers grasp the idea*
> *of the visits, which is not just to provide a jolly or a lark, but for boys to see and study the things we*

do. Thus to say after five minutes at the Queen's Gallery that you have "done" the stamps or to boast that you made the circuit of the White Tower at the Tower of London four times while the rest of the party has done it once, shows a misunderstanding of the whole idea. However it is rare that we have to decline the honour of someone's company and the fact that so many boys give up their Wednesday afternoons to go to Westminster Abbey or the Commonwealth Centre is commendable – one might say highly commendable.

C-B's Wednesday trips became legend and when he retired in 1976, Michael Rowett took on overall responsibility for them in addition to his annual tours to Greece. He himself said that there could be no question of one person filling the gap which C-B's retirement had created and at least half a dozen members of staff took trips on different weeks, notably Peter Ashenhurst and the Revd John Llewellyn. A more classical, and one might say cultural, approach was adopted with visits to places such as the Victoria and Albert Museum and Westminster Cathedral with its campanile. The annual picnic trip to Lullingstone Roman Villa was restored to the programme and was always popular. Throughout the 1970s and into the 1980s, Wednesday trips continued to be a weekly feature of school life and the momentum and enthusiasm for them was maintained. James Osborne (DCPS 1978-1986) a regular and enthusiastic Wednesday tripper, summed them up in 1984 when he wrote:

Geoffrey Close-Brooks and a group of boys on a Wednesday trip visiting the Daily Mirror presses - 1974
(Courtesy Mirror Group Newspapers)

The Wednesday trip is an opportunity to discover more about our heritage. What do you know about Queen Anne's Footstool? How many steps are there in The Monument? All this is on your doorstep and can be obtained for a mere fifty or eighty pence. The Wednesday trip also visits galleries and museums and in the summer term goes further afield and is able to spend more time out of doors. Mr Rowett is the source of information and our guide and we all thank him for the time and energy he gives us.

In 1984 it was Rowett's turn to retire and responsibility for Wednesday Trips fell to Barbara Dalton from the music department, often aided by Anne Earle. Between them they visited some interesting venues in London but as C-B had noted earlier, several boys each year who opted for Wednesday trips were definitely those from the more eccentric fringe. As a result there were several occasions when boys separated themselves from the party or who left the train at the wrong station causing major headaches for the organizers. It was not surprising therefore that Anne Earle asked the headmaster in 1990 if she could be relieved of the duty of taking Wednesday trips, a recent debacle with the roof of a school transit in an underground car park no doubt playing a part.

But it was not just the staff who were finding the trips less attractive, for despite James Osborne's earlier enthusiasm times were changing. Boys no longer had the option of going home on a Wednesday afternoon if they were not required at school, and a greater emphasis on alternative facilities meant that more opportunities were available for those who did not wish to play games. Beyond the school's control, the threat of strikes and bomb scares in Central London, which were prevalent at the time, made parents uneasy and the trips became more difficult to arrange. To start with they became less frequent and smaller groups of boys were taken to places out of Central London such as Chislehurst Caves, more often than not using one of the school's vehicles. By 1992, Wednesday Trips had come to an end and what had once been an institution became just a memory. Barbara Dalton changed her loyalties from tripping to conservation and for a while the only Wednesday trip was to Brightlands where boys were encouraged to build nest boxes and learn how to manage the environment. Sometimes visits were made to Dulwich Woods for the same purpose. Henry Newman and Mark Boullé, both of whom left the school in 1995, were enthusiastic founder members, but as one door closed so another opened, and the boys of today have far more choice about how to spend their Wednesday afternoons than was ever the case before.

1968 saw the innovation of an idea which involved travel for the masses – Expedition Day, but that too has run its course. The idea behind Expedition Day was that all boys in the Upper and Middle School (Years 5, 6, 7 and 8) went out for a day in the summer term when Common Entrance and school exams were over. The first in June of that year included destinations such as Southampton, the Royal Marine Depot at Deal, Stratford-on-Avon and Whipsnade. Journeys were by coach and although it poured with rain, the day was described as an unqualified success and it became a regular and popular part of the school calendar for many years. Initially boys were given a choice of destinations, but since staff were inclined to vie with each other for the most popular trip, this did not work very well. Ferris always had the grandest ideas, taking his chosen group across the Channel for a day in France where at Wimereux he insisted that the boys ordered their lunch in French. Rumour soon came back that this proved difficult since the restaurateur was British and did not want to waste time while each boy individually struggled with his vocabulary to place an order. After some very late returns and adverse comments from those who were not chosen to go, destinations were limited to the UK. Individual staff still chose their destinations and with help from others, took their own classes out for the day so boys no longer had a choice, but there was still a degree of bickering about some classes having a better deal than others.

In the early years, destinations were far and varied and were to places as far afield as York, Chester and Bristol. On three occasions whole trains were chartered and on arrival at the destination, coaches were waiting to take class groups to places of interest in the vicinity. The most ambitious of these was in 1973 when a special train was chartered from Sydenham Hill to take DCPS direct to Norwich. It was a long day and a far cry from those early days on Hayes Common in the 1920s. The railway authorities were very obliging and even printed special tickets for each boy. Whole trains were chartered again when the upper part of the school was taken to Oxford in 1977 and to Portsmouth in 1987, these special trains starting at Gipsy Hill. The cost of Expedition Day was always met by parents who had little say in the matter, but as costs went up, the destinations became nearer and less ambitious. By 1992 the cost of this day out, which expected a compulsory attendance, was borne by the school as part of the fee structure and destinations were limited to London and the South East. This was not detrimental to their success and a day out after exams was always welcome. Ann Revell's energetic expeditions to the depths of Epping Forest each year were always popular, especially as she managed to gain special dispensation for her group not to wear school uniform on the grounds that it was impractical.

In June 1986, the Sixth Form boys (Year 8) went to Wales for a week of activities in Snowdonia when their exams were over, so were no longer a part of Expedition Day. So successful was this venture that in due course it led to other year groups having a few days away from Dulwich during term time. In 1994 all boys from the Fourth Forms (Year 6) were taken to York as a year group in two separate parties, each of four days' duration and both following the same programme. These proved to be very worthwhile so much so that similar year group trips were subsequently arranged for boys in Years 5 and 7. In 2004, Year 8 followed established practice by going to Llanberis for a week of physical activities in June, one day of which included the climbing of Snowdon with the Headmaster, but as the number of boys in the year group regularly exceeded a hundred each year, the Chippeways and Deerfeet went one week and the Mohicans and Ojibwas the next. This reflected the divisions made in the early days to Hayes Common and was seen

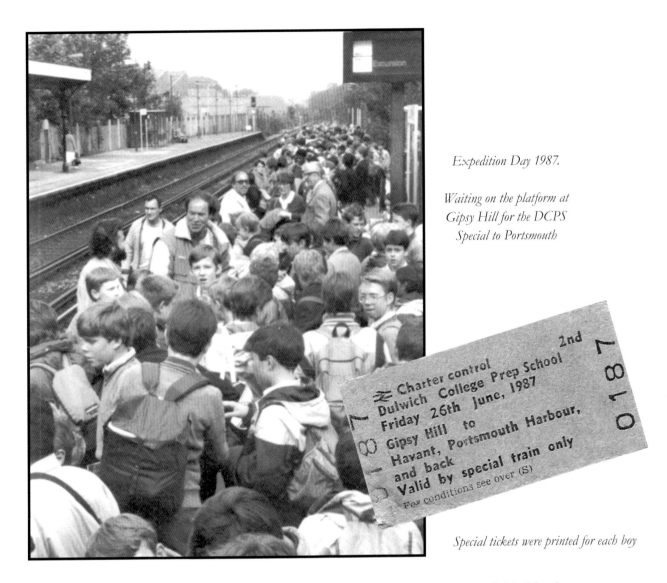

Expedition Day 1987.

Waiting on the platform at Gipsy Hill for the DCPS Special to Portsmouth

Charter control
Dulwich College Prep School   2nd
Friday 26th June, 1987
Gipsy Hill   to
Havant, Portsmouth Harbour, and back
Valid by special train only
For conditions see over (S)
0187

Special tickets were printed for each boy

as the fairest way of dividing the year equally. Other year groups were divided by forms for their visits. Year 7 went to Amersham for a programme of group problem-solving activities and Year 6 continued to go to York to study the history and geography of that great city. Finally Year 5 went to Sheringham for a few days by the sea and an introduction to learning to live away from home, maybe for the first time. Each year group thus had a few days of corporate involvement during the course of a year, the boys gaining benefit from what the school calls Social Education. These ventures are part of the curriculum from which boys cannot opt out and the cost is borne by the school. They have become established annual events, and although not taking place at the same time, they became, to some extent, extensions of Expedition Day which was thus considered redundant, the last being in 2001.

Occasional day visits during school hours have taken place for a long time for boys of all ages. London, with its museums and galleries, has much to offer and the Science Museum has long been a favourite, but journeys into the countryside, such as the pond-dipping days with the younger boys, have been arranged too. Practical experience is a valued tool for learning and Geography in particular lends itself to this with classes being taken out periodically for the day to study a river, a stretch of beach or the workings of a factory. Just once (in 1969) strings were pulled when a party of boys was taken down a working coal mine in Nottinghamshire, but that would never be allowed to happen now. Throughout the 1970s and 1980s, History and Geography combined for the then Sixth Form boys (Year 8) to go for a day out either to the Ironbridge Gorge in Shropshire or the Potteries of Stoke-on-Trent, this included a mining museum where boys went underground officially. Taking large parties on service trains is never easy, but there are advantages and the annual trips to York for Year 6 continue to choose the rail option. Fieldwork has become an integral part of the syllabus in Geography and boys of various age groups have gone out regularly for shopping or pedestrian surveys or to study local traffic flows. In addition to days out for whole classes, there have been optional excursions in holiday time for different year groups. Sheringham in Norfolk and the Dorset coast have provided ideal locations for practical study and places visited and techniques applied have depended upon the requirements of the day. History and Geography are perfect partners for combined study and since 1999 Year 5 has visited Hastings for a day where aspects of both subjects have been studied. Trips out as part of school work have not been their sole preserve and there have been visits to galleries and exhibitions, science lectures and concerts. The Nursery, Annexe and

*Freddie Peakman and James Taylor interviewing passers-by as part of
their Geography fieldwork, in what appears to be a deserted Bromley*

Lower School boys have also benefited from the occasional day out as extensions to their work, sometimes on a form basis, the London Zoo being a good example.

Arranged for less academic reasons has been a programme of visits to places of interest in London for the Year 8 boys at the end of June each year when all exams are over and they are approaching the end of their time at DCPS. These started in 1981 and have varied over the years to include such locations as the Imperial War Museum and the Museum of the Moving Image. The days out have been supplemented at school by discussions ranging from drug misuse to the correct procedure for ironing a shirt. In 1996 Year 8 boys were fortunate to receive a lecture from Michael Palin who enthralled his audience with excerpts and slides from his *Around the World in Eighty Days* series of television programmes.

Boys taking a break from studying coastal erosion at Durdle Door - 2003

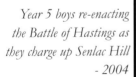

Year 5 boys re-enacting the Battle of Hastings as they charge up Senlac Hill - 2004

Although the ways by which boys have been taken out of school to local places have changed, school journeys abroad have steadily increased as new opportunities have been made available and as members of staff have come up with new ideas. The end of school cruising in 1982 conveniently coincided with the arrival of Alan Chidwick as Head of French. Like his predecessors he needed little persuasion to take boys to France and he wanted as many as possible to share his enthusiasm, and indeed his passion, for the culture and traditions of all things French. The first notable change from that of his predecessors was that he passed responsibility for the ski-ing trips to the PE Dept where it logically belonged, and he concentrated purely on trips to France. Progressively he built up a following and a wide range of destinations, the trips becoming collectively known, with some affection, as 'Chidwick Tours Inc'. His first trip in his first term was to Paris where school journeys outside Britain had started all those years ago. It was deemed a great success and was repeated a year later, but in 1984 he chose a different location by taking DCPS to Provence and thereafter he alternated by taking a group to Paris at Easter one year and to Provence at the next. By 1990, the Loire region and Normandy had been included into what had become a rolling programme, but the trips still only took place once a year and were open to Years 6, 7 and 8 only. So popular were his 'tours' and so vigorous his energy that trips began to be undertaken at half-terms in addition to those during the longer holidays, and it was not uncommon for there to be several in a year, each catering for a specific age group. The 1989 trip to Paris marked a turning point in the way Chidwick arranged his

Boys examining relics from World War I at Vimy Ridge - 2001

tours. On this trip the hotel was some distance from the centre, the Metro was on strike and the whole operation proved stressful and difficult. As with London and the Wednesday trips, visiting capital cities presented problems which had not been apparent a decade earlier, so Paris was dropped from his programme and the safer environment of Alsace and Strasbourg was offered as an alternative, the first trip there being in 1990. Thereafter the Normandy trips were arranged for Year 5 only and destinations for other year groups varied from year to year between the Loire, Provence and Alsace. In 2001, he branched out again by taking a large party to the Somme Battlefields of the First World War for the first time, the site of the Battle of Waterloo also being included. The new millennium saw further developments in school journeys abroad, especially in specialist trips combining several disciplines within the school. Often these were initiated by recently appointed members of staff who had arrived with fresh ideas. In 2001 Simon Severino, with Simon Head, led a trip to Sorrento in Italy combining the geography of the area with some of its classical history. Severino's annual trips to Sorrento rapidly became established. In 2003 Sarah Gibson, from the school's languages department, with Sean Savides and Dennis Spammer led a trip to Planète Futuroscope in the Vienne region of France, combining French with Science as well as providing an enjoyable holiday. In 2001 the veteran Alan Chidwick joined forces with the Director of Music and, with Philip Brooke and others in support, led a group of musicians on a tour to Strasbourg and Baden Baden where they gave performances. So successful was this that subsequent music tours followed. This was not the first time that musicians had travelled abroad for in 1993 Stephen Woods, then Head of Strings, had taken a party of musicians to perform at a concert in Minnesota, USA. The highlight of this tour was when they met the well known violinist Nigel Kennedy. Unusually for a DCPS holiday venture, this trip gained the support of a sponsor and the participants were grateful to Merrill Lynch for providing it.

Ski-ing holidays, nearly always at the start of the Easter holidays, have been popular ever since Malcolm Curtis put them back on the DCPS map in 1962 and few years have passed since then when a ski trip has not been arranged. In April 1985, Ian Martin as Head of PE took his first ski trip to Les Collons in the Swiss Alps. He must have been impressed with that particular resort as he took parties there every year until he moved to the staff of Dulwich College in 1992. Each organizer has a favoured destination and there are many companies which cater for school ski-ing trips. When David Adkins assumed responsibility for them in the following year, having already assisted Martin on previous trips, he decided it was time for a change so boys were taken to Courmayeur, an Italian ski resort near Mont Blanc in the Aosta Valley. From an organizer's point of view there is much to be said for going to a known location once it is established that the facilities are up to the mark. Adkins found that Courmayeur suited him and the school well, so assisted by wives, partners and colleagues, it became a regular destination. Many trips were oversubscribed and for a few years there was room for an overflow. During the February half-term in 1998, Simon Severino, then recently appointed Head of Geography, took 17 boys on a ski-ing trip to the Austrian Alps and just a few months later Adkins took a much larger party again to Courmayeur. This pattern continued for a few years with Severino varying his destinations to include the Dolomites in 1999 and the Italian Alps in 2002.

At the end of the summer holidays in 1989, Stephen Woods, aided and abetted by several members of staff, took a party of boys on a very different type of school journey to the South of France. Living under canvas, they all enjoyed five days of sailing, windsurfing and canoeing and so successful was it that a repeat trip was arranged for the following year, this time led by David Adkins as Stephen Woods was away on a sabbatical. There were further trips to Gastes in subsequent years, but as the summer Bank Holiday is in late August and the autumn term starts earlier in September, the time proved difficult and the trips stopped. These holidays proved to be popular and sailing holidays have been resumed. Not all trips are milk and honey and there can be problems from time to time which disrupt the programme and which cause major headaches for the staff involved. In 1992 one of the boys, Simon Scott, slipped while at Gastes and rendered himself unconscious. It was a genuine accident resulting in concussion, and although it proved not to be serious, it did mean that Simon could not return with the others and had to be flown home later, Adkins staying behind with him. Because of problems like these, national regulations and recommendations have been introduced to provide guidelines for those leading school journeys and many schools have a teacher who acts as an Educational Visits Co-ordinator (EVC). At DCPS this became the responsibility of David Adkins from 2003.

Tours outside mainland UK for a particular sport had already been instigated by the cricket ventures to South Africa already mentioned and earlier to Jersey by Robin Whitcomb. Not wanting to be outdone, and wishing to give different boys a chance to play games in other countries, Adkins arranged a series of soccer matches for boys in Venice and Rome in 2002, led by Mitchell and Morland. As the new millennium gathers momentum and world sporting events gain in popularity, there is scope and as yet untapped enthusiasm for more tours abroad to be arranged with a bias towards sport. Yet possible problems lie ahead.

Although virtually all aspects of school life have progressed beyond recognition since that first school trip to Paris in 1927, taking children out of school during school holidays has presented problems despite the range of opportunities on offer. Trips arranged during term time which may be regarded as part of a day's work, and the residential ones currently arranged each year for whole year groups, are well established and likely to continue. In the holidays, ski-ing remains as popular as ever as do the trips to France; sporting and cultural tours have become fashionable, each trying to outdo the other for originality and enterprise, and doubtless there will be others as promoters come up with new ideas. So why the lack of optimism? Diminishing numbers of willing participants is not the reason, nor is there unwillingness by parents to pay for school trips when they are outside the curriculum. The problem, not so apparent as yet within the independent sector, is the increasing responsibility being thrust upon teachers who arrange school journeys during holiday time. Given the pace of life at DCPS and the demands made upon staff, it is perhaps surprising how popular holiday trips continue to be, and sometimes there are too many options from enthusiastic group leaders keen to instigate holiday ventures, than there are staff to accompany them. The greatest reason for a possible decline in holiday trips in the long term could arise from the litigation culture which has developed. Taking children anywhere is a major responsibility and they do become ill, get lost or have accidents however stringent the precautions, and this applies to holiday and term-time expeditions alike. Simon Scott's incident at Gastes in 1992 is a case in point and well illustrates the onus which falls upon the shoulders of group leaders and those who accompany them. Teachers can easily become liable for any misfortune, a risk which increasing numbers are not prepared to take and teachers' unions are beginning to recommend that their members do not participate in any activity which is beyond the school campus. The need to enforce statutory regulations can also lead to difficulties and, as a result, it is not surprising that some teachers are beginning to think twice about the wisdom of volunteering in the first place. Sporting tours which have greater physical involvement, especially those for rugby, have even greater risks and correspondingly higher insurance, and risk assessment has to be evaluated for all trips. These may be logical and sensible requirements, but fulfilling them has become an increasingly onerous task, to say nothing of gathering deposits and balances by required dates. Parents are often willing, and sometimes encouraged, to accompany school trips in a semi-supervisory way, but they do not know the children, are subject to the same restrictions and are not always suitable. Negligence on anyone's part can never be acceptable and there is need for a degree of regulation, especially as there are risks now which did not exist before and greater precautions have to be taken. Supervision is thus increased and the amount of freedom given to pupils is reduced. School trips both abroad and at home will continue unquestionably, but will they be as much fun or be as beneficial in the future as they have been in the past? There seems little likelihood that they will be for those who choose to administer them.

Reservation notice for DCPS on their return from 'Wolves' after a visit to the Ironbridge Gorge

15   Wheels within Wheels

Within a school, there are many departments and activities which are an integral part of school life, yet they often go by unnoticed or without the recognition they deserve. The maintenance department, for example, has produced some very colourful and long-standing members of staff over the years. Longest standing of all to date has been Ian Larkin, not from the Dulwich school but from the one in Cranbrook, who worked continuously there from the age of sixteen until his retirement in 2003 at the age of sixty. No member of the teaching staff can match that. Ian, and others like him, managed to keep the buildings and grounds of both schools in good shape, sometimes under trying conditions, and it is easy to take the work they do for granted.

Important though the school's maintenance may be, there are far more people involved working behind the scenes than meets the eye. The domestic staff, who tend to see a little more of the boys, particularly at lunchtime and at social occasions, are equally important. In Dulwich, the catering department provides lunches for almost a thousand people every day in term time and is sometimes criticised, unfairly, for producing too much institutional food. The administrative staff, which includes the bursary and the school secretaries, also play an important role yet few of the boys know who any of them are. The book room provides stationery for staff and boys alike, now at almost any time of the school day. Nor should the medical department be overlooked. The boys know who the school Sisters are because there are times when they are much in need and the school without them would be unthinkable. These, then, are just some of the cogs within the DCPS wheel, without which the whole place would simply grind to a halt.

To be considered also are the extra-mural activities conducted by members of the teaching staff during out of school hours in the form of clubs, often after school but sometimes during breaks as well. These have taken place from the very start on an optional basis, and boys have always been encouraged to take advantage of them. Today the cost of equipment necessary to organise most of the clubs and extra-mural activities is built into the fee structure, but in the past parents paid for boys to join clubs on an *ad hoc* basis. The variety of clubs offered has invariably depended on the enthusiasm of staff employed at the time. Boys (and girls) in preparatory schools are at a responsive age and if a member of staff suddenly announces that a bee club is to be formed, there would be no shortage of members wishing to join. There have been some unusual clubs over the years, a rocketry club being a recent example, and that will almost certainly give way to another when the person in charge of it moves on. In 1919, which is as far as records go back, there is mention of four clubs being offered, none of which exists today. They were map reading, signalling, woodcraft and boxing. Boxing continued until the 1970s and is a casualty of changing attitudes, but traces of the rings which once held the rope around the boxing ring in the school hall can still be found if you know where to look. Other school clubs just faded as social habits changed so that stamp collecting and model railways, as examples, no longer have the appeal amongst youngsters that they once had.

During the 1920s little mention is made of activities which would now be known as clubs and it is clear that they were on the fringes of school life. Many boys went home for lunch in the pre-war period so there was neither the scope nor the opportunities for clubs as there are now. By 1930, the original woodwork club had become carpentry, chess was introduced in 1933 and Livingston introduced a drama club in 1935. In that year also a model railway club started and was always oversubscribed. This was principally an 'O' gauge layout which had the luxury of a room all to itself in the roof above the Lower School. The room was totally destroyed in the 1982 fire by which time it was being used as a stationery store. There was also a science club although no science lessons appeared

Model Railway Club - 1935

in the timetable at that time. An aspect of extra-curricular activity during the 1930s was the school's involvement with an organisation known simply as 'JRF'. All was explained in the autumn 1936 edition of the school magazine:

> *What does it all mean? What is it all about? Those magic letters JRF stand for Junior Road Fellowship. When it is realised that 500 young people under fifteen years of age are killed on the roads every term, and that 40,000 a year are injured, it is obvious that the time has come to do something about it. This JRF is that something. It aims at giving youngsters a real road sense and showing them what sportsmanship and consideration for others on the road mean. In this way when the time comes for those youngsters to drive their own cars and ride their own motorbikes, they will not be found wanting, but will become good drivers. Road accidents will then automatically become less.*

JRF was a commendable idea although there is no evidence to show whether the figures quoted were national, global or pure guesswork, and one wonders just what was meant by '*sportsmanship*' on the road. To start with, membership to JRF within the school was voluntary but by 1937 every boy in the school had automatically become a member and there was a JRF Tribe Competition. Badges and licences were issued based on sound road sense and cycle tests on the road, and licences could even be endorsed! The climax came that year when the school was visited by Sir Malcolm Campbell, then famous for his attempts to

Sir Malcolm Campbell (second from right) came to DCPS to present a bicycle to the winner of the 'JRF' Competition. Leakey is on the extreme right - 1937

break world speed records, both on land and on water. He was subsequently killed in one of his attempts. Sir Malcolm came to the school in the summer term to award a bicycle to the winner of the JRF competition. He was accompanied by representatives of the press and treated very much as a guest of honour and for the school it was a great occasion. With the coming of war, JRF disappeared and although it was not reinstated afterwards, an inter-tribe Highway Code Competition, later to become Road Safety, continued for some years. More recently, the PTA has arranged for boys to take part in cycle courses in school holidays at the cycle track at Herne Hill and these have proved popular.

When the school evacuated to Cranbrook in the autumn of 1939 there was still a need to offer boys leisure activities, and as all were then boarding, the need was even greater. Music was relayed through loudspeakers by way of gramophone records and there was some corporate community singing to patriotic tunes. With the co-operation of Cranbrook School, evening clubs for handiwork and science were quickly formed and at the camp itself clubs for table tennis, billiards, stamps and chess were among those to be resurrected. With the move to Betws the following June, the need for leisure was just as necessary and these same activities were soon under way again. A music club flourished in Wales under the hand of Elaine Barnett and there was scope for new activities such as mountaineering, although these were not normally arranged on a club basis.

When the school re-assembled in Dulwich after the war, clubs soon started again although the choice on offer was different and limited. Some like the out-of-doors club were short lived, but carpentry was back on stream within weeks and continued for many years.

Captain Fleming's Archery Club - 1947

Attempts were also made to resuscitate an art club but it '*dwindled in numbers because we can only meet after school which presents problems about going home in the dark for some would-be members*'. It didn't dwindle for long, but because of the problems of boys going home in the dark, often on their own, lunchtime clubs tended to be more popular than those held after school, and for many years there was a consistency of clubs on offer. Some had a long run while others came and faded as interests changed. Captain Fleming, one of the school's more flamboyant teachers, introduced an archery club in 1947. This was held on the school field and was popular for a while, but it never re-appeared once he had left. He also started a photographic club and a year later a science club was re-introduced. Biology and pottery had appeared earlier and a table-tennis club involving day boys versus boarders made a brief appearance in 1948. The Lower School too introduced clubs for the younger boys, two early ones being for nature and handwork. Jill Caster introduced weaving in 1956 and at the same time Horace Rowbotham started a metalwork club: both were to last many years. One club, which also had a long run, was puppetry. This flourished for almost twenty years and among its members was the broadcaster and actor Martin Jarvis. Known now for his clear diction, he wrote when he was eleven years old that *'speaking plays a very important part in our puppet shows'*. For many years the puppetry club was in the hands of Muriel Spokes, formerly in charge of the Annexe, but when she retired interest gradually declined. Folk dancing too was surprisingly popular for a long time in the post-war period, this being inspired by F C Hambleton who had the masterly skill of being able to promote and share his interests with others. Not quite so surprising was stamp collecting which had a considerable following, both inside and outside school at the time. T F Merritt introduced a club for philatelists in 1953 which was principally to swap stamps and exchange information between members. R A Shakeshaft took this over six years later and the club lasted until he left the school in 1973. As well as these, art, boxing, carpentry, chess and gymnastics all became long-lasting clubs. Gymnastics had a particular problem as the building used was totally inadequate, the 1958 magazine informing its readers that there was barely enough room for the twenty-six members! When the then spacious new gymnasium was opened in 1966, membership shot up to 120.

As the years passed, earlier popular clubs such as metalwork and carpentry gave way and are now incorporated into Design Technology, which exists both as a club and as a timetabled subject. The same can be said for science which started as a club long before it appeared in the classroom. Worthy of mention

Chess on the Lower School playground - 1989

is chess, which George Szaszvari brought to the fore in the 1980s, several boys being successful in international championships. So enthusiastic was he, that he created a giant chessboard on the playground for a while, thus encouraging boys to show an interest in the game and maybe to try it in their break times.

As well as being responsible for teams in the major sports as mentioned earlier, teaching staff from outside the PE Department have introduced, or reintroduced, a diversity of clubs in recent years. Some, like Greek, have been more or less continuous, whereas golf was introduced in 1988 by Richard Lynn, then re-introduced by Bunky Symmes and is currently under the hand of Philip Brooke, Director of Music. Ecology, bridge, philosophy and badminton are all examples of clubs which have appeared in recent times and some have become options on games afternoons. Under the jurisdiction of Elaine Vestey, the canoe club has steadily extended its influence beyond the bounds of DCPS. Although the swimming pool has been used for regular training sessions, and the club has its own canoes carefully stowed nearby, it has become involved in events away from school such as the Regional Youth Paddlesport Event held annually at Crystal Palace. Boys have also enjoyed Sunday visits to a canoeing centre at Yalding on the River Medway in Kent, and there have been regular canoeing holidays to places as far afield as the Galloway Sailing Centre in Scotland. Canoeing can be a dangerous sport and great care has always been taken to maintain its safety. In 1919 there were just four clubs on offer and the many options available for 2004 showed how opportunities have evolved and proliferated. Not all are

Elaine Vestey with the Canoe Club on the Medway - 1995

strictly clubs, and times have been broadened to the extent that a few have been available at 7.50 a.m. - a far cry from earlier days when one of the school rules, printed in the prep register, proclaimed that no boy should arrive at school before 8.30 a.m. No boy has ever been expected to participate in every club and activity, that would not be possible, but all are expected to be involved in at least two and the options, as ever, depend to a large extent on the interests of staff at the time.

An activity which is no longer with us, but which was very popular for over thirty years, was scouting and there was always a long waiting list. After the war, Leakey employed to the staff a former RN Lieutenant, T J Williams. He had an interest in scouting and as a result of his life and experience at sea, DCPS soon had a group of sea scouts. When they arrived in uniform each week for their scout day, to the other boys they were considered the elite and were the envy of many. Camps and a wide range of activities were arranged by Williams for his scouts and among his possessions were an old army lorry 'Annie'

Chris (the dog) and Annie (the lorry) off with the scouts and cubs for an outing - 1951

and a large St Bernard dog, Chris. Without seats, safety belts or a care in the world the boys piled into the back of 'Annie' and a great time was had by all wherever they went. Sometimes they went off to sea and the '13th Camberwell', as the group was properly called, flourished long after Williams left in 1951. There was a cub pack as well for the younger boys, although these were 'land' cubs. Williams built up a great following with the sea scouts and his departure left a gap which was hard to fill and scouting went through a lean time until R E Ferris arrived on the staff in September 1960. He quickly resuscitated it and his enthusiasm and masterly touch for organisation put the sea scouts well and truly back on the DCPS map. As well as weekly meetings, there were annual summer camps, the locations varying from year to year. A private garden at Lowestoft was a popular venue for a while providing comparative safety and easy access to the sea. The boys slept in tents and cooked by patrols, the food itself being provided for them. In term time, there were weekend camps and those to the scout centre at Longridge near Marlow on the Thames were easily accessible and always well supported. After such strenuous weekend activity which invariably involved more excitement than sleep, there were some weary heads for

DCPS scouts on parade at camp in Lowestoft - 1965

school on Monday morning. There was great parental support and sea-scouting activities became a series of outward bound courses with a nautical orientation, while the scout parents formed a kind of parent association within the school long before either the PTA or outward bound activities had been established. It could be said, perhaps, that the enthusiasm among the scouting parents and the goodwill they generated within the school was the embryo from which the PTA was born. When Ferris died in 1976, scouting was already on the wane, and although the cubs continued for a few years, times were changing and the boys were attracted to other things. By then Ann Revell and other members of staff were offering outward bound activities to boys in the holidays and these, to some extent, filled the breach.

An extra-mural activity with which the school has been involved over the years has been the raising of money for charity. This has been done in all sorts of ways by many people, ever since Leake had the idea of sponsoring a cot at King's College Hospital in 1923. This evolved into each boy bringing a shilling to school once a term, the money being donated to various charities, usually at the Headmaster's discretion. Produce brought in for the Harvest Festival Service was distributed from the start to the Home for the Incurables at Crown Point and continues to this day, although now there are other recipients as well. During the war money was raised for the war effort, and for several decades afterwards the school's principal beneficiary was the National Society for the Prevention of Cruelty to Children (NSPCC). Money was collected in blue egg-shaped boxes and different badges were given to boys for the amounts they had collected. Boys whose fathers were doctors, and who agreed to leave the box in the surgery waiting room, often gained many badges. Once a year a representative from the NSPCC came to the school to thank the boys for the money which had been raised and for many years Jill Caster and Bridget Woodcock meticulously emptied the boxes and sent the money off. As the terms went by, money was raised for worthwhile causes in a variety of ways. The school was much involved with a local old people's home (now closed) called Inglewood at Crystal Palace and there have been sponsored swims. One was held at James Allen's Girls' School before the DCPS pool was built and later, using the school's own pool in 1992, Robin Whitcomb raised money for Guide Dogs for the Blind and so inspired the boys that enough money was raised for no fewer than eleven dogs.

Robin Whitcomb (l) looks on as Michael Pitt (head boy) presents a cheque to
a representative of Guide Dogs for the Blind Association in 1992

In 1993 Red Nose Day was marked for the first time. This combined with 'non-uniform day', already established, when Upper and Lower School boys paid 50p to come to school in clothes of their own choice and, replacing lessons from morning break until lunch, there were stalls and amusements arranged by the boys themselves on a form basis. Jonathan Monroe (DCPS 1986- 1993) wrote simply of Red Nose Day that *'it was an hour of disorganized, disorderly good fun for the whole school, pupils and teachers alike'*. One of the staff, Piers Tobenhouse, shaved off half his beard and at the end of the day £2,117 was sent to Comic Relief. National Red Nose Day was supported in subsequent years and as before was combined with a non-uniform day. Richard Witts organised several of these with much gusto and they were always successful and provided a few hours' break from the routine of school. Quite separately, the Lower School held 'penny bazaars' each year, although whether it was still legal to sell home-made cakes without wrapping was a matter for some conjecture! On another occasion money was raised for a kidney dialysis machine at Dulwich Hospital, thus maintaining links with the local community.

In 1998 Witts had the idea of raising money by organising a twenty-four hour run at the school field. The principles were that participants gained sponsors for the number of laps they ran, there would be at least one person on the track at any one time with a baton, and that it would be fun. Almost at once it became known as the 'Fun Run'. Boys, parents and

The 24 hour Fun Run - 1998

staff entered into the spirit of the occasion and later Witts described the support he gained as being *'totally unexpected and the result startlingly successful'*. The run began at noon on Friday June 19th. Some runners came in wigs, others gave piggy-backs, and much fun was had by all, the atmosphere and sense of occasion prevailing through the night. The last lap was run the next day at noon by Philip de Glanville, former DCPS pupil and at the time Captain of England's rugby squad. Fine weather blessed the occasion and at the end over £28,000 was raised, but the day was not without incident. Just before de Glanville ran his lap, he asked Witts to look after his car keys. Richard Witts was so elated and weary from the events of the previous 24 hours that at the end he just slipped quietly away to the depths of Kent - with the keys in his pocket and without a mobile phone. Philip de Glanville stayed on to give away the prizes at Sports Day which followed in the afternoon and there was then some clever Sherlock Holmes detective work to trace Richard and retrieve the keys.

Encouraged by the Fun Run, Witts decided the following year to have a 'Fun Day' which incorporated a Fancy Dress Parade with Red Nose Day. This time boys from the Annexe through to Year 8 paid £1 to take part and there were some sensational outfits. At the end of the day the judges had a difficult task deciding which boys had the most original outfits from each year group. These days of fun, which raised money for various charities each year, were not limited to the boys and members of staff also often entered into the spirit of the occasion.

Members of staff making the most of Fun Day - 1999
(from l to r: Bunky Symmes, Sarah Gibson, Piers Tobenhouse, Chris Smith)

In 2000, and in conjunction with the PTA and the millennium celebrations, Witts arranged another Fun Run at the school field. There was a fireworks display and a barbecue which continued through into breakfast and as before a baton was continuously carried around the school field for 24 hours. This time the weather was poor and not quite so much money was raised as two years earlier but it was still fun, and a great team effort by all who took part. Among the chosen beneficiaries were the Demelza Hospice for children at Sittingbourne, St Christopher's Hospice in Sydenham, the Tuke School and the Sparrow Foundation in South Africa.[1]

Ever since its formation in 1969, the PTA has been involved in fund-raising initiatives, not only for the benefit of the school, but for external beneficiaries as well, although raising money has never been a stated objective in its constitution. For the school, it has provided activities and equipment over and above those which would normally be supplied and each section has gained benefit in rotation. Recent examples have been the purchase of a digital camera and books for the refurbished Annexe library, and the purchase of play equipment for the Annexe and Lower School playgrounds which had been enlarged. A new outdoor sound system was also provided, of which the whole school could take advantage. But it was not just the school which benefited from the PTA through the generosity of parents. Each year just before Christmas there has been a Senior

Senior Citizens' Party at DCPS - 1998

Citizens' party at which over a hundred elderly people from the locality are hosted and entertained by the school. A few of those who attend are former employees, and local GPs have been approached for recommendations as to who else could be invited. Parents, staff

1 Initiated by George Marsh, this is described more fully in Chapter 16

and current pupils, through the PTA, all contribute to make these annual parties enjoyable for all who visit the school on these occasions.

The Sparrow Schools in Johannesburg have also gained benefit from PTA funding and donations have been made to The Andrew Previté Foundation to provide a new specialist multiple sclerosis unit at King's College Hospital, as well as REACH, the Great Ormond Street charity. In order to pay out, money must come in. Originally the PTA accrued funds through subscriptions, but now the principal source comes from fund-raising events. Of these the most profitable has been the annual Fireworks and Bonfire Extravaganza as it has become known, held at Brightlands each November. Once a small affair, those who organise it now require an obligatory day of training in order to satisfy the requirements of Health and Safety. In addition to the fireworks, there are themed evenings such as the *Night of The Raj* ball in 2003 which provided an evening of fun as well as a lucrative source of funds. So successful was this that a Caribbean evening is on the agenda, this being in aid of Cystic Fibrosis Research at the Royal Brompton Hospital, chosen because a current pupil is a sufferer. Apart from fund-raising activities, the PTA is an important channel of communication between home and school.

The school has always needed to be maintained, but until about forty years ago it was much smaller than it is now and it was often more economic to employ contractors or people from outside to undertake the simplest of jobs. In the Headmaster's minutes of an internal meeting held in 1936, for example, and one of only a few to survive, there is mention of a firm called Cafflins who came to the school each Friday afternoon to wind the school clocks. Cafflins were found to be unreliable and it was further minuted that Harrods should be approached instead. In the same year bushes needed to be removed from a corner of the school field to make room for a new cricket pitch and again outside labour was sought. The school had always employed a porter who carried out all sorts of practical jobs within the school, from putting up the blinds in the hall before a lantern slide show, to summoning boys to visit the headmaster for 'Tolly' (the cane). Some of these porters served the school for many years and several former pupils remember the name of one called Walpole – maybe from their personal association with 'Tolly'!

Sometimes the few men the school did employ for maintenance work were far from unskilled. Soon after Leakey married in 1932 and while visiting his wife's parents in Cranbrook, he spotted Horace Rowbotham who was working at a garage there. Rowbotham had been an electrical engineer during the First War, but when the recession came, he found himself out of work. Leakey persuaded him to move to Dulwich with his family and offered him a part-time job at the school. At the time the school possessed four large Daimler cars which were used to convey boys to and from school, a service for which the school charged two old pence per mile – a little less than 1p in today's money. These cars needed to be licensed as Public Service Vehicles, so Rowbotham was responsible for their maintenance as well as all electrical work within the school. By the outbreak of war, Austins had replaced the Daimlers and Rowbotham was called up again, but returned afterwards and organised a most successful after school club for would-be metalwork enthusiasts. When he retired in 1967, George Edmed carried on the club and it continued for a few more years. Now working with metal is part of the DT department syllabus so every boy has become involved and it is not just for the enthusiastic few.

The school cars outside 42 Alleyn Park - 1938

Tom Emment came from a local firm of builders in Dulwich and from 1925 he also worked for the school in a part-time capacity. He carried out minor repairs to the school buildings from that time and during the Second War he was invaluable when repairs were needed after air raids. As a sideline, he also ran a carpentry club both during the lunch hour and once a week after school. Before the war, and apart from the field at Grange Lane, the school grounds were nothing more than a playground and the headmaster's garden, with the paddock beyond near the Annexe. Leake, until he left Dulwich, and Leakey too, employed their own domestic staff, several of whom worked in the school as well. Charlie Beesley looked after Leakey's garden at his home at Six Pillars, also spending some time at the school, and like Leakey's personal cook, Mabel Drewry, he accompanied the school on its evacuation both to Cranbrook and to Wales. Beesley returned after the war to become the gardener at Brightlands where his pride and joy was the kitchen garden where he grew vegetables for the boarders. In due course garden produce became more readily available and it was on the wane when he retired in 1967. Maybe this was just as well for two years later the vegetable garden was swept aside when the Nursery School was built on its site. Phyllis Glazier, who played a large part at the Cranbrook school after the war, was also originally one of Leakey's personal staff, and she was another who went with him and the school when it evacuated.

After the war circumstances had changed and it became obvious to Leakey that with so much of the school fabric needing attention it would be more economic to employ a carpenter on a full-time basis. Leakey always looked within before he looked without and when he approached Mabel Drewry's brother, Stan Smith, to see if he would be interested in this work, he struck gold and did not know at the time how fortunate he had been with his choice. Stan Smith, or just 'Smithy' as he was universally known, was a real character and stayed at the school for thirty years. When 'Smithy' made something it was made to last, but he did things in his own way and in his own time. As an example, he totally rebuilt the back staircase at Brightlands in 1967 when it needed replacing and it will last for many a year yet. One of Stan Smith's first jobs in 1946 was to repair the desks which had been brought back from Wales. These had been in use at the school for a long time before the war and by going first to the camp and then to Wales, they were well travelled and well worn. It would be several years before the school was in a position to buy new furniture – always an expensive item. The boys sat on form benches for lunch and these were difficult and costly to obtain at the time. As a result 'Smithy' set to and made a couple of dozen and these lasted well beyond those which were purchased later. Many of the window frames were rotten or damaged and the whole school was in urgent need of a lick of paint. 'Smithy' kept the school together for many years and will be remembered too for his dry sense of humour. When asked to comment one day after he had been asked to paint a room in black for new trends in drama then being practised, he simply said that he would hang around and wait for the fashion to change! Then there was 'Eagle' or Mr Eagle as he was occasionally

Stan Smith (Smithy).
As school carpenter from 1945 to 1986, he was indispensable

*Clearing
snow from the
playground
- 1962*

Boy Labour!

*Brushing rain
water off the
nets - 1994*

*They make
good waiters
too! - 1995*

and more properly known. He was Leakey's 'man' who would don a black shiny cap if he were Leakey's chauffeur, but who on another day would be equally at home clearing the drains. He also doubled up as school porter. With fewer staff employed to maintain the school it was not considered inappropriate to ask the boys to perform menial jobs sometimes and clearing snow away from the playgrounds, for example, was a job they often enjoyed. After a concert or play when the hall was urgently needed again for another purpose, boy labour was often the quickest way to make a rapid transformation. There were occasions when they made good waiters too!

Cleaning, catering and maintenance all grew as the size of the school increased and in 1946 Miss Guest was appointed to oversee them. She superintended these areas until she retired in 1956 and she had numerous successors. Among those who lasted more than a few years were Irene Ingram, Norrie Macdonald and Barbara McIntosh, the position in due course becoming known as Domestic Bursar. Staff directly employed by the school prepared boys' lunches, as did those who worked at the servery. Until the hall was enlarged in 1959, space for lunch had always been a problem and boys who lived locally were encouraged to go home for their midday meal, the school fee being reduced accordingly. Those who stayed at school to eat sandwiches from home in a classroom supervised by a member of staff were charged one (old) penny a day. The formality of lunches from Leake's days was swept aside in wartime when self-service and queuing became the norm, and that was the way it was to be when school resumed in 1945. For a long time there were lunches at set times. First Lunch was for the Lower School at 12.30 (as it still is). Second Lunch began for the older boys at 1.00 when the Lower School had left and was principally for those playing games and involved in clubs. Last Lunch for the rest began at about 1.30, and which boys attended which lunch varied from day to day. Food for the Annexe and Nursery was also prepared in the kitchen. Although school lunches were not always universally appreciated, for many years, and certainly in the immediate post-war period, they were mundane but wholesome.

By 1970, the school's premises had become more extensive and as costs rose it became prudent for the school to employ more men on a full-time basis to carry out routine maintenance, although outside contractors were used as well for major work. Much of the decoration, both inside and out, and at Brightlands as well, was carried out by Jim Anderson, an ex-para who ran his own small decorating business. Scrupulously honest and a jack of all trades, Anderson could be relied upon to be called out at any time night or day, and his wife was head cook in the kitchen for many years. Decisions had to be taken as to whether it was cheaper, and whether there was time, to have work done by what was colloquially known at the time as 'OOL' (Our Own Labour) or call in outsiders. Jobs like carpet laying, the installation of electrical equipment and major structural alterations were done by specialist contractors, but much internal work was done by OOL, especially during school holidays. The bursar had overall charge of maintenance and strange as it may seem now, the teaching staff often became involved as well. Among the many portfolios held by Bert Finn, the Second Master, was one on maintenance. He went round the school every holiday to see which rooms needed decorating and which desks needed to be removed or replaced. During the 1980s the janitor-cum-porter was Joe Cairns whose title officially was School Caretaker, but as well as making the school secure at night, he would do anything from putting away the benches after lunch to running errands in the school van, a small Ford Escort in those days. Security was not as tight as it might have been and the school was broken into on numerous occasions, the most serious resulting in the fire which destroyed the Lower School in 1982, already referred to.

The school grounds at Grange Lane and at Brightlands were in the hands of a full-time groundsman and one of them, Wally Musyka, was another great character. Employed in 1965 and originally from the Ukraine, he stayed until he died in 1989 during which time he gained the respect of all for his hard work. Although the pitches were always immaculate, he could not accept or understand that numerically it was customary to count from 'zero'. As a result it became the norm on Sports Day to subtract one foot from each long jump event because the measurements at the side started at 'one'! More recently the school has acquired the use of the former Lloyd's playing fields in Gallery Road and those of the Mary Datchelor field in Hunts Slip Road, so coupled with the existing grounds at Brightlands and at Grange Lane, it became necessary for there to be two groundsmen and currently Bob Feint is assisted by Mark Mallory. In addition, there are gardeners who look after the grounds at Alleyn Park and at Brightlands. Prominent among these in the 1980s was Richard Pleace who gave elegance to the job by always wearing a tie, and more recently John Davies who has been at the school since 1988. At that time responsibility for the maintenance of Brightlands itself was in the hands of the housemaster who employed a full-time odd-job man to make day-to-day repairs and carry out other routine work. The kitchen and domestic staff were also employed by Brightlands but paid by the school. All these people worked autonomously but were answerable ultimately to the Bursar.

With the acquisition of new buildings, the installation of expensive equipment such as computers and legislation involving fire regulations and health and safety, restructuring the way by which the school was maintained became an increasing necessity. A start was made in 1987 when the provision of lunches and all other food was put into the hands of caterers. When the domestic bursar, Celia Sullivan later to be Celia Case, left the school in 1987, neither she nor her position was replaced. One of Hugh Woodcock's last appointments was that of Shirley O'Loughlin to be responsible for the day-to-day cleaning of the school and the serving of lunches. Originally employed at Brightlands as a cleaner in 1976, she quickly moved up to the main school where she made her mark as a linchpin, ultimately becoming Domestic Supervisor. As well as cleaning, she also arranged domestic staff for gatherings such as parents' evenings, Sports Day and PTA functions. Cleaning was thus separated from maintenance and Shirley became responsible for all those who cleaned the school, many of whom doubled up to serve lunch. Like Celia Case before her, 'Shirl' was soon respected by her 'ladies' and neither was a person to be trifled with. Catering, domestic cleaning, and maintenance, once the responsibility of one person, had by 1990 thus evolved into three separate departments.

In 1991 Glenn Purdy was appointed as Clerk of Works to superintend school maintenance. He inherited Joe Cairns, who clearly did not like the upheaval to his life and chose to move on, and Peter Edmunds the school's carpenter who stayed and who continued as the only specialist within the maintenance department. There were also a number of odd-job men, who were replaced when Terry Bunsell was employed as a full-time porter. Scope within his employment soon broadened, and currently as School Keeping Assistant he can undertake any reasonable work which he is capable of doing. No two days are ever the same for Terry. Ray Overington, who became the School Keeper, replaced Joe Cairns. His responsibilities were considerably greater than those of his predecessor and he worked in tandem with Glenn Purdy. Health and safety became a big issue in the 1990s and much more attention was given to it and the legislation resulting from it. As in all public buildings, there must be regular testing of emergency lighting, and fire escapes and means of evacuation have to be constantly upgraded. Seventy-five per cent of the school is alarmed at night and much of the school is equipped with smoke detectors. Electrical appliances have to meet legal requirements of safety and the four mini-buses, three vans and three tractors all have to be maintained to the highest standards. The swimming pool also has to be maintained to strict safety standards, as do the two lifts within the school. The school is now manned from early morning until late at night every day, weekends included and the buildings kept secure when not in use. All these obligations require much paperwork which has to be kept up-to-date and submitted to the Bursar who has overall responsibility. Glenn Purdy, whose proper title became Maintenance Supervisor, has seen many changes and although the actual number of persons employed in his department has not increased significantly, the work performed by individuals under his jurisdiction became more flexible and extensive.

In any organisation someone has to be responsible for paying the bills and sorting out the finances of the business. Little mention of this side of the school's affairs was recorded or documents kept until the school became a Trust. Until about 1930 and when it was proprietorily owned and smaller than it is now, much of the paperwork was done by the headmaster himself assisted by his wife, with each boy's account written out individually in longhand at the end of each term. Although there were three headmasters during the 1930s, matters had reached a point by then when they were needed increasingly on the educational side. In effect there were only two after 1934 because Leake Senior had gone into semi-retirement, but he retained a large financial interest and to some extent continued to hold the purse strings. In 1931 Leake appointed Miss E M Leitch to the then grand title of Bursar. She received the fees, balanced the books and paid the bills, except salaries which remained in the hands of the headmasters. There were no pay scales and employees accepted the terms of their employment when they started although there were pay rises from time to time, not always universally given. There was no registrar or entrance test until the mid 1950s and boys were admitted on application at the headmaster's discretion. Miss Leitch served the school well. She went with it to Cranbrook in September 1939 and then on to Betws. There, at the Royal Oak, she had her office, appropriately, in what had formerly been the hotel's reception area. She returned to Dulwich in 1945 where she stayed until her retirement in 1949. In 1946 Leakey decided that it would be easier within the limits of clothing control and coupons if school uniform were purchased at the school and not from an outside supplier as had been the case before the war, when first Selfridges and then Harrods had been chosen, and Miss Guest embraced this with her other duties. Her office thus became the school shop, currently the room used by the headmaster's secretary, and she was surrounded by large cupboards holding supplies of blazers, socks, caps and the like. She also arranged second-hand sales when boys left the school, these being forerunners of the clothing sales which were to follow in later years. When the school became a Trust in 1957, the bursary was in the charge of Miss Dorothy Lightley but soon afterwards there followed a run of bursars who took up the position on their retirement from one of the armed services. Among them was Major T A Kennedy Davis who was succeeded in 1960 by Kenneth Leaver, also an ex-Major, but who was never known to use his former rank at school. As the school grew so the paperwork grew with it and extras such as trips, lunches, clubs and stationery were all additional to the basic termly fee and had to be entered individually on each boy's account. Ann Henderson had worked in the Bursar's office from 1957 and had seen several bursars come and go, so when Leaver retired as a result of poor health early in 1964 she became Acting Bursar for two terms until his successor, Captain Douglas Ardron RN, was appointed later in the year.

Captain Ardron was a man of some standing, not only by stature for he was well over six foot, but also by nature. He had a commanding presence which gained him the respect of many, and under his stewardship the school entered a period of financial stability. Ardron brought a style of meticulous precision with him from the Royal Navy and he was a stickler for detail. He respected those who stood their ground and fought for their corner, but he had little time for those whom he considered inefficient or lightweight. He held the purse strings tightly and although there were no departmental budgets in those days, he ensured that money was not wasted and no particular project became out of hand financially. As a result, fees were kept at a reasonable level and sound housekeeping meant that money was available for development and school improvements. To start with, Ardron's responsibilities were limited to Alleyn Park, but in due course he became the first in-house Secretary to the Trust, a position which hitherto had been held by the school's solicitors. This change meant that Ardron became responsible for financial affairs at Cranbrook as well. There a 'local bursar', Margaret Davies, held a chequebook account for wages and local needs, but salaries and fees were dealt with from Dulwich. Ardron did not only stand his ground with those who worked beside him as colleagues. It had always been the practice for weekly wages for domestic staff to be paid in cash. One day in 1973 he had just returned to his office from the bank with cash for wages when an assailant burst into his office and attacked him with a knife. Towering high over the intruder, Ardron held firm and although suffering a slashed wrist, managed to keep the money on his side of the desk with the result that the attacker left empty handed. Ardron made little of what had happened implying that it was not so much bravery on his part as impudence of a man who had had the cheek to enter his office uninvited! The incident started a move towards paying staff wages by cheque, but since not all held bank accounts, it took some while for it to be implemented.

Marion Reeves became the Bursar's part-time secretary in 1979, responsible for wages, salaries and day-to-day expenses. Also part-time was Joan Chamberlain who was already administering the receipt of fees. Although electric typewriters were used, much paperwork was done by hand and methods and equipment, although sound, were cumbersome and in some cases almost Dickensian. For example, there was an addressograph machine which held the names and addresses of every pupil, both in Dulwich and in Cranbrook. To address an individual invoice, a handle had to be pulled each time. In 1984 Ardron announced his forthcoming retirement and John Vince was appointed to succeed him although the two worked side by side for a year. Almost at once Marion Reeves officially became Assistant Bursar and Vince, who had come from the world of commerce, introduced a more modern approach as well as being able to secure large amounts of second-hand, but very usable, furniture for the school's benefit. Jane Joyce replaced Joan Chamberlain in 1986, by which time the receipt and administration of fees had become a full-time job, soon to be using the latest computerised technology. Before Stephen Born was appointed in 1996, Marion Reeves performed the duties of Bursar during a period of inter-regnum and in 1998, the bursary took up residence in 42 Alleyn Park occupying rooms which had formerly been classrooms. So much had the workload and paperwork grown that by 2000 there were three staff working within the department, as well as the Bursar himself. Born created a new and different image by showing more interest in the social life of the school and partaking in activities involving both parents and boys, thus becoming a more familiar face around the school than had been the case with previous Bursars. As Bursar, he is also Secretary to the Trust and to the governing body.

Since the formation of the Trust in 1957, many highly skilled and talented people have voluntarily given their time to the two schools by agreeing to be Governors and the part they play, though largely unseen, is another important cog within the DCPS wheel. As Secretary to the Trust, Stephen Born is in a position to recognise the significant input made by the Governors and he is an important link between them and the school. He writes:

> *The contributions the Governors bring from the worlds of medicine, law, engineering, science, religion, education, finance, the arts and others, have helped to shape 'the school business' of today. Seldom interfering, but supporting the Headmasters of both schools with experience and practical application*

from beyond the normal horizons of prep schools, Governors' time amounts to weeks of free consultancy each year. There is no sinecure and they carry significant liabilities in respect of the legal constitution of the Trust, as Charity Trustees, as Trustees of the pension schemes as well as ultimate responsibility for financial probity and compliance with the range of laws affecting schools.

For some Governors, their association with the schools spans decades, one notable example being Michael Prince who, as a chartered accountant, was involved with DCPS at the time of the formation of the Trust in 1957. Michael Prince attended Governors' meetings from that time in an advisory capacity, became a Governor in 1972 and finally retired as Chairman in 1996. Clearly both schools benefit from such continuity of service.

In September 2004, David Pennock was Chairman of the Governors, assisted by twelve members of the Board, several of whom hold eminent positions at schools to which boys go on leaving DCPS.

Another important administrative nerve centre is the school office which for many years was in cramped conditions also using obsolescent equipment. In the immediate post-war years, Katherine Leakey, Leakey's second wife, conducted much of the secretarial work although after 1957 she had less involvement when Mary Hammond was appointed as headmaster's secretary. She was succeeded by Wendy Waldram but when Leakey became headmaster at Coursehorn in 1961 he took her with him and the position in London was filled by Joan Pettit who stayed for many years. Immediately after the war the room currently occupied by the headmaster's secretary was the main school office and was shared by Miss Guest and her cupboards, but by 1950 they were separated and the then school office was housed in the small room which today is the headmaster's office adjacent to his study. In that small space were two secretaries, a telephone switchboard, a large duplicator and numerous filing cabinets.

In 1982 Jean Laxton arrived from the College bringing with her a certain amount of technical know-how and some of the office equipment was updated. Within two years she moved back to the room which had earlier been used as the main office, but this time it was not shared by any other department and the small original office became a reception and waiting area for visitors. It was customary for former parents to be employed as secretaries whenever this was possible as they had knowledge of the school and were not involved in current politics or matters of confidentiality. Joan Pettit and Jean Laxton had both had boys in the school, as had Pam Hayden who worked with Jean Laxton as registrar for new pupils, by this time almost a full-time job. As well as routine correspondence, the office produced circulars to parents on all matters, including school trips, and examination papers for internal exams. These were typed onto waxed skins and then duplicated on a Gestetner machine which was often a messy business when there was too much ink on the roller. Electric typewriters replaced manual ones and when the first photocopier arrived no one was allowed to use it except the office secretaries. Although adequate twenty years earlier, the office with more and more filing cabinets had become cramped, and by 1991 another assistant secretary had arrived. When the Link Building was opened with its paved entrance hall in 2002, what had once been the staff work room by the old front door became a fully modernised secretarial office with controlled access to the main entrance and the registration of visitors. The Headmaster's Secretary in 2004 Angela Jackson, who arrived when Jean Laxton left in 1992, occupied the original room all to herself giving a degree of privacy. She was supported by three other secretaries, one of whom is the Registrar. Although all the rooms in the original Victorian buildings have had numerous uses, one which has remained constant from the start is the headmaster's study. This was chosen by Mallinson over a hundred years ago and still retains its original marble fireplace. Roofless now, thanks to war damage, the verandah outside remains as does the ancient wisteria which grows around it

Another area within the school which has seen gradual growth is the provision of stationery from what has simply become known as the Book Room. In 1932 a larger room for the use of staff was provided (known as the Common Room) and the place where it had formerly been at the top of the stairs on the 1st floor of Number 42 became the school's book room. It was to remain there for over sixty years. In charge initially was M A Glenn ('Maggie') who was already working administratively within the school and teaching younger boys to read. In those days, boys bought their own textbooks which were bought back again by the school at a 'reasonable' price depending on condition at the end of each school year. As well as providing simple items of stationery, 'Maggie' Glenn encouraged boys to save money by establishing a school savings association which was a part of National Savings and which flourished until the start of the war in 1939. After the war Miss Glenn went to work at Brightlands, so from 1945 stationery and the distribution and ordering of books was placed in the hands of Dorothy Kay who taught Maths, and who was given the task in lieu of performing staff duties. Boys and staff could thus only have access to stationery requirements during morning break or part of the 'dinner hour' as it was then called. At other times of the day Miss Kay was simply not available. Newly published textbooks were hard to come by at that time and replacements were usually reprints of existing editions, so that Nelson's *First French Course*, *Algebra For Beginners* and Kennedy's *Shorter Latin Primer* went on and on. Existing books constantly needed to be repaired and made serviceable again for later users. Staff had to work hard to obtain what they wanted in those days. If twelve pictures were to be put on a wall, forty-eight drawing pins were methodically counted out. By 1960 the work involved had become too great for a member of the teaching staff and Marjorie Hewitt and Peggy Coldwells both had long spells in charge of the book room. By the time Christine Riley arrived in 1977, the purchase of school equipment, as well as books, had come within the book room domain and the sale of stationery in the form of pens, rulers, rubbers, geometry sets, crayons etc, to say nothing of the occasional hymn book, had become big business, not only to the boys but for the staff as well. After absorbing nearby cupboards and spare nooks and crannies, the room had to move to somewhere larger and a fully equipped book room with computer and photocopier is now provided on the ground floor of Number 40. The distribution of prizes and cups became the responsibility of the book room and prep registers, school calendars and the coloured tribe 'slips' are all produced from there 'in house'. This has resulted in the work becoming full-time, not only during the term but in school holidays too.

Not to be confused with the book room is the book shop. Started in the late 1960s by the then Head of English, Charles Guttmann, this involved selling suitable paperbacks to boys at certain times of the week from a room set aside specifically for the purpose. Developed enthusiastically by his successor, Carl Gilbey-McKenzie, sales reached a peak in the late 1970s when DCPS was selling more books to its pupils through *Books for Students* than any other school in Britain. One reason for the success was that boys could obtain books by having vouchers signed by parents who were only too willing to encourage their sons to read, the final cost being added to the school bill at the end of each term. Open Day in December was always big business, but it was not unknown for boys to ask their parents to sign for vouchers for books which they, the boys, would then give to their parents as Christmas presents! With the ending of Retail Price Maintenance on books, sales have never been quite so high, but the book shop has become an integral part of the English department and continues to offer a valuable and worthwhile service which enables boys to see and handle books which hopefully they will want to read.

Boys have always eaten and the school has always needed maintaining, but the growth of medical care given to the boys over the years has changed out of all recognition. Before 1920, when boarders were accommodated within the school, there was a sanatorium for boys who were ill, overseen by Mrs Marshall who, so far as can be ascertained, was not medically qualified. When the boarders went to live with members of staff in various houses in the locality, the sanatorium was put to other uses and the only medical care offered was given by non-teaching administrative staff, in the 1930s by people like Maggie Glenn and Phyllis Glazier. Treatment was simple on a 'cuts and bruises' basis. At this time a boy could only attend school if a medical certificate had been signed for the start of each term to the effect that he had not been in contact with any infectious or contagious disease over the holiday. So strictly was this rule enforced, that a boy arriving at the start of a term without his certificate would not be allowed admission and was sent home to fetch it. Even so there were frequent outbreaks of mumps, measles, rubella and chicken pox. These have since been contained by immunisation but outbreaks of chicken pox were not uncommon at Brightlands even as late as the 1980s. After the war when the boarders were under one roof again at Brightlands, a State Registered Nurse (SRN) who lived in, was employed to look after their health and attend to their medical needs. The room set aside for this purpose was known as the 'Sick Hut' for many years, a name it inherited from the camp days of 1939. During the daytime when the boarders were away, the nurse went to school from 10 a.m. until 3 p.m. to attend to the needs of day boys. Outside those hours, and still mainly on a cuts and bruises basis, medical problems were dealt with by a member of the administrative staff. In 1967 a resident matron was employed at Brightlands for the first time while Dawn Blaikley, as the SRN, worked for slightly longer hours at the school, being still available during the daytime for a sick boarder if the need arose. The room from which the school sister operated was far too small, and as a professional she needed better facilities and played a big part in designing a new medical room as it was soon to become. During the 1970s, Dawn Blaikley's work, and that of her successor Anne Flute, was about 85% medical, dealing with children who came through the doors with bumps, bruises, headaches, sports injuries and the like, and that was the way it still was when Mary Rudge arrived in 1985, but big changes to the role played within the school by the school sisters were on the way.

The 1989 Children Act put greater onus on schools to monitor pupils for emotional problems as well as medical ones, and children were actively encouraged to be more open about difficulties of any kind which they might be experiencing. Boys with worries, sometimes just about their school work, had already 'gone to see Sister' for a quiet chat long before 1991, so the foundations of pastoral care, as it was to become, were already being laid. Implementation of the Children Act was one of the first major tasks facing George Marsh when he became headmaster in 1991, and a procedure for pastoral care within the school was soon established. There was a clear need for there to be a sister on duty at all times while the boys were in school, so from 1993 two Sisters worked three days each per week, the overlap day being on Wednesday, and Belinda Twort thus appeared on the scene. Mary Rudge and Belinda Twort formed a formidable but much respected partnership until the former retired in 2002, but a precedent had been set and Clare Leach soon became an equally cheerful part of DCPS life in her place.

The time had already come for there to be a need for a Sister to accompany boys on many of the school's trips and expeditions and the presence and wisdom

Sisters Belinda Twort (l) and Mary Rudge

of a school Sister was always a welcome addition to any group. In school, more and more counselling was given to the boys, and to staff too sometimes, and new regulations brought about a considerable increase in paperwork in that department as in others. When the medical room was built in 1970, it was a vast improvement on what had gone before, but it proved inadequate for modern needs and in 2002 it was doubled in size to incorporate a counselling room, a treatment room, a larger office and a quiet area with beds where boys could rest and recover. Numerous medical examinations, hearing and eye tests are just some of the activities conducted each year in the medical room, and it seems likely that these will increase in the years ahead.

Forty years ago, the medical room, the school office, the book room and the bursary operated from rooms barely the size of large cupboards, and catering, cleaning and maintenance were all the responsibility of one person. As the school has grown and classrooms have moved from cramped Victorian bedrooms to spacious new teaching areas, so the facilities and staff needed to support them have grown too. It is tempting to contemplate what improvements and changes will be necessary in the next forty years in these important areas outside the classroom. New technology and legislation may well come about, but whatever befalls all will continue to play an important integral part in the day-to-day functioning of the school in an unglamorous, and sometimes almost unnoticed, way.

Boys receiving attention in the extended Medical Room 2005

16 Marsh and an Eye to the Future

On 6th September 1991, at morning assembly, George Marsh faced the school for the first time as headmaster, only the sixth person within almost a hundred and twenty years to hold that position. Even though he was Hugh Woodcock's preferred choice, taking over from a person who had become virtually an institution in his own right was by no means easy, yet like other headmasters who had gone before him, Marsh was determined to lead the school in his own way and in his own style. By coming from Edgarley, the Prep School of Millfield School in Somerset where he had been headmaster for five years, he was not new to the game. So with his wife Ann and their two children, the Marsh family became the new occupants at 35 Alleyn Park.

George Marsh
Headmaster 1991 -

There were two hiccups even at the very first assembly. The new headmaster entered the hall, turned to face the boys and said 'Good Morning'. The boys responded. Then there was a silence, which seemed to be very long indeed to the headmaster. Eventually David Whytehead, Head of Religious Studies, said a prayer and assembly was up and running. No one had told Marsh he was expected to say a prayer. The second hiccup came at the end of the assembly. It was the tradition for boys to come into the hall for the first assembly of the school year to be told which class each would be in. The new headmaster was at least warned of this task on his way into Assembly and was handed a school list. This was printed in very small type and contained over 300 names. Reading long lists of names out cold without any practice is always taxing. The first name on the list was a boy called Ebonolu Akintade. Every eye was on the newcomer as he read out the name. It would have been kind if he had been pre-warned, but no one had thought to do so.

Marsh came from a different generation from his predecessor and expected his staff to use his forename when talking in private. This caused problems to certain long-standing staff, one of whom took nearly three years to adjust to the change. Boys were also expected to be known by their forenames in class, which was a harder lesson still for some staff to learn. The boys of course retained the normal courtesies when addressing staff.

The first term, and indeed the first year, were times for Marsh to observe and learn how the school worked. With a staff, many of whom were well set in their ways, it was a matter of deciding how and when to implement the changes which were clearly necessary without alienating or upsetting them. Bert Finn, the Second Master, realised that the school needed to move forward on several fronts if it was to remain a leading prep school. Marsh and his second master spent many hours discussing a strategy for change and Finn quickly became the trusted confidant of the new Head. Changes to the curriculum, lunch system, assemblies, sports, clubs, teaching, learning, pastoral care and relationships between the four sections of the school were all initiated within two years of the new Head arriving. Sadly Bert Finn did not live to see the changes put into practice.

Employed by Leakey as long ago as 1956, Finn had seen headmasters come and go so he was the very person whose views Marsh could listen to. Then in March 1992, just as the second term of the new regime was coming to an end, tragedy struck. With heavy heart, Marsh had to break the news to the boys at assembly one Monday morning that Bert Finn had died suddenly and unexpectedly, leaving his friends, family and the school in shock. Somehow one could relate to how it must have felt in 1922 when the much-respected H O Glenn had died in similar circumstances. Finn was months from retirement and during his time the school had undergone many changes, both structurally and administratively, and he had picked up a large number of portfolios on the way. Many tributes were paid to him, but perhaps one of the simplest and most poignant came from Stephen Robinson (DCPS 1967-1975), one of his former pupils:

> *Bert Finn was a great figure. He knew everything that was going on and was a constant presence around the school, and although he had a temper, he was immensely kind. I always thought he was much under-rated as an academic teacher: I was a duffer at Maths but he nursed me through the Westminster Entrance Exam with extreme patience.*

David Whytehead who had joined the staff in 1967 and who had filled many breaches in the past, undertook some of Finn's responsibilities until a new second master, to be designated Deputy Head, was appointed. It is the practice of IAPS to inspect schools within two years of the appointment of a new Head to confirm that person as a member of IAPS. Their 1994 inspection, not surprisingly, was favourable, but one recommendation was that there should be greater integration between the school's various departments. Finn's death and the inspection report gave Marsh the further ammunition he needed to change the way the school operated. More by chance than by design, the school in Cranbrook was already undergoing similar change following the appointment of Mike Wagstaffe as headmaster in 1990, a year earlier than the change in Dulwich. Although both headmasters had autonomy from the governors to administer their schools in their own way, there was much common ground between them. Foremost in the minds of both, and current in other walks of life, was the principle that major decisions should be the result of collective discussion, or put another way, 'team management', although as head of the team, ultimate decision making lay with the Headmaster and him alone, and he would take the praise – or the stick – resulting from it. So a group of senior staff was brought together to form what became known as the Senior Management Team (SMT). There were plenty of matters for it to consider as well as day-to-day routine matters. Not least among these were the application of the National Curriculum and all that it entailed, the Children Act, legal requirements which needed to be implemented regarding health and safety, Information Technology (IT) and in-service training for teachers (INSET). Thomas Noble, who had joined the school as Head of Classics in 1984, became Director of Studies and responsible for all matters relating to the school curriculum, its involvement with the National Curriculum and implementation of keystages associated with it. This brought about a considerable increase in paperwork for the Headmaster downwards, each department having a detailed scheme of work and every teacher within it having to produce a short or medium term plan of projected work. Gone were the days when it was left to individual teachers to interpret the syllabus in their own way and be answerable to no one.

Closer links with the educational world outside the independent sector brought about anomalies. One was the nomenclature used to distinguish the various year groups which had been in existence from the start and was universal in preparatory schools. It seemed sensible and logical to rename the year groups to match those used in the National Curriculum, so a break with tradition was made in 1995 resulting in the 6th Forms becoming Year 8, the 5th Forms Year 7, and so on down to the Nursery School with its reception class. At the same time, and as a further step towards greater integration, the terms Upper and Middle School were abandoned to become Main School, each year group having a staff member nominated to oversee the welfare of the boys within it. Other sections remained as they were, but closer links were developed between them. Not long after the formation of the SMT, Henry Kirk was appointed as Deputy Head to fill the gap left by Bert Finn, but it was not an appointment which was to last. One aspect of school life which was not totally lacking, but which needed greater emphasis, was the welfare of boys when they had personal problems. This had come under the umbrella of the school Sisters, so when the position of Deputy Head was advertised again in 1997, Marsh put emphasis on pastoral care into the wording of the appointment.

From the very start, and while all these changes were going on, Marsh was as anxious as the governors to continue with the building development plans. The opening of the Music School in 1989 had set standards which at the very least had to be matched or bettered. A plan had been in the pipeline to demolish 38 Alleyn Park and the building next to it, currently used for maintenance, and in their place build a new teaching block which would extend from the music school and be at right angles with Alleyn Park. There were then two significant developments. When Marsh arrived he quickly visited a number of schools to which DCPS sent on boys but, in addition, he wanted to establish a closer relationship with the Kingsdale Comprehensive School, the school's immediate neighbour. The two heads began to meet informally several times a term and a rapport grew up between them. Government involvement also took a hand, not directly but indirectly. One of the legacies of Margaret Thatcher's government was to establish what became known as LMS – Local Management of Schools. By being independent, this did not involve DCPS, but it did affect the neighbouring Kingsdale School. Kingsdale had originally been built to accommodate two thousand pupils, some of whom stayed on originally after school leaving age to study A Level. As the years went by and fewer pupils chose this option, the arrangement became uneconomic and ultimately A Level students from Kingsdale attended a Sixth Form College elsewhere. This meant that it had fewer pupils than was originally intended and so had surplus buildings which were adjacent to DCPS. As a result of LMS and Marsh's closer links, an offer was made to the London Borough of Southwark for DCPS to purchase some of the adjacent buildings and land which had become redundant. Marsh was delighted and somewhat surprised when Southwark agreed. There were one or two conditions. There would have to be a space of 'no-man's land' (on the DCPS side) and a twelve foot high fence of separation would also be required. It took several years for the legalities to be worked out, all of which resulted in a delay. Plans had already been prepared by Woodcock for a classroom block to be built in the vicinity, but with the acquisition of more land the plans were re-arranged so that the new building would be parallel to Alleyn Park and not at right angles to it as was the original idea. The proposal to demolish Number 38, which had been part of the original plan, was dropped, not only because it was no longer necessary but, by being one of the few remaining Victorian buildings in Alleyn Park, its retention was considered desirable.

The delay in construction enabled there to be a complete re-think as to what form the building should take inside, and Marsh had considerable influence over this. New classrooms were urgently needed and although initially the building was designed to be of three storeys, a fourth was included which resulted in the whole roof space being used as well. The new building was eventually ready for the September term in 1995 and as that was the fiftieth anniversary of the return of the school from Betws-y-Coed, it was decided to call it the Betws Building. It was formally opened by Sir Bryan Thwaites, former pupil and governor, at Open Day in December of that year. The classrooms were spacious to say the least, but the greatest innovation was the wide areas between them on each floor which became known as 'social areas'. Here boys have been encouraged to relax during break times and no longer were they compelled to go outside.

The Betws Building as built in 1995, before the library was added next to it

The opening of the Betws Building allowed redevelopment of all the old teaching spaces. For example, three spacious Science Labs with staff offices replaced five small classrooms above the School Hall. At the same time it was decided to incorporate these works with a bridge between the original buildings at 40 and 42. This had been considered many times over the years but had never been done. The result was a complex which included a new entrance hall to the school paved with York stone, old rooms merged into spacious new ones, and at the top floor of the Link Building yet another home for Art. At the same time the bursary moved into offices on the first floor which had once been classrooms. The old Victorian buildings, though looking unchanged from the outside, were so totally transformed inside that a pupil from a decade earlier would hardly recognise his former school, and the locality of any particular room could only be detected from the view from the window.

The building of the Betws Building allowed ICT to have the facilities this fast growing subject deserved. The top floor became a computer suite. After it had been in use for only a few days, one of the boys remarked that it was like going up to Heaven, the unofficial name it has kept ever since. The use of computers had grown rapidly and although Ann Revell had pioneered their use in school ten years earlier, the room devoted to them had

Not bomb damage, but the side of Block 40 being adapted for the new Link Building between 42 and 40 - 2001

Inside the new Entrance Hall with its plasma information screen - 2004

Design Technology - 2004

Information Technology - 1995

quickly become too small. The spacious new suite was equipped initially with Risc PCs which was an extension of the previous system, but this was superseded in 1999 when PCs using Microsoft Windows NT were installed, these in turn were replaced by machines with flat screens and the latest XP operating system. It is a fast moving world and it is logical to assume that computer software, and the equipment associated with it, will constantly need updating. To start with computer periods were timetabled and in due course the use of computers also became integrated into subject lessons for the older boys. The room was open and staffed from early in the morning until an hour after school ended, including morning and lunch breaks, for boys to use and develop their skills. New technology was not overlooked and facilities such as colour laser printers, digital cameras, scanners and interactive white boards were introduced as they became available.

Although not part of the Betws Building, the other subject to mushroom rapidly from humble beginnings a decade earlier was Craft Design and Technology (CDT). Soon after Marsh's arrival, the National Curriculum referred to this simply as DT, thus emphasising the importance of the design of materials as well as their application, and skills in electrics, electronics and plastics were added to those of wood and metal. Woodcock encouraged his staff to promote new and developing subjects to other schools, and in the same vein Marsh supported Elaine Vestey when she became a prime mover in the formation of the Independent Schools Design Technology Association (ISDTA). This was a forum for preparatory schools to meet and discuss common goals and methods for DT within an acceptable budget. At DCPS, Art had moved to a new location in 2002, so DT was able to make use of the space vacated. The double period allocation each week for Years 8, 7, 6 and 5 did not change, although Years 7 and 8 shared the double period with Art for half the year, giving greater timetable scope for the increased demands required for the older boys. The improved facilities provided a main workshop, computer area and rooms for storage and preparation. The so called new subjects of IT and DT gained much from the construction of new buildings and the refurbishing of old ones, but so did the long established ones. Each subject was at last able to have its own area with classrooms equipped with televisions and video recorders as well as departmental offices and storage areas. Boys gained the advantage of each having their own lockable locker in a classroom within one of the subject areas.

As well as improved facilities for senior Science, DT and Art, the Betws Building and the Link Building with its fine entrance hall between 42 and 40, a new fully equipped library with spacious reading space and computer terminals was opened in 2002 between the Betws Building and 38. The original school had been a collection of separate Victorian houses which had been acquired progressively and which had spaces in between. Mallinson filled in the first of these when the hall was built between 44 and 42 in 1897, but the remaining gaps not only provided space for new structures, but also gave uncontrolled access, making the school insecure. Mindful of the need to be more safety and security minded, Marsh was able to use these spaces to advantage by providing new and better facilities, at the same time making the school more secure. Parking space, and the controlled movement of cars within the school, was also improved and made safer.

The decision taken some years ago by the Board of Governors to set aside a percentage of income for future development meant that there was more cash in the kitty for progressive improvements and Marsh was in the fortunate position of being able to implement them, many of which have been referred to in previous chapters. It was his philosophy, for example, for as many boys as possible to have the opportunity to play in matches against other schools in one sport or another if it were possible. More matches meant more teams and more space would be required for them to be played. The first move was to become a partner with Kingsdale School at the Mary Datchelor playing field in Hunts Slip Road. This was another example of co-operation between the two schools which is very much to the benefit of both. The acquisition in 2004 of the former Lloyd's playing field in Gallery Road, including a fine pavilion which went with it, enabled this to be achieved. In the same year, the Lower School playground was enlarged when adjacent land was purchased from Southwark. As well as providing a larger play area, it also resulted in the removal of an unsightly concrete former boundary fence which had been in place since Bowen Drive was built in 1952 on what had once been Lord Vestey's private drive to Kingswood House. Within the school, the large play area known as 'The Cage' was strengthened and made more secure with floodlighting and this has proved a valuable asset on dark evenings.

The new library - 2004

The former Lloyd's playing field and pavilion in Gallery Road, acquired for the use of DCPS in 2004

While major structural additions and improvements were taking place outside to the fabric of the buildings, important changes, some of them quite radical, were taking place inside. When Elizabeth Hill was appointed Deputy Head in 1997, a social change in the way responsible adults were expected to look after young people was under way and this particularly concerned the teaching profession. Liz Hill was appointed specifically to extend and develop the pastoral side of the school. This has included the tutorial system of pastoral care and the delivery of Personal, Social, Health and Citizenship Education (PSHCE). A planned and co-ordinated programme has evolved. It includes matters such as anti-bullying, a positive behaviour policy, self responsibility and relationships with others.

Procedures, many of which were already being followed but which were unwritten, became established school policy. Cornerstone to change has been the Nurturing Programme delivered through Circle Time. This has been introduced into schools in recent years, although it has not always been met with universal acclaim. At DCPS it has involved boys discussing issues with one another in an informal way, thus enabling them to learn how to accept the other person's point of view without necessarily agreeing with it. Themes such as 'praise and criticism', 'managing difficult feelings' and 'choices and consequences of behaviour' have been considered. Tolerance and empathy are encouraged and the management of personal skills is developed. These objectives are far-reaching and extend across the whole spectrum of human activity from awareness of such matters as personal health and safety to the responsibilities and morals of good citizenship. Raising awareness about behaviour and anti-social behaviour, as well as learning about simple human graces, are also key aspects of the Circle Time programme. It starts in the Nursery and is structured throughout the school with boys having a 35-minute period allocated to it each week. It is a time for boys to focus on themselves, providing a forum for them to have a "voice". It also enables class tutors to come to know the boys in their charge that much better. Weekly themes are followed but individual teachers have been able to adapt it to their own style. Through Circle Time, the care of children has come a long way since the days of Mr Bumble!

In Circle Time the teacher is the facilitator. The aim is for boys to be encouraged to have a key input, to take responsibility, increase awareness and hopefully help to raise their own self-esteem. The principles discussed in Circle Time extend across the curriculum, both in and out of the classroom. Each term there is also a specific theme which is reinforced through assemblies. In the summer of 2004 it was Trust and Team-Work. Staff at all levels have received In-Service Training (INSET) and this in itself has brought the various departments of the school closer together. Issues which were common to all had a common code to follow, and this has resulted in there being a pastoral co-ordinator HOY (Head of Year) for each year group. In conjunction with the PTA, evenings have been arranged for parents at which school policy in these matters has been discussed and there is a parallel parents' programme offering training in the Nurturing Programme for them to operate in their families. The principles behind Circle Time are sound and implementing them has required fundamental and philosophical changes in the ways by which children are managed, and these have not always been easy to accept. New concepts need time to become established, and time will tell if the boys of today will become better citizens than those of yesterday.

As well as having concern for the well being of boys in his own school, Marsh became involved, almost by chance, in the welfare of a group of others far less privileged. This came about as a result of the cricket tour to South Africa in 1997. He felt that it would be wrong for a DCPS team to go all the way to South Africa without playing in a township, so within the programme a match against a Gauteng cricket team was arranged at the Alexandria Township in Johannesburg. As more funds had been raised than were necessary, it was decided to donate £3000 to develop cricket for youngsters in Gauteng and there was a moving ceremony at the end of the match when the cheque was handed over at the Alexandria Oval. Eighteen months later, Marsh received a telephone call from a Mrs Jackie Gallagher in Johannesburg reiterating earlier thanks to DCPS for providing her school with £3000. Marsh was a little surprised at first to see the connection, but the Gauteng Cricket Board had used the money given earlier to educate promising young black cricketers through what was known as The Sparrow Schools Foundation, an organisation educating almost a thousand children from the ages of 3 to 19, thus ensuring that promising cricketers have the educational skills to survive if they became national or international sportsmen. During the course of the conversation the dream of a tour for some of the Sparrows to visit England was raised. Almost spontaneously Marsh said, '*What a wonderful idea: I will raise the money and organise the tour*', only considering afterwards what he had let himself in for. He never looked back and with involvement from the PTA, the Sparrows visited DCPS in 2002. Since then a Sparrows choir has visited DCPS and there have been other cricket tours to South Africa.

Relations were cemented still further when Ruth Cole, formerly from the Annexe staff, spent a few days visiting sections of the Sparrow Schools while in South Africa and this included observing and becoming involved with several classes. It was an uplifting experience for her, and for Marsh too when he accompanied the 2003 tour. The PTA has provided further donations which have gone towards the cost of a new basketball pitch for the Sparrows and a plaque marking their generosity has been unveiled. The links and friendships made with this deprived part of Africa seem set to last and other schools in the UK have become involved as well.

In view of the contributions which Marsh was making in the prep school world generally, it came as no surprise when he was elected to be Chairman of IAPS for the academic year 2000-2001. He made it known to parents, boys and staff that this would not involve long absences from Dulwich, but the moment seemed right for Thomas Noble to assume from then the position of co-Deputy Head, the curriculum and timetable continuing to be included in his portfolio.

The face of DCPS in London has changed substantially over the last hundred years, from new land being gained to the construction of new buildings, and with the financial resources to do both. Structurally and numerically the school has grown in size, although the original buildings at 42 and 44 Alleyn Park, with the hall in between, still form the core. Disciplines, teaching techniques, methods and facilities have all changed too. But how has the life of a twelve-year-old pupil changed? A comparison between the life of a senior boy in 2004 with that of his counterpart a hundred or so years earlier is reflected in the school timetable. There are a few similarities and many differences, but boys have always had full days at DCPS and they have been kept busy. In 1888, for example, and just three years after the school's foundation, the school day started at 9 a.m, but there was school on Saturdays with three subjects for 'prep' on that evening as well. Wednesdays and Saturdays were deemed half holidays when lessons ended at 2.45 p.m. German was an alternative to some Greek lessons and drawing was an alternative to singing, although whether this was an option which boys could choose, or if there was a switch in mid-year as happens now with DT and Art, is not recorded.

" Deus adest laborantibus."

DULWICH COLLEGE PREPARATORY SCHOOL.—LIST OF WORK.

SIXTH FORM, SECOND TERM, 1888.

Hours.	MONDAY.	TUESDAY.	WEDNESDAY.	THURSDAY.	FRIDAY.	SATURDAY
9—9.15.	Psalms. Prayers.	Hymn. Prayers.	Psalms. Litany.	Hymn. Prayers.	Psalms. Litany.	Hymn. Prayers.
9.15—10.	Algebra.	Arithmetic.	Euclid.	Algebra.	Arithmetic.	Euclid.
10—10.45.	Greek.	Latin.	Latin.	Latin.	Latin.	Latin.
11—11.45.	Latin.	Latin.	Swimming.	Latin.	Latin.	Swimming.
11.45—12.30.	French.	History.	Greek.	French.	History.	Greek.
2—2.55.	Bible.	Greek.	French.	Geography.	Greek.	French.
3.5—4.	Latin.	English.	Half Holiday.	Singing.	English.	Half Holiday.
Preparation.	Latin. Arithmetic. History.	Greek. Euclid. French.	Latin. Algebra. French.	Latin. Arithmetic. History.	Greek. Euclid. French.	Latin. Algebra. History.

On Wednesday and Saturday the hours are from 9—1.

Sixth Form (Year 8) 1888

Year 8   2004

Miles Underwood 8S **Timetable** Autumn Term 2004

	Monday	Tuesday	Wednesday	Thursday	Friday
1	English	Maths	French	Maths	Maths
2	Maths	Maths	Maths	Biology	Geography
3	French	French	Latin	Biology	Geography
4	Latin	English	History	English	RS
5	RS	Art/DT	History	Latin	Physics
6	Form	Art/DT	Music	PE	Physics
7	Games	Latin	Games	French	French
8	Games	Chemistry	Games	History	English
9	Games	Chemistry	Games	Geography	English
Prep	French/RS	English/Latin	French/Hist.	Sci/Geog	Maths (French vocab)

The school timetable for a Year 8 boy in 2004 (until 1995 he would have been in a Sixth Form) showed a broader diversity of subjects. He had lessons in Information Technology, Art, Chemistry, Physics, Biology, and Design Technology, with more time given to sport and games. Although he had fewer subjects for 'prep' each evening and no school on Saturday mornings, his school day was longer. Finding time for the new demands of the timetable was not easy. Marsh, assisted by his Director of Studies, had the task of trying to squeeze more and more into the timetable, achieving it to some extent by extending the length of the school day. He felt that DCPS should offer a broad education, and slanting the timetable heavily towards those subjects which were ultimately examined was not a desirable option. There was also a partial move away from streaming classes by ability.

The school's catchment area and methods by which boys reached school have changed too. A hundred years ago most boys lived locally and there were fewer of them, but as public transport improved boys came from further afield, the nearby railway (which was electrified in 1924) making places like Bromley and Beckenham more accessible. Many walked or came by cycle as a number do now, but few if any came by car. Tom Hendriks (DCPS 1998-2004) noted some of these differences when he wrote:

> *I ran down to the bus stop, caught my usual bus at 6.58 and sat in my usual seat. After a short journey I arrived in Brixton. The indicator informed me that my second bus would arrive in eight minutes. When it arrived, I flashed my bus pass and swung round into a seat. Twenty minutes later I was off and heading towards Alleyn Park. I went into school and into the dining hall for breakfast, 'My usual please - bacon and a baguette'.* After breakfast Tom went on to write: *I strode up the stairs two at a time into the Betws Building and when I reached my classroom I spun the dial on my locker before swinging the door open and packing my bag for the first three lessons.*

There were no bus passes, no bus indicators, no dials on lockers, nothing resembling the Betws Building and certainly no breakfasts a hundred years ago. Then boys had wooden desks with iron frames and kept their books inside. Masters went from room to room, boys stayed inside the same room all day for most lessons and many of them went home for lunch. Tom was one of a small number who came to school by public transport, but for reasons of convenience and safety many travel to and from school these days by special coaches, in some cases shared by boys from Dulwich College and Alleyn's School. This means that places like Clapham and Blackheath have become more accessible too. Breakfasts were introduced in 1997.

Marsh noticed that boys were arriving in school early, not having had an adequate breakfast, so he approached the caterers to see if providing breakfast on an optional basis was a viable proposition. As a result, a choice of cooked or uncooked food has been provided in the hall between 7.40 and 8.20 each morning, paid for in cash at the time. Breakfasts have proved popular not only with boys, but with staff, parents, brothers and sisters and anyone connected with the school. DCPS has led the way again and is one of the first schools in the locality to provide this facility. Occasionally the school holds what it calls 'The Big Breakfast'. This is when as many people as possible are asked to attend and part of the proceeds are set aside for a charitable cause. Billy Stansbury (DCPS 1993 - 2003) explained all in 2002 when he wrote:

> *The Big Breakfast was an occasion for all ages to enjoy from kindly grey-haired grannies, through suave-suited businessmen to mothers and tiny babies in pushchairs. People who had never come before were excited because of the atmosphere and the scrumptious food on offer. In a way the Big Breakfast was rather like a Marrakesh souk as we were always being hassled to buy raffle tickets and other various competitions. Most people did do their part for charity. I do not think there was anyone in the room who didn't enjoy the morning, especially the boys as we missed our first lesson!*

Shirley O'Loughlin at the till during the Big Breakfast - 2002
(Courtesy Ann Revell)

The advent of television and video recorders meant that lessons for a boy in 2004 were very different from those of a hundred years earlier when 'chalk and talk' was to the fore, learning by rote was common and the cane was the answer for those who did not learn their verbs properly. The school's first video recorder, which has survived to the archives, went to the French department in 1974 and was large and cumbersome, but at the time it was considered a wonder. Thirty years on, every classroom for Years 5 to 8 has a television and a video recorder, their use and advantage being noted by Jeremy Holt (DCPS 1998 - 2004) who wrote while reflecting on his time at DCPS:

> *I returned to an 8S English lesson to watch 'To Kill a Mockingbird', a magnificent film full of suspense, adapted from the Harper Lee classic. With French came the start of our 'Marcel Pagnol Season' as we*

began to watch 'La Gloire de Mon Père', the first of two autobiographical films based on the director's childhood in the beauty of the hills in Provence.

Any teacher will emphasise that television and video recordings are aids to teaching and not teaching methods in themselves, and at the time Jeremy was enjoying his post-exam period. Soon DVDs will have replaced video recorders as the technical march of progress continues, and all parts of the school have easy access to these media resources.

Another change which Marsh instigated early on was the Leavers' Service for Year 8 at the end of the summer term. Here in the Music School in front of parents and staff, boys read short reflections from highlights of their time at the school which they choose to recall. Accompanied by a religious service and some uplifting music, this provides a grand finale to a boy's time at the school. Prize Giving had become a cramped affair in the hall with long periods when not many were involved so prizes are currently awarded to the Year 5 and 6 pupils on the penultimate afternoon while Years 7 and 8 have a ceremony following the Leaver's Service, on the last day of term.

Marsh will not be at the school for as long as some of his predecessors, but he has implemented substantial changes. These may not have been outwardly so dramatic as some of the events which occurred earlier, but he ensured that the school maintained its reputation and kept pace with current developments in both techniques and facilities. It could be said that Leake had to deal with the tribulations of the First War; Leakey had the Second, Woodcock had two major fires (and the school's centenary) and Marsh had the National Curriculum! That may be so, but all called for a clear head and an understanding of what needed to be done. When Leakey created the Trust in 1957, one consequence was that the school was no longer owned by an individual and any profits were ploughed back for future development. Leakey predicted that this would happen but it took a little time, and the first major post-war development in 1966 did not appear until five years after he had left Dulwich, although plans had been in the pipeline long before. Similarly, Marsh had been in post for four years before the Betws Building finally materialised. In short, the income from today pays for the needs of tomorrow and each generation of boys benefits in that way.

What about an eye to the future? In July 2005 the Nursery School was pulled down and rebuilt, whilst at the main school site work started on the construction of a Sports Hall. DCPS is now well into its second century and who knows what the future will hold for education generally, and for the independent sector in particular?

The school which Thomas Henry Mason was invited to start in 1885 has set standards and has facilities today which are the envy of many, thanks largely to the fortitude of its headmasters, supported by the governors, and the goodwill which each has developed in his own characteristic way. The same can be said for the companion school at Cranbrook which, though younger, has a reputation in its own area second to none. Like the school in Cranbrook, the one in Dulwich may one day admit girls and it may have a theatre. One day it may be led by a Headmistress and not a Headmaster. The original Victorian buildings have survived two wars and have been substantially refurbished, and other buildings will come and go, and uses for them change, as demands of the times change. There will be problems undoubtedly, but it is to be hoped that none will be as harsh as those which resulted in two world wars with much of the school having to evacuate during one of them. At that time, personal survival and the long-term future of the school, especially survival of the one in Dulwich, was foremost and today's problems seem almost trivial by comparison.

It is the pupils which make a school what it is, led by its head and all the staff within it. On leaving the Prep they go beyond to secondary and tertiary education and over the years many have gone far to reach distinguished positions. It is thus fitting that the last words in this History of DCPS should go to a couple of them, their comments perhaps reflecting those of many. In 2002, Gareth Rhys (DCPS 1994-2002) wrote:

> *I feel that anyone who has been to the Prep for any length of time has been presented with many chances and opportunities, be it playing in orchestras or concert bands – with fantastic venues - to fencing, water polo, chess, swimming, art and even weaving. Whatever angle you look at the school, it provides something for everybody. As there is so much diversity, there are so many chances to meet firm friends. Although not all of it was plain sailing, a lot of it was, and it was fun too! All the teachers, even dare I say the Headmaster too, are friendly and – especially the Headmaster – have very amusing senses of humour. I have made friends from teachers and boys alike and I have many happy memories to treasure for the rest of my life.*

Three years later, in 2005, Tom Renner summed up his time at DCPS in an equally appreciative way:

> *I have really enjoyed my time at the Prep for a number of reasons. Firstly, the teachers make a real effort to make the work enjoyable for the boys. Secondly, the school isn't geared strongly towards passing end-of-year exams. Obviously they matter, but there are so many extra-curricular activities and sports going on, that the overall effect is that the exams take a back seat until the half term before them. The school is not only exceedingly good academically, but it is also a fun environment to be in, a happy community and a great place to start school life.*

When Dr Welldon approached his friend Thomas Mason in 1885 to start a school in Dulwich, which has become known as DCPS, little did he know that very quickly it would become one of Britain's leading preparatory schools.

Aerial view of Dulwich College Preparatory School in 2002

THE DCPS COMMUNITY 2004

GOVERNING BODY

Mr D R M Pennock (*Chairman*)   Mr T J Davis (*Deputy Chairman*)   Mr C M P Bush   Mrs S Garnett

Mr J M Hammond   Mr T C Monckton   Mr R K E Nicholson   Mrs P Owen   Sir D Penry-Davey

Mrs R Pringle   Mrs S E Simon   Secretary to the Trust: Mr S R Born

TEACHING STAFF

Headmaster: Mr G Marsh, MA

Deputy Head (Pastoral) Mrs E A Hill   Deputy Head (Curriculum) Mr T A Noble: Classics

Senior Master Mr P C Tobenhouse: History i/c Year 7   Director of Administration Mr C R Gordon: History

UPPER SCHOOL: HEADS OF DEPARTMENT

Mr D J Adkins: *Sport*   Mr R W Aitchison: *English*   Mr P C W Brooke: *Music*   Revd A R Chidwick: *Mod. Lang.*

Mr D Johnson: *Maths*   Mrs K Kent-Smith: *Science*   Mrs A M Revell: *ICT*   Mr S Severino: *Geography, i/c Year 6*

Mr G Smart: *Art*   Mr C R Smith: *RS*   Mrs E Vestey: *DT*

Brightlands: Housemaster Mr J Banks: Geography, Maths Assistant Housemaster Mr A O'Loughlin: *Swimming, PE*

ASSISTANT TEACHERS

Mr A R Adams: *Music*   Mrs S Banks: *Science*   Miss H Booth: *Maths*   Ms J de Pear: *Art*

Miss E Fairway: *English, Drama*   Mlle S R Gibson: *Mod. Lang., i/c Year 5*   Mme J Gire: *Mod. Lang.*   Mrs G Hewitt-Jones: *Music*

Mr E Johnson: *English*   Mr G King: *Latin*   Miss E Krafft: *Maths*   Ms J M McElroy: *English*

Mr M G Mitchell: *Maths*   Miss S Rallan: *Maths*   Mr S P Savides: *Science*   Mr D Spammer: *Science, PE*

Mr K Street: *Music*   Mr P Topham: *Geography*   Mr J J Veitch: *Science, Maths, Ass. DoS*

Mr R Villars: *History, RS*   Mr R P Whitcomb: *Library, PE*   Mrs A Wregg, MSc: *Maths, DT*

LOWER SCHOOL

Mrs K M Wilkins: Head of Section   Miss J Maynard: Deputy   Miss F Anderson   Miss N Carter

Mrs L Davidson: SEN   Mr A Fielder   Miss D S Freeman   Miss C Gibson   Mrs J Hepher

Miss A Klahn   Mrs M A Langford   Miss R C Marcheselli   Mrs S D Noble   Ms L Otway

Mrs S J Sampson   Mrs A Spammer   Mrs J E Westmacott: Ass. DoS   Miss B Williams   Mr P Williams

ANNEXE

Miss E Adriano: *Head of Section*   Mrs R Trotman: *Deputy*   Miss I Costaras   Miss F Delaney   Mrs M-E Everit

Miss K Partridge   Miss M Pearson   Mrs J Pinnell   Mrs P Rusling   Miss S M Sutto

Mrs L A Symmes: *SEN*   Mrs C Beaty   Mrs S D Ellway

NURSERY

Mrs H C Strange: *Head of Section*   Mrs S Barrick   Mrs S Born   Mrs L Gabriele   Ms L A Hopewell

Mrs C Janda   Mrs R Owen   Ms J Taylor   Miss K van Berckel   Miss V Weall   Miss J Bone

Mrs P Burridge   Miss S Lee   Mrs C R Main   Mrs T McCabe   Miss A Salter   Miss A Samworth

Miss J Lovett: *Nursery Administration*

ADMINISTRATION/ADDITIONAL STAFF

Mr S R Born: *Bursar*   Mrs J Mustafa: *Assistant Bursar*   Mrs J G Joyce: *Bursar's Secretary*

Mrs S Smyth: *Bursar's Office Ass.*   Mrs A L Jackson: *Headmaster's Secretary*   Miss S J Astbury: *Admin. Assistant*

Miss G Peaple: *Receptionist*   Mrs F V Aitchison: *Registrar*   Mr M A Woodall: *Book Room Co-ordinat*

Mr N D Smith,: *Archivist*   Dr J French: *School Doctor*   Mrs B Twort: *School Sister*

Mrs C R Leach: *Deputy School Sister*   Mrs K Warren: *Assistant School Sister*   Mrs S Banks: *Houseparent*

Mr P Chi Ekeigwe: *DT Technician*   Mr P Saunders: *Network Manager*   Mr D Lewis: *Systems Administrator*

Mr M O Mokuolu: *ICT Technician*   Mrs F Khan: *Science Technician*   Mrs K Fletcher: *Assistant Librarian*

Mrs S Ward: *Catering Supervisor*   Mrs S O'Loughlin: *Domestic Supervisor*   Mr G Purdy: *Maintenance Supervisor*

Mr R Overington: *Schoolkeeper*   Mr F Tarrant: *Assistant Schoolkeeper*

Mr R Faint: *Grounds Supervisor*   Mr M Mallory: *Head Groundsman*

UPPER SCHOOL TEACHING STAFF 2004

Mme J Giret, Miss J McElroy, Mrs A Revell, Mr P Brooke, Mr D Spammer, Mr K Street, Miss E Fairway, Mr C Smith, Mr G Smart, Mrs B Twort, Miss S Rallan
Mr R Villars, Miss R Muir, Mr G King, Mrs S Banks, Mr P Topham, Mr D Adkins, Mr A Adams, Mr A O'Loughlin, Miss E Krafft, Mlle S Gibson, Mr E Johnson, Mr S Savides
Mrs K Kent-Smith, Mr R Aitchison, Mr C Gordon, Mr P Tobenhouse, Mrs E Hill, Mr G Marsh, Mr T Noble, Rev'd A Chidwick, Mr S Severino, Mr D Johnson, Mr J Banks

Index